Frommer's®

Brittany

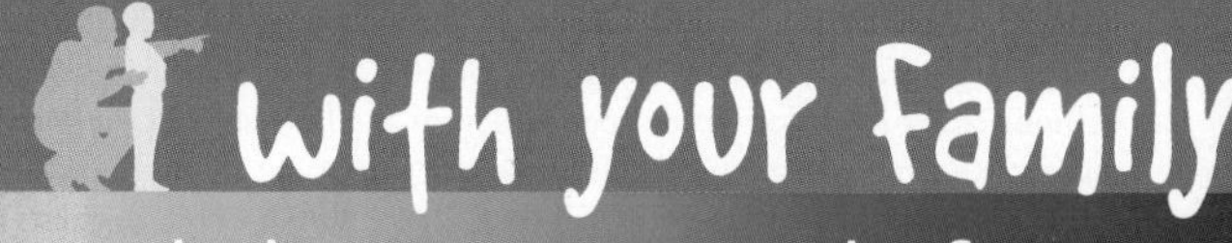

From rural charm to seaside fun

by Rhonda Carrier

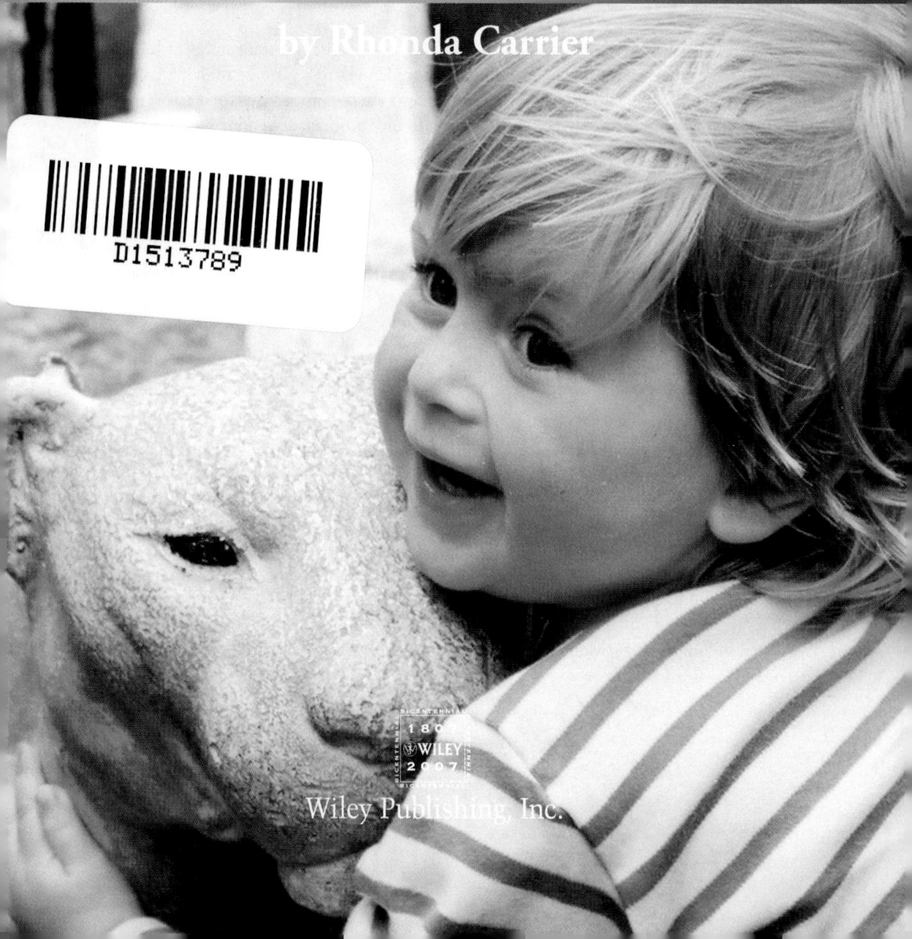

1807 WILEY 2007

Wiley Publishing, Inc.

Wiley Publishing, Inc.
111 River St.
Hoboken, NJ 07030-5774

ISBN: 978-0-470-05525-0

UK Publisher: Sally Smith (Frommer's UK)
Executive Project Editor: Martin Tribe (Frommer's UK)
Development Editor: Anne O'Rorke
Content Editor: Hannah Clement (Frommer's UK)
Cartographer: Tim Lohnes
Photo Research: Jill Emeny (Frommer's UK)
Production by Wiley Indianapolis Composition Services

For information on our other products and services or to obtain technical support, please contact our Customer Care Department within the U.S. at 800/762-2974, outside the U.S. at 317/572-3993 or fax 317/572-4002. Within the UK Tel. 01243 779777; Fax. 01243 775878.

Wiley also publishes its books in a variety of electronic formats. Some content that appears in print may not be available in electronic formats.

Printed in Singapore by Markono Print Media Ptc Ltd
5 4 3 2 1

Contents

About the author iv
An additional note vi

1 Family Highlights of Brittany 1

Brittany Family Highlights 3
Best Accommodation 9
Best Eating Options 13

2 Planning a Family Trip to Brittany 17

Visitor Information 20
Essentials 31
Accommodation & Eating Out 42
Getting Children Interested in Brittany 49
Fast Facts: Brittany 49

3 Ille-et-Vilaine 55

Essentials 57
Visitor Information 58
What to See & Do 61
Family-Friendly Accommodation 90
Family-Friendly Dining 101

4 Côtes d'Armor 107

Essentials 108
Visitor Information 108
What to See & Do 112
Family-Friendly Accommodation 131
Family-Friendly Dining 138

5 Finistère 143

Essentials 145
Visitor Information 146
What to See & Do 148
Family-Friendly Accommodation 176
Family-Friendly Dining 189

6 Morbihan 197

Essentials 198
Visitor Information 200
What to See & Do 201
Family-Friendly Accommodation 224
Family-Friendly Dining 231

Appendix: Useful Terms and Phrases 235

Index 259

About the author

Rhonda Carrier studied French language, literature and culture at the universities of Cambridge and the Sorbonne in Paris. After travelling widely, both around France and further afield, she spent 10 years working in London as a writer and editor for local guides and listings magazines, as well as producing award-winning short fiction. In 2005, after living in France for a year, she rediscovered London with her young sons while researching the first edition of *Frommers' London with Kids*. She now divides her time between France and Manchester, and is also the author of the companion to this guide, *Normandy with Your Family*.

Acknowledgements

As ever, unending thanks to my husband Conrad Williams, who somehow manages to be a brilliant dad by day and write wonderful novels by night.

Immense gratitude goes also to Daniel, Yoyo and Sophie Amaglio, for long-ago summers that sparked my love affair with France and its language, and to Madame Haynes, my teacher at Leicester High School, for nurturing and inspiration.

I'd also like to express fondest thanks to Teresa Hardy and Richard Dale for help with research, to Fiona Dunscombe for the kind of encouragement every writer needs, to my brother David for cat-sitting duties, to Conrad, Hester and Hildelith Leyser and Kate Cooper for a house and for Finistère leads, to Jane Watt for another house in another country and for local knowledge, and to Nick Royle for holiday reading and much, much more.

The following people have also offered greatly appreciated support, input and/or feedback over the years.

Gemma Hirst; Holly, Alan, Jarvis and baby McGrath; Kate, Charlie and Bella Royle; Szylvi, Laurence, Leo and Melody Davey; Jan Parker and Chris, Lucy and James Newman; Paula Grainger and Michael and Nate Marshall Smith; Judy and Joe Reynolds; Liz Wyse; Malcolm Swanston; Christi Daugherty, Pete Fiennes and Sarah Guy; Diana Tyler; Heather Brice and family; Dea Birkett; and all the talented Lumineuse writers around France.

Thanks too to our parents David, Mary, Leo and Grenville, and to my stepfather Tim, for support and faith over the years.

Lastly, *sincères remerciements* to all the hardworking professionals in tourist offices all over Brittany, for their unfailingly prompt advice and assistance.

Dedication

For Conrad, Ethan and Ripley – the perfect travel companions.

An additional note

Please be advised that travel information is subject to change at any time and this is especially true of prices. We therefore suggest that you write or call ahead for confirmation when making your travel plans. The authors, editors and publisher cannot be held responsible for experiences of readers while travelling. Your safety is important to us, however, so we encourage you to stay alert and be aware of your surroundings.

Star Ratings, Icons & Abbreviations

Hotels, restaurants and attraction listings in this guide have been ranked for quality, value, service, amenities and special features using a star-rating system. Hotels, restaurants, attractions, shopping and nightlife are rated on a scale of zero stars (recommended) to three (exceptional). In addition to the star rating system, we also use four feature icons that point you to the great deals, in-the-know advice and unique experiences. Throughout the book, look for:

FIND	Special finds – those places only insiders know about
MOMENT	Special moments – those experiences that memories are made of
VALUE	Great values – where to get the best deals
OVERRATED	Places or experiences not worth your time or money

The following **abbreviations** are used for credit cards:

AE	American Express
MC	MasterCard
V	Visa

A Note on Prices

Frommer's provides exact prices in each destination's local currency. As this book went to press, the rate of exchange was 1€ = £0.67. Rates of exchange are constantly in flux; for up-to-the minute information, consult a currency-conversion website such as www.oanda.com/convert/classic.

An Invitation to the Reader

In researching this book, we discovered my wonderful places – hotels, restaurants, shops and more. We're sure you'll find others. Please tell us about them, so we can share the information with your fellow travellers in upcoming editions. If you were disappointed with a recommendation, we'd love to know that too. Please write to;

Frommer's Brittany with Your Family, 1st Edition
John Wiley & Sons, Ltd
The Atrium
Southern Gate
Chichester
West Sussex, PO19 8SQ

Photo Credits

Front cover photos: © Agripicture Images / Alamy; © Agripicture Images / Alamy; © Directphoto.org / Alamy; © Goodshoot-Jupitarimages France / Alamy; © Conrad Williams; Back cover photo: © PCL: © Agripicture Images / Alamy; p ii: © Agripicture Images / Alamy; pii: © Directphoto.org/Alamy; p ii: © Goodshoot-Jupitarimages France / Alamy; p iii: © Agripicture Images / Alamy; p iii: © Agripicture Images / Alamy; p iii: © Directphoto.org/Alamy; p iii: © Goodshoot-Jupitarimages France / Alamy © PCL; p. 1: © The Travel Library; p. 2: © The Travel Library; p. 4: © The Travel Library; p. 4: © Conrad Williams; p. 7: © Parc des Grands Chênes; p. 8: © The Travel Library; p. 8: © Bruno de la Sablière; p. 10: © Le Lodge Kerisper; p. 11: © Ian Sanderson / Kura Images; p. 12: © PCL; p. 14: © PCL; p. 17: © PCL; p. 55: © The Travel Library; p. 59: © Conrad Williams; p. 62: © PCL; p. 63: © PCL; p. 65: © The Travel Library; p. 66: © Stockfolio / Alamy; p. 67: © The Travel Library; p. 67: © Conrad Williams; p. 70: © Stockfolio / Alamy; p. 71: © Conrad Williams; p. 73: © AA World Travel Library / Alamy; p. 75: © Phil Wahlbrink/WahlbrinkPHOTO / Alamy; p. 77: © Conrad Williams; p. 81: © PCL; p. 82: © fstop2 / Alamy; p. 83: © Parc des Grands Chênes; p. 86: © Parc des Grands Chênes; p. 87: © Conrad Williams; p. 91: © Alain Machet / Alamy; p. 96: © Holgar Ehlers / Alamy; p. 103: © PCL; p. 107: © PCL; p. 111: © The Travel Library; p. 113: © Office de Tourisme de Saint Cast Le Guildo; p. 113: © The Travel

Library; p. 116: © The Travel Library; p. 117: © GARYCOOPERL / SM National Stud Lamballe; p. 120: © PCL; p. 121: © Bildarchiv Monheim GmbH / Alamy; p. 123: © Conrad Williams; p. 124: © La Vapier du Trieux Steam Train in Paimpol; p. 127: © The Travel Library; p. 128: © Marion Kaplan / Alamy; p. 129: © Peter Allen – Kura Images; p. 132: © Conrad Williams; p. 135: © Conrad Williams; p. 136: © The Travel Library; p. 139: © PCL; p. 143: © The Travel Library; p. 147: © Conrad Williams; p. 149: © The Travel Library; p. 150: © Hemis / Alamy; p. 151: © Conrad Williams; p. 154: © The Travel Library; p. 155: © The Travel Library; p. 156: © Art Kowalsky / Alamy; p. 157: © Claude Thibault / Alamy; p. 158: © images-of-france / Alamy; p. 161: © Kathleen Norris Cook / Alamy; p. 163: © Mark Boulton / Alamy; p. 165: © The Travel Library; p. 167: © CW Images / Alamy; p. 170: © The Travel Library; p. 172: © The Travel Library; p. 173: © CW Images / Alamy; p. 174: © Conrad Williams; p. 175: © Conrad Williams; p. 176: © Ian Sanderson / Kura-Images; p. 188: © Allan Ivy / Alamy; p. 190: © Arco Images / Alamy; p. 194: © Photononstop / Photolibrary Group; p. 201: © Comité Départemental du Tourisme du Morbihan; p. 201: © Bathilde Chaboche / Office de Tourisme de Belle Ile en Mer; p. 202: © Bathilde Chaboche / Office de Tourisme de Belle Ile en Mer; p. 203: © Robert Harding Picture Library Ltd / Alamy; p. 204: © Fabienne Fossez / Alamy; p. 205: © Stockfolio / Alamy; p. 208: © Comité Départemental du Tourisme du Morbihan; p. 210: © Conrad Williams; p. 211: © Geoffrey Morgan / Alamy; p. 213: © Cro magnon / Alamy; p. 215: © The Travel Library; p. 216: © Phil Wahlbrink/ WahlbrinkPHOTO / Alamy; p. 217: © Kevin Howchin / Alamy; p. 221: © Conrad Williams; p. 222: © The Travel Library; p. 223: © Bruno de la Sablière; p. 225: © Le Lodge Kerisper; p. 227: © Ian Sanderson – Kura Images; p. 230: © Thierry Retif / Hotel Gavrinis – www.gavrinis.com; p. 232: © Conrad Williams; p. 235: © Conrad Williams

1 Family Highlights of Brittany

France has represented different things to me at various crucial stages of my life: as a teenager spending long indolent summers in the country home of a French family; as a carefree student drunk on Gallic culture in Paris; as a thirty-something enjoying my first holiday with my husband-to-be; and as a house hunter while pregnant with my first baby five years ago. But I've come to experience this wonderful country the most deeply as a mum, living in and exploring France with my two young sons, and learning to appreciate to the full its manifold charms: stunning landscapes, a laidback attitude to life, and – last but by no means least – superb food and drink!

I'm not alone – 75 million foreign visitors to France each year make it the world's most popular holiday destination. A great many of these are British families, attracted by a number of factors – notably, France's proximity to Britain, especially with the blossoming of low-cost air travel, and its lower living costs, which make eating out and staying in interesting accommodation much more affordable than in the UK.

Brittany, easily accessible from Britain and boasting kilometres of stunning coastline, has long been a favourite with visitors from across the Channel. Unspoilt beaches, untouristy inland sites bursting with authentic Breton culture, and child-friendly crêperies are just a few of its draws. This is also a region awash in myths and legends: countless

Breton festival

sites are said to be linked with Merlin, Viviane, Sir Lancelot and other Arthurian figures, or with *korrigans* – shapeshifting Breton fairies with red flashing eyes, who like to substitute human children with changelings. The tales of mermaids and cities lost beneath the waves, recounted throughout this guide, are bound to enchant children of all ages.

Coming back down to earth, I'd like to stress that visiting France with children is not without its frustrations – for me, spoilt by having lived in central London with its round-the-clock facilities, the hardest aspect of French life has been the rigid and rather limited restaurant opening times and the tendency of shops, banks and businesses to shut down for three hours in the middle of the day. However, once you've got your head around this and adjusted your routines accordingly, you'll find Brittany one of Europe's most delightful regions to visit with children. Just bear in mind that the weather can turn nasty on you whatever the season, and make sure you save some of those wonderful museums and aquariums for rainy days!

BRITTANY FAMILY HIGHLIGHTS

Best Family Events The 'festival of children in Brittany', **Bugale Breizh**, brings together most of the region's children's traditional dance groups – around 1,000 youngsters in all – in the Côtes d'Armor town of Guingamp, renowned for Breton dancing. Over a single day in early July, participants as young as five dress in historical costume, while young visitors can take part in dance and workshops including puppet-making, cooking, traditional games and Breton wrestling. See p. 110.

Later that month or in early August, Lorient in the Morbihan hosts the **Festival Interceltique**, a week-long gathering of Celts from all over Western Europe. In addition to Celtic traditional, classical, folk, jazz and rock music and dancing, there are Breton games and sports galore, including demonstrations of and free tuition in *boules*, skittles, tug-of-war and more, plus workshops on woodland games. Some evenings are 'Nuits Magiques', with pipe bands, dancers, choirs and firework displays. See p. 200.

Best Cities **St-Malo** in the Ille-et-Vilaine is a combination of ancient walled pirates' city and gorgeous seaside resort. It also offers some of the best shopping in Brittany or Normandy, and has a fantastic aquarium. See p. 63.

Finistère's naval port of **Brest** may not be the prettiest city but it has a cracking sealife centre – one of the world's best – and a stunning natural bay, the Rade de Brest, which you can sail through in the company of cargo and military ships. Its former Nazi submarine pens are just one

Harbour, St-Malo

fascinating sight among its museums and other attractions. See p. 148.

Best Natural Attractions The Côtes d'Armor's **Côte du Granit Rose**, with its pinky-brown rocks eroded into odd shapes resembling skulls, tortoises and piles of crêpes, is one of France's most famous stretches of coast. A signposted circuit takes you past gorgeous turquoise bays, and some of the houses appear to be squashed between boulders. See p. 115.

The valley of **Huelgoat** in Finistère is strewn with as many legends as it is strangely shaped rocks. The best known, the Roche Tremblante or 'trembling rock', weighs about 100 tonnes but is balanced so precariously a child can make it move. Some people claim to make out wild boars' heads in the rocks of the Mare aux Sangliers and see fairies bathing in the Mare aux Fées. See p. 156.

In the Morbihan, the inland sea of the **Golfe du Morbihan** has a magical landscape of tiny

Côte du Granit Rose

Speaking in Tongues: The Breton Language

About 300,000 inhabitants of Brittany (and some people in the Loire Atlantique, which used to be part of Brittany) still speak Breton, which is descended from a branch of Celtic languages brought to the region by Roman–British settlers. Cornish and Welsh are the modern-day languages to which it's most closely related, and it's comprised of four dialects, though there are no set areas in which these are spoken – the language as a whole varies slightly between one village and its neighbours. It's never been an official language of France, despite efforts by supporters for state recognition, and this is one factor in its decline (1.3 million people spoke it in 1930, and around half of the population of southern Brittany spoke no other language, not even French). On the other hand, there have been some positive developments – in the 1970s Diwan schools (unfunded by the state) were set up to teach children Breton, and in 2004 the *Astérix* books (p.114) were translated into Breton and Gallo (another language of Brittany, based on Latin) – an important symbolic step given that *Astérix* is said to be based in Brittany. And as you venture deeper into Brittany, from about the Côtes d'Armor onwards, you'll begin to see street signs and place names in Breton as well as French.

It's by no means an easy language to pronounce, and you don't need to speak any to get by in Brittany, but you may have fun looking out for, recognising and trying out some of the following phrases on your travels:

Breizh – Brittany
brezhoneg – the Breton language
demat/devezh mat/salud dit – hello
kenavo – goodbye
ken emberr – see you soon
trugarez – thank you
mar plij – please
deuet mat oc'h – you're welcome
degemer mat – welcome
kreiz-kêr – town centre
da bep tu – all directions
porzh-houarn – train station
skol – school
ti/ty – house
ti-polis – police station
ti an douristred – tourist office
ti-kêr – town hall
krampouezh – crêpes
chistr – cider

islands that you can see by boat or from a plane or hot-air balloon. See p. 205.

Best Animal Park The **Domaine de Ménez-Meur** in Finistère is a conservation park with farm, forest and country circuits where you can see wolves, boar and deer, and endangered Breton breeds. Observation hides and viewing points are ubiquitous, and there are pony-and-trap rides and nature-related activities. See p. 159.

The Morbihan's **Ferme du Monde** is a remarkable farm with more than 400 domestic animals from around the world (including yaks, buffaloes and camels), created entirely by disabled workers. The eclectic programme of events includes calf races, balloon sculpting and traditional bread-making, and there's a children's farm, a *petit train*, pony rides, an animated scale model of a Breton village, puppet shows, and a play area. See p. 208.

Best Aquarium The **Grand Aquarium** in St-Malo in the Ille-et-Vilaine has an amazing **Nautibus** mini-submarine ride and a Bassin Ludique for young children, with a touchpool and funky interactive installations. See p. 72.

In Finistère, Brest's space-station-like **Océanopolis** is one of the world's very best sealife centres, with a penguin colony, a multiscreen helicopter trip over Antarctica, a glass lift down past the shark tank and much, much more. See p. 160.

Best Beach Resorts
Untouristy **St-Lunaire** in the Ille-et-Vilaine is a tranquil family resort with four lovely beaches, children's clubs and watersports, open-air family film screenings and lots of activities. See p. 66.

On its own peninsula in Finistère, **Carantec** is an intimate, relaxed, quite chic resort with masses of children's activities in summer, including beach clubs, free concerts, dance shows, circus acts, drawing and painting lessons, and a nature trail. You can tour the bay with its bird reserve and sea fort by canoe or cruiser, and there are six beaches, including the Plage de Kélenn with its sailing centre, play area, striped bathing huts and cafés. See p. 152.

Best Islands Wild and wind-lashed **Ouessant** 20km off the Finistère coast is home to the world's most powerful lighthouse, a lighthouse museum and unique dwarf black sheep. Explore it on foot, by bike, on horseback or by pony and trap. See p. 153.

Brittany's largest island, **Belle-Ile** off the Quiberon peninsula in the Morbihan, is a chic favourite among Parisians for its mild climate and idyllic beaches. Join local youngsters bodyboarding at Port Donnant, or climb a lighthouse, take a bus or taxi tour, hire a pony-and-trap or go horse-riding. See p. 202.

Best Boat Trips The ***bâteau-promenades*** on the lovely Rance estuary between St-Malo and Dinard in the Ille-et-Vilaine takes you past islands, coves, watermills, *malouinieres* (merchants' country dwellings), fishing villages and marine wildlife, including – if you're lucky – seals. Lunch and dinner trips include a 'Pirate's Menu' for children. See p. 81.

Trips in the ***Capitaine Némo***, a catamaran with submarine viewing 'salons', allow you to get up close and personal with marine life around the Iles Glénan off the coast of Finistère, with guided commentary in French by a marine expert. See p. 170.

Best Forest The **Fôret de Brocéliande** (or Paimpont) in the Ille-et-Vilaine is a wonderland of Arthurian myths and atmospheric ancient monuments, as well as a scenic area for walking, riding and mountain biking. See p. 67.

Best Outdoors Activities The forest of Villecartier in the Ille-et-Vilaine is home to the **Parc des Grands Chênes** with its acrobatic routes through the trees. Bring a picnic for lunch by the lake with its **Port Miniature**, where you can ride replica ferries, tugs, steamboats and fishing boats amidst scale models of Breton landmarks. You can also orienteer, walk and ride ponies. See p. 87.

The Ille-et-Vilaine also has a **Vélo Rail** – a system of quirky two-person bikes, joined side-by-side, that you ride along old train tracks through the heart of nature. See p. 88.

The Côtes d'Armor has a summer **Cap Armor** programme of free or cheap activities for locals and tourists across the *département*, including riding, mountain biking, sea canoeing, diving, volleyball, tennis, horse-and-carriage riding and Breton dancing. See p. 128.

Océanopolis, Brest

Parc des Grands Chênes

Best Museum The expanded **Musée de Bretagne** in Rennes in the Ille-et-Vilaine is a must-see for visitors to Brittany, tracing the region's history and identity through objects (including old toys), costumes, videos and more. It shares a building with the **Espace des Sciences**, a science museum with a planetarium and the Laboratoire de Merlin – a discovery zone with 30 hands-on installations. See p. 78.

On a coast bristling with majestic lighthouses, the **Musée des Phares et Balises** on Ouessant off Finistère is the world's only museum on the history of lighthouses and maritime signals. As well as navigation aids, there are models demonstrating the dangerous process of building lighthouses, plus objects from shipwrecks and displays on the harsh lives of lighthouse-keepers. See p. 168.

Fort la Latte

Best Castles The partially-ruined 13th century **Château de la Hunaudaye** in the Côtes d'Armor has child-friendly guides, a booklet with discovery trails, and free daily archaeology and weaving workshops in summer so parents can explore the medieval remains while the children get creative. Summer also sees spectacular *son-et-lumière* shows, and in September there's a Children's Day with games and workshops. See p. 123.

Also in Côtes d'Armor is one of the most dramatic sights on the entire Breton coast: the fortified medieval **Fort la Latte** rising from jagged cliffs against a backdrop of blue sea. Famous as a location for the final scenes of the 1958 film *The Vikings*, it has two drawbridges and the dungeon, plus an 18th century oven used to 'cook' cannonballs (to set enemy ships on fire). See p. 123.

Best Themepark The **Village Gaulois** in the Côtes d'Armor is a collection of Celtic-themed games in a setting out of an *Astérix* book, run by an association that channels profits into schools in Africa. See p. 128.

Best Art Site For just one day a year, in June, the hamlet of Nizon in Finistère hosts **Hangar't**, a quirky 'Fête des Cabanes' with installation pieces by modern artists placed in little huts that have been created from leaves, branches and other natural materials by local children. See p. 168.

Best Markets Best known for its mysterious megaliths, Carnac in the Morbihan has a stylish beach resort that – in addition to lots of children's activities – hosts **Nocturnes** evening markets in July and August, with stalls full of local produce and crafts. See p. 203.

Best Shops An unexpectedly great place for gifts and toys is **La Droguerie de Marine** in St-Malo in the Ille-et-Vilaine, an ancient marine hardware store that resembles an exotic ship. Alongside classic products for sailors there's a treasure trove of tin Pop Pop boats, games, ship's models, compasses, tin whistles, homewares and books. There's even a grocery section with local delicacies, from fish ravioli to salted-butter caramels. See p. 89.

In Concarneau in Finistère, the **Biscuitier Chocolatier Glacier Lanicol** has huge decorative chocolate animals to admire as you help yourself to some of the riotously colourful giant and mini meringues, tempting slabs of chocolate, mouth watering *kouignettes* (moist little cakes in praline, chocolate and almond, lime and other flavours), and *torchette* biscuits containing Breton seaweed. See p. 174.

BEST ACCOMMODATION

Best Family-Friendly Option The **Résidence Reine Marine** in St-Malo in the Ille-et-Vilaine has pristine modern apartments with sea views, direct beach access and use of an indoor pool, sauna, bar, games room, breakfast service, babysitting and laundrette. You pay a fraction what you would at the *résidence's* big sister, the Grand Hôtel des Thermes, but can use its famous seawater therapy centre and children's and beach clubs. See p. 97.

Best Grand Hotels The **Grand Hôtel des Bains** at Locquirec on the northern Finistère coast is an elegant 18th century seafront hotel with a fashionable New England feel and awesome bay views from its family rooms and beautiful decked terraces. As well as direct access to a sandy beach, it has an indoor saltwater pool, a Jacuzzi and spa, and there's a nearby sailing and diving school for all the family. The restaurant serves healthy food based on local seafood and organic produce. See p. 176.

In the Morbihan, close to Lorient, the **Château de Locguénolé** has 2km of private shoreline, a large outdoor pool beside its 'winter garden', which houses saunas, a Turkish bath and massage rooms, a tennis court, bike hire, a private pontoon for those arriving by boat and even its own helicopter offering trips to the Golfe du Morbihan, Belle-Ile and more. You stay in the castle itself or in its 18th century stone cottages 4km (2.5 miles) away towards the beaches but sharing its amenities, which include a Michelin-starred restaurant. See p. 224.

Château de Locguénolé

Le Lodge Kerisper

Best Seaside Hotels The **Castel Régis** at Brignogan–Plages in Finistère is a moderately priced option with a little sandy beach of its own, as well as lush gardens with children's play equipment and a panoramic waterside lounge with books and children's games – a great place to watch the sunset over a glass of wine. There's also a tennis court, canoes for hire, a sauna and an outdoor pool in high summer; rooms include family suites and a four-person 'gîte'. See p. 179.

At the northern end of Finistère's Baie d'Audierne, in the town of Audierne itself, the **Hôtel-Restaurant Le Goyen** is a genteel blue-shuttered harbour-front hotel with elegant rooms, most with a balcony facing the sea. There are spacious suites, some with panoramic views from their living rooms, a conservatory restaurant with a port view and a sophisticated children's menu, plus room service and babysitting. See p. 184.

Most Stylish Hotels In the unlikely setting of the ferry port of Roscoff in Finistère, the **Hôtel du Centre** has a fresh modern look in its 16 rooms, some of which can interconnect to form 'family apartments' – think traffic-light red and grey decor and walls embellished with quotes about the sea by Breton poets. Its former sardine bar has been transformed into a tapas restaurant from which you can watch *boules* matches as you eat breakfast, sandwiches and salads, or local seafood. See p. 178.

Le Lodge Kerisper in the yachting town of La Trinité-sur-Mer in the Morbihan has trendy 'beach hut' decor but doesn't overlook childrens' or parents' needs – there's an outdoor pool that's heated year round and equipped with games and waterwings, beach games and

Le Ty Nadan

waterproofs to borrow, bikes (and child seats) for hire, children's books and films to watch on your in-room DVD player, babysitting, a stunning bar and a massage and beauty treatment space. Staff organise outings, including sailing trips to nearby islands, and make up picnics, or you can just doze under the fruit trees while the children run around. See p. 226.

Best B&Bs **Au Char à Bancs** near St-Brieuc in the Côtes d'Armor has five shabby-chic rooms for up to four people, filled with quirky objects (old birdcages, radios and crockery), an utterly charming inn famous for its ham and sausage hotpot and rhubarb crêpes, a wooden fort and other original play equipment for children, Shetland ponies to pet (and ride in summer) and a river with pedalo hire in the warmer months. See p. 134.

At Rosnoën in Finistère, you can stay on a working honey farm with its own free museum, the **Ferme Apicole de Térenez**. The doubles and four-person rooms are fairly spartan, as you'd expect for the price, but all kinds of baby equipment is available, and there's also a playground, mountain bike hire and Ouessant sheep, hens, geese and other animals to pet in the wooded garden. Beaches are a 10-minute drive away. The farm shop sells gingerbread, nougat, biscuits and more. See p. 183.

Best Gîtes The chic *gîtes marins* at **Les Maisons de Bricourt**, part of superchef Olivier Roellinger's empire at Cancale in the Ille-et-Vilaine, are in a league of their own – seaside cottages with New England decor, they boast log fires, cute sleeping nooks for children, deluxe bathrooms, and superb kitchens with ovens designed by Roellinger and lots of complimentary goodies. A few steps away lies a vegetable and herb garden where you can pick ingredients for dinner on your private terrace. See p. 90.

More affordably, **La Villeneuve**, a complex of eight gîtes on the gorgeous Bélon estuary in Finistère, has an outdoor pool, a play area, a *boules* pitch and table tennis, woods to build dens in and lawns to run around on, plus practicalities such as cots, highchairs, child-safety gates, babysitting and a communal laundry. See p. 188.

Best Campsites **Le Ty Nadan** at Locunolé in Finistère has an outstanding range of activities, including canoeing on the river or sea, horse and pony rides, watercycling, treetop acrobatic courses, tennis and pedaloing. As well as four-star campsite standards such as a pool complex with waterslides and a paddling pool, it has babysitting and great children's clubs offering zoo trips, insect hunts, puppet shows, crêpe-making, films and more. Guests with tents can hire fridges, cots and highchairs, or there are mobile homes, a couple of apartments, and wooden chalets by the river. See p. 187.

Also in Finistère but a totally different kettle of fish, the **Aire Naturelle de Keraluic** at Plomeur is a small 'green' campsite based around a renovated Breton farm in the heart of the countryside and surrounded by forests yet only 6km (3.75 miles) from the coast. Facilities are kept to a minimum, but there's an unobtrusive play area, table tennis, a *boules* terrain, a games room with chess, cards and so on, and a cosy stone-walled library with books for all ages. B&B accommodation and studios are also available. See p. 186.

BEST EATING OPTIONS

Best Children-Friendly Restaurants On the busy Plage du Kélenn at the chic family resort of Carantec in Finistère, **Le Petit Relais** is a brasserie/pub/bar/*glacier* with a fine terrace, long opening hours, free Internet access, games, books and colouring sheets for children, and bottle-heating and baby-changing facilities. Come for late breakfasts/brunches, snacks (sandwiches, pastries and ice creams), and an unusually wide-ranging menu that includes tarts, *croques*, pasta dishes, salads, *chili con salsa*, Italian platters, Russian caviar and *moules Bretons* (mussels with cider). See p. 190.

Also in Finistère, at Landerneau with its famous bridge, the **Restaurant de la Mairie** goes all out to ensure relaxed family mealtimes, with a baby-changing room, toys and a pretty patio with a resident tortoise. Children get a good-value menu of tried-and-tested favourites, while parents can enjoy the speciality *timbale Neptune* – prawns, scallops and mushrooms in Cognac and

Seafood Restaurants, Cancale

cream – or other hearty local fare such as duck or veal kidneys. See p. 191.

Best Seafood **Au Biniou** in the family resort of Le Val-André in the Côtes d'Armor is a stylish fish restaurant popular with locals for its shellfish platters, mussels from a nearby bay and fresh local fish cooked simply or in more surprising ways – perhaps with coriander and chive noodles and Vietnamese fish sauce butter. The under-10s menu features excellent fish and top-notch desserts. See p. 138.

La Corniche at Brignogan-Plages on the northern Finistère coast looks like a sailors' dive but serves incredible seafood against panoramic bay views. The changing menus, written up on large chalkboards, might feature exquisite skate wing and delicious 'fisherman's stew', while the children's creamy monkfish comes with some of the best *frites* they'll ever taste. See p. 190.

Best Crêperies The super-friendly **Crêperie des Grèves** at Langueux in the Côtes d'Armor uses local farm produce, much of it organic, in its faultless galettes and crêpes, whether egg, ham or cheese, sugar and butter or chocolate versions for children, or more grown-up recipes such as smoked sausage, scallops with *julienne* vegetables or plump cod. Books for children are piled by the hearth, or they can wander out to the seaside play area as you enjoy a *bolée* of cider and keep an eye out from the window. See p. 141.

Also in the Côtes d'Armor, in the resort of St Cast-le-Guildo, the **Crêperie Chez Marie** has eccentric ornaments, including goblins, witches, frogs and pigs, walls covered with outsized flower frescoes, and a front terrace safely set on a pedestrianised street. Its all-day service makes it a good option for early dinners – especially given its wide-ranging menu, which includes galettes and crêpes but also the likes of steak and chips, fish or cheese tartlets, feta and olive salads, omelettes, and the town's mussels. See p. 139.

Best Vegetarian Food Not exclusively vegetarian, **Le Café Bleu** within St-Malo's walled city in the Ille-et-Vilaine offers great veggie salads and other non-meat options among its tasty galettes, savoury and dessert crêpes, and hearty sandwiches. Sometimes customers get a free *dégustation* (taster) of veggie pâté and bread, and most ingredients are organic and/or Fair Trade. If you're self-catering, you can stock up on organic mueslis, tuna terrines, Fair Trade coffee and so on while you're here. If you can't tear yourself away from the beach a minute's walk away, all dishes can be provided as takeaway. See p. 105.

Best Ethnic Restaurant Amid a sea of crêperies and seafood joints, the **Via Costa**, a camp Brazilian-themed 'fashion lounge' by the beach at Etables-sur-Mer in the Côtes d'Armor, stands out. In a decor of fairy lights and exotic flowers, you can enjoy everything from tandoori chicken brochettes and Thai salad to the speciality 'Brazilian' pizza with mozzarella, chocolate and banana. Save room for outlandish desserts such as crêpe 'tagliatelle' with red fruits, *sirop de menthe* and basil. You can also get tapas in the bar. See p. 140.

Best Outdoor Eating **Le Surf** at St-Lunaire in the Ille-et-Vilaine masquerades as a humble snack bar but somehow produces an amazing variety of wonderful dishes from its tiny kitchen, at bargain prices. You can enjoy anything from nutella and banana paninis to Indonesian king prawn salad with seaweed butter on its covered terrace or at one of its tables lined up along the sea wall, looking down over the untouristy Plage de Longchamp with its rock pools. See p. 106.

A great picnic spot is the **Fôret de Villecartier**, also in the Ille-et-Villaine. You can work up an appetite on the treetop adventure course, or orienteering, walking or riding ponies, and after your picnic you can relax in a pedalo or a replica ferry or steamboat on the lake. See p. 87.

Best Views At the **Château d'Eau** at Ploudalmézeau in Finistère, a 50m (165 ft) high former watertower with 360-degree views of the ocean and countryside, food is almost an irrelevance. But the galettes and crêpes, some of which are named in honour of keepers of local lighthouses, are good, and there's all-day service. See p. 192.

Also in Finistère, the more elaborate **Restaurant Patrick**

Jeffroy at Carantec has a panoramic dining room looking out over the yacht-filled Baie de Morlaix. The food is expensive and gorgeously presented – the daily-changing children's menu might include such delights as hermit crab and avocado salad, local pollack with new potatoes, and chocolate cake with strawberry sorbet. See p. 189.

Best Breakfasts In the picturesque oyster-farming port of Cancale in the Ille-et-Vilaine, the laidback little **Café du Port** has a decked harbour terrace where those tired of Continental pastries can get cooked breakfasts and freshly squeezed juices at fair prices. On a sweltering day, don't miss the iced chocolate drinks. See p. 102.

2 Planning a Family Trip to Brittany

BRITTANY

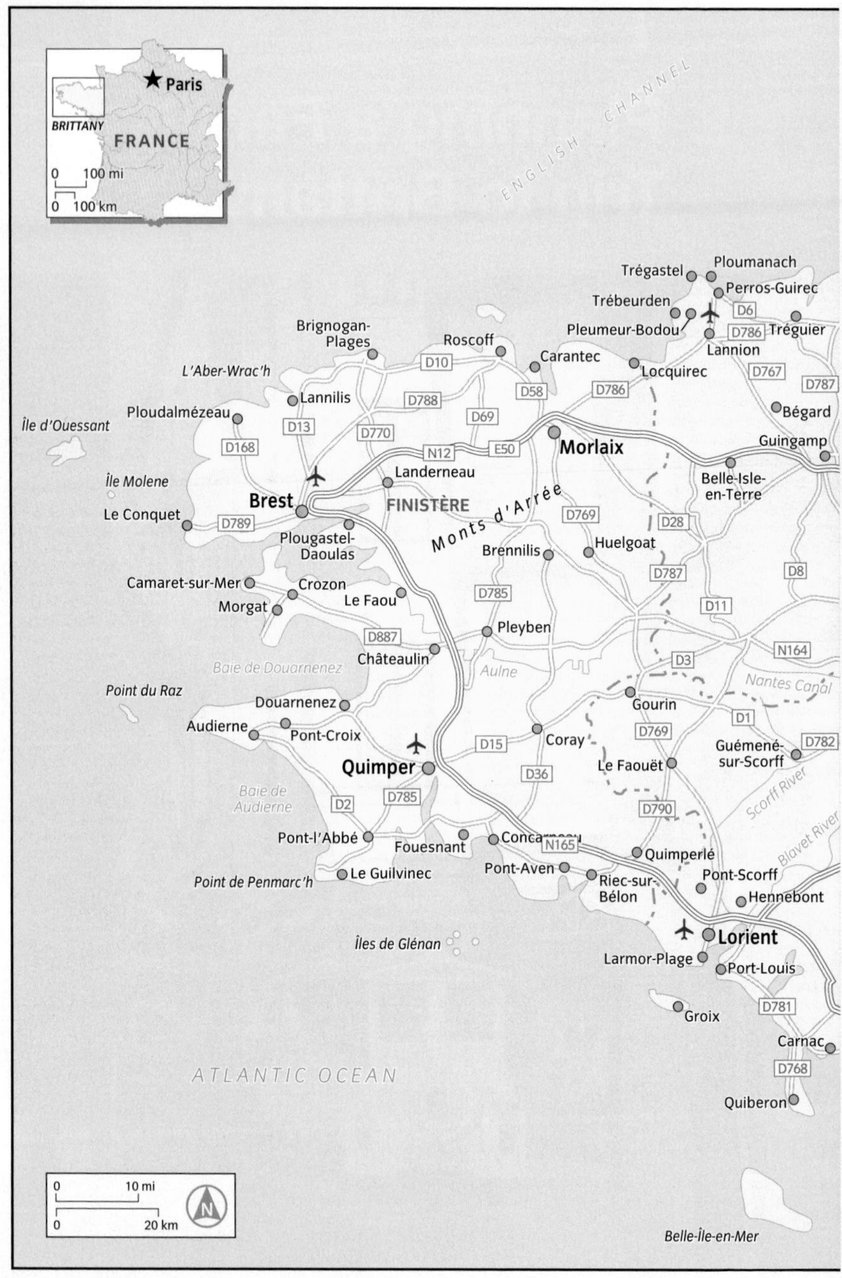

Paris
BRITTANY
FRANCE
0 100 mi
0 100 km
ENGLISH CHANNEL
Trégastel
Ploumanach
Perros-Guirec
Trébeurden
D6
Pleumeur-Bodou
D786
Tréguier
Lannion
Brignogan-Plages
Roscoff
Carantec
Locquirec
L'Aber-Wrac'h
D10
D767
D58
D786
D787
Lannilis
D788
Bégard
Ploudalmézeau
D69
Île d'Ouessant
D13
D770
Guingamp
D168
Morlaix
N12
E50
Landerneau
Belle-Isle-en-Terre
Île Molene
Brest
FINISTÈRE
Le Conquet
D789
D769
D28
Monts d'Arrée
Plougastel-Daoulas
Brennilis
Huelgoat
D787
D8
Camaret-sur-Mer
Crozon
Le Faou
D785
D11
Morgat
Pleyben
D887
N164
Châteaulin
D3
Baie de Douarnenez
Aulne
Nantes Canal
Point du Raz
Gourin
Douarnenez
D1
D769
Audierne
Pont-Croix
Coray
Guémené-sur-Scorff
D15
D782
Quimper
Le Faouët
D36
Scorff River
Baie de Audierne
D785
D790
D2
Blavet River
Pont-l'Abbé
Concarneau
Fouesnant
N165
Quimperlé
Pont-Scorff
Pont-Aven
Le Guilvinec
Riec-sur-Bélon
Point de Penmarc'h
Hennebont
Îles de Glénan
Lorient
Larmor-Plage
Port-Louis
Groix
D781
Carnac
ATLANTIC OCEAN
D768
Quiberon
0 10 mi
0 20 km
N
Belle-Île-en-Mer

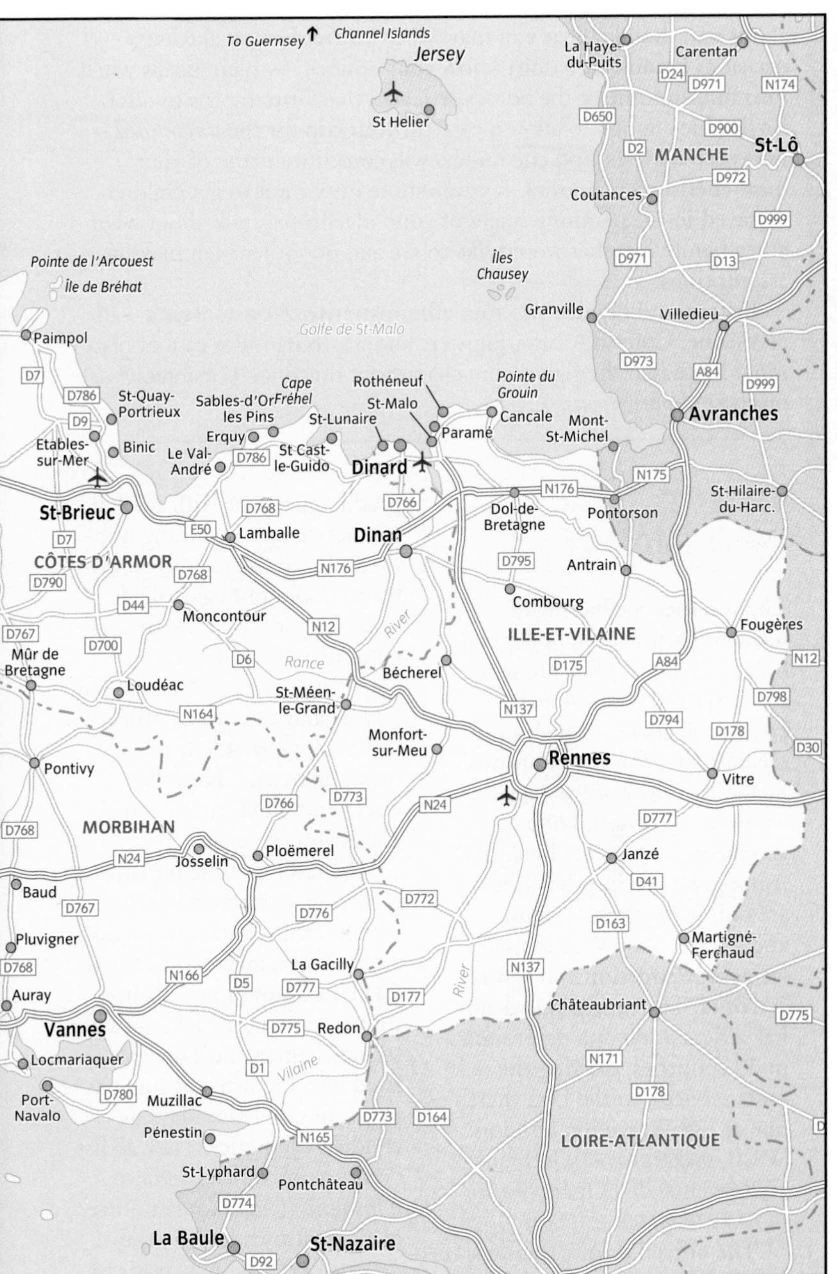
To Guernsey
Channel Islands
Jersey
St Helier
La Haye-du-Puits
Carentan
MANCHE
St-Lô
Coutances
Îles Chausey
Granville
Villedieu
Avranches
Pointe de l'Arcouest
Île de Bréhat
Paimpol
Golfe de St-Malo
Cape Fréhel
Rothéneuf
Pointe du Grouin
St-Malo
Cancale
St-Quay-Portrieux
Sables-d'Or les Pins
St-Lunaire
Paramé
Mont-St-Michel
Erquy
Etables-sur-Mer
Binic
Le Val-André
St Cast-le-Guido
Dinard
St-Brieuc
Dol-de-Bretagne
Pontorson
St-Hilaire-du-Harc.
Lamballe
Dinan
CÔTES D'ARMOR
Antrain
Combourg
Moncontour
ILLE-ET-VILAINE
Fougères
Mûr de Bretagne
River Rance
Bécherel
Loudéac
St-Méen-le-Grand
Monfort-sur-Meu
Rennes
Pontivy
Vitre
MORBIHAN
Josselin
Ploëmerel
Janzé
Baud
Pluvigner
Martigné-Ferchaud
La Gacilly
River
Auray
Châteaubriant
Vannes
Redon
Locmariaquer
Vilaine
Port-Navalo
Muzillac
Pénestin
LOIRE-ATLANTIQUE
St-Lyphard
Pontchâteau
La Baule
St-Nazaire
D24
D971
N174
D650
D900
D2
D972
D999
D971
D13
D973
A84
D999
D7
D786
D9
D786
N175
N176
D768
D766
E50
D7
N176
D795
D790
D768
D44
N12
D767
D700
D6
D175
A84
N12
D798
N164
N137
D794
D178
D30
D766
D773
N24
D768
N24
D777
D41
D767
D776
D772
D163
D768
N166
D5
D777
N137
D177
D775
D775
D1
N171
D178
D780
D773
D164
N165
D774
D92

Planning any family trip means finding a happy medium between inflexible military-style advance plotting and being so *laissez-faire* about your holiday that you may, when you're there, make lousy decisions because you don't know your options – which means you'll miss out on some of the best experiences that Brittany has to offer. Be flexible enough to allow a place in your trip for the *unplanned* – unexpected events and encounters will constitute many of your most cherished memories. It's even more important to get children involved in the planning stages of your adventure – talk about what every family member would like to see and do rather than making assumptions.

Brittany subdivides into four administrative ***départements*** – Ille-et-Vilaine, Côtes d'Armor, Finistère and Morbihan. For ease of planning, I've based the sightseeing chapters of this book (Chapters 3–6) on these *départements.*

VISITOR INFORMATION

The Internet age has made researching/planning holidays a breeze. France's official tourist board website, ***www.franceguide.com***, clicks through to separate sites for 30+ countries, including ***http://uk.franceguide.com/*** for the UK and ***http://ie.franceguide.com*** for Ireland. Among the services they offer are online brochure ordering and a travel shop with booking for accommodation and sports activities. The tourist board also has offices, **Maisons de France**, in 29 countries, offering the same services. In the UK, there's one at 178 Piccadilly, **London** W1 (*09068 244123*), in France at 20 avenue de l'Opéra, **Paris** (*01 42 96 70 00*).

The official tourist websites let you pick the region you're heading for – including Brittany – from a scroll-down menu, producing a page with the full contact details, including website links, of the regional tourist board (Comité Régionale de Tourisme or CRT), departmental tourist offices (Comités Départmentales de Tourisme or CDTs) and the tourist offices (*offices de tourisme*) of major towns and cities. Note that CRTs and CDTs aren't actual places you can visit.

The CRT website for Brittany is ***www.tourismebretagne.com***, which is translated into English and other languages. I've listed CDT websites under 'Visitor Information' in the relevant sightseeing chapter; most are translated into English and some have pages on family holidays or children's activities. They all list every tourist office, *syndicat d'initiative* (small tourist office) or *mairie* (town hall) in the *département*. You may want to print out the page for any *département* you plan to visit.

Another source for tourist offices is ***www.tourisme.fr/recherche/e_main.hm***.

Child-Specific Websites

Brittany's tourist board website (above) has a '**Breizh Trotters**' section for 15–25-year-olds. Another useful resource, ***www.france4families.com***, has lots of general information about France, plus guides to various French regions, including Brittany.

More general family-oriented sites are ***www.takethefamily.com***, with tips, destination guides (including lots on camping in France) and a discussion board; ***www.babygoes2.com***, with general tips and location reports; and ***www.deabirkett.com***, a handy forum for exchanging tips and views, run by the former *Guardian* children's travel specialist.

For route planning ahead of a trip, or even just general interest, ***http://maps.google.com*** has zoomable maps of just about anywhere, directions to and from places, and even detailed satellite images – look at Brest's Océanopolis from above, for instance, or even the hotel you're going to stay in! If you have the time to be really organised in advance, the excellent ***www.viamichelin.com*** can give you detailed directions (plus maps) from your home town to your destination in France, or between places in France, including the location of speed cameras.

Entry Requirements, Customs & Bringing Pets

Passports & Visas

Citizens of other **European Union** (EU) countries need an **identity card** to enter France – for the time being, this means a passport for UK citizens. **Non-EU citizens** need a passport but few nationalities require a **visa** – South Africans are among the few. However, stays of more than three months by non-EU citizens do require a visa. For French embassies/consulates round the world, see ***www.diplomatie.gouv.fr/venir/visas/index.html***.

Taking Your Pet

Under the **Pet Travel Scheme** (PETS), UK-resident dogs and cats can now travel to many other EU countries and return to the UK without being quarantined. Dogs and cats are issued with a **passport** (by a vet) after being fitted with a microchip and vaccinated against rabies at least 21 days prior to travel. On re-entry to the UK, you need to get your pet treated against ticks and tapeworm (by any EU vet 24–48 hours before being checked in with a transport company approved by the scheme). For full details, check ***www.defra.gov.uk/animalh/quarantine/index.htm***.

Most French hotels and some self-catering properties accept animals, usually with an extra fee (averaging € 7 (£ 4.65) per night). The commercial website *www.visitfrance.co.uk* is a good source of pet-friendly self-catering options.

Coming Home

Visitors to France from other EU countries can bring home any amount of goods for personal use, except new vehicles, mail-order buys, and more than 800 cigarettes, 10 litres of spirits, 90 litres of wine and 110 litres of beer. Travellers from outside the EU must declare all transported goods and pay duty or tax on those worth more than € 175 (£ 118). All visitors leaving with more than € 7600 (£ 5135) must declare the amount to customs. The French customs website, *www.douane.gouv.fr*, is translated into English, German and Spanish.

Money

The Euro

France – in common with 11 other countries at the time of writing – has the **euro** (€) as its currency. There are 100 **cents** in a euro, with **notes** for € 5–500 and **coins** for 1 cent–€ 2.

As of writing, the **euro-sterling exchange rate** was € 1.48 to £ 1 (68p to € 1), making mental calculations fairly easy (drop a third to get a rough figure in pounds). For current rates and a currency converter, see *www.xe.com*.

Credit & Debit Cards

Most French shops, restaurants and hotels take credit or debit cards, or at least **Visa** and **Mastercard** – **American Express** and **Diner's Club** are only really accepted in expensive hotels and restaurants. There is often a lower spending limit of € 7–15 (£ 4.65–10) for cards. The only **places unlikely to accept cards** today are B&Bs, small campsites and inexpensive rural inns.

You now use your **PIN** number when making a purchase with your card as well as when using it at a cashpoint, except at automated pumps at **petrol stations** out of hours, which, frustratingly, still refuse foreign cards.

Before you leave, tell your credit card company you're going abroad, as they sometime put a **block on cards** that deviate from their normal spending pattern.

For **lost or stolen cards**, see p. 52.

Traveller's Cheques

These are becoming a thing of the past now that cities and most towns have 24-hour ATMs, and you need to show ID every time you cash one. If you do choose to take some traveller's cheques, perhaps as a backup, you can get them at some banks, building societies, travel agents and the Post Office, among other outlets. Keep a record of their serial numbers

What Things Cost in Brittany	€	*£
1 litre unleaded 95 petrol	€ 1.27	£ 0.86
Hire of medium-sized car (per week)	€ 200–1350	£ 134–910
Taxi ride	€ 2 base fare; € 1 per km	£ 1.35; £ 0.67
City/town bus fare, adult	€ 1.20	£ 0.80
City/town bus fare, child 5 or over	€ 1.20	£ 0.80
Single train fare Quimper–Brest (75km (46 miles))	€ 21.50	£ 14.50
Single train fare child 4–11 (75km (46 miles))	€ 16	£ 11
Single TGV fare, Rennes–Vannes (110km (69 miles))	€ 30	£ 20
Single TGV fare child 4–11 (110km (69 miles))	€ 23	£ 15.50
Single Air France fare, Paris–Brest (600km (375 miles))	€ 62–155 (inc taxes)	£ 42–105
Single Air France fare, Paris–Brest, children over 2	€ 62–155 (inc taxes)	£ 42–105
Admission to zoo, adult	€ 13	£ 9
Admission to zoo, child 4–12	€ 6.50	£ 4.50
Admission to public museum	free	free
Cinema ticket, adult	€ 8	£ 5.40
Cinema ticket, child	€ 5.60	£ 3.75
British newspaper	€ 0.55	£ 0.47
Local telephone call (per minute)	€ 0.03–0.09	£ 0.02–0.06
European phone call (per minute)	€ 0.22	£ 0.15
Fixed-price menu at mid-priced restaurant	€ 14–18	£ 9.50–12
Under-12s menu at mid-priced restaurant	€ 9	£ 6
1 litre milk in supermarket	€ 0.78	£ 0.52
1 litre apple juice in supermarket	€ 0.78	£ 0.52
1.5 litre bottle still water in supermarket	€ 0.20	£ 0.15
1kg bananas in supermarket	€ 1.20	£ 0.80
Ham & cheese baguette from takeaway counter	€ 3.50	£ 2.40
Packet of 20 small Pampers in supermarket	€ 8.50	£ 5.75
330ml infant milk in supermarket	€ 0.60	£ 0.40

*Assuming a conversion rate of £ 1= €1.48

in case of loss or theft, and carry them separately from money and/or cards.

Cashpoints

There are 24-hour cashpoint machines or ATMs outside all French banks and in many supermarket lobbies – even relatively small ones in out-of-the-way towns – and withdrawing cash is rarely a problem unless you've gone over your limit. You usually get a better rate at a cashpoint than you would at an exchange booth (which may also take a commission), but your bank will probably charge you a fee for using a foreign cashpoint, so don't withdraw small sums every day or two as you may at home.

It's also a good idea to bring some cash into France as a backup, and to have two or more cards in case of a hiccup – you can make withdrawals from cashpoints using credit cards, paying interest on the advance from the moment you receive the cash.

When to Go & What to Pack

The weather in Brittany can be wildly **changeable**, switching from glorious sunshine to pouring rain in the blink of an eye. As in the UK, winters are very cold and summers increasingly hot. May can be a grey drizzle-fest, particularly on the west coast, and even in summer you need to pack light sweaters, waterproof coats and hats, and wellie boots alongside swimming gear (or buy some while you're in France). If you plan to eat in some of the fancier hotel restaurants during your stay, you also need to pack quite smart clothes, including shirts and trousers for males of the species.

A very helpful tool for planning days out is ***www.meteofrance.com***; even with only basic French (you need to know the days of the week) you get a general idea of what to expect in your area from its click-on maps. Or call ☎ *08 92 68 02 XX* (XX is the number of the *département* – 35 for Ille-et-Vilaine, 22 for Côtes d'Armor, 29 for Finistère, 56 for Morbihan). A good English-language website is ***http://weather.uk.msn.com***.

Since Brittany is most popular among tourists for its beaches and coastal resorts, it is at its busiest – and most expensive – in **July and August**.

Remember that the French holiday *en masse* in August, meaning congested roads and resorts, and big family attractions such as Brest's Océanopolis get very crowded. On the other hand, this is when most **festivals and events**, including **children's beach clubs**, take place. I've listed many of these beach clubs, which are often called 'Clubs Mickey', in the relevant sightseeing chapters; otherwise, they are detailed on tourist office websites or centrally on the national beach clubs federation's website, ***www.fncp.fr***.

Otherwise, **spring, early or late summer** or **autumn** can be

Average Daytime Temperature & Rainfall in Brittany

	Jan	Feb	Mar	Apr	May	June	July	Aug	Sept	Oct	Nov	Dec
Temp. (degree C)	9.3	8.6	11.1	17.7	16	22.7	25.1	24.1	21.2	15.5	9.5	6.2
Rainfall (cm; St-Malo)	8.06	5.24	4.79	6.4	5.72	3.58	4.97	4.26	4.84	8.29	7.81	8.72

Children's Kit

The following items can make travelling with babies or young children in Brittany easier or more relaxing:

Bébétel Baby Monitor Unlike battery-powered listening devices, this is not limited by range and suffers no interference, so you can use it in all hotel restaurants. You plug it into a standard phoneline (there are foreign adapter sets) and programme in your mobile number (you may have to add the international code); if your child gets up or cries, the monitor calls you. It costs a hefty £ 180 or so (see ***www.bebetel.com***); a few hotels have them but none, at the time of writing, in Brittany.

Littlelife Baby Carriers These backpacks-with-children-in are great if you're walking or hiking a lot and don't want to be encumbered with a buggy – include 'Voyager', with a zip-off bag for drinks, snacks and wipes, for about £ 170; lighter models start at half that. They're sold at ***www.johnlewis.com*** and outdoor pursuits shops, as are the firm's very handy compact superabsorbent **travel towels**.

Portable Highchairs Most French restaurants provide at least one highchair, but if they don't, or it's taken, or it's a weird old-style one without a front bar, you may be left trying to eat with one hand and hold a squirming baby or toddler with the other. Lightweight options you can carry around include the supremely compact 'Handbag Highchair' (a loop of fabric that secures your baby to the chair), the foldable Handysitt toddler seat, and The Early Years' inflatable booster seat. All are sold at ***www.bloomingmarvellous.co.uk***, with prices £ 15–75.

Boardbug Baby and Toddler Monitor Great for the beach (p. 28) or for shopping, this award-winning wristwatch-style monitor alerts you whenever your little one (or ones – the parent unit can be paired with up to three child units) strays from you, with adjustable distances from 2–150m. It costs about £ 55 from ***www.travellingwithchildren.co.uk***.

charming times to visit, when you have many animal parks and beaches virtually to yourself. But you'll need contingency plans for those days, all too frequent, when the weather lets you down, and smaller attractions may not be open – you're best advised to save Brittany's wonderful museums, aquaria and other indoor attractions for rainy days.

Public & School Holidays

French **national holidays** are called *jours feriés*; banks and small shops close but larger supermarkets increasingly open in the morning. Most museums close but many other visitor sites stay open, as do the majority of restaurants. If there's a public holiday on a Thursday or Tuesday, many people take the

Friday or Monday off as well – this is called *faisant le pont* ('making a bridge').

The main public holidays are **New Year's Day** (1 Jan), **Easter Monday** (Mar or Apr), **Labour Day** (Fête du Travail; 1 May), **VE Day** (8 May), **Whit Monday** (late May), **Ascension Thursday** (late May/40 days after Easter), **Bastille Day** (14 July), **Assumption of the Blessed Virgin** (15 Aug), **All Saint's Day** (1 Nov), **Armistice Day** (11 Nov) and **Christmas Day** (25 Dec).

There are five **school holidays** a year in France: 2 weeks in February, 2 weeks at Easter, all of July and August, 1 week at the end of October, and 2 weeks at Christmas. As in the UK, holidays are staggered round the country: Brittany is in Zone A. However, some tourist sites take into account the holiday in force in their own area, Parisian holidays (Zone C) and sometimes holidays in neighbouring areas (the Loire Atlantique and western Normandy bordering Brittany are also in Zone A).

The following are sample dates for general guidance:

18 Feb–6 Mar (A), 11–27 Feb (B), 4–20 Feb (C)

22 Apr–9 Mar (A), 15 Apr–2 May (B), 8–24 Apr (C)

4 July–2 Sept (all)

22 Oct–3 Nov (all)

17 Dec–3 Jan (all)

Tourist sites and roads are busier during these periods, especially July and August, and hotels often more expensive, but remember that many museums, galleries and other venues host **extra children's activities** in the holidays, and resorts have children's beach clubs (p. 24) and special events and entertainment.

If you do visit at a busy period, note that the French tend to go out mid-afternoon, after the lunch break, so mornings can be good times to see the more popular attractions.

Special Events

For my pick of the best family-friendly happenings throughout the year, from puppet festivals to *son-et-lumière* extravaganzas, see the 'Children-Friendly Events and Entertainment' section of each sightseeing chapter.

One festival that you'll find all over Brittany, in just about every town and village, is the **fest noz** – evenings of traditional Celtic music and circle dances revived in the 1950s, often with a bonfire. You'll find one near you on any Saturday evening (look for flyers on town hall notice boards and in shop and supermarket windows), with visitors welcome to join in the dancing and general merrymaking for free; you pay for drinks and food.

Insurance & Health

Travel Insurance

Travellers to France from other EU countries now need to carry their **European Health**

Insurance Card (EHIC), which replaced the E111 form as proof of entitlement to free/reduced-cost medical treatment abroad. The quickest way to apply for one is online (*www.ehic.org.uk*), or call ☎ *0845 606 2030* or get a form from a post office. You still pay upfront for treatment and related expenses; the doctor will give you a form you use to reclaim most of the money (about 70% of doctors' fees and 35–65% of medicines/prescription charges), by filling in a form you request by phone when you get home.

Note, however, that the EHIC only covers '*necessary* medical treatment', and it does not cover repatriation costs, lost money, baggage or cancellation, and so is no replacement for **travel insurance**. Before you buy the latter, though, check whether your existing insurance policies, credit cards or bank account covers you for lost luggage, cancelled tickets or medical expenses. If they don't, an example of cover for a family of four travelling to France for 2 weeks, without any adventure sports, with a reputable online insurer such as *www.travelinsuranceweb.com* is £ 20.49; an annual multi-trip policy costs £ 41.49, so is well worth it if you make more than two trips a year. Make sure your package includes **trip-cancellation insurance** to help you get your money back if you have to back out of a trip or go home early (both more likely if you're travelling with youngsters), or if your travel supplier goes bust. Allowed reasons for cancellation can range from sickness to natural disasters or a destination being declared unsafe for travel.

Other **non-EU nationals** – with the exceptions of Canadians, who have the same rights as EU citizens to medical treatment within France – need comprehensive travel insurance that covers medical treatment overseas. Even then, you pay bills upfront and apply for a refund at home.

Staying Healthy

There are no real health risks while travelling in France, and you don't need vaccinations. For general advice on travelling with children, read *Your Child Abroad: a Travel Health Guide*, by Dr Jane Wilson-Howarth and Dr Matthew Ellis (Bradt).

If You Fall Ill

For **emergency treatment, doctors** and **chemists**, see p. 50 and p. 51.

Bring along copies of **prescriptions** in case you or anyone in your family loses their medication or runs out. Carry the generic name of prescription medicines, in case a local pharmacist is unfamiliar with the brand name. You should also bring along an extra pair of contact lenses or prescription glasses.

When flying, pack any **prescription medicines** you'll need while in the air in your hand luggage in their original containers, with chemist's labels. At the time of writing, anti-terrorism precautions required some medicines to be verified by airport chemists.

If you or your child has an illness that may make explanation of what's happening impossible, and that needs swift and accurate treatment (such as epilepsy, diabetes, asthma or a food allergy), the charity **MedicAlert** (***www.medicalert.org.uk***) provides body-worn bracelets or necklets. These are engraved with the wearer's medical condition(s)/ vital details, ID number and a 24-hour emergency telephone number that accepts reverse charge calls so his or her medical details can be accessed from anywhere in more than 100 languages.

Travelling Safely with Children in Brittany

France – especially outside Paris and other major cities – is generally a very safe country. A traveller's main worry, as in most countries, is the risk of being targeted by **pickpockets and petty thieves**, and so travel with your car doors locked as a precaution. As a parent, be especially wary of French drivers; many pay no heed to the speed limit, exceed the alcohol limit and drive aggressively. Virtually no one in France stops at **pedestrian crossings**, so tell your child to wait until vehicles are motionless before proceeding.

As everywhere, **hold hands with young children** and don't let them out of your sight unless someone you trust is supervising them – they can move faster than you think. Avoid situations where your child could get swept away in a **crowd**, and with older children agree on **a place to meet** should you get parted – at the information desk at a museum, for instance. Make sure they have your mobile number and accommodation address on them, with instructions to ask for a member of the police force (*agent de police* or *gendarme*) should they not be able to find you. Their name should never be visible on their bag/clothing, and tell them the importance of **never divulging their name to a stranger**.

Beaches can be lethal: you lay back and close your eyes for what seems like a second, and when you open them your child is nowhere to be seen. With the sea close by, the potential for disaster is clear. The rule is to take it in turns to flake out while one parent keeps watch. If you're alone, you have no option but to stay hyper-alert. For peace of mind, especially if you have more than one child to keep an eye on, invest in **Boardbug** wrist-worn monitors (p. 25) with adjustable distance alarms for children of varying ages. You could also try a set of walking reins if you have a toddler who likes to go walkabout.

Specialised Resources

For Single Parents

For a useful 'Holidays' page with contact details of useful associations and operators in the UK, see *www.singleparents.org.uk*. The US-based *www.singleparent travelnet* is also good for travel advice.

One Parent Families (*0800 018 5026 www.oneparentfamilies.org.uk*) is a British charity offering info and advice for lone parents; **Gingerbread** (*0800 018 4318*, *www.gingerbread.org.uk*) is similar, with members getting regular emails with discounts and holiday ideas. Members of both get discounts with tour operator **Eurocamp** (p. 36), which has an Arrival Survival service to help lone parents unpack and settle in. Other camping operators, including **Siblu** (p. 36), offer discounts, as do most **youth hostels** (p. 43).

For Grandparents

Grandparents travelling with children are a rapidly growing market, but specialist operators in the field tend to be US-based, and there are no current tours including Brittany.

Grandparents – many of whom may be retired and living in France – are most likely to holiday with their children and grandchildren in gîtes (p. 44). If you take your grandchildren on outings, remember that over-60s generally get **discounts** on travel tickets, museum and zoo entry and so on.

For Families with Special Needs

Many of France's historic buildings, including museums and hotels, have limited or non-existent **wheelchair access**. Older town hotels, in particular, lack lifts. That said, modern facilities are up-to-scratch, and most hotels have at least a couple of accessible or ground-floor rooms. **Holiday Care** (*0845 124 9971*, *www.holidaycare.org.uk*) publishes overseas information guides (about £ 5) listing accommodation they believe to be accessible but haven't inspected in person.

Although the Channel Tunnel is a long way from Brittany, if you come to the region via Normandy, it is within easy reach of the latter. Travelling on the **Eurotunnel** (p. 34) is easier than ferries for wheelchair users because you stay in your car. Alternatively, **Eurostar** (p. 34) offers first-class travel for second-class fares for disabled people.

The 21st Century Traveller

Mobile Phones

It's indispensable to have your mobile phone with you if you're driving with children. Luckily, these days it's usually hassle-free to use a British mobile phone in France: it will simply switch over to a **French network** when you reach France, and you can call British numbers and French numbers directly, or sometimes using the international dialling code (it seems to vary). It's wise to **check in advance with your service provider** that your phone is set up for 'international roaming', and have them explain the procedure for accessing voicemails while abroad (again, this is usually trouble-free, but do double check).

Call charges to UK or French numbers will be higher than within the UK, and you will also pay for any incoming calls from your home country. If you're going to be making or receiving a lot of calls, or go abroad often, it might be worth buying an **international SIM card** to temporarily replace your UK one; see, for instance, ***www.0044.co.uk***. This will give you a local number and lower calling rates. Check first though, that your phone is not locked to its UK network. Or, if you're staying more than a few weeks or come to France repeatedly, you could just buy a pay-as-you-go mobile phone from a communications shop such as France Télécom/Orange, found in all largish town centres, or even from a large supermarket.

For those from further afield, such as the **USA**, the situation is basically the same provided you have a world-capable multiband phone on a **GSM** (Global System for Mobiles) system, with 'international roaming' activated. Again, installing an international SIM card can save you money if you use the phone frequently.

Recharge your phone whenever you get the chance (many come with travel adapters you can plug into your car's cigarette lighter).

Other Phones

For information about **area** and **international dialling codes** and **public phones**, see p. 53.

The Internet

Large cities and most towns of any size have a choice of Internet access points, whether in **cyber cafés**, public **libraries** or the **tourist office**; tourist offices will provide you with a list, or sites such as ***www.cybercafe.com*** and ***www.cybercaptive.com*** can be helpful. A good French site is ***www.cybercafe.fr***. You can also get (expensive) Internet access in some **post offices**, and some major cities have **Internet kiosks** in the street.

To **retrieve your emails**, ask your Internet Service Provider (ISP) if it has a **web-based interface** tied to your existing account. If it doesn't, set up a **free web-based email account**, with, for instance, ***www.yahoo.com*** or ***www.hotmail.com***. You might want to start one up anyway, as backup in case of hiccups with your existing account.

Most **hotels**, mid range and up (and sometimes also budget ones), have either a terminal where you can access the Internet for free (or for a small charge) or means by which you can access it from your laptop – through a **modem connection/dataport** in your room (meaning you pay as you would a phone call, which is expensive in hotels; you may also need an adapter) or, increasingly, through free **Wi-Fi** ('wireless fidelity') access throughout the hotel. Wi-Fi access is also available in many airports and cafés. Most new laptops come already wireless-enabled; otherwise you need to install an access card, from, for instance, *www.shop.bt.com* or computer stores.

If you're a touch typist and need to do a lot of emailing, **French keyboards**, which have letters in different places, will slow you down.

ESSENTIALS

Getting There

By Plane **Low-cost airlines** have opened up Brittany to air travellers: the situation fluctuates, but at the time of writing you could fly from points in the **UK and Ireland**, including the Channel Islands, to:

Dinard (Ille-et-Vilaine)

Rennes (Ille-et-Vilaine)

Brest (Finistère)

Lorient (Morbihan)

Companies that operate regular flights to destinations in Brittany from Britain and/or Ireland are **Ryanair** (UK ☎ *0871 246 0000*, Ireland ☎ *0818 303030*, France ☎ *0892 232375*, *www.ryanair.com*); **Flybe** (UK ☎ *0871 700 0535*, Ireland ☎ *01890 925532*, outside UK ☎ *00 44 13 922 685 29*, *www.flybe.com*), **Aer Lingus** (Ireland ☎ *08181 365000*, UK ☎ *0870 876 5000*, Europe ☎ *00 353 818 365 044*, *www.aerlingus.com*); **Aer Arann** (Ireland ☎ *0818 210210*, UK ☎ *0800 587 2323*, and rest of world ☎ *00 353 6170 4428*, *www.aerarann.com*). For who flies where, see the 'Getting There' section of the relevant sightseeing chapters.

As a general rule, **under-2s fly free**, if they sit on your knee; older than that, they pay the same fare as you. **Fares** can start as little as £ 0.01 depending on your destination and when you book, but don't include **airport taxes and other charges**, which can add up to about £ 60–80 for a family of four. Also, some airlines, including Ryanair, might charge extra for checked-in baggage.

You can also fly to **Paris** from the UK or Ireland with a number of operators, including **British Airways** (UK ☎ *0870 850 9850*, France ☎ *0825 8254400*, *www.britishairways.com*) and **Air France** (UK ☎ *0870 142 4343*, France ☎ *0820 820820*, *www.airfrance.com*). From Paris, there are flights to **Rennes** (Ille-et-Vilaine), **Lannion** (Côtes d'Armor), **Brest** and **Quimper** (Finistère) and **Lorient** (Morbihan) with Air France (above).

Among airlines that fly regularly between the **USA** and Paris are: **American Airlines** (☎ *800 433 7300*, *www.aa.com*), **British Airways** (☎ *800-AIRWAYS*), **Continental Airlines** (☎ *800 525 0280*, *www.continental.com*), and **Delta Air Lines** (☎ *800 241 4141*, *www.delta.com*). **Air France** (above) flies to Paris from the USA and Canada, and **Air Canada** (☎ *888 247 2262*,

www.aircanada.com) flies there from Toronto and Montreal.

There are currently no direct flights from **Australia** to Paris; most people go to London and get a connecting flight. **South African Airways** (✆ *0861 359722*, **www.flysaa.com**) flies to Paris from Cape Town and other cities in South Africa.

What can you take on flights: Passengers between the UK and France are allowed one laptop-sized bag. You are only allowed to take small quantities of liquids in your cabin luggage or on your person. These liquids must be in individual containers with a maximum capacity of 100 millilitres each. You must pack these containers in one transparent, re-sealable plastic bag of not more than one litre capacity. Drinks and toiletries can, however, be purchased in airport shops once you've passed through security. Remember that the situation may change at short notice for security reasons. Check with your airline prior to packing about current regulations so you don't waste time repacking at the airport.

By Road

Ferries

Brittany has ferry ports at **St-Malo** in the Ille-et-Vilaine and Roscoff in **Finistère**. For more details, including crossing times, see the 'Getting There' sections of the respective sightseeing chapters.

The major ferry operator between Britain/Ireland and northern France, **Brittany Ferries** (UK ✆ *08703 665333*/ France ✆ *02 98 29 28 00*, **www.brittanyferries.com**), has crossings to St-Malo and Roscoff, as well as Caen-Ouistreham and Cherbourg in Normandy, both of which can be handy for eastern Brittany. All vessels have children's facilities, and some are positively luxurious – the *Pont-Aven*, for instance, which sails between Roscoff, Plymouth and Cork, has a swimming pool, cinemas and some plush accommodation, including Commodore Class rooms with a double bed and sofabed, TV/DVD player, balcony and free breakfast.

Although long sailings (as compared to the most popular routes from Dover to northeastern France; p. 33) are evidently the costliest, with small children in the car you will probably be keen to reduce driving time – it doesn't make sense, for instance, to take a cheap ferry to Boulogne and then drive all the way across northern France to holiday on the western Breton coast, unless you're visiting other places en route. What you save in ferry fares, you lose in petrol money (especially with current prices), possible overnight stays in hotels, countless snack stops and general shredded nerves. Try to think of a long ferry crossing as part of the overall adventure of your holiday, not simply the act of getting there.

Prices vary widely according to whether you travel by day or night, the standard of accommodation you choose (it's obligatory on overnight sailings), the number of passengers, the size of your car and other details. However, as a rough guide, a return trip (overnight both ways, late Aug–mid-Sept) between Plymouth and Roscoff for two adults and two children aged 4–15 with a standard car, 4X4 or MPV without a roof load, trailer or bike carrier, in an outside four-berth cabin, costs about £ 530. An outside cabin (that is, with a window) is only slighter more expensive than an inside one but makes the experience all the more exciting for youngsters (and often for adults too!). The cheapest option is an inside couchette with shared facilities. The same journey with a **motorhome** is £ 560, with a car and the smallest model of **caravan** £ 640.

The **online booking system** is generally good, with the occasional blip, and there's a £ 10 discount for online booking. Some people prefer the transparency of talking to an operator about the cheapest options; however, Brittany Ferries' online system does give you a colour-coded guide to the scale of prices around your preferred date so you aren't trapped into the most expensive crossing. And make sure to play around with the buttons when getting an online quote: you may find, for instance, that a cabin with a TV is no more expensive than one without. Note that Brittany Ferries is also an award-winning **tour operator** (p. 35).

Other ferry firms operating to Brittany are **Condor Ferries** (Poole/Weymouth–St-Malo, plus Portsmouth–Cherbourg in Normandy; ☎ *0870 243 5140*, ***www.condorferries.co.uk***), and **Irish Ferries** (Rosslare–Roscoff, or Cherbourg in Normandy; Ireland ☎ *0818 300400*, France ☎ *01 56 93 43 40*, ***www.irishferries.com***). Accommodation and facilities are more basic than on Brittany Ferries but there are children's amenities. Again, purely as a guide, in late Aug/early Sept you might expect to pay £ 300 for a Weymouth–St-Malo return with Condor Ferries, for a family of four with a standard car and no trailer (there are no overnight crossings).

The shortest, cheapest and most popular Channel crossings are **Dover** to **Boulogne**, **Calais** and **Dunkerque**, which are on the other side of northern France from Brittany but may be useful if you are touring Normandy first (in which case, see the companion to this guide, *Normandy with Your Family*).

In addition to **Caen-Ouistreham** and **Cherbourg**, Normandy has ferry ports at **Dieppe** and **Le Havre** further east.

You might save by booking ferries (and Eurotunnel; p. 34) through the 'one-stop shop' ***www.ferrybooker.com***, but it's difficult to make direct price comparisons because its search facility may not throw up the same sailings and accommodation availability. Families who can be flexible about when they travel will nearly always find that fares are cheaper mid-week.

By Eurotunnel If you come to Brittany via Paris or Normandy, the **Eurotunnel** shuttle train service (☏ *08705 353535*, ***www.eurotunnel.com***), which takes cars through the Channel Tunnel between Folkestone and Calais, can be the least painful crossing option, since the journey takes just 35 minutes and you don't even need to get out of your car. Sample prices in late Aug/early Sept can be anything from £ 49 to £ 155 each way, with lower fares early in the morning or late at night. These are standard fares rather than more expensive Flexiplus fares, but you can still get a different train from the one you're booked on for free provided you arrive within 2 hours of your scheduled departure time.

By Rail You can travel from London or Ashford Kent to Calais, Lille or Paris on **Eurostar** (☏ *0870 530 0003*, ***www.eurostar.com***); London–Paris takes about 2 hours 50 minutes (2 hours 15 minutes when the terminal moves from Waterloo to St Pancras International in autumn 2007), with fares varying according to how far ahead you book and the degree of flexibility you require regarding exchanges or refunds – they can be as low as £ 59 per adult and £ 50 per child aged 4–11 for a return ticket in standard class.

Eurostar can also book **onward journeys** from Lille or Paris to Rennes, Brest, Quimper, Lorient and Vannes in Brittany. Alternatively, ***www.raileurope.co.uk*** offers combined booking for Eurostar tickets and onward journeys.

By Bus This is your cheapest but slowest and least comfortable means of getting to the Continent, and with children in tow you may be asking for one long headache of a journey. It may be bearable with teenagers, if you bring the requisite iPods, game gadgets and books.

Eurolines (☏ *08705 808080*, ***www.nationalexpress.co.uk***) runs from London-Victoria to Paris, taking between 7 hours 15 minutes and 13 hours, depending on how long you have to wait at the port (the trip back takes from 6 hours 20 minutes). Some buses have extra legroom; all have air-con and toilets. Return prices start at £ 28 ('funfares' for all ages from 0). There are also daily buses to **St-Malo** in the Ille-et-Vilaine; taking about 16 hours; prices are about £ 80 return for over-26s, and for overnight trips you need to pay at least an extra £ 5 for accommodation on the ferry.

Package Deals & Activity Holidays

Package deals let you buy your plane, ferry or train ticket, accommodation and other elements of your trip (that is, car hire or airport transfers) at the same time, often at a discount. Alternatively, they may include hidden charges that you would avoid by booking direct with a hotel or carrier. The appeal for parents is that they *save you time* researching and booking.

Activity holidays are roughly the same with the addition of some kind of sporting, creative or cultural activity, though sometimes you make your own travel arrangements. **Escorted tours**, where you are taken around the various sites, are to my mind anathema to family holidays, where you need to remain flexible in case the children get bored/tired/ill. Such holidays also take away the exhilaration of getting out there and discovering a destination for yourself – one of the best lessons you can give your children.

The following are a few of the best organisers; you will find many more on the Internet and advertised in **Sunday papers**. Again, check that your travel insurance (p. 26) covers you if an operator goes bust.

Breton Bikes ★★★ In 2005, 25% of bookings with this small and very friendly Brit-run cycle-tours firm were by families with young children, so you can be sure it's well equipped for your needs. Several routes (1 or 2 weeks) are suitable for those with children, on quiet roads or cycle paths; accommodation is on campsites with play areas and lakes to swim in (or in hotels or the firm's own gîte if you prefer). Every conceivable piece of kit is available, including baby seats, baby trailers (one- and two-seat), trailer-bikes, small touring bikes, tandems small enough at the back for a 6-year-old, and sleeping bags for all ages. In Whitsun Family Week the six 'fixed centre' tents at the firm's base at Gourec (near the Lac de Guerlédan; p. 114) are reserved for families.

Prices for a week in high season are £ 190 per adult, £ 140 per 10–17-year-old, £ 85 per 4–9-year-old and £ 50 for children up to three, including bikes, maps, tents/camping equipment, and backup (repairs, advice, etc); campsite fees (£ 1–5 per adult per night) aren't included. Some travel can be arranged, and advice on your options is given.
*☎ 02 96 24 86 72, **www.bretonbikes.com***

For other family-friendly cycling holidays in Brittany, plus walks and short breaks on the coast, contact **Headwater** (*☎ 08700 622650, **www.headwater.com***).

Brittany Ferries ★★★ This ferry company is also an award-winning tour operator that can make parents' lives easier by booking hotels, apartments, gîtes, camping chalets, theme parks, cycling and boating holidays and so on in conjunction with travel on its ferries, in Brittany or elsewhere in France. All properties are inspected, and – handily for those anxious about the language – there's a 24-hour telephone hotline with English-speaking staff to deal with plumbing problems or the like. The excellent online search facility lets you refine, say, your gîte search by distance from a beach, availability of baby equipment and so on, and masses of detail is provided about each property. You can also mix-and-match holidays – for instance, you might treat yourselves to a posh hotel after a week in a chalet.

*0870 556 1600, **www.brittanyferries.com***

Crown Blue Line ★ This UK-based firm offers 1 or 2 week self-driven river and canal cruisers from Messac in the Ille-et-Vilaine to the Côtes d'Armor, the Morbihan, or the Loire Atlantique south of Brittany. Some are one-way; your car is transferred while you are en route. The vessels are easy to steer and require no experience, and you can hire bikes to help you stop off and explore. To cover the distances requires no more than 4–5 hours cruising a day, but you need to factor in 20 minutes to get through each lock. Prices start at £ 676 per week for a four-person cruiser. The website gives travel advice and the firm can organise transport from airports and stations.

*0870 240 8393, **www.crownblueline.com***

Siblu Formerly Haven Europe, this company offers tent, mobile homes and chalets at four sites in Brittany, including its own Domaine de Kerlann close to Pont-Aven in Finistère (p. 187). All sites have children's clubs, water parks with indoor and outdoor pools, a toddlers' pool and slides, play areas, and sporting and practical amenities. You can see the attraction of this kind of a holiday for those with young children – lots of ready-made playmates and a range of things to do when the weather isn't so great. Expect a five-night stay in a three-bedroom mobile home with linen in late May to cost about £ 500 (mid-week ferry crossings are included; you can get a small discount for independent travel).

*0870 998 2288, **www.siblu.com***

INSIDER TIP

Look out for special offers with Siblu on parents' websites such as ***www.netmums.com***.

Similar firms are **Canvas Holidays** (***www.canvasholidays.com***), who deal with 13 sites in Brittany; **Eurocamp** (***www.eurocamp.co.uk***), with 16 sites; **Keycamp** (***www.keycamp.co.uk***), with 15 sites; and **Thomson Al Fresco** (***www.thomsonalfresco.co.uk***), with six. Many deal with the same campsites, including Le Ty Nadan (p.187) and La Grande Metairie (p. 228). All can book your travel (ferry/Eurotunnel/flydrive).

VFB Holidays ★ This highly reputed and longstanding firm is a good source for gîtes in Brittany, as well as hotel breaks. A sample price for an old shoemaker's cottage in the Ille-et-Vilaine countryside 10km (six miles) south of Fougères for a family of four plus a baby in late May is £ 495 without ferry crossings, which you can book at preferential rates with the company after reserving your accommodation. This includes an online booking discount of £ 25.

☎ *1242 240340, **www.vfbholidays.co.uk***

VVF Vacances ★ The draw of using this French family holiday specialist is that although its website is also available in English, the resorts are generally full of French people – great if you speak reasonable French and don't want to be surrounded by other tourists. It specialises in low-cost holiday 'villages' – in Guidel-Plages in the Morbihan, for instance, it offers self-catering modern duplex apartments by the sea with onsite children's clubs, a play area, sports facilities and a laundrette for around € 335 (£ 226) per week for four. Not all of its options are self-catering, though.

☎ *00 33 1 55 01 36 62, **www.vvf-vacances.fr***

Getting Around

By Car Though far from environmentally friendly (or cheap, given today's petrol prices), having your own set of wheels allows you the necessary flexibility when it comes to exploring Brittany, especially more rural areas.

Most visitors from the UK bring their own cars on the ferry (p. 32) or – less handy for Brittany – Eurotunnel (p. 34); if you're among them, you need to bring your **driving licence**, the original of the **vehicle registration document**, a current **insurance certificate** and, if the vehicle isn't registered in your name, a letter of authorisation from the owner. Your British insurance will give you the minimum legal cover required in France, but it's advisable to ask your insurer for a **green card** (international insurance certificate) – these are no longer compulsory but provide fully comprehensive cover. Get yourself some extra peace of mind by arranging **24-hour breakdown assistance** too (p. 40). Note that if you break down on a motorway (of which there is only one in Brittany), however, you can only call the official breakdown service operating in that area; there are orange emergency telephones every two kilometres. They have a fixed fee of € 68.60 (£ 46) for repairing or towing a vehicle, € 85.75 (£ 58) at night (6pm–8am). You can call your breakdown firm after towing you off the motorway.

Those coming into France must display an international **sign plate** or sticker (i.e. 'GB') as near as possible to their rear registration plate. Carrying a **red warning triangle** is strongly advised even if your car has hazard warning lights because breakdown may affect your electrics (they're compulsory for cars towing a caravan or a trailer). You should also buy a complete **spare-bulb** kit before you go, as it's illegal to drive with faulty lights. You need to **adjust your beams** for right-hand drive, which means buying special stickers to affix on your headlights. All gear is available at shops at the port.

The **French road system** is generally excellent, although

Brittany has only one of its excellent **motorways**, a short stretch out into Normandy. The largest roads here are mostly *routes nationales* (RN or N) – main roads, usually single lane, that sometimes take you through scenic towns. They have fairly frequent parking/rest areas (*aires*) and petrol stations (be aware that automated out-of-hours pumps don't take cash or foreign credit cards).

Driving rules and advice: Traffic rules in France resemble those in force in Britain – the key difference is that in France you *drive on the right*. Be wary of forgetting this for a moment when you come out of a petrol station or junction. In built-up areas, you must give way to anybody coming out of a side turning on the right (the infamous **priorité à droite**); this rule no longer applies at roundabouts, where you give way to cars that are already on the roundabout. Common signs you will see are *chaussée déformée* ('uneven road/temporary surface'), *déviation* ('diversion') and *rappel* ('continuation of the restriction'). The official text of the **French Highway Code** is available in English at ***www.legifrance.gouv.fr***. For **road signs**, see ***www.permisenligne.com***, or your road atlas will probably picture many of them. Note that you must be at least 18, not 17, to drive in France. For **child car seats**, see p. 40.

Don't **drink and drive** at all – apart from the safety of yourself and your children, there are frequent random breath tests and the alcohol limit is just 0.05%. The **speed limits** are 130km/h (80mph) on toll motorways, 110km/h (68mph) on dual carriageways and motorways without tolls, and 90km/h (56mph) on other roads except in towns, where it's 50km/h (30mph). On wet roads it's 110km/h (68mph), 100km/h (62mph) and 80km/h (50mph) respectively; in fog with visibility of less than 50m, the speed limit is 50km/h (30mph) even on toll motorways. For cars towing a caravan, the limit is 65km/h (40mph) if the weight of the trailer exceeds that of the car by less than 30%, 45km/h (28mph) if the excess is more than 30%. Speeding is supposed to always result in fines *and* a court appearance, but it's not clear what this means for foreign drivers.

Car hire: The best way to hire a car in France is in advance, via the Internet, so you have **proof of your booking** when you arrive – a Hertz office once denied all knowledge of a phone booking of mine despite two preliminary calls. When collecting your car, as well as your reservation printout, you need a **driving licence** for each driver, additional photo ID (your national identity card, or your British passport), your passport if you're a non-EU resident, and a credit card in the main driver's name (sometimes two cards for expensive models). Different hire firms have different **lower age limits for drivers**; it's generally 21–25, but it can depend on how expensive the model is, and you may have to pay a young drivers surcharge. For child seat hire, see p. 41.

Car hire in France has got much less expensive in the past few years – I've been quoted as little as £ 119 for a week's hire of a compact four-door car in early September. But **prices** seem to vary enormously, even between cars of a similar size, so make sure you get a few quotations from different firms – and check that they include unlimited mileage, full insurance, tax and 24-hour breakdown assistance. With some cheaper deals, you may need to buy **damage excess liability waiver** so you're not liable for a considerable initial chunk of loss or damage to the car. This starts at around € 6.50 (£ 4.40) per day. Good deals are often available if you book via low-cost airline websites (p. 31) at the same time as buying your air ticket. All of the major car hire companies operate in France, including the following. The websites will tell you which operates where.

Avis *www.avis.co.uk*

Easycar *www.easycar.com*

Europcar *www.europcar.com*

Hertz *www.hertz.co.uk*

National/Citer *www.citer.com*

If you bring a car hired in the UK into France (for instance if your own car is involved in an accident just before your holiday), you must inform the hire firm that the car is being taken to France to ensure you're covered there. You might need to show the French police the rental agreement to prove you have this insurance.

Motorhomes Motorhomes are subject to the same road rules as cars. You can stop for a few hours in a motorway service area but note that toll tickets are only valid for a limited time. You are also not allowed to stop overnight at the roadside: to find out about the 1700 places adapted for motorhomes (i.e. providing waste disposal and water) in France, including campsites, see the French-language *Camping-car Magazine* (available at newspaper kiosks, or print out sites for your area from its website, *www.campingcar-magazine.fr*, ahead of your trip).

If you're not bringing your own motorhome, you can hire one in Brittany from Brest or Lorient, or from Paris: try *www.motorhome-hire-france.com*. A 4–5-person motorhome with unlimited mileage for 1 week in high season can cost from around € 190 (£ 128), with special rates for long-term rents (two months or longer). Damage excess liability waiver and 24-hour breakdown assistance are optional but highly advisable; you can also get child seats, bedding sets, bike racks, folding picnic tables and satellite navigation (with a hefty deposit).

By Air There are no low-cost airlines operating within France, but a single ticket between Paris

Tips for Travelling by Car

When travelling long distances by car, it may be worth timing your trip to coincide with your child's **naptime** or even leaving after dinner and unloading youngsters into bed at your pre-booked accommodation. Think about investing in an **in-car satellite navigation system**; they are now relatively affordable (from about £ 190), and many people claim they are marriage-savers. They're particularly handy for parents who are trying to map-read *and* deal with the demands of children in the back, but be vigilant about removing the system from your car when you leave it parked on the street, or someone else will do it for you. Other desirables or essentials are:

- A fully charged **mobile phone**.
- **Breakdown cover/roadside assistance. Europ Assistance** (*01444 442211*, ***www.europ-assistance.co.uk***) has very fair prices and an excellent reputation. If you do break down, tell the operator you have children so they prioritise you, and if you're where other cars could run into the back of you, such as on the hard shoulder of the motorway, it's wise to get children out of the car. If you have a **hire car**, make sure the booking includes 24 hour roadside assistance.
- **Child seats.** Under-10s must be seated in the back in France, except for babies in rear-facing safety seats, though the latter must not be used if the front passenger seat is fitted with an airbag. New laws that came into force *in the UK* in Sept 2006 require children under 13 (or under 136cm in height) to use a specialist seat for their

and Brest can cost as little as € 62 (£ 42) with **Air France** (p. 23). Children pay the full fare from the age of two; below that they occupy your lap. When travelling with a baby, you may want to invest in a **Baby B'Air Flight Safety Vest**, which attaches to your seatbelt to protect lap-held children during turbulence, and allows you to sleep knowing your baby can't fall from your arms. It costs about £ 27; see ***www.babybair.com***. But check with your airline first; some loan baby-carriers for free.

The following **domestic routes** are operated by Air France (p. 31) to Brittany:

Paris (CDG/Orly)–**Rennes** (p. 58)

Paris (Orly)–**Lannion** (p. 108)

Paris (CDG/Orly)–**Brest** (p. 145)

Paris (Orly)–**Quimper** (p. 145)

Paris (Orly)–**Lorient** (p. 198)

Note that Paris' Charles de Gaulle (CDG) airport is sometimes referred to as Roissy.

age, except in certain mitigating circumstances. There is no such law in France, and the types of car seat provided by **car-hire companies** vary: Easycar, for instance, provides infant seats for babies up to 9 months (or 9kg) and boosters for children up to 10, Europcar provides seats for the ranges 0–12 months, 1–3 years and 4–7 years. You need to reserve them when you book your car; expect to pay about € 17–30 (£ 12–20). If that seems expensive, it's relatively hassle-free to bring your own seat or booster by plane – they just go in the hold with your other luggage (though may come out at a separate point in the baggage hall at the other end; ask staff at the airport if yours doesn't materialise). A good source of information on car seats both for the UK and abroad is ***www.childcarseats.org.uk***.

- Other miscellaneous equipment includes: a **first-aid kit; window shades**; children's **travel pillows**; a portable **highchair** (p. 25); a **cooler box** to replenish with drinks and snacks each time you set off; **wipes**, **nappies** and **plastic bags** (for nappies or motion sickness); **blankets**, **sweaters** and a **change of clothes; audiotapes/CDs** of your children's favourite stories or songs; **sticker books**, **crayons/paper** or a **magic slate**, or a **compact travel book** with games and activities, such as the *Amazing Book-a-ma-thing for the Backseat* (Klutz, available from ***www.amazon.co.uk***).

By Rail France's national rail system, run by the **SNCF** (***www.voyages-sncf.com***, with versions in other languages), is efficient and inexpensive compared with the British network, and a very good way of getting between cities and larger towns. Its famously zippy **TGV** (*train à grande vitesse* or 'very fast train') network is ever-expanding – see ***www.tgv.com***, also available in English, for an excellent clickable up-to-date route map combined with a quotation (it then takes you back to ***www.voyages-sncf.com*** to book). There you will see that Brittany is very well covered by the TGV.
See 'Getting Around' in the sightseeing chapters for your options between the main cities and towns in each *département*, with journey times. Branch lines serve some smaller towns (again, see the SNCF website), though to explore Brittany properly you really do need your own wheels.

Expect to pay about € 30 (£ 20) for a single ticket from Rennes to Vannes (110km (69 miles), € 23 (£ 15.50) for a child 4–11 (under-4s travel free on a parent's lap on all trains, unless you want to pay for an extra seat). The very clear online booking system will tell you if you need a seat reservation or not (on some trains they're compulsory, on others you can't reserve). Note that onward tickets within France can be bought at the same time as your Eurostar ticket to Lille or Paris, via Eurostar or RailEurope (p. 34).

By Bus This is your least satisfactory means of getting around Brittany. For more rural areas, in particular, it's not worth the hassle, especially for those with children. You're most likely to use French buses within large towns or cities, such as Rennes; in this case, the basic system is that you get a ticket (about €1.20 (80p), under-5s free) that allows you any number of trips by bus and any other urban transport system (Rennes has a tram-style metro) within the following hour. That said, most Breton cities have fairly compact and walkable centres containing most of the sights, hotels and restaurants.

By Bike If you don't bring your own bikes, tourist offices can give you lists of hire outlets, or you may find that your hotel, B&B, gîte or campsite offers bike loan or hire. All hire shops have helmets, and most can also provide **child seats** and perhaps **child trailers**. My comment on French drivers (p. 28) should discourage you from cycling with your family on all but the quietest country lanes. A better bet are **Voies Vertes** – walking, cycling, rollerblading and wheelchair-accessible tracks on former railtracks or canal towpaths. For information on Voies Vertes and **Véloroutes** (cycle routes), including masses on Brittany, check out ***http://troisv.amis-nature.org/sommaire.php3***. It also has advice on **taking your bike on trains** (a complex issue; you basically need to talk to the SNCF in each individual case), and in turn recommends ***www.randobreizh.com*** (for walking, cycling and other 'nature sports') and ***www.voiesvertes.com***. Tourist office websites also list routes in their area.

ACCOMMODATION & EATING OUT

Accommodation

There are some stratospherically expensive hotels in Brittany, but on the whole accommodation represents seriously good value to anyone used to hotel prices in the UK, which means that even if you're on a budget you might allow yourselves the occasional splurge. I've based the **price categories** used within the Accommodation sections of the sightseeing chapters on the following ranges, based on lodgings per night for two adults and two children, without breakfast except in the case of B&Bs and the occasional hotel (as noted in individual reviews):

Very expensive: More than € 290 (£ 195)

Expensive: € 220–290 (£ 148–195)

Moderate: € 110–220 (£ 74–148)

Inexpensive: Less than € 110 (£ 74)

Very expensive options tend to be **châteaux-hotels** or grand old **seaside hotels** with gastronomic restaurants, swimming pools, babysitting services and more – fabulous places for the odd night or two, with a truly French feel and a welcoming attitude to children. In the expensive and moderate categories you'll find many very good seaside hotels, often with pools, though beware that most insist on **half board** (breakfast and lunch or dinner in the hotel-restaurant) in high season, which can be limiting for those with children.

B&Bs (*chambres d'hôte*) are split between the moderate and inexpensive categories; as a general thumb, the more rural they are, the cheaper they'll be. Most are cosy and welcoming; often they're on farms where youngsters can pet the animals and sometimes join in with farming tasks. The inexpensive category also includes campsites, youth hostels and **gîtes** (see p. 44). The latter have long been the most popular option among families holidaying in France, since even relatively luxurious examples with pools, when broken down per head per night, represent very good value compared with hotels, and the self-catering facilities mean you save money on eating out too.

Campsites run the gamut from rowdy four- and five-star affairs with huge aquaparks, manifold sports facilities and children's entertainment to quiet sites situated within the grounds of historic châteaux, or green sites where the onus is on leaving a minimal 'environmental footprint'.

I've not included many **youth hostels**, but if you're prepared for your accommodation to be a bit rough and ready (generally in rooms with two bunk beds, with a sink and perhaps an ensuite shower room), they can be good places to stay, with readymade playmates on hand for the children, communal kitchens, laundrettes and games rooms, and sometimes activities laid on. Single-parent families (p. 29) often get special rates. The French hostelling association website, ***www.fuaj.org.uk***, translated (badly) into English, has links to individual hostel websites where they exist but doesn't list private hostels or those run by other organisations, such as La Mine d'Or. Expect to pay approximately € 12 per person (about £ 8) in a four-person room, including breakfast, plus € 23 (£ 15.50) for annual family membership of FUAJ.

Just about every hotel and B&B I've reviewed in this guide offers **family rooms** for up to four people; if not, then interconnecting rooms or suites with comfortable sofabeds are available. Note that '**appartement**', when used in the context of hotels, usually means a suite rather than a flat with self-catering facilities. **Cots** are usually provided, either free or for a small extra fee (see p. 49). **Breakfasts**, though generally of high quality whatever the price range (almost invariably Continental or occasionally in the form of a buffet, they usually feature fresh, sometimes organic, farm produce), can get a bit monotonous – you may not think it now, but there will come a day when you can barely countenance a croissant, no matter how buttery and delicious. Hotel breakfasts, in Brittany as elsewhere, can be wildly expensive.

Hotels You're generally better off dealing directly with the 60 or so hotels and accommodation options that I recommend throughout this guide (or others listed on **tourist board and tourist office websites**; p. 20), rather than via a booking agency, and doing it by **email**. This allows you to explain your requirements as a family and check exactly what's provided for children, from bottle warmers and cot linen to games consoles, and to have the details in writing in case of queries or discrepancies when you get there. Hotels very often offer **special offers** or **last-minute deals** on their website, but even if they don't, always ask if a better rate is available.

Centralised booking services are best in turning up late deals. On ***www.guidesdecharme.com*** (available in English), for instance – where the options aren't necessarily that 'charming' (they work with a partner site offering more downmarket properties) – you might find a modern self-catering studio-apartment for four in the resort of Carnac (p. 203) in the second half of September for as little as € 864 (£ 584) for 2 weeks, including use of a swimming pool. The site ***www.logisdefrance.com*** also reserves approved hotels around France, including late deals, but its booking system is prone to bugs.

Hôtel-Résidences This has been my revelation of 2006 – apartments in *résidences* attached to hotels, so you have the flexibility of self-catering but can also use the hotel facilities. A very good example is the Reine Marine at St-Malo (p. 97), where you can stay in a sea-view apartment with use of a pool, sauna, bar, laundrette and breakfast delivery service, enjoy direct access to the beach, and also use the thalassotherapy (seawater cures) centre and crèche and children's club of its five-star sister hotel and restaurant. At present there aren't too many around, but I predict they'll proliferate in coming years.

Gîtes & Apartments Many readers of this book will probably be looking for self-catering accommodation in a quaint old

Breton cottage not too far from the sea, where they can relax and feel at home abroad, with the option of cooking for themselves. You get more space and lower prices than at a hotel, your children won't disturb people in neighbouring rooms, and you save money on restaurants (which children get sick of pretty quickly anyway). The downside can be a lack of things to do on a rainy day, especially if you're in a gîte without a TV/videoplayer or covered pool – it's worth having a few contingency plans up your sleeve (save indoor treats such as aquariums and museums for bad weather). Some gîtes can also be a bit grotty, filled with owners' unwanted furniture. Look carefully at website photographs, and check exactly what's included – if you're there for 2 weeks, it's a shame to have to waste precious holiday hours in search of a laundrette if your gîte doesn't have a washing machine.

Luckily – at least for visitors – the gîtes market is oversaturated in many parts of France, which means you get copious choice and good deals, especially if you can hold out and wait for a last-minute deal. Good websites include ***www.interhome.co.uk***, ***www.frenchconnections.co.uk*** and ***www.cheznous.com***. With the last two you can check availability on the website but you book direct with the owner, which means they can be better value. All three offer travel discounts. The British Sunday newspapers carry ads for countless other firms arranging self-catering

Breaking Journeys without Breaking the Bank

For cheap **overnight stops en route**, budget hotel chains **Etap** (***www. etaphotel.com***) and **Formule 1** (***www.hotelformule1.com***) offer rooms with a double bed and a single bunk running over the top of it (suitable for over-5s) for around € 37 (£ 25) a night € 28 (£ 19) in a Formule 1, where rooms have sinks but share showers and loos). Many also have enclosed carparks. If you're travelling in hot weather, it's worth finding one with air-con; as rooms are often next to busy roads they can be noisy if you sleep with a window open.

I've used Etaps when driving far into the night with sleeping children, pulling up at the nearest when I've wanted to call it a day. If reception's closed, there are rather wonderful automated check-ins – you feed in your credit card and it spits out a room code. On one occasion I found no rooms available, but just relocated to a Formule 1 two minutes away. However, the really great thing about Etap is that you can book rooms in advance and cancel them up to 5pm on your day of arrival without paying a bean, meaning you can have the security of a reservation but back out if you fall behind schedule. Buffet breakfasts are € 4 per person (£ 2.65).

Children's Gîtes (*Gîtes d'Enfants*)

This school-holiday programme allows children aged 4–16 to enjoy country life and outdoor activities with other children (often including the host's own family) at an establishment – usually a farm – inspected by the French department of health and social services. Activities might include buttermaking, rambling, making herb gardens, picking flowers, going on picnics, dance and foreign-language lessons, handicrafts: canoeing, riding and sailing. You're probably thinking you came on holiday to spend time *with* your children, not to fob them off on somebody else, but if they're independent and enjoy discovering nature and wildlife, they might enjoy doing this for a week while you stay in a hotel nearby, so you can pop in and see them every day but grab some 'adult time' and perhaps even a bit of pampering. It's generally a good idea – at least the first time – to send a child with a sibling, cousin or friend of a similar age. There are **Mini-Gîtes** for ages 4–10, generally accommodating just two to five children on a farm, **Junior-Gîtes** for six or more children aged 6–10, where the owner is helped by a trained assistant, and **Clubs Jeunes** for between 12 and 35 children aged 11–16, with more active sports. Expect to pay around € 285 (£ 193) a week; some places also offer activities by the day.

For children's gîtes by *département*, see ***www.gites-de-france.fr***. Some owners speak English, where indicated, but this is obviously a great way for children who speak some French to improve their language skills. For **farm stays** in the Ille-et-Vilaine, see p. 96.

accommodation. Or official **French organisations *www.clevacances.com*** and ***www.gites-de-france.com*** have websites in English.

You can, don't forget, just type 'gîte' and the name of the area or nearest town into a search engine such as ***www.google.com*** and see what it throws up – many owners now have their own websites. Make it easier for yourself by adding extra search-words such as 'child-friendly' or 'toddler' or 'swimming pool', though this may exclude suitable places that haven't set up their website properly (their problem, not yours).

Prices vary according to location, facilities (including pools, play areas, the availability of babysitting and so on), luxuriousness and time of year, but as a guideline expect to pay £ 190–400 (£ 128–270) per week for a gîte for four without a pool in the Côtes d'Armor.

Finally, it's a long shot, but you may strike lucky at a **home-swap** site such as ***www.homeexchange.com***, where you try to match up with someone who will swap houses with you. You can sift through, say, the Brittany listings looking for someone who has listed your home country (or city) as somewhere they'd like to stay. If they like the look of your house as much as you do theirs and you can agree on a date, you get free accommodation and someone to housesit for you while you're away. Basic annual membership of this website is US$25 (about £ 14); if you want to list your own property, it's US$59.95 (about £ 33).

Camping France has about 11,000 campsites, all of them listed on the excellent directory ***www.campingfrance.com***, with versions in English and other languages and a clickable map for searches by region or a themed search facility (sites with direct beach access, scenic inland sites, sites with indoor pools or water parks, sites with children's clubs, sites with fitness and spa facilities and so on). It gives detailed descriptions and fees for each, and lets you book online, though it also gives telephone numbers, websites and email addresses of the sites so you can do it direct. It even has mini area guides and links to tourist offices.

In the Accommodation sections of the individual sightseeing chapters of this book, I provide my own picks of the nearly 1,000 sites in Brittany; my personal preference is for smaller 'green' sites and sites in the grounds of châteaux, but I recognise the attraction of large sites with indoor pools and children's clubs and have recommended some accordingly.

For companies specialising in camping and mobile home holidays in these sorts of sites, including ferry travel, see p. 36 and p. 37.

Eating Out

Some people come to France for the food alone, and one of the joys of exploring this country is that you can generally walk into the most modest-looking café in any small town and be assured of getting a good meal of fresh, well-prepared food, even it's just an omelette, a *croque-monsieur* (p. 245) or a *salad composée* (main-course salad). Under such circumstances, it's amazing that companies such as McDonald's have been able to get a foothold in France, though I admit to using them as handy stopoffs when on the road with my children, for the playrooms and loos.

Most French restaurants and cafés are welcoming to children, and many have **children's menus** (generally about € 7.50 (£ 5)) though often these feature little more than *steak haché* (a hamburger patty) or ham and chips, then ice cream, and can get very repetitive. **Vegetarians** are still poorly catered for in this largely carnivorous country; omelettes, some main-course salads (above) and margherita pizzas are helpful standbys, but it's always wise to double check with your waiter that, for instance, pieces of ham won't sneak their way into such dishes. Naturally, in Brittany with its wonderful fresh **seafood**, those who eat fish but not meat won't go wanting. Brittany's famous **crêperies**, specialising in buckwheat pancakes (*galettes de blé noir*) and lighter crêpes, are another godsend for veggies, offering fillings such as woodland mushrooms in cream. In fact, crêpes are the perfect fast food – they take less than five minutes to prepare, are fairly nutritionally sound and cost next to nothing! But again, you'll get a point where you can't face another crêpe.

For **food vocabulary**, including **Breton specialities**, see p. 243.

Restaurants and cafés generally have at least one **highchair**, but if you're travelling by car bring a portable one (p. 25) for places that don't or where the existing one is taken. Your only real problem as a parent in France is that mealtimes are very rigid, and you're unlikely – at least outside cities or resorts in high season – to find somewhere serving food outside standard **lunch and dinner hours** (generally noon–2.30pm and 7–10pm). For those, like me, spoilt rotten by cities such as London with their all-day eating options, this can be very frustrating. If you want to have dinner out, your only solution may be to encourage your children to have an early-afternoon nap so they can make it through to dinner without going into meltdown. **Brasseries** and **crêperies** often have all-day service (*service continu*), but again, only at the seaside in season or in larger towns. Brasseries can also get smoky because they have bar areas. On no account be tempted by a roadside **Buffalo Grill**; these look fun and have all the child-friendly trappings, including all-day service and sometimes even bouncy castles, but when we once succumbed, the food was so shockingly bad we tremble every time we pass one now.

I've tried to cover the whole range of options in my 'Eating Out' sections in the sightseeing chapters, recognising that if you're not staying in accommodation with self-catering facilities, the cost of eating out at least one or twice a day, even in France, is going to mount up. But alongside unpretentious crêperies, you'll find reviews of some stunning gastronomic restaurants that welcome children – perfect for occasional treats, especially if you take advantage of **fixed-price lunch** or **dinner *menus* (set menus)** rather than ordering from the ***carte* (à la carte menu)**. I've based my **price categories** on the following ranges, based on two adults and two children consuming two courses plus drinks:

Expensive: More than € 75 (£ 50)

Moderate: € 45–75 (£ 30–50)

Inexpensive: less than € 45 (£ 30)

GETTING CHILDREN INTERESTED IN BRITTANY

Involving children in planning your trip is the best way to get them interested. As well as using this book to show them what to look forward to in Brittany, whether it be the crazy rocks of the Côte du Granit Rose (p. 115) or the submarine ride at St-Malo's Grand Aquarium (p. 72), introduce them to books such as **Bonjour France!** (Rebecca Welby, Beautiful Books), with maps, games, quizzes and activities on France for 7–12-year-olds, who can register their scores on the Young Travellers Club website (***www.youngtravellersclub.co.uk***). Its contents include 'Beach Olympics and Rainy Day Games'.

Though most of the well-loved Madeline books by Ludwig Bemelmans, about the escapades of a French schoolgirl, are set in Paris, **Madeline Says Merci: The Always Be Polite Book** (available from ***www.amazon.co.uk***), republished in paperback in late 2006, is a good way of getting youngsters aged about 4–10 interested in France and in learning some French phrases. Another classic character is **Astérix**; the location for his fictional settlement is thought to have been inspired by part of the Breton coast (p. 114). Astérix's countless adventures are available in French, Breton, English and lots of other languages.

Bécassine, a cartoon character from the early 20th century, is a Breton farmer's daughter who becomes a servant in Paris: among her tales, available in French only from ***www.amazon.fr***, are *L'enfance de Bécassine*, about her peasant childhood in Brittany.

For smaller children, you can pick up locally themed **coloriage** (colouring) books in most local newsagents: topics include the Brittany and Lighthouses.

Lastly, familiarise your family with the culinary delights of northern France by getting a copy of *Cuisine Grandmére* by Jenny Baker and trying out some of the authentic Breton recipes including flamed sugared apples.

FAST FACTS: BRITTANY

Area Codes See 'Telephone', p. 53.

Baby Equipment Most hotels, B&Bs and gîtes can provide **cots,** often for a charge (an average of € 8 (£ 5.50), and some offer other equipment such as bottle warmers and changing mats. Some places don't provide linen for their cots because of allergy risks. Supermarkets, especially large ones, are good for baby equipment (*matériel de puériculture*), from nappies and jarred food to baths and car seats, but if you want to go to a specialist retailer, many out-of-town *centre commerciales* (shopping parks) have baby-and-toddler supermarkets such as **Bébe 9** (***www.bebe9.com***).

Babysitters Most expensive and some moderate hotels arrange sitters for guests, usually a tried-and-tested local (or someone from an agency) rather than one of their staff. Most need at least 24 hours notice. You usually pay the sitter directly; rates average € 8–10 (£ 5.40–6.70) per hour. Some gîte-owners also offer babysitting, either themselves or by a family member such as a daughter. Alternatively, ***www.fr.cityvox.fr***, a 'going out guide', has 'Garde d'enfant' *annonces* (in French, even on the English-translation pages) by local babysitters, but you'll need to satisfy yourself as to their credentials and references.

Breastfeeding Breastfeeding in public is much less common in France than the UK, and you may get stared at, especially if you're feeding an older infant. You may want to brazen it out, since breastfeeding is your right, or you might prefer to find an out-of-the-way spot.

Business Hours **Shops** outside large towns generally open at 9 or 10am (7 or 8am for bakeries) and close at 6 or 7pm, with a 2 hour break at lunchtime (usually 12.30–2.30pm). Many also open on Sunday morning (in conjunction with a market) but close Monday mornings or all of Monday. Very large **supermarkets** often stay open until late (9 or 10pm), and larger towns have convenience stores open until late in the evening. Supermarkets increasingly open in the morning on public holidays too, except Christmas Day.

Banks always close on public holidays; the rest of the time they're generally open 9.30am–4.30pm, with a lunch break in smaller towns. In the latter they may be closed Monday afternoons but open Saturday mornings. Most have 24-hour **ATMs** (p. 22).

Restaurants generally open noon–2.30pm and 7–10pm; larger towns and resorts usually have some with *service continu* (p. 48). Public **museums** usually close on Monday or Tuesday and on public holidays, but most tourist sites open on public and school holidays. Brittany is a seasonal region and many attractions and hotels close for part or all of the **winter**; many businesses, though not hotels and rarely restaurants, close for the whole of August, when the French take their holidays *en masse*.

Car Hire See p. 38.

Chemists Staff at chemists (*pharmacies*), recognisable by a green cross, can provide **first aid** in minor emergencies. **Rotas** of pharmacies operating out of normal hours (9am–1.20pm and 2.30–8pm, Mon–Sat) are posted in every chemist's window and in local papers. It's a good idea to take a first-aid course yourself; there's a CD-Rom version (about £ 30) developed in collaboration with St John's Ambulance: see ***www.firstaidforkids.com***.

Climate See 'When to Go & What to Pack', p. 24.

Currency See 'Money', p. 22.

Dentists For emergency dental treatment, go to your nearest hospital or health centre.

Doctors Some upmarket **hotels** have doctors on call, though they can be expensive private ones. Alternatively, local newspapers list **doctors on call** (*médécins de service*) and chemists (p. 50) open outside normal hours, or there may be information posted outside the local *mairie*. If you're staying in one place for a while, it's a good idea to **make a list of emergency contact details** and pin them up by the front door (check first that your host hasn't already provided one in their welcoming pack).

Driving Rules See p. 38.

Electricity Electricity in France runs on 220-volt, 50-cycle AC. Visitors from the UK and Ireland need a two-pin European adapter (easily available at French supermarkets) to use their own appliance; those from North America need a voltage transformer (unless the appliance has a dual voltage switch) and plug adapter. Many hotels can loan guests adapters.

Embassies & High Commissions There are embassies or consulates for the UK, Ireland, USA, Canada, Australia and New Zealand in Paris; these are your point of contact for passport and legal problems. For contact details, see ***www.expatries.diplomatie.gouv.fr/annuaires/annuaires.htm***.

Emergencies Staff in most hotels are trained to deal with emergencies, so call the front desk before you do anything else. Otherwise, for an **ambulance**, call ☎ *15*, for the **police** ☎ *17*, for the **fire service** ☎ *18*. Note that you will be expected to pay upfront for an ambulance and try to claim back your money later on your insurance. In rural areas it will probably be quicker to drive to the nearest **hospital** yourself anyway, unless it is dangerous to move the injured person. Note that **hospitals** are sometimes signposted *hôtel de dieu* rather than *hôpital* or *centre hospitalier*.

Holidays See p. 25.

Internet Access See p. 30.

Legal Aid Contact your embassy or consulate (p. 51).

Lost Property Unless you know where you dropped an item and can ask there, go to the nearest police station. For important documents such as passports, contact your embassy or consulate (p. 51). For lost credit cards, see p. 52. If you think your car may have been towed away for being illegally parked, ask at the local police station.

Mail Post offices, recognisable by their yellow signs with blue birds, are generally open Mon–Fri 8am–7pm and Sat 8am–noon; in towns and villages they tend to open Mon–Fri 9am–12.30pm and 2–5pm and Sat 9am–noon but close some afternoons. Postcards or letters to the UK weighing less than 20g cost € 0.55 (37p) and take 1–5 days. Stamps are sold at tobacconists (*tabacs*) as well as post offices. If you need to receive mail while travelling, ask the sender to address it to your name c/o Poste Restante, Poste Centrale, in the relevant town. You will need to show proof of identity and pay a small fee.

Maps For online sources to plot your route, see p. 21. On the road, arm yourself with a good French road atlas: the Michelin Tourist & Motoring atlases (available from **www.amazon.co.uk** and at petrol stations and port shops) have the best level of detail.

Money & Credit Cards See also 'Money', p. 22. For **lost/stolen cards**, call the relevant company immediately: for **Amex** call *01 47 77 72 00*, for **Visa** *0892 705705*, for **MasterCard** *01 45 67 84 84*, for **Diners** *0810 314159*. For emergency cash out of banking hours, you can have money wired to you online, by phone or from an agent's office via **Western Union** (*0800 833833*; ***www.westernunion.com***).

Newspapers & Magazines
National **dailies** include *Le Monde*, *Libération* and *Le Figaro*, and all have online versions; **regional newspapers** are *Ouest-France* (***www.ouest-france.fr***) covering Brittany and part of Normandy, and **Le Télégramme** (***www.letelegramme.com***), with local editions for 14 cities and towns in Brittany. These newspapers are good sources for local listings of markets, cinema showings and so on. Newsagents also stock a choice of glossy magazines covering the region in French. Otherwise, **English-language newspapers** from the UK and USA are widely available at newsstands and newsagents, usually a day old, without the supplements and at a premium price; the British **Guardian** has an international edition sold in Europe.

Police In emergencies, call *17*. For theft, you have to file a report at a local police station.

Post Offices See 'Mail', above.

Safety See also p. 28, 'Travelling Safely with Children in Brittany'. The usual common sense tips apply – don't leave money or valuables on display on your person or in your car, and be wary of **pickpockets** in confined public spaces; don't allow yourself to be distracted by anyone while withdrawing money at a **cashpoint**; and don't walk alone in unlit open spaces such as parks (most of which are locked out of hours anyway) or even on seemingly innocuous residential streets after dark.

Taxes A 19.6% national **value-added tax** (VAT; *taxe valeur ajoutée* or **TVA** in French) is included in the price of most goods and hotel and restaurant services in France. Non-EU residents can reclaim most of this if they spend € 175 (about £ 118) or more at a participating retailer – ask for *détaxe* papers and present them at the airport; the refund can go to your credit card.

Taxis In major towns and cities and at airports, taxis can be caught from ranks (look for square signs with 'Taxi' in white on a blue background); they can also be hailed in the street if the 'Taxi' sign on the roof is lit and the small lights under it are switched off. Away from main centres or airports, ask at your hotel or restaurant desk, or call a local firm – see *www.pagesjaunes.fr* (French *Yellow Pages* online) or ask at the tourist office. Check all taxis have a meter, and for airport taxis and out-of-town trips, ask the driver for an estimate before setting out. For average rates, see p. 53.

Telephone Within France, all telephone numbers are 10 digits, including a 2-digit **area code** (☎ *02* in Brittany) that you must dial even if you're calling from within that area. Numbers starting with 06 are **mobile numbers** that it will cost you more to call; numbers starting with 0800 and 0805 are free to dial but are only available within France (other numbers beginning 08, such as 0892 and 0820, have differing rates).

To **call a French number from abroad**, drop the initial 0 of the area code after dialling the international code (☎ *00 33* from the UK, ☎ *011 33* from the USA). To **dial the UK from France**, call the international code (☎ *00 44*) then the British number minus the first 0 of the area code; to call the USA dial 00 1 then the number. If you don't bring your mobile (p. 29), avoid using hotel phones as charges can be high; buy a **phonecard** (*télécarte*) from a post office, tobacconist or newsagents, starting at € 7.40 (about £ 5) for 50 units. Incoming calls can be received at **phoneboxes** where the blue bell sign is shown.

Time Zone France is one hour ahead of **British time**, with clocks going forward by an hour for summertime or 'daylight saving', as in the UK, on the last Sunday in March and reverting on the last Sunday in October. France is six hours ahead of North American **Eastern Standard Time** (EST).

Tipping *Service compris* means a service charge has been included on your bill, but you may wish to leave an extra tip (about 15% of the total).

Toilets & Babychanging There are public *toilettes* on the streets of most larger towns and cities, and in some smaller places; if you can't find one, bars and cafés are normally happy for you to use theirs but for politeness' sake make a small purchase while you're there. Alternatively, try a large shop such as Printemps (p. 176) or a public museum. Few places except big family-oriented tourist sites such as zoos, aquaria and museums have babychanging facilities, so be equipped with a portable folding mat.

Water French water is safe to drink. Many restaurants automatically serve you a carafe of chilled tap water (*eau du robinet*). Bottled water is *eau minérale plat/sans gaz* (still) or *gazeuse/pétillante* (sparkling).

Weather See p. 24.

3 Ille-et-Vilaine

ILLE-ET-VILAINE

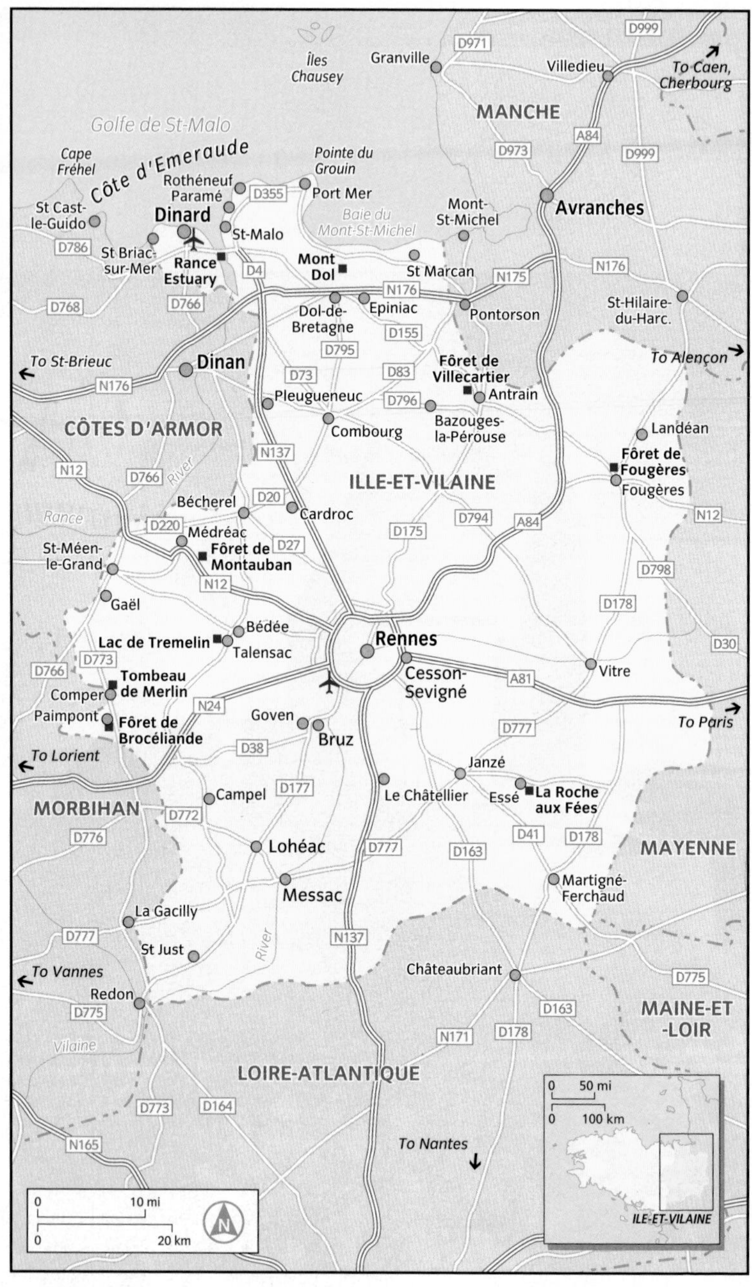

The Ille-et-Vilaine's green, wooded countryside is largely similar to that of Normandy just over the border, and the coast doesn't yet feel truly 'Breton' – rocky, wild and windswept. Yet this is still an excellent place for a beach holiday: the oyster-farming town of Cancale and its resort Port-Mer are just the start of the stunning Côte d'Emeraude, with views over the awe-inspiring Baie du Mont-St-Michel shared by Brittany and Normandy. A short drive away, stunning St-Malo combines a walled pirates' city with a gorgeous seaside resort. St-Malo also offers some of the best shopping in northern France, and has a fantastic aquarium. Lesser-known St-Lunaire further west is a blissfully peaceful setting for a family holiday.

Heading south, away from the coast, you'll pass the picturesque Château de la Bourbansais with its very good zoo en route to the pretty little secondhand book town of Bécherel. Further south still, lovers of stories and myths can get a further fix in the forest of Brocéliande (Paimpont), a wonderland of Arthurian myths and atmospheric ancient monuments. The *département* can also be a good base for those visiting the world-famous Mont-St-Michel, one of the world's biggest tourist attractions, which lies just over the border with Normandy (see p. 68, and the companion guide to this book, *Normandy with Your Family*).

Brittany's capital, Rennes, is a good place to head for culture – the Musée de Bretagne, the region's cultural storehouse, is here, there are some great family-oriented events, and you might also want to stock up on English-language books. But it's surprisingly un-enticing in terms of family accommodation; you're far better off staying in the surrounding countryside, especially Brocéliande.

Around here are some great animal parks and rural activity centres with something to offer all ages, plus a wide variety of stunning accommodation and some fabulous restaurants serving local produce, including oysters, mussels and other seafood from the Baie du Mont-St-Michel. You'll come away from the Ille-et-Vilaine with more than a breath of fresh air in your lungs, and the feeling of really having got away from it all.

ESSENTIALS

Getting There

By Boat **Brittany Ferries** (p. 16) sails once a day from **Portsmouth** to **St-Malo**, leaving St-Malo late morning and Portsmouth mid-evening and taking almost 11 hours. Like all Brittany Ferries' crafts, the *Bretagne* offers children's entertainment and a games room. You're also within about a 60–90 minute drive of Caen-Ouistreham and Cherbourg in Normandy, to which Brittany Ferries sails as well.

Condor Ferries (p. 17) runs fast ferries between **St-Malo** and **Poole or Weymouth** daily from

May to October, less frequently the rest of the year, taking 4 hours 35 minutes–5 hours 15 minutes. Some crossings require a change of vessel in Guernsey in the Channel Islands. Boats have a children's area.

By Air **Ryanair** (p. 15) runs budget flights between **Dinard** on the north coast and **London Stansted** (1 hour 5 minutes) and the **East Midlands** (1 hour 25 minutes).

At the time of writing, **Aer Lingus** (p. 15) had just launched twice-weekly 1 hour 15 minute flights between **Dublin** and **Rennes** airport just west of the city. There are also budget flights to Rennes from Southampton with **Flybe** (p. 15), and flights to Rennes from Paris (CDG) with **Air France** (p. 15).

By Train **Rennes** is 2 hours from **Paris** on the **TGV**, and there's a new direct TGV from Paris to **St-Malo** too, taking 2 hours 55 minutes (some trains also stop at **Dol-de-Bretagne**). For SNCF details, see p. 25.

VISITOR INFORMATION

The website of the CDT (the tourist office for the *département*), ***www.bretagne35.com***, is a mine of information unto itself, and has a links page (click on 'Préparez Votre Sejour' then 'Liens Utiles') listing all tourist offices (or town halls where relevant) and their websites in towns and cities throughout the *département*.

Orientation

The city of **Rennes** is bang in the middle of the *département*, with its main roads radiating out from it: the **N137** takes you to **St-Malo** (about an hour to the north), the **N12** goes west to **St-Brieuc** in the Côtes d'Armor and on to **Brest** in Finistère, and the **N24** travels west to **Lorient** in the Morbihan. To the east, the **D175** leads to the Mont-St-Michel just over the border in Normandy, while the **A84**, Brittany's only stretch of motorway, takes you into the heart of Normandy. The **N157** turns into the **A81** to Le Mans in the Sarthe, your fastest route to cover the 220km (137 miles) to Paris from Rennes.

Getting Around

As with all of Brittany, a **car** is the best way of getting around unless you plan to be based in one place. Even in the cities of St-Malo and Rennes, some of the best attractions are a little way out of the centre and a hassle to reach by public transport, especially if you have children in tow.

If you don't bring your own car across the Channel, **Hertz** (p. 23) has pickup at Dinard airport (you can book a car at the same time as your Ryanair flight). If you catch the TGV to St-Malo, **ADA** (☎ *02 99 56 06 15*) and **Europcar** (📞 *02 99 56 75 17*) have car-hire offices on boulevard des Talards.

Local tourist offices will provide details of **taxi** and **bike-hire** firms.

Children-Friendly Events & Entertainment

Most towns of any size have fireworks and parties on **14th July – Bastille Day**. The coast is a good place to enjoy a display, or **Rennes** has a very large celebration on the Plaine de Baud (📞 *02 99 28 55 55*, ***www.ville-rennes.fr***).

Centre Culturel Juliet Drouet

Set in pretty Fougères with its huge fort, this exciting cultural space is a good place to take up some culture *en famille*: the programme varies, but look out for 'family operas' such as *L'enfant et les sortiléges*, a collaboration between composer Ravel and writer Colette about a child's cruelty toward the objects, plants and animals around him. There are also family dance shows and visits by contemporary circus companies, which you can enjoy even if your French isn't brilliant. The website gives age indications.

Year round. Théâtre Victor Hugo, rue Gué Maheu, Fougères, 📞 *02 99 94 83 65,* ***www.centreculturelfougeres.fr****. Tickets: adults € 10–18 (£ 7–12), under-12s € 7.50–12 (£ 5–8).*

Etincelles Aquatiques ★★

'Aquatic sparkles' is an open-air extravaganza of music, dance and fireworks involving around 250 amateur performers (and a total team of 950 volunteers, plus an audience of more than 5,000) in a stunning lakeside setting. The 'story' blends various local mythical or historical figures – fairies from the nearby Roche aux Fées (p. 75), 'rush-pullers' (who used to call locals to a feast by vibrating rushes), and imps – and is great fun for all ages, though you may have

Half-timbered buildings in Rennes

trouble keeping tots up 'til the starting time of 10.15pm. You can come to the site earlier (you can even camp here) and have a dinner of galettes, crêpes, sausages or sandwiches.

Bring a cushion and warm clothing, and book well ahead (you can do so online), as the four performances are always heavily subscribed.

*Aug. Etang de la Forge, Martigné-Ferchaud, 35km (22 miles) southeast of Rennes on D41, ☎ 02 99 47 83 83, **www.etincelles-aquatiques.org**. Tickets: adults € 12 (£ 8), children 5–12 € 5 (£3.50).*

Quai des Bulles St-Malo's festival of *bande dessinée* (comic strip) and the projected image has been running for more than 25 years and attracts exhibitions by a huge variety of authors, as well as about 80 stands set up by publishers, bookshops and fanzines. Each year there's a new film theme, with showings for all ages, plus book launches, auctions and debates. Real connoisseurs can sign up for workshops on *bande dessinée* techniques run by the organisers twice-monthly year round.

*Nov. Palais du Grand Large, Espace Duguay-Trouin, St-Malo, ☎ 02 99 40 39 63, **www.quaidesbulles.com**. Adm free.*

Quartiers d'Eté ★★ This free, three-day, open-air festival in an east Rennes park is organised by young volunteers with a youthful audience in mind – music has an ethnic slant, with lots of hip hop, ragga and slam – and there are plenty of fun and games, including quirky performance pieces, open-air cinema, a 'human jukebox' to regale you with your favourite songs, *vélo polo* (polo on mountain bikes, of all things), a graffiti wall, pony-rides and local farm animals, fishing, ecology lessons, figurine painting followed by battle games, temporary tattooing, jewellery-making, juggling and much more besides. In short, it's a bit of a mish-mash but great fun for a slightly eccentric day out. Camping is possible if you want the full-on festival experience; reserve ahead. The park also has play areas.

*July. Parc des Gayeulles, avenue des Gayeulles, Rennes, ☎ 02 99 36 81 08, **www.crij-bretagne.com/qe2006/**. Adm free.*

Rennes sur Roulettes ★ This weekend festival brings together some of the best rollerblading teams and individuals in the world, competing in the women's and men's International Marathons over about 50km on the streets of central Rennes. But non-pros are not overlooked: there's also a *randonnée populaire* in which anyone can take part, free of charge and without the need to register in advance, on the Sunday (you do need a helmet and a doctor's certificate stating you are generally fit). You do as few or as many circuits as you like. Blades and pads can be hired (for instance, from Super Sport, ☎ *02 99 31 39 50*, at the central Centre Commercial Colombia), and the organisers provide free T-shirts and refreshments. If you're a novice, there are free lessons, with blade and pad loan. The event also sees ramp demonstrations and a late-night roller-party.

*May. Central Rennes, ☎ 02 99 27 74 00, **www.rennessurroulettes.com**. Adm free.*

Tombées de la Nuit This large open-air festival has taken over the centre of Rennes for a week in July for more than 20 years. As the name suggests, it only gets going at sunset, so it may not be one for the younger children, but older ones will love the combination of music, dance, poetry, theatre and other street performance, much of an avant-garde nature. Most events are free, but some of the concerts require tickets, sold at the Fnac bookshop (p. 223) or at the tourist office on rue Saint-Yves. The website gives age guidance for individual shows.

*July. Rennes, ☎ 02 99 32 56 56, **www.lestdnuit.com**. Adm mainly free, some events € 2–10 (£ 1.35–6.65).*

WHAT TO SEE & DO

Children's Top 10 Attractions

❶ **Riding in** the Nautibus submarine at the **Grand Aquarium** in St-Malo. See p. 72.

❷ **Chugging out** across the sands in the tractor-drawn **Train Marin**, to see mussels growing on *bouchots*. See p. 82.

❸ **Swinging from** tree to tree at the **Parc des Grands Chênes.** See p. 87.

❹ **Cycling along** an old railway track on a family **Vélo Rail** at Médréac. See p. 88.

❺ **Exploring** the **forest of Brocéliande** with its ancient stones and Arthurian legends. See p. 67.

❻ **Finding out** about woodland toys at the **Musée de Bretagne** in Rennes. See p. 78.

❼ **Observing** silkworms close up at Campel's **Secrets du Soie** museum. See p. 79.

❽ **Navigating** a pirates' maze, the **Labyrinthe des Corsaires,** at St-Malo. See p. 86.

❾ **Seeing** the carved sea monsters at the **Rochers Sculptés de Rothéneuf**. See p. 69.

❿ **Sleeping in** a safari-style treehouse at the **Domaine des Ormes**. See p. 92.

Towns & Cities

Bécherel, Cité du Livre ★

A town devoted to secondhand bookshops – it's a bit like a smaller, less frenetic version of Wales' Hay-on-Wye – may not sound like an obvious choice for those with children, but Bécherel has the makings of a great family day out if you share a love of books, or a half-day if you combine it with a visit to the **Zoo de la Bourbansais** (p. 73). Except for the first Sunday of the month, when

Bookshop at Bécherel

there's a book fair, or at the Easter book festival or August 'book night', it's a sleepy little place full of ambling cats and old ladies peeping at strangers from behind net curtains, and as such it's best to call the **tourist office** (see p. 63) ahead of time to check that at least some of the bookshops will be open: their hours, which often aren't posted in the windows, are sporadic. Ask at the tourist office, too, for their beautifully illustrated free French-language booklet, which tells children (aged seven and up) all about the traces of the town's compelling history (it contains vestiges of a Plantagenet castle and towers, and grand houses dating from its incarnation as a linen-exporting centre), rewarding them with a goody bag with pencils, a ruler, a compass and so on. The helpful staff will also let you know of any relevant events, such as exhibitions on old children's literature.

The most child-friendly of the dozen or so shops is the delightful **Librairie Guriziem** (rue de la Chanvrerie, ☎ *02 99 66 87 09*), which stocks old and modern French books for adults and children, on all kinds of subjects. Children's fare can include Tin Tin, old Mickey Mouse annuals, illustrated Dickens' tales, comic strips and more, but if they don't want to browse while you peruse the shelves, there's a special little table and chairs heaped with new books (such as 'Oui Oui' – Noddy) and letters to play with. Book-browsing being thirsty work, the owners have thoughtfully added a *salon de thé* where you can relax to classical music while the children doodle with the paper and pencils provided. You can take your pick from juices, organic teas, beer and cider, and hot chocolate prepared on a corner hob from melted chocolate slabs and milk – highly recommended. Tables and chairs are also provided on the pavement looking out onto the town's pretty central square, which has benches and a piece of children's playground equipment (and a fair amount of unscooped poop when we last visited).

For English-language and other non-French books, walk up the side of the square, to the **Librairie Neiges d'Antan** (rue de la Beurrerie, no phone), recognisable by the donkey's face peering down from its sign. This also stocks books on Brittany, old crime novels and travel books, and children's books (on its first and second floors), but opening times and even days seem highly arbitrary.

About 25km (16 miles) northwest of Rennes on D27. Tourist office: ☎ 02 99 66 75 23, ***www.becherel.com****.*

St-Malo ★★ Famous for its gnarled 17th and 18th century *corsaires,* dubbed 'pirates with a permit' (they had royal warrants to attack foreign commercial vessels), St-Malo sprawls outwards from its historic hub, the *ville intra-muros*. It's here that visitors – many of whom are just biding their time until their ferry home – tend to flock, for the often-touristy restaurants and the good shops (p. 88). The place has considerable charm: you can stroll the wide ramparts and enjoy good beaches, including the **Plage du Bon Secours**, from which you can sometimes walk out (after studying the tide warnings), to **Grand Bé island**, where the French writer Chateaubriand is entombed (as a child he played on the rocky Plage de l'Eventail a few minutes' walk away). In summer you can also walk out to the **Fort National**, a largely 17th century military stronghold and one-time execution site with a drawbridge, jail and powder magazine (there are English-speaking guides), and breathtaking views back over St-Malo. Children might also like to see the **Petit Aquarium** (place Vauban, ☎ *02 99 56 94 77*), set into the very ramparts themselves, but there's a much better 'Grand' one on the fringes of town (p. 72). There's also a **petit train touristique** and a lovely if pricey carousel by the Grand Porte. **Place des Frères Lamennais** is a peaceful square with a fine little playground where youngsters can mix with local children and work up the appetite for an organic crêpe or two in the nearby **Café Bleu** (p. 105).

St-Malo

Beastly Doings

Europe's largest mammoth skeleton was found on the Mont-Dol, a former island, now landlocked, that you will see rising from the flat landscape around Dol-de-Bretagne on the way between the Mont-St-Michel (in Normandy; p. 68) and St-Malo. The Mont-Dol was also once home to rhinos, cave lions and wolves, and is said to be the place where St Michael battled Satan before victoriously leaping over to the Mont-St-Michel (the more imaginative claim that you can see his footprint, and marks made by the devil's claws).

Accommodation (p. 97) is better outside the walled centre – notably in the city's seaside resort of **Paramé** stretching northeast as far as **Rothéneuf** with its amazing sculpted rocks (p. 69). As well as being a ferry port, St-Malo is a good place from which to make trips by *vedettes* (little ferries) to the nearby resort of Dinard, the town of Dinan, the Cap Fréhel (p. 124) and the island of Cézembre; the extremely helpful tourist office (which can even, on a Sunday, tell you where your husband can watch the British FA Cup Final!) has details of all.

Tourist office: Esplanade St-Vincent, ☎ 0825 135 200, ***www.saint-malo-tourisme.com****.*

Beaches & Resorts

Paramé, the seaside resort of St-Malo (p. 63), has excellent sands for children.

Anse Du Guesclin On the quiet coastal road between St-Malo and Cancale lies this glorious, slightly wild, croissant-shaped stretch of sandy beach. Make sure to bring nets for foraging in the sparkling rockpools; good swimmers might also like to seek out the bank of wild oysters about 200m offshore. The little island at the eastern end of the beach, cut off at high tide and topped by the dramatic Fort Du Guesclin (built on the site of a 12th century fortress) was home for some of the 1950s and 1960s to singer Leo Ferré and his famous pet chimp Pépée, about whom he wrote a song. There's also, rather delightfully, a hermit occupying an old customs shelter on the Pointe des Grands Nez ('Big Noses Point') – take care not to disturb him!

Just east, the **Plage de la Touesse** will please teenage fans of Colette, who found inspiration for *Le Blé en Herbe* – about a family holiday in Brittany and the love between two adolescents – while living in a villa here in 1911–26.

About 18km (11 miles) northeast of St-Malo on D201.

Cancale Cancale can seem touristy, with its curving bay

crammed with seafood restaurants and cafés, but come at low tide to watch the tractors out in the oyster beds just offshore of its **Port de la Houle** (and to enjoy the distant view of the Mont-St-Michel in Normandy; p. 68) and you will really get the feel of being at the working seaside. In fact, go the whole hog and buy a plastic tray of oysters and wedge of lemon from one of the stalls (at € 2.50 (£ 1.70)) for six, costing a fraction what they do in the restaurants just steps away) and enjoy them as natives do, with a bottle of cider on the steps down the beach, tossing the shells back to the ocean. Your children might not yet have a taste for squidgy seafood (the fancy groceries along the front have plenty of biscuits and other fare they can picnic on), but they may well enjoy visiting the nearby **Ferme Marine** (p. 82). There are also trips out in an old *bisquine*, **La Cancalaise** (see p. 83). And if you can't stretch to a night or two in the **Maisons de Bricourt** (p. 90), at least stop off for an ice cream or crêpe at its delightful **Grain de Vanille** tearoom.

To the north, and still part of Cancale, **Port-Mer** is a sweet and picturesque bay with a handful of cafés and brasseries and lots of yachts. The sailing school (✆ *02 99 89 90 22*) runs courses for everyone aged six to 77, and there's a Club Mickey for children in summer. Further north still, the **Pointe du Grouin** is a jagged headland with brilliant views, including close-ups of the Ile des Landes, a reserve for great cormorants and other birds, with a lighthouse. In summer you might also spot dolphins. But sadly, even out of season tourists tend to overrun this spot.

15km (9 miles) east of St-Malo on D355. Tourist office: 44 rue du Port, ✆ 02 99 89 63 72, ***www.ville-cancale.fr.***

Oysters for Sale, Cancale

St-Lunaire ★★ Named after an evangelising monk who supposedly lived to the age of 115 (his Gallo-Roman sarcophagus can still be viewed in the town's 11th century church and his sandal marks are supposedly visible on the Pointe du Décollé where he stepped offshore after chopping through fog with his sword), St-Lunaire was transformed in the 1860s, with the addition of wide boulevards, grand villas, hotels and a casino, from a humble fishing village into a chic resort. A couple of decades later, a Haitian, rich from sugar cane, added the Grand Hôtel (now apartments), tennis courts and 17 villas to house his many children. Things calmed down after the 'Années Folles' ('Mad Years') of the 1920s, and now this is a placid family resort retaining the stunning sea vistas that – some claim – inspired Debussy to write parts of *La Mer*.

The four lovely beaches include **La Grande Plage**, which has a children's club in July and August and a mini-golf course; on nearby Boulevard de la Plage in the same months you can enjoy free **Cinema Familial** daily showings (9pm) of well-known child-friendly films. The longest beach is the **Plage de Longchamp** stretching out of town to the east, where you can hire sea canoes, bodyboards and sand yachts from the **Point Passion Plage** (✆ *02 99 46 30 04*, ***www.ycsl.net***). The same firm runs a sailing school on all sorts of vessels, with a starting age of

St-Lunaire

seven, plus a 'Jardin des Mers' activity programme for 5–8-year-olds. Don't miss the surprising wonderful 'snack bar', **Le Surf** (p. 106), towards the western end of this beach.

You can buy beach gear and hire bikes at **La Cabine** (80 rue de la Grève, ✆ *02 99 46 31 76*), and the **Tennis-Club** (✆ *02 96 46 31 11*) offers lessons and courses for children, and, in summer, junior and family tournaments. **Les Ecuries** (✆ *02 99 46 06 20*, ***www.les-ecuries.net***) offers a '*poney* club' for ages five and up and rides in the area. For places to stay, see p. 99.

Nestling up against St-Lunaire is the very pretty estuary town of **St Briac-sur-Mer**, with great beaches and a delightful centre full of *brocantes* (junk shops) and the largish Tant Qu'il y Aura la Mer, which stocks children's wear. At the church, children might enjoy spotting the green stone mackerels that adorn its exterior (the fish used to be seen here as a herald of spring).

*3km (2 miles) west of Dinard on D786. Tourist office: boulevard du Général de Gaulle, ☎ 02 99 46 31 09, **www.saint-lunaire.com**.*

Other Natural Wonders & Spectacular Views

Fôret de Brocéliande ★★

Also known as the Fôret de Paimpont, this area of woods and moorland west of Rennes is the centre of Breton Arthurian legends – possibly after an 11th century lord of the forest brought back tales of King Arthur and the Knights of the Round Table after fighting in England during the Norman Conquest. Today there are tourist trails taking in atmospheric sites where events involving characters from the legends are said to have taken place, plus

Ancient Stones in Brocéliande Forest

Neolithic remains such as menhirs and dolmens. **Paimpont** tourist office provides maps and itineraries, including a driving tour, plus details of guided tours in French. Or head for the Château de Comper nearby (just

The Mont-St-Michel

Bay of Wonders

The **Baie du Mont-St-Michel**, a bay of glittering sandflats stretching out between Brittany and Normandy, is one of France's most awesome sights – and one of its deadliest, with quicksand and Europe's fastest-moving tides still claiming lives today as they did those of medieval pilgrims attempting to reach the **Mont-St-Michel**. This rocky islet 2km off the coast of Normandy, topped by a dramatic Benedictine abbey, is a UNESCO World Heritage Site and France's most-visited attraction outside Paris. It's often thought to be in Brittany – in fact, many Bretons still challenge Norman ownership of it, claiming that it's only there now as a result of the river Couesnon, the historic border between Brittany and Normandy, having changed course.

Only about 50km (30 miles) east of St-Malo, the Mount (✆ *02 33 60 14 30*, ***www.ot-montsaintmichel.com***) is easily visited by those holidaying in Brittany. It's not the most child-friendly of sights, with its steep cobbled lanes and tourist hordes, but if you come outside high season or in the evening you can still catch inklings of its mysterious aura. The best bit for children is the **Archéoscope**, a multimedia space with a *son-et-lumière* show about the mount's history, construction and legends (in French, but with great footage from a helicopter). You can also visit the **abbey** itself, including the spooky crypts, a **Musée Maritime** with model boats and displays on local tides and ecology, and the **Musée Historique**, with waxwork prisoners, reconstructed *oubliettes* (prison cells set in dungeon floors), torture instruments, weapons, and a 19th century periscope that lets you look at the bay.

inside the Morbihan), which houses a **Centre de l'Imaginaire Arthurien** (✆ *02 97 22 79 96*) with annual exhibitions about the area and the legends, including waxwork scenes. This is a good way of getting your bearings before setting out, though the texts and videos are in French only; it also hosts frequent medieval re-creations, festivals and tournaments.

Other Arthurian sites include the idyllic **Lac de Comper** (or 'Grand Etang') next to the château, at the bottom of which the magician Merlin is reputed to have created a castle of crystal for the fairy Viviane, and the **Fontaine de Barenton**, a spring where Merlin and Viviane are said to have met, and which is reputed to have powers for bringing rain and curing madness (hence the name of the nearby village of Folle Pensée – 'Mad Thought'). **Merlin's Tomb** ('Tombeau de Merlin'), where Viviane reputedly imprisoned him for eternity, is signposted a short drive north of here, but these days there's nothing more to see than two slabs of stone (the site was ravaged by treasure

Midway between St-Malo and the Mount, the **Maison de la Baie du Vivier sur Mer** (*02 99 48 84 38*, ***www.maisonbaie.com***) is a nature centre that brings alive the bay of the Mont-St-Michel, especially its main trade of mussel farming, for all ages – partly through imaginative and interactive displays and a new film on marine life in the bay. A visit is best combined with a 2 hour tour of the bay in the 'Mytili-Mobile' – a tractor-drawn cart taking you to see mussels growing on *bouchots* amidst the sands – or, better still, with one of the guided walks lasting 4–7 hours (over a distance of 8–15km). One walk, the *Balade Découverte* (4–5 hours over 8km: i.e. moving at a snail's pace!), was conceived specially for families and includes shell-hunting. For the contact details of all companies running guided trips in the bay, see ***www.mont-saint-michel-baie.com***. There is also an annual grand **Rando-Baie** programme (*02 33 89 64 00*, ***http://randobaie.free.fr/***) of fantastic family-based events in the bay, run from the Maison de la Baie at Genêts in Normandy but with some activities taking place in the Ille-et-Vilaine. A warning: Victor Hugo described the tides in the bay as being 'swift as a galloping horse' (they come in at 1 metre (3 feet) a second, with roughly 14 metres (46 feet) between high and low water marks). **Never walk in the bay without a guide**.

For more on the bay of The Mont-St-Michel and the Mont, walks and other outdoor activities in the area, and the Rando-Baie event, see the companion guide to this book, *Normandy with Your Family*.

seekers in the 1890s). For books and crafts on Arthurian and other Celtic and medieval themes, visit **Au Pays de Merlin** (rue du Général de Gaulle, Paimpont, *02 99 07 80 23*).

Besides the ancient and legendary sites, this is a scenic area for walking and riding (tourist offices sell 'Topo-Guides' detailing 3–20km circuits), as well as for hiring mountain bikes (*02 99 54 67 54*). Look out for the red schist, due to the presence of iron, a mineral also responsible for confusing walkers' compasses.

For places to stay, see p. 93–97.

Paimpont tourist office (syndicat d'initiative), 5 esplanade de Brocéliande, 02 99 07 84 23, ***www.brocelandetourisme.info.***

Rochers Sculptés de Rothéneuf ★★ In a region known for its weird natural rockscapes, the faces, figures and creatures adorning the rocks at the far end of the coastal strip leading away from St-Malo *intra-muros* (p. 63) could almost pass unnoticed. Created by a deaf-dumb priest as a way of

Rochers Sculptés de Rothéneuf

expressing himself, they tell the tale of a local family of *corsaires* who end up being devoured by sea monsters after a battle with other pirates. It's a bit like viewing a collection of gargoyles, crowded together and lashed by the waves, and ghoulish-minded children will find both them and the setting fascinating. Descending the vertiginous rock face (beware: those with toddlers or babes-in-arms might find the rough-hewn steps too much of a challenge, and everyone needs sensible shoes), it's astonishing to imagine the priest clambering down here every day for 25 years, chiselling away.

INSIDER TIP

Come first thing in the morning, especially on a weekday, to have the Rochers to yourself and best appreciate their beautiful weirdness.

If you do come later in the day, **Restaurant Le Bénétin** (see p. 103) at the top of the path has a wonderful terrace where you can enjoy afternoon tea or dinner.

Rothéneuf harbour nearby has good sheltered beaches, as do the Pointe de la Varde headlands just east, together with some World War II pillboxes (be wary of the steep drops), rabbits, winding paths popular with joggers, and canoeists.

5km (3 miles) north of St-Malo intra-muros on D201, no tel. Open daily 9–7. Adults € 2.50 (£ 1.70), under-12s free.

Aquaria & Animal Parks

La Chêvrerie du Désert You're never far from a friendly (often a somewhat overfriendly) goat in Brittany, but this little 'discovery farm' is worth a visit if you're in the area – children can get up close and personal with dwarf goats in their enclosure, as well as admiring Vietnamese pigs, Poitou donkeys, Ouessant sheep (p. 153), Jersey cows and a variety of birdlife, while parents can peruse the goats' cheese, jam and honey, cider, apple juice and other handmade farm produce in the shop. There are free quiz sheets for 7–12-year-olds, and you can watch the goats being milked at 5.30pm. Afterwards, you can get enjoy galettes, cheese platters, and goats' milk crêpes and other desserts.

Plerguer, 8km (5 miles) west of Dol-de-Bretagne off D676. ☎ 02 99 58 92 14. Open Apr–June and Sept Mon and Wed–Sat 2.30–6.30pm, Sun and public hols 11am–6.30pm, July and Aug daily 11am–6.30pm. Adm: adults € 5 (£ 3.35), children € 4 (£ 2.70).

Ecomusée du Pays de Rennes ★ La Bintinais on the outskirts of Rennes was once one of the city's largest farms, and this three-storey museum now housed there retraces its five-century history, through arte-facts, machinery and furniture, enlivened – for children and adults alike – by audiovisual displays, interactive games and films. The permanent exhibits are complemented by temporary exhibitions on regional themes, though these tend to be rather weighty for children. In any case, your children will probably be most interested by what's outside the four walls – 19-hectare grounds in which 19 threatened local breeds graze, including some rather fetching spotted pigs, and in which you can take horse-and-carriage rides. There's a pleasant lakeside picnic area (and an indoor one for bad weather), plus a little shop. Allow about 2 hours in total for your visit.

Ferme de la Bintinais, route de Châtillon-sur-Seiche, Rennes (from centre, take avenue Henri-Fréville, then follow signposts in direction of Noyal-Chatillon-sur-Seiche), ✆ *02 99 51 38 15.* ***www.ecomusee-rennes-metropole.fr****. Open Apr–Sept Tue–Fri 9am–6pm (museum building closed noon–2pm), Sat 2–6pm, Sun 2–7pm; Oct–Mar Tue–Fri 9am-noon and 2–6pm, Sat 2–6pm, Sun 2–7pm. Adm: adults € 4.60 (£ 3.10), children 6–14 € 2.30 (£ 1.55).*

Ferme du Tessonnet This 6 hectare (15 acre) farm is a breeding centre for 50-plus threatened breeds, including Girgentana goats from Sicily, recognisable by their spiralling horns reaching a height of 70cm, Mangalitza pigs, distinguishable by the very dense curly black hair on their back, and miniature pigs from the USA. Children-oriented activities are organised, including pony rides for the very young.

Grand Aquarium, St-Malo

*Goven, 20km (12 miles) southwest of Rennes on D21, ☏ 02 99 42 02 55, **www.animal-agrements.com**. Open 2–7pm Sun and public hols mid-Apr–June and Sept, Sun–Fri July and Aug. Adm: adults € 3.50 (£ 2.40), children € 2.50 (£ 1.70).*

Grand Aquarium ★★★ There's a small aquarium within St-Malo's walled city (p. 63), but this out-of-town complex really is the business, not least because of its amazing **Nautibus** ride, about which my eldest son was still raving a full month after our visit (''member the submarine, Mummy?'). Not for the claustrophobic, this consists of mini submarines that make six-minute tours of an underwater pool full of marine flora, fauna and mock wrecks (the turbulence is designed to be part of the fun, apparently...). Then there's the wonderful Bassin Ludique especially for young children, with a touchpool with rays, turbots and more, a walkway over a larger pool, and funky interactive installations such as the Sirène Anémone, which calls out to its siblings if you get too close.

In the Anneau des Requins or 'Shark Ring', a massive circular aquarium, you can recline on soft mats and watch lemon sharks, nurse sharks, sandbar sharks, sand tiger sharks, turtles and a giant grouper swim around you in 600,000 litres of water, to soft music and subtly pulsating lighting (call ☏ *02 99 21 19 00* for details of overnight stays in the Ring; adults € 110 (£ 75), children aged 6–14 € 80 (£ 54)). Other rooms are cleverly themed (oil rig, lab with bubbling test tubes, wreck and so on), with stories told by a fictional explorer (in French only) but an emphasis on serious ecology. Among the small fry, don't miss the black-and-white striped common cuttlefish, which my son described as a 'squashed zebra', the humpback grouper, which we discovered bears the much more interesting name *mérou Grace Kelly* in French (note that not all the information on the display boards is translated into English), and the lanternfish whose eyes shine with luminescent bacteria.

Allow a good 2–3 hours for your visit. The restaurant, **L'Escale Gourmande**, offers good seafood, including fishermen's stew with rice (€ 13.20 (£ 8.90)), plus an under-12s menu (€ 6.30 (£ 4.25)) that includes fish croquettes with chips.

*Avenue du Général Patton (towards Dinard), St-Malo, ☏ 02 99 21 19 00, **www.aquarium-st-malo.com**. Open on average daily 10am–6pm or 10am–7pm, but call for complicated seasonal opening hours (including late-night openings). Adm: adults € 13.90 (£ 9.35), children 4–14 € 9.90 (£ 6.60).*

Musée de l'Abeille Vivante This offbeat little 'museum of the living bee', set in an old stone dwelling and open in high summer only, appeals to visitors of all ages: the 200 square metres of displays on apiculture might be strictly for older children and parents, but little ones love peering into the five active hive colonies (safely behind glass) and, in

August (3pm daily), seeing honey being extracted. There's also a video, guided tours, and a shop where you can taste hive produce.

18 rue de la Briqueterie, Vitré, about 30km (19 miles) east of Rennes on D857, ☎ 02 99 75 09 01. Open July and Aug Mon–Sat 2–6pm except public hols. Adm: € 3.20 (£ 2.15), under-12s free.

Parc Ornithologique de Bretagne This wooded park brings together birdlife from all over the world, from Siberian geese to Australian black swans, which means there's quite a racket going on for most of the day. Some creatures – such as the parrots – will be familiar from zoo visits; others, including the golden pheasants from China and Lady Amherst pheasants from Tibet and Burma, may come as more of a surprise. The beady-eyed birds of prey also exert a fascination. Strolling around the duck- and geese-filled lake is pleasant on a sunny day, and there are tables and benches where you can sit and survey the scene or have a snack, plus a cute bar with a terrace and a gift shop. Allow about 90 minutes for a visit.

*53 boulevard Pasteur, Bruz, about 10km (6 miles) south of Rennes off D177, ☎ 02 99 52 68 57, **www.parc-ornithologique.com**. Open Apr–June and Sept daily 2–7; July and Aug daily 10am–noon and 2–7pm; Oct–mid-Nov and mid-Feb–Apr Sun 2–6pm. Adm: adults € 6.20 (£ 4.15), children 3–12 € 3.80 (£ 2.55).*

Zoo de la Bourbansais ★★ If you feel a little guilty ogling exotic animals in captivity, this charming zoo with its almost tropical atmosphere might be for you, given that it's part of a castle and park that lets you take in some history and culture in the

Château de la Bourbansais

same outing. Bounded by a rich, shady forest (the deer and wolf enclosures merge into the trees), La Bourbansais is lush with palms, colourful flowers and other plants, to the point where it's sometimes difficult to see the animals (including, since 2006, tamarind monkeys) through the foliage, but they seem to have a decent amount of space, and there are daily feedings to watch.

If you do join a 40 minute guided tour of the beautiful castle with its period interiors (there are combined or separate tickets for the zoo and castle), reward the children with a turn on the bouncy castles and play equipment (and a maze July–Sept) or a 15 minute spin on the *petit train* (afternoons only), though you may be surprised how much fun they have just running around the formal gardens with their pyramid hedges and weathered statuary. The grounds also host anachronistic daily displays (Apr–Sept) involving falconry and hunting hounds (defended as a passion of French kings, as if that impressed anyone).

The zoo has a counter serving *steak frites*, Italian ices, *barbe à papa* (candyfloss) and more, plus a shady picnic area, but nobody seems bothered if you eat in the castle gardens – a civilised alternative.

Pleugueneuc, 38km (24 miles) north of St-Malo off N137, 📞 02 99 69 40 07, www.zoo-bourbansais.com. Open daily Apr–Sept 10am–7pm; Oct–Mar 2–6pm. Adm: adults € 14.50 (£ 9.80), children 4–16 € 10.50 (£ 7) (€ 18.50/14.50 (£ 12.50/9.80) with castle).

Nature Reserves, Parks & Gardens

Parc de Port Breton The resort of Dinard itself may appear to have had its day, but its 23 hectare (57 acre) municipal park is out of the ordinary in that in addition to a couple of children's play areas, a sports field, a rose garden, a water feature and about 2,000 trees, it has lovely sea views, a 'pets corner' with around 60 animal and bird species, including llamas, wallabies, deer, donkeys and pheasants, and a walkway in the shape of the tree-based Celtic zodiac, from which Druids believed you could deduce your main personality traits.

Avenue de la Libération, Dinard, 📞 02 99 46 74 64. Open daily 8am–6.30pm. Adm free.

Jardin du Thabor ★ One of the loveliest public gardens in all of France, on a site abandoned by Benedictine monks after it become a favourite spot for duels (in the sloping area known as Enfer, or 'Hell'), Rennes' Jardin du Thabor is a great picnic and walking spot, with diverting topiary animals and statues, a carousel and outdoor *babyfoot* (table football), as well as a botanical garden and an orangery hosting changing exhibitions. Don't miss the enchanting Jardin des Catherinettes with its fountains, grottoes and mysterious island. Come on a Sunday and blend in with the Rennes families walking off their lunch. Or if you're here in summer, especially

La Roche aux Fées

during the Tombées de la Nuit festival (p. 61), try to catch a concert or a Breton music and dancing show (Wed in July).

Place St Melaine, Rennes, 02 99 28 56 62. Open daily summer 7.15am–9.30pm; winter 7.30am–6pm. Adm free.

Historic Buildings & Monuments

La Roche aux Fées ★

Delighting lovers of the prehistoric and of fairytales alike, the 'Fairies' Rock' (20m long, 6m wide and 4m high (65 by 20 by 13 feet)), is one of the most impressive dolmens (Neolithic gallery tombs) in France – all the more so given that fairies are said to have flown the 40-or-so huge red-schist slabs here about 5,000 years ago (they weigh up to 40 tonnes, so those fairies must have had some biceps!). Other legends hold that this was a dragon's lair, the tomb of a Roman emperor, and a site of human sacrifice. According to some locals, it's impossible to walk round it and count the same number of stones twice; unless, that is, you are about to wed and do the counting by full moon, in which case, if the numbers do tally, your marriage will last. One thing that *is* sure is that its entrance is aligned with the rising sun at the winter solstice, which means the interior is illuminated on 21 December. Wear sensible shoes, as this is an uphill walk (you're rewarded with great views over the countryside).

Just south of Essé, 25km (16 miles) southeast of Rennes off D41, 08 20 20 52 35. Open all the time. Adm free.

St Just This is another exceptional Neolithic site famous for the diversity of its dolmens and megalithic buildings (which range in date from 5000 to 1500 BC), set on a beautiful area of heath. Comparable in many ways with Carnac (p. 212) but completely untouristy, its sites of interest are dotted over several kilometres. A highlight is the **Demoiselles de Cojoux** or **Roches Piquées** – quartz standing stones that may have been part of a larger alignment, and that according to legend are actually young girls turned to stone for dancing at prayer time. A 7km 'discovery circuit' gives an insight into human activity here, starting from 7,000 years ago, and lets you appreciate the natural surrounds; there are green arrows to follow, plus information points along the way, but you can pick up free leaflets at **La Maison Nature et Mégalithes** at St Just itself (allée des Cerisiers, *02 99 72 69 25*). The latter is also your contact point for information on events, such as evening walks to see nocturnal birds of prey.

45km (28 miles) southwest of Rennes off D177. Open all the time; adm free.

Télégraphe de Chappe This stone building amidst marshland in the bay of Mont-St-Michel (p. 68) is one of the last vestiges of a late 19th century telegraph system that linked Paris and Brest on the far west coast – a precursor of the modern telephone line. It was one of about 50 posts dotted across the country at 15–20km intervals; they relied on the manoeuvring of the mobile arms at the top of each building, with each position corresponding to a coded message. It's incredible to think that messages could be relayed in this way over the 600km (375 mile) distance between Paris and Brest in just 20 minutes. The restored building is open for visits in summer, when you can watch the replica arm functioning and see displays about the system. With any luck, by the time of your visit the interactive interpretation centre (being created at the time of writing) will have opened too.

St Marcan, 10km (6 miles) northeast of Dol-de-Bretagne on D797, 02 99 48 53 53. Open June–Sept Wed–Sun 10am–noon and 2–6pm. Adm: adults € 3 (£ 2), children 8–12 € 1 (£ 0.70), under-8s free.

The Top Museums

Atelier–Musée de l'Horlogerie Ancienne This 16th century building devoted to timepieces old and modern is most interesting for its workshops, in which you observe a watchmaker practise his painstaking craft. There's also a re-created watchmaker's *atelier* from the early 20th century, where you can see the tools used. The exhibition rooms contain more than 200 items, which in addition to clocks and watches dating from 1600 to the present include music boxes and animated tableaux, which children tend to like best. A clock/watch shop completes the picture. Allow about 30 minutes for a visit, an hour if you watch the video.

37 rue Nationale, Fougères, 02 99 99 40 98. Open mid-June–Aug Mon–Sat 9am–12.30pm and 2–7pm, Sun 2–6.30pm; Sept–mid-June Tue–Sat 9am–noon and 2–7pm (last adm 1hr before closing time). Adm: adults € 4.50 (£ 3), children 10–17 € 3.70 (£ 2.50), under-10s free; family ticket € 16.40 (£ 11).

Ecomusée du Pays de Montfort Set in a tower that is all that remains of the town's 14th century castle, this museum provides a salutary lesson in life's simpler pleasures with its displays on childhood toys from pre-Industrial times. In place of Playstations and the plastic contraptions of our era, you can see toys made from wood and other natural country materials both for and by children. Like mine, your children will probably be inspired to see just what can be created from leaves, flowers and even fruit and vegetables; if you're lucky, you may catch a workshop in which toys are being made. In addition, the museum has displays on medieval Montfort, regional costumes from 1840 to 1940, Arthurian legends in the surrounding Brocéliande forest (p. 67) and other local legends, architecture and photography. Temporary exhibitions are sometimes held too.

2 rue du Château, Montfort-sur-Meu, 25km (16 miles) west of Rennes on D125, ☎ 02 99 09 31 81. Open Tue–Fri 9am–noon and 2–6pm, Sat 10–noon and 2–6pm, Sun and public hols 2–6pm. Adm: adults € 3.50 (£ 2.35), children 6–16 € 2 (£ 1.35), under-6s free.

Espace Ferrié ★ FIND Opened in 2005, this 'transmissions museum' charts the evolution of human communications from prehistoric smoke signals to microchips, some of it in a military context. It's all very hi-tech and interactive, with eight multimedia 'islands' and a variety of

Canoeing on the Vilaine River

themed zones plus plenty of hands-on exhibits designed for children. The displays on cryptology are always a winner, while clunky old radios and telephones often invoke a snigger or two. There are also some light-hearted temporary exhibitions and special events such as a display of totems and sculptures made from discarded electronic components by a contemporary artist. Avail yourself of one of the free audioguides (in French, Breton, English, German and Spanish) to get the best from your visit.

*Avenue de la Boulais, Cesson-Sévigné, east Rennes, ☎ 02 99 84 32 43, **www.espaceferrie.fr**. Open Wed–Mon 2–6pm, closed some public hols. Adm: adults € 3 (£ 2), children free.*

Manoir de l'Automobile et des Vieux Métiers This vast museum, in the grounds of a 17th century manor, houses a collection of 400-or-so cars, from chunky 1930s Talbots to sleek Ferraris and modern Formula 1 cars, plus a few thousand scale models. Around 230 waxwork tableaux with utterly unlifelike mannequins in period costume add a touch of humour to proceedings, and liven things up for family members who might not be as car-crazy as others. As well as old forms of transport, including horse-drawn carts, they evoke a variety of bygone trades. There's a good half-day's visit here if you have a genuine interest in cars; if so, the receptionist will tell about opportunities for karting, quad-biking and race-car driving (there's a racetrack adjoining the museum). There's also boat hire and canoeing on the Vilaine river in nearby Messac.

Route de Lieuron, Lohéac, 35km (22 miles) southeast of Rennes on D177, ☎ 02 99 34 02 32. Open 10am–1pm and 2–7pm daily July and Aug; Tue–Sun Sept–June. Adm: adults € 8.50 (£ 5.70), children 10–16 € 7 (£ 4.70).

Musée de Bretagne/Espace de Sciences ★★★ Since spring 2006, Rennes has been home to the **Les Champs Libres**, which as well as housing the city library contains the Musée de Bretagne (previously located in the Beaux-Arts museum, and a third of the size) and the all-new Espace des Sciences (Science Centre). The **Musée de Bretagne**, as Brittany's regional storehouse, is a must-see on any visitor's list, particularly the exhibition 'Bretagne est Univers', which, designed to resemble a city, with 'streets' and 'squares' between the main displays, traces the region's history and identity through objects, costumes, videos and more, from paleolithic tools to a Minitel computer. **Mille et Une Images**, another permanent exhibition (this time with free admission), evokes the region from a more poetic point-of-view, with sound and light effects helping to create a 3D universe in which paintings, posters, photos and old engravings are experienced as a 'flow' of sensations, rather than in any chronological or thematic order. Children are naturally most interested by the many Breton toys and games on display, including a wooden Poule Picorante ('Pecking Hen') from 1935, a 1930s 'bottle-fishing' game, also made of wood, and a Bécassine doll made in 1905. The temporary exhibitions on topics such as comic strips (*bandes dessinées*) in Brittany might also be of interest.

The **Espace des Sciences** comprises a state-of-the-art planetarium, which puts on three one-hour shows (on the sky at night, legends about the sky, and the solar system) in the afternoons, plus three exhibition rooms. The first, the **Salle Euréka**, hosts six-monthly exhibitions on topics such as Time and Water. The **Salle de la Terre** ('Earth Room') looks at the geology of northern France's Armorican peninsula through big-screen films, 3D models, multimedia displays, a mini earthquake simulator, a little amphitheatre hosting daily shows and discussions, and 50-or-so rocks collected from the area between Cherbourg and the

Ile de Groix. Lastly, the **Laboratoire de Merlin** is a discovery zone with 30 hands-on scientific installations that allow you to, for instance, create electricity, make a ball hang in the air, or learn about water pressure. Again, there is a little amphitheatre where you can watch daily science displays.

INSIDER TIP

Visits to the Laboratoire are restricted to one hour, with a maximum of 40 people, so put your names down for a slot at reception as soon as you arrive at the museum (there's a single ticket office for the Musée de Bretagne and Espace des Sciences).

Access to the **city library** is free; as well a large range of children's books and magazines it has regular storytelling and music sessions. There's also a **café** for meals and light snacks, with a lovely terrace, and a **shop** selling items relating to the cultural and scientific exhibitions, including books, DVDs and postcards.

Technology-lovers should note that since 2002 Rennes also has an automated **metro** system that is well worth a ride.

*10 cour des Alliés, Rennes, ☎ 02 23 40 66 70 (Musée), ☎ 02 23 40 66 40 (Espace des Sciences), **www.leschampslibres.fr**. Open Tue noon–9pm, Wed–Fri noon–7pm, Sat and Sun 2–9pm. Adm Musée de Bretagne or Espace des Sciences: adults € 4 (£ 2.70), children 8–16 € 3 (£ 2), joint ticket adults € 7 (£ 4.70), children 8–16 € 4 (£ 2.70) (planetarium: adults extra € 3 (£ 2), children € 2 (£ 1.35). Ask about special rates for groups of 5 aged 8 and up.*

Musee Louison Bobet This offbeat, lovingly run little museum dedicated to a local hero who won three consecutive Tours de France (1953–55) may be of interest to sporty children, or those entranced by the sight of lycra-clad cyclists giving it some va-va-voom on French roads. As well as some of Bobet's bikes, you see medals, photos, paintings, videos, press articles, books, letters, cycling attire and other items associated with his sporting career and the Tour de France in general. Show your children the picture, in Bobet's own album, of the future World Champion in his first cycling competition (he is said to have got so fast by delivering bread for his dad, the local baker). The lady who runs the place knew Bobet in her youth and will reminisce fondly if you ask her any questions. Mums and Dads might also be interested in the displays on Bobet's later incarnation as a businessman who brought thalassotherapy (seawater cures) to Brittany.

5 rue de Gaël, St-Méen-le-Grand, 45km (28 miles) west of Rennes off N164, ☎ 02 99 09 67 86. Open 2–7pm daily July–Sept; Sun–Mon Oct–June. Adm: adults € 3 (£ 2), children 10–14 € 2 (£ 1.35).

Les Secrets du Soie ★★ A 'museum of silk' may not sound like the kind of thing to set children alight, but even – or perhaps especially – tots are enthralled by its glass case full of live silkworms (or larvae) munching on mulberry leaves. After finding out some amazing statistics, including the fact that silkworms increase 10,000-fold in weight over 4–5 weeks, visitors get the chance to pass a thread of raw silk between their fingers. The displays are imaginative, evoking exotic lands and the adventures and ardours of the Silk Route. You learn about the route taken by explorer Marco Polo, for instance, by handling figurines without seeing them (to emphasis the importance of the sense of touch), and a shadow theatre using Chinese puppets tells the story of the Asian princess said to have discovered silk while drinking tea under a mulberry bush 5,000 years ago. There is also a room exploring the use of silk in theatre costumes and fashion, from Egyptian kaftans to contemporary catwalk styles. Each year sees a temporary exhibition too. Guided tours, available in English, take about 90 minutes; if they are oversubscribed, or you don't think your children will last the course, the receptionist will give you a free booklet. The shop stocks scarves, ties, bags, cushions and more, plus sewing and crafts materials.

Campel, 40km (25 miles) southeast of Rennes on D65, ☎ 02 99 34 93 93, ***www.secretsdesoie.fr****. Open 2nd half Apr, Sept and 1st half Oct Sun–Fri 2–6pm; May and June daily 2–6pm; July and Aug daily 10am–noon and 2–6pm. Adm: adults € 6 (£ 4), children 5–15 € 4 (£ 2.70).*

Art & Craft Sites

L'Atelier Manoli ★ This museum and sculpture garden on the site where the artist Manoli lived until his death in 2001 is a surprisingly good bet for children, displaying about 400 outsize works and models based around three main themes: the human figure, 'assemblages' and animals (the 'Bestiaire'). It's fun to look at the 'assemblages' (displayed in La Chapelle, one of eight exhibition rooms) and try to work out what discarded objects they were created from (including saws and nails), but children generally have the most fun exploring the pathways and green lawns, where sculpted animals (including owls, horses, elks, panthers), gravity-defying human figures and strange creatures lurk amidst the vegetation. Don't miss the *Hommage à la Rance* – a sheep with a fleece made up of little metal boat propellers, built to commemorate the tidal electric dam on the Pointe de Brebis ('Ewe Point') of the estuary nearby.

9 rue du Suet, La Richardais, 2km (1.25 miles) southeast of Dinard on D114, ☎ 02 99 88 55 53, ***www.manoli.org****. Open Apr–June and Sept Sat, Sun and public hols 3–7pm; July and Aug daily 10.30am–noon and 3–7pm. Adm: € 4 (£ 2.70), under-12s free.*

Musée des Beaux-Arts This austere building conceals a warm museum with brightly coloured walls and important artworks and artefacts covering a huge span

An Old French Cart

from Ancient Egypt to the present day, including pieces by contemporary Breton artists. Youngsters who are into art should find much of interest, whether it be the calm of George de la Tour's famous *Le Nouveau-né*, a glowing oil painting of two women with a newborn baby, the garish ferocity of Rubens' *La Chasse au tigre* ('Tiger Hunt'), the nightmarish *Massacre des innocents* by Cogniet, in which a mother tries vainly to protect her child from King Herod, or the distorted woman's body in Picasso's *Baigneuse*, one of several he painted at the resort of Dinard in the 1920s. If your children speak good French, try to time your visit to coincide with a monthly **Croqu'musée** ('Bite-Sized Museum') workshop (Wed 2–3.30pm, € 2.30 (£ 1.55)), for children aged 5–7, 8–11 and 12–14, on themes such as Fantastic Animals, The Sky and Hats. You need to book ahead, as there are only 15 places for each age group. Alternatively, free French-language family leaflets on themes such as Egypt and 20th century art are available at reception.

Note that the tourist office runs 90-minute guided tours of the museum in French, English, Spanish and German by arrangement.

20 quai Emile Zola, Rennes, 📞 *02 23 62 17 45,* ***www.mbar.org****. Open Tue–Sun 10am–noon and 2–6pm. Adm: adults € 4.20 (£ 2.85), under-18s free.*

Children-Friendly Tours

Croisières Chateaubriand

Though it's great not to follow the well-beaten trail, it can also be enjoyable at times to accept that you *are* a tourist and do something that locals would probably avoid like the plague. That goes for these *bateau-promenades* on the lovely Rance estuary that divides St-Malo from Dinard. The route takes you past islands, sheltered coves, old watermills and *malouinières* (merchants' country dwellings), abandoned boats, fishing villages, and lots of marine wildlife, including herons, cormorants

Oyster Beds at Cancale

and – if you're very lucky – seals. All trips have live commentary, and there's a covered panoramic terrace and sun decks from which to take in the scenery. Straightforward trips last 90 minutes or three hours, but there are also very pleasant three-hour lunch or dinner trips with a choice of seafood-oriented menus. None are cheap, but the food is high quality, and there's an under-12s 'Pirate's Menu'.

Gare Maritime du Barrage de la Rance, Dinard, 02 99 46 44 40, ***www.chateaubriand.com****. Open all year, call for times. Reservations recommended; arrive 30mins ahead of sailing time. Tickets from: adults € 15 (£ 10), children 13–18 € 12 (£ 8), 2–12 € 10 (£ 6.60), family € 43 (£ 29).*

Ferme Marine What better place to tour a working oyster farm than scenic Cancale (p. 64) with its broad oyster beds?

Visitors to this family enterprise get to see farming techniques, including the hauling in of the mesh bags, and oyster sorting by hand (an arduous task), plus an exhibition of seashells from around the world that appeals more to youngsters – toddlers love the giant shells that are sometimes as big as themselves. You may have to carry tots, though, as some of the display cases are set quite high in the walls. The little shop has decorative objects made from shells, including some costume jewellery and accessories that may appeal to little princesses, as well as some regional produce. In addition to the times given below, there are daily tours in English and German in summer (July–mid-Sept), at 2pm and 4pm respectively.

L'Aurore, Cancale, 15km (9 miles) east of St-Malo on D355, 02 99 89 69 99. Visiting times mid-Feb–June and mid-Sept–Oct Mon–Fri 3pm, July–mid-Sept daily 11am–3pm and 5pm. Adm: adults € 6.10 (£ 4), children € 3.10 (£ 2), family ticket (2 adults and 2 or more children) € 16.80 (£ 11).

Train Marin ★★ This fishy jaunt comprises rides in yellow tractor-drawn trailers 5km into the otherworldly landscape of the bay of Mont-St-Michel to see mussels clustered on *bouchots* – the wooden posts on which they are cultivated, and which disappear beneath the water at high tide. It's incredible to see how tiny they start out. You also get to watch a demonstration of dredging for shrimps (children can join in if they like) and see some huge wooden traps dating from around 1000 AD and still used to catch fish. The whole trip takes two hours; the live commentary in French takes in the history of the bay and its legends as well as mussel farming. Advance booking is essential, but you also need to arrive a half-hour ahead of your slot otherwise your place might be sold to someone else. Remember your wellies, too, as this is a muddy outing!

Note that the Maison de la Baie at nearby Le Vivier-sur-Mer (p. 69) also runs tractor-drawn trips out to see mussel farming. Don't miss the string of picturesque old windmills on the coast road between Cherrueix and Le Vivier, now converted into chic homes.

*Cherrueix, 30km (19 miles) east of St-Malo off D797, ☎ 02 99 48 84 88, **www.train-marin.com**. Times vary hugely due to tides; call for details. Tickets: adults € 10.50 (£ 7), children 4–11 € 7.50 (£ 5), family of five € 40 (£ 27).*

For Active Families

See also '**Beaches, Resorts & Islands**', p. 202–205.

La Cancalaise ★ This old *bisquine* – an elegant sailing boat used by local fishermen from around 1810 to the 1940s – now offers half-day or one-day 'discovery trips' of the beautiful bay of Mont-St-Michel (p. 68). Half-days are more manageable for those with children, as a full day lasts from 9am to around 6pm, and food is not provided so you need to take your own. Once you're aboard, the four-strong crew demonstrate traditional sailing techniques, or you

La Cancalaise

can just sit back and admire the scenery. Under-6s are allowed at parental discretion, at no charge. The hut at Cancale sells clothes, posters and items bearing the boat's logo.

*La Halle à Marée, Cancale, 15km (9 miles) east of St-Malo on D355, or Port-Mer 3km (2 miles) north of Cancale, ✆ 02 99 89 77 87, **www.lacancalaise.org**. Dates call for sailings. Tickets: half-day adults € 24 (£ 17), children 6–14 € 12 (£ 8), full-day adults € 42 (£ 28), children 6–14 € 24 (£ 17).*

Centre d'Activités et de Loisirs de Chênedet ★★ This wonderful rural centre deep within the Fougères forest with its atmospheric megaliths and other Druid remains welcomes everyone from solitary walkers to families and school groups, though you need to speak French to profit fully from the range of activities. Visitors can explore the forest and its ecosystem, take classes on environmental awareness, hire mountain bikes, go orienteering or walking, or ride horses, whether you need to learn from scratch or want to enjoy treks through meadows and woods. To get the most of the centre, stay for a couple of days – accommodation is offered in communal gîtes or on the lakeside campsite, and there's a restaurant with family-friendly fare if you don't want to cook. If you do stay longer and your children love riding, there are themed programmes: beginners (including animal care, walks and a show put on by the children on the last day); circus skills (equestrian acrobatics, juggling and more); and horse camps (with overnighters in teepees and an evening of Native American tales and legends).

*Route Forestière de la Villeboeuf, Landéan, 6km (4 miles) north of Fougères on D177, ✆ 02 99 97 35 46, **www.chenedet-loisirs.com**. Open all year. Prices vary according to activity.*

Centre Nautique de Rance

This is a well-reputed sailing school popular largely because of its setting in a sheltered estuary, which makes it brilliant for beginners, although English-language training is not offered so you and your children will need a good command of French. Individual lessons and boat hire (including canoes) are offered for most of the year; the school holidays see five-day courses for a maximum of 10 pupils, resulting in a certificate – comprising general watersports initiation/familiarisation courses for 4–6-year-olds and 6–8-year-olds (Le Jardin des Mers et Les Moussaillons respectively), and courses on different types of sailing boat for those eight and over. Or you might just want to leave the children to play while you get a hang of things, in which case there's a beach club with morning and afternoon sessions costing from € 5 (£ 3.30).

*Quai de Rance, St Suliac, 8km (5 miles) south of St-Malo on D117, ✆ 02 99 58 48 80, **http://perso.orange.fr/cn.rennes**. Open all year. Prices vary according to activity.*

Cobac Parc One of those activity parks with a rather 'homemade' feel that the French seem to specialise in, Cobac Park is nevertheless a good place for a family day out when everyone's had their fill of beaches. Of the 30 or so attractions, the big draws are the traditional carousel, the rope bridge over the boating lake and the 'monkey bridge' between the trees. Although most things are aimed at children roughly five and over, there's no shortage of possibilities for tots, from petting goats to noodling about in the toddlers' pool (open May–Aug from 1pm) or 'children's village'. There's also a baby-changing/ feeding cabin. The three restaurants include a self-service café with waffles, crêpes, ice creams and the like (including a children's menu), but there are picnic spaces too.

Le Parc de Haute Bretagne, Lanhélin, 12km (7.5 miles) southwest of Dol-de-Bretagne on D78, ☎ *02 99 73 80 16. Open on average 10.30am–6pm, but call for seasonal variations and closures (Oct–Mar, most of Apr, May and Sept, and about half of June). Adm: adults € 14 (£ 9.40), children 3–14 € 12.50 (£ 8.40).*

Domaine de Tremelin ★★

This leisure base on a wooded site on the shores of a 50 hectare (123 acre) lake caters to all age ranges, from toddlers to thrill-seeking teens and adults. Younger visitors like the clean, supervised beach, the pedaloes and electric boats, the karts, the bouncy castles, the play areas, the mini-golf and the *petit train*; older ones can ride quads or motorbikes, swing through the trees on special circuits (separate ones were introduced in 2006, starting at age three), climb the giant tree ladder or fly high on the 'Mégabooster' (a trampoline to which you are affixed with elastic reins). You can also horse ride, hire bikes, walk or hike, play tennis, canoe on the lake, and take windsurfing lessons.

With so much going on, you may want to stay for a few days, in which case there are 20 basic gîtes for 6–8 people (available by the night, weekend or week, from € 49 (£ 33) per night for a six-person gîte), or a campsite (no advance booking). A bar–restaurant with a sunny terrace caters to those who don't want the hassle of shopping and cooking, with full meals and snack fare. In high season, there's a holiday feel to the place, with *guinguette* (traditional dance hall entertainment), storytelling evenings and walks, discos, *fest-noz* (p. 10) and *pétanque* contests. By the way, if you wonder about the cheesy fake sword sticking out of one of the rocks, remember that this is King Arthur country (see Brocéliande; p. 67).

Lac de Tremelin, just south of Iffendic, 30km (19 miles) west of Rennes off D72, ☎ *02 99 09 73 79,* ***www.domaine-de-tremelin.fr****. Open 24hrs daily Apr–Sept. Adm: free to site; individual rates for each activity.*

Enigmaparc Scheduled to open as this guide went to press, this leisure park for children aged about six and up promised to offer family fun with an original slant: basically, you will journey through scenes from ancient Egypt, the Middle Ages, the Celtic world and Asia, ensuring that the adventurer Enigmus doesn't succumb to the traps his enemy Grignouse has in store for him. Mazes, puzzles and games requiring physical and/or mental dexterity will keep you going for 3–4 hours.

Zone d'Activités du Bois de Teillay, Janzé, 18km (11 miles) southeast of Rennes on D41, ☎ 02 99 47 07 65. Open/adm call for details.

Labyrinthe du Corsaire ★ The *corsaires* were 'pirates with a permit' operating out of St-Malo (p. 63), and this summer corn maze by the sea has corresponding nautically themed routes (one specially for tots), plus the 'Casse-tête' ('Brainbuster') with its illusions and traps. There's more of an incentive for your children to find their way to the middle than in most mazes, since they'll find a choice of bouncy castles there. Elsewhere in the grounds are a mechanical rodeo bull, a gladiator inflatable, giant wooden games, strategy games, a little farm with Ouessant sheep (p. 153), goats and geese, and pedal-karts. Exhausted by all that, you can repair to a snack bar.

INSIDER TIP

The best times to come to the Labyrinthe are the spooky night sessions in August (phone for details; you need to bring a torch).

There's another Labyrinthe du Corsaire in Guidel in the Morbihan (p. 198).

Route de Quelmer La Passagère, St-Malo, ☎ 02 99 81 17 23, ***www.labyrintheducorsaire.com****. Open daily late June–mid-July, late Aug–early Sept and a few days mid-Sept 11am–7pm; mid-July–late Aug 10.30am–7.30pm. Adm: € 6.80 (£ 4.60), under-3s free.*

Maison des Jeux et Sports Traditionnels de Bretagne Le Jaupitre, a federation of traditional Breton sports and games

Parc des Grands Chênes

The Port Miniature de Villecartier

such as skittles, will open this permanent games venue in the latter half of 2007, with indoor and outdoor play areas, café games, exhibitions on the history of games, training in *gouren* (wrestling) and other athletic Breton sports, and games-making workshops.

Rue de la Vieille Forge, Monterfil, 30km (19 miles) west of Rennes on D240, ☎ 02 99 07 47 02, ***www.jeuxbretons.org.***

Parc des Grands Chênes/Port Miniature ★★★

FIND Paradise for little monkeys, 'Big Oak Park' in the Villecartier forest offers acrobatic routes through the trees using specialist halters that snap on to ropes. There are three levels of *parcours* for adults and, since 2006, three for children, with barrels to crawl through, ropes to swing on and aerial walkways; the expert staff give full safety briefings. You're far from civilisation, so bring a picnic for lunch by the lake and plenty to drink.

If you factor in a whole day for your visit, you can also go for a ride on an electrically powered replica ferry, tug, steamboat or fishing boat amidst scale models of Breton landmarks such as the Phare de la Vieille lighthouse at the **Port Miniature de Villecartier**. Or you can go orienteering or walking along the signposted paths, ride ponies or go out in a pedalo.

Base de Loisirs Forêt de Villecartier, 15km (9 miles) southeast of Dol-de-Bretagne on D155, ☎ 06 88 72 73 40, ***www.parcdesgrandschenes.fr.*** *Open 9.30am–7pm (last entry 4pm) Apr–June and Sept–Nov Sat, Sun and public and school hols; July and Aug daily. Adm: adults € 20 (£ 13.50), children 10–13 € 15 (£ 10), 4–10 € 10 (£ 6.70).*

Ranch de la Foucheraie This French-speaking equestrian centre on the edge of the forest surrounding the Château de Montmuran is a superb place for family rides amidst bucolic scenery and picturesque châteaux, whether by the hour, the day, the weekend or the week – the latter rides go as far Mont-St-Michel just over the border in Normandy (p. 68) or the Forêt de Brocéliande (p. 67), or further afield in France or even abroad, with nights spent in communal gîtes along the way. Children aged eight and up also have the option of signing up for specially designed weekend or four-day trips. Highly qualified and friendly guides accompany all rides, whether for total beginners or more experienced riders.

*Cardroc, 25km (16 miles) northwest of Rennes off D27, ☎ 02 99 45 82 55, **www.ranch-de-la-foucheraie.com**. Rides € 15 per hour (£ 10), € 130 for 10 hours (£ 87), grande randonnée to Mont-St-Michel in Normandy € 600pp (£ 400).*

Vélo Rail ★★★ These wacky two-person bicycles (actually two bikes welded together) run on old rail tracks on a choice of two circuits, one covering 6km and taking about an hour to complete, the other covering 14km and taking two hours, or more if you break for a picnic along the way. Under-8s ride in a sort of hammock swung between the parents' bikes; older children get special mini bikes of their own, also ridden in pairs. People with reduced mobility can enjoy the same scenery (the Néal valley, forest of Montauban and some megalithic remains) from a special motorised wagon for up to 20 people (advance booking and a minimum of eight people required), and there's also a road train for everyone, with a comical little soundtrack of rural tunes. Brilliant fun.

Train station, Médréac, 45km (28 miles) northwest of Rennes on D220, ☎ 02 99 07 30 48. Open June–Sept daily 10am–6pm; Apr, May and Oct Sun and public hols 2–6pm (departures on the hour); rest of year by arrangement. Fee: € 8–12.50 (£ 5.30–8.30) per pair, € 2–3.50 (£ 1.40–2.40) per child.

Shopping

There's a **Fnac** bookstore (p. 223) in **Rennes** (Centre Commercial Colombia, ☎ *02 99 67 10 10*), plus a **Printemps** (p. 176) department store (Centre Commercial Alma, ☎ *02 99 32 57 70*).

La Boutique Sentimentale ★

FIND The proprietress of this shop, which opened a few steps from St-Malo's Grande Porte in late 2005, is on a mission to persuade locals and tourists alike to adopt a 'new way of living' – which means Fair Trade products made from natural (often organic) materials are the order of the day. Yet there's no hippyish feel to the range of products displayed: everything has been chosen with an expert eye for style. In among the tempting homewares (cushions, crockery and so on) are well-selected clothes for both adults and children, such as bright yellow and orange Indian organic babygros (€ 14 (£ 9.40)) and colourful hand knitted children's jumpers (€ 55 (£ 37)). You'll also find soft toys and carved colouring pencils, plus essential oils and other toiletries, Fair Trade recipe books, delectably soft organic cotton towels and gorgeous, capacious beach bags (€ 14 and € 19 (£ 9.40 and £ 12.80)) in a range of colours, made by a cooperative in Bangladesh.

Just opposite the shop is Pop, a boutique for mums-to-be and new babies.

3 place du Poids du Roy, St-Malo intra-muros, 📞 02 23 18 35 85. Open Mon 2–6pm, Tue–Sat 10am–12.30pm and 2–7pm.

La Droguerie de Marine ★★ This ancient marine hardware store a few minutes' walk from St-Malo's walled city has stayed true to its origins – at least on the ground floor, where you'll still find classic products for sailors such as Marseille soap, brushes, paints, varnishes and waxes, knives and storm matches. But look deeper inside and you'll find that this is a definition-defying treasure trove – and an unexpectedly brilliant place for gifts to take home. Children's eyes are inevitably drawn to the Pop Pop boats – little tin craft that move when you place a little candle into them – taking up one whole window display, but there's a whole array of other toys and games, plus ship's models, compasses, barometers, tin whistles and decorative objects, from linen to mirrors. A grocery section stocks local delicacies such as fish ravioli from Le Guilvinec, lobster soup, salted-butter caramels and beer. Appropriately, it's like being on an exotic ship. If it inspires you to sail forth, there's a book section focusing on three main themes – the Sea, Brittany and Travel – including English-language books.

66 rue Georges Clemenceau, St Servan-sur-Mer, St-Malo, 📞 02 99 81 60 39. Open Tue–Sat 10am–12.30pm and 2.30–7pm, plus Mon in high season and Sun and Mon in Dec.

La Grande Ourse A top spot for fashion-conscious children (from birth to 16), this St-Malo boutique stocks a wide variety of designer labels, including Lili Gaufrette, Diesel, Ikks and Essential Girls. Naturally, it doesn't come cheap: think € 50 (£ 33) for a pair of Burberry baby shoes that might fit them for all of a month, and € 99 (£ 66) for a pair of Burberry check slacks.

4 Rue Porcon de la Barbinais, St-Malo intra-muros, 📞 02 99 40 46 83. Open Mon 3–7pm, Tue–Sat 10am–12.30pm and 2.30–7pm, Sun 3–7pm.

Nouvelles Impressions It's not easy to find a shop stocking English-language books outside Rennes, so it's worth coming out to this friendly little place in Dinard, even if the resort itself is no longer any great shakes. It's a general bookstore, so you'll find everything from *roman policiers* to cookery tomes, but travel and books on Brittany and the sea are its strengths, and you'll find a good range of postcards. The very good children's section ranges from pre-school books to *bande dessinée*.

42 rue Levavasseur, Dinard, 📞 02 99 46 15 95. Open Mon 2.30–7pm, Tue–Sat 9.30am–12.15pm and 2.30–7pm (slightly longer hours and Sun morning in high season).

Sportmer This classic toyshop in the centre of St-Malo has no pretensions, and is all the better for it – it's just crammed full of toys and games, from ships' models and radio-controlled cars to up-to-date TV-related merchandise – Dora the Explorer dolls feature prominently. It's a useful stopoff on the way to the nearby Plage du Bon Secours (p. 63), with plenty of beach gear buckets and spades, balls, nets for dabbling in rockpools, kites and more.

Opposite, **Brise Lames** has classic Breton stripes for all ages, from babies up.

5 place aux Herbes, St-Malo intra-muros, ☎ 02 99 40 23 32. Open Mon 2.30–7.30pm, Tue–Sat 10am–12.30pm and 2–7.30pm, Sun 3–7pm.

FAMILY-FRIENDLY ACCOMMODATION

Baie du Mont-St-Michel

For more accommodation around this beautiful bay, see *Normandy with Your Family*, a companion to this guide.

VERY EXPENSIVE

Les Maisons de Bricourt

★★★ Famous chef Olivier Roellinger was brought up in Cancale, and having returned to set up a restaurant, **Le Relais Gourmand**, in the house where he was born, has colonised much of the town with his chic establishments: **Les Rimains**, a four-room hotel near the restaurant in the north of the town; the **Gîtes Marins**, four seaside cottages for 2–8 people close by; the **Château Richeux**, a slightly larger hotel at the southern end of town, with its own restaurant; the **Grain de Vanille** tearoom; and **L'Entrepôt Epices Roellinger**, a shop selling his spices, chutneys, seaweed creations and so on.

Families should shy away from the romantic retreat of Les Rimains in favour of the **Château Richeux**, set in an imposing 1920s villa and offering 11 rooms and two apartments in lemony or marine hues, with gardens and orchards containing beehives, a donkey and Ouessant sheep. Or better still are the **stunning Gîtes Marins** with their stylish but homely New England decor. They're a bit more expensive, but you're self-contained so don't have to worry about disturbing other guests. Rooms are huge, with subtle nautical touches; children get their own special beds, either posh bunks or cute nooks where they love to play hide and seek. Bathrooms are super-luxurious, the kitchens fully fitted (ovens were designed by Roellinger), and the living rooms fitted with large TVs and CD players. Books, including children's story and colouring books, can be found in the corridor. French windows open onto a private terrace with loungers, a table and chairs, and barbecue equipment. A stroll down the winding paths leads you to the vegetable and herb garden (where you are free to pick ingredients for dinner) and past Les Rimains to the cliff top, where you can follow a customs officers' track down to Cancale's port or along to the Pointe du Grouin (p. 65), or just contemplate the oyster beds laid out below like patchwork. Take the shrimp nets from the cottage if you want to garner further ingredients for your evening meal.

Breton breakfast (which costs € 18 (£ 12) in the other establishments) is included in the price, and discreetly left in a basket outside your door at 7.45am, so that you can choose when to take it. It is a feast of cake, crêpes, soft rolls and half a large loaf, and can be complemented by the goodies left thoughtfully in your fridge on arrival – eggs, the most heavenly salted butter (also sold in L'Entrepôt Epices), fresh oranges and grapefruits to squeeze, milk, juice, water, wine and beer. Little essentials such as gourmet hot chocolate powder are also provided. Should the sea wind bite, you can snuggle up next to a roaring fire (chopped logs are left beside it). If you want your room to be cleaned, it's an extra € 28 (£ 19) a time.

As for the restaurants, you'll need to book aeons in advance to secure a table at the **Relais Gourmand**, where Roellinger specialises in seafood with spicy touches, but the Château de Richeux's 'marine bistro', **La Coquillage**, is a little more informal and a lot less expensive (the 'Marine Menu' is € 29 (£ 19.50)). Children will be happiest of all at the **Grain de Vanille**, a casual 'meeting place' with books, serving superb galettes, ice cream, cakes and hot chocolate with or without spices.

*Cancale, 15km (9 miles) east of St-Malo on D355, ☎ 02 99 89 64 76, **www.maisons-de-bricourt.com**. 21 units. Château Richeux double room € 160–290 (£ 108–196), apartment from € 290 (£ 196), extra bed € 28 (£ 19); Gîte Marin for 4 or more from € 380 (£ 256), extra bed free. Cot*

Le Maisons de Bricourt, Cancale

free. Amenities: two restaurants, tea-room, spice shop, babysitting, laundry service. In room: TV, CD player, hairdryer.

MODERATE

Domaine des Ormes ★★ This 200 hectare (495 acre) tourist park may overwhelm those who like intimate holidays, but it does offer an extraordinary choice of accommodation, activities and facilities, meaning it's unlikely you'll ever be stuck for something to do here, even on the rainiest day. Although it's not the place for those who really want to feel they are in France (you'll be rubbing shoulders with mainly British guests), it is remarkably free of the corporate feel you might expect from such a large-scale venture. This is reflected in some of the original accommodation options, which include two **family tree houses** for up to six (in two bedrooms), suitable for those with children aged six and up. Attractive wooden structures overlooking the cricket pitch, accessed by ladders or steps, they have ecological loos and heating in cool weather. Decor is bright, and there is definitely the feeling of being in a safari cabin. Guests do need to bring their own sleeping bags or blankets, but breakfast is included in the (very reasonable) rates – it's delivered to the foot of the tree for you to collect when you're ready.

If that all sounds a little adventurous, you can choose from a **three-star hotel** with an outdoor pool and fitness facilities, a plush **Clubhouse hotel**, a *résidence-hôtel* with **studios and apartments**, four peaceful stone **gîtes** for 3–5 people with private gardens, two-storey wooden **chalets** for up to six, well-appointed **mobile homes** for up to six, and a **four-star campsite** with 800 pitches (150 for those touring with caravans or tents). You're not right by the sea here (the site is about 15km inland from Cherrueix), but the vast parkland – set around an imposing 16th century château – offers a waterpark, horse and ponyriding, a treetop adventure course, tennis, cycling (you can hire bikes, baby seats and helmets), an 18-hole golf course and crazy golf, an archery range, table-tennis, pedaloes, kayaks and surf bikes, football tournaments, basketball, cricket and fishing, plus a whole raft of summer 'animations', from treasure hunts to sumo wrestling. Some activities are free, for others there is an extra charge, but overall this is a good-value option given the range of facilities.

The site has a choice of restaurants: relatively upmarket ones at the hotel and Clubhouse, a campsite restaurant serving pancakes and grills, including a children's menu, and a pizzeria where you can eat in or take out.

Domaine des Ormes, Epiniac, 6km (4 miles) south of Dol-de-Bretagne on D4, ☎ 02 99 73 53 00, ***www.lesormes.com****. Family tree house € 152 (£ 101) per night for 2 adults and 2 children 6–16; double hotel room € 75–130 (£ 50–87) plus € 15 (£ 10) extra person; studio or apartment € 373–940 (£ 252–635) per* *week, gîtes € 480–1135 (£ 320–766) per week, chalets € 465–985 (£ 314–665) per week, mobile homes € 306–1010 (£ 207–682) per week, camping pitch € 19.95–29.25 (£ 12–18) one person, additional person € 4.95 (£ 3.30), children 2–12 € 2.50 (£ 1.70). Amenities: four restaurants, shop, games and activities, laundrettes, Internet access, postal service, bureau de change, cashpoint.*

INEXPENSIVE

Ferme de la Vieuville ★ VALUE This charming 18th century farmhouse and its outbuildings stands out for its flexibility where families are concerned: choose from two sunny stone gîtes with private terraces, both for 4–6 people (a larger one was in progress at the time of writing), or two B&B units, which – unusually – benefit from self-catering facilities (a corner kitchen with fridge and electric oven and hob, plus barbecue equipment). Of the latter, the Grenier à Blé unit has private access and its own terrace; in addition to a double bedroom and a mezzanine with a single bed, two further single children's rooms can be added.

Alternatively, Orge is a double bedroom to which one or two single children's rooms can be tacked on. The decor, throughout all the accommodation and public spaces, is rustic without being cluttered. Best of all, and surprisingly given the low prices, there's a pretty heated indoor pool, surrounded by comfy chairs and hammocks, although it's only open for a couple of months in summer. The friendly but unintrusive hosts also offer unlimited free Wi-Fi Internet access, and are happy to help you arrange activities such as cycling or recommend local restaurants.

About five minutes' walk from Cancale's bustling port (p. 65), the Ferme is in a little dead-end alley, meaning it's virtually free of traffic and noise, and there's direct access to the GR long-distance walking path.

*Cancale, 15km (9 miles) east of St-Malo on D355, ☎ 02 23 15 19 30, **www.fermedelavieuville.fr**. B&B € 45–70 (£ 30–47) double, € 15–25 (£ 10–17) per child's bedroom; gîtes € 375–700 (£ 250–470) per week (nightly rates available). Amenities: indoor pool (June–Sept). In room: gîtes TV and videoplayer, washing machine, dishwasher, kitchen, BBQ equipment; B&B tea- and coffee-making facilities, shared kitchenette and BBQ equipment.*

Around Bécherel & the Forêt de Brocéliande

EXPENSIVE–VERY EXPENSIVE

La Motte Beaumanoir Handy for the Bourbansais castle and zoo (p. 73), this hotel will please those with hankerings to stay in a true French château, with its turrets, antique panelling and furniture, and sumptuous, slightly chintzy fabrics. Dating from the 15th century, it's not so posh that you'd constantly feel the need to keep a rein on the children, but it's probably not the kind of place you'll feel relaxed with toddlers. That said, there's plenty to do outside: 20 hectares (50 acres) of forest, an outdoor heated pool, a tennis court, bikes for hire, and two boats you can take out on the lake. In cooler weather there are spacious lounges with open fires, including a billiards room. Mum and Dad might like to take it in turns to enjoy a Thai or shiatsu massage, and there's a small fitness suite.

The eight individually furnished rooms have views of the garden or the lake. Families have the choice of the Suite Loft with a cute little living room in a tower, a very large double bedroom and a mezzanine with twin beds, or the Suite Privilège, with a double room, a twin and a single. The hosts serve good, if expensive, Continental breakfasts (€ 18 (£ 12) adults, € 12 (£ 8) under-12s) – you're paying for the privilege of sitting in the rather formal breakfast room. Gourmet lunches and dinners are also available with 24 hour advance booking. Astonishingly, you have to pay € 10 (£ 6.70) for the use of a highchair.

*Pleugueneuc–Plesder, 38km (24 miles) north of Rennes off N137, ☎ 02 23 22 05 00, **www.lamottebeaumanoir.com**. Double € 155–200 (£ 105–135), family suite € 230–310 (£ 155–209), extra bed € 20 (£ 12), cot € 20 (£ 12). Amenities: outdoor pool, fitness suite, massage, Internet access, babysitting. In room: Sat TV, telephone, minibar, hairdryer. Closed Jan–early Feb.*

MODERATE

Château du Pin This sober 19th century country house surrounded by tall oaks and meadows isn't the place for those with rambunctious toddlers, but if your children are older, bookish types (in which case you're in the right place – a few kilometres from 'Merlin's Tomb' and other Arthurian sites; p. 67), they may love the literary-themed rooms resembling something from a bygone, more elegant era. Of the four B&B rooms, two (Marcel Proust and Marguerite Yourcenar) are straight doubles; the others are family suites, each with a double and a twin room sharing a bathroom. The first, Victor Hugo, has a smart, very large double room with wooden floors, furnished with strong colours and stripes; the children's room is a little chintzier. George Sand is more muted, in yellows and neutrals. Both are scattered with books and other items relating to the respective writers, plus quirky touches such as straw teddy bears. Breakfast is a copious Continental affair served in a smart little *salon* by the self-effacing host; you can run it off in the large lawned grounds surrounding the house. The kindly hosts also offer very good evening meals by prior arrangement (€ 28 (£ 19); € 10 (£ 6.70) under-10s), with a highchair provided. Alternatively, there's a pretty gîte for five people.

*Iffendic, 30km (19 miles) west of Rennes on D30, ☎ 02 99 09 34 05, **www.chateaudupin-bretagne.com**. four rooms. Double € 75–90 (£ 50–60), family suite € 93–100 (£ 62–67), gîte € 350–500 (£ 236–337) per week. Cot free. Amenities: evening meals by request.*

INEXPENSIVE

La Clef du Four ★ VALUE Another handy option for the Bourbansais zoo (p. 73), this cute B&B in a 19th century stone house represents remarkable value given that guests have use of a kitchenette, and, between April and October, a fine little swimming pool surrounded by deckchairs, parasols and plants. The five rooms, relatively plain but spruce after renovation work in 2005, include a family suite for two adults and up to three children (with a double and two single beds, and space for a cot). All have showers rather than baths, but they do have the benefit of independent entrances, and there is a shared garden with toddlers' play equipment (slides, tractors and trikes). The large Continental breakfasts are served on the pool terrace, giving them a slightly tropical feel, and a highchair can be provided. There's a minimum two-night stay Nov–March.

La Touche Pichard, Plesder, 38km (24 miles) north of Rennes off N137 ☎ *02 23 22 01 35,* ***www.laclefdufour.com****. Double € 48–53 (£ 32–35), family room for four € 80–90 (£ 53–60), extra bed € 15 (£ 10). Cot free. Amenities: outdoor pool, toys.*

Domaine du Logis ★★ This four-star campsite in the grounds of a turreted 15th–17th century castle is set back from roads and very shady, making it a safe, cool option. One section has space for tents, caravans and motor homes, another contains well-maintained mobile-homes. In the latter you can hire baby-kits (highchair, cot and bath) for a bargain € 3 (£ 2) a day. The main draw are the two pools, one for toddlers, but you can also hire bikes to ride by the nearby canal, or canoes to paddle along it, and fish in a neighbouring lake. Little children get a relaxation room in which to cool off on hot days, a TV room and play areas, and you can play volleyball, basketball, *boules*, mini-golf, archery, giant chess, table tennis, billiards, table football and video games. A library is at guests' disposal, and in high season there are concerts and themed evenings. There's a good, clean family feel to it all, and a touch of character that's missing from some larger sites.

La Chapelle-aux-Filtzméens, 13km (8 miles) northeast of Bécherel on D13, ☎ *02 99 45 25 45,* ***www.domainedulogis.com****. 180 pitches. Camping € 10–21 (£ 7–14) per night 1st adult, € 4–5 (£ 2.70–3.35) subsequent adults, € 2–3 (£ 1.35–2) children 3–12; mobile home € 290–650 (£ 196–439) per week (weekend rates available). Amenities: outdoor pools, canteen, bar, grocery, laundry with ironing facilities, baby-changing area, Internet access.*

Le Gîtes de Kersillac These stone cottages in the grounds of a tranquil dairy farm are not only named 'Arthur' and 'Judicäel' in reference to local folklore – their walls are adorned with charming murals of fairies, forest scenes and more. Though whimsical, they're practical and comfy, with solid rustic furniture, good beds, and dishwashers

TIP Down on the Farm

If your children love animals, are independently minded and speak good French, they may enjoy a stay on a French farm, in which case try the area east of Rennes, the 'Pays des Portes de Bretagne'. **La Haute Hairie** (Saint M'Hervé, *02 99 76 72 88*, ***www.ferme-pedago.fr.st***), for instance, offers week-long stays for 6–12-year-olds in the school holidays; they look after and ride ponies, milk cows, and feed and care for small animals such as rabbits and ducks. There are also songs around a campfire, games, a visit from a clown, a contest for the best-decorated pony, horse-and-cart rides, and crêpes and a party on the last night. Accommodation is in a large gîte, with bedrooms for 2–7, each ensuite. Adults, meanwhile, can pamper themselves somewhere plush and relatively child-unfriendly: perhaps the Romantique attic room in **Le Coq-Gadby** in Rennes (156 rue d'Antrain, *02 99 38 05 55*, ***www.lecoq-gadby.com***), an intimate hotel with a spa and gastronomic restaurant.

For other farm stays in the area, see ***www.pays-des-portes-de-bretagne.com***. Alternatively, **La Ferme de Trénube** (*02 99 09 10 51*) offers similar stays at Talensac west of Rennes, with farm life, nature discovery and art activities for 6–12-year-olds, and exploration of the Brocéliande forest (p. 67) and ecology projects for 12–15-year-olds.

---

and washing machines. Judicäel has two double bedrooms and a twin, Arthur one double and a twin. Both have two bathrooms and a terrace, and they share table tennis and table football facilities. Guests are free to look round the farm and watch the cows being milked.

Riding a Farm Pony

*Gaël, 45km (28 miles) west of Rennes on D30, 02 99 07 76 78, **http://giteskersillac.com**. Rates: € 248–435 (£ 167–294) per week (nightly rates also available). Amenities: games. In room: TV, washing machine, dishwasher.*

Le Grénier d'Ernestine ★★

FIND In keeping with the surrounding area with its elves, fairies and mythical knights, this B&B is a kind of childhood paradise for children and adults alike, with five homely rooms dotted with old dolls, teddies and toy cars, and even its own little farmyard, with donkeys, ponies and horses, dwarf and Alpine goats, and more. The welcoming owner often makes time to regale young visitors with stories about the animals and their antics. The five spacious rooms – a ground-floor one for those with reduced mobility, two doubles with room for a extra bed, and two rooms with a double bed, a single bed and a small double on a mezzanine level – are filled with antiques inherited by the owners. Alphonsine has direct views onto the farmyard, for better or worse. Breakfast includes homemade cake and jams created to old recipes. The cosy breakfast room and *salon* extends out onto a terrace when the weather permits, and here you can enjoy evening meals by request. The hosts have five children of their own so won't be the least bit fazed by yours running around.

*Les Basses Barres, Bréal-sous-Montfort, 13km (8 miles) southwest of Rennes off N24, ✆ 02 99 60 34 03, **www.grenier-ernestine.com**. Cot free. Room for four € 72 (£ 48) (weekly rates available). In room: TV, telephone.*

St-Malo

VERY EXPENSIVE

Le Grand Hôtel des Therms, the swish four-star mother establishment of the Résidence Reine Marine (see below), is St-Malo's most luxurious option.

MODERATE

Résidence Reine Marine

★★★ VALUE FIND Opened in 2005, this is the latest addition to St-Malo's health and hotel empire, the **Thermes Marins**, which also includes the **Grand Hôtel des Thermes, Hôtel Jersey** (two-star), **Hôtel Antinéa** and **Résidence Neptunia**. The beauty of the set up is that you can stay somewhere much cheaper than the Grand but use the seawater therapy centre for which it's famous – which includes a very good children's club (€ 22 (£ 15) per half-day) so your little darlings can have fun while you relax. Among the programmes are an increasingly popular 'new mum and baby' option – mum gets pampered with seaweed wraps and the like while baby is cared for in the children's club for five hours a day; there are also a couple of baby massage sessions. (Dad can come too, and use the sauna, 'Aquatonic' pools and so on). Young guests can also enjoy windsurfing, sand-yachting and catamaran sessions and courses, and in July and August there's a beach club for 3–10-year-olds in front of the Grand Hôtel.

The self-catering *résidences* are the best options for families, but the Neptunia, right next to the Grand Hôtel, offers only studios (double bed and sofabed), so can get a little cramped. It's worth upgrading to the Reine Marine; it's further away from St-Malo *intra-muros* towards Rothéneuf, but has secure parking. Its pristine modern one- and two-bedroom apartments for up to six (living rooms have sofabeds) have sparkling bathrooms and kitchenettes (with dishwashers), satellite TV, oodles of storage space, and incredible views (from some rooms) over the sea and beaches sweeping away to each side. Steps take you down the wide clean sands in seconds, and if the tide's low you can walk to the Grand in about 20 minutes.

Prices are exceptionally keen for the standard of accommodation offered; they vary widely according to whether you have a sea view and the time of year you come, but as a rough guide, expect to pay € 167 (£ 112) per night for a two-bedroom, light-flooded apartment with a sea-view in June – a steal, especially given that you get free use of the residence's indoor pool, sea-facing sunbathing terrace and sauna. There is also a useful on-site laundry, a bar with those same beautiful views, a huge games room with a widescreen TV and board games, and an order-in breakfast and pâtisserie service, with seaweed bread, *tarte provençale* and caramelised Breton butter cake among the offerings. Those with babies can reserve highchairs, cots and changing mats from the highly obliging staff, and babysitting can be arranged. Given the location, standard of accommodation – the beds are supremely comfortable – and facilities, this is my top recommendation for family accommodation in Brittany. The minimum three-night stay won't seem long enough once you're here!

If you do want to splash out on the Grand Hôtel, there are family suites with interconnecting bedrooms and a *salon*, but the décor is rather bland for a hotel of this standing. Golf-loving dads might like to hear that the group also owns the **Saint-Malo Golf and Country Club** 20 minutes' from the city; this too allows access to the sea-water centre and children's club.

*65–67 avenue John Fitzgerald Kennedy, Paramé, St-Malo, ☎ 02 33 18 48 58, **www.reinemarine.com**. 67 units. Rates: 1-bedroom apartment for up to four € 69–215 (£ 47–145) per night, 2-bedroom apartment for up to six € 78–292 (£ 52–197); ask about combined accommodation/ thalassotherapy rates. Amenities: bar, restaurant (at Grand Hôtel), baby-sitting, thalassotherapy centre with children's club, indoor pool, swimming lessons and pool fitness, sauna, solarium, laundry, games room, bike hire, windsurf hire, alarm calls, breakfast delivery. In room: TV, DVD player hire, baby equipment, kitchenette.*

INEXPENSIVE

Camping d'Alet This large campsite just outside St-Malo *intra-muros* (past the ferry port) may only be two star, but certain features within its grounds make it unique – a ruined 18th century fort and a German blockhouse from World War II, when the Germans used the site as a stronghold, now containing a little museum tracing St-Malo's occupation and liberation. History aside, amenities are limited to children's play areas and mini-golf, and there are only three toilet and shower blocks between the 300 places, but this is a municipal site, which means that it's very cheap and you're more likely to be mingling with French people than in more touristy four-star sites. It's also right by the beach, with lovely views over the Rance estuary and plenty of watersports facilities on hand.

*Allée Gaston Buy, St Servan, St-Malo, 02 99 81 60 91, **www.malouins.com/campings/**. 300 pitches. Tent pitch € 12–16 (£ 8–12) up to two people, then € 5.50 (£ 3.70) per person or € 2.60 (£ 1.75) children 2–10; motorhome pitch € 3.80 (£ 2.55). Amenities: play areas, mini-golf.*

St-Lunaire & Around

EXPENSIVE–VERY EXPENSIVE

There's an **Accor Thalassa** hotel in the faded resort of Dinard; its three-star *résidence* with 2–3-person studios, **Les Villas La Falaise**, shares access to its sea-water cure centre.

Grand Hôtel Barrière ★ Part of an ultra-posh mini-chain, the Grand is popular – like its sister establishment the Normandy Barrière in Deauville in Normandy – with well-to-do French parents, who come to splurge and relax while their children make friends at its Club Diwi & Co (open Tue–Sun in the school holidays and most weekends following or preceding a public holiday). If you've stayed at the Normandy Barrière, though, note that the Grand's children's activities are not as extensive – the club, for 4–12-year-olds, is only open mornings (9.30am–12.30pm/€ 10 per session per child), and there's no crèche for babies or children's restaurant. That said, the activities, which might include constructing a marine-themed mobile, building sandcastles on the beach and learning circus skills, are well thought out. There's also a range of seasonal events, including a Halloween supper followed by a sweet hunt through the corridors of the elegant hotel, which looks over the ramparts of neighbouring St-Malo. There's also a largish indoor pool, and mums and dads appreciate the sauna and hammam (Turkish bath), and perhaps the fitness suite.

Families tend to stay in interconnecting rooms, which have sea or garden views; they're light and airy, with nautical stripes in pastel shades and small balconies. Prices are considerably lower than in the Deauville hotel, but this is still the place that French and foreign stars choose to stay during Dinard's annual British film festival, so you know you can count on first-class, ultra-discreet service, whether in the swish restaurant, where seafood naturally predominates or in 333 Café, a more relaxed café-bar with a seaview terrace, serving sandwiches, salads and so on.

The under-12s menu in the restaurant (€ 17 (£ 11.40)) includes the likes of tomato and mozzarella salad as a starter, main courses of fish fillet and green vegetables, or tagliatelle Carbonara, and desserts such as Ile flottante (meringues on a 'sea' of custard). Alternatively, there's a daily-changing 'Initiation au Goût' menu that allows children to try out the chef recommendations with their parents. Breakfast at € 18 per adult and € 10 per child under 12 years.

Check the website for family breaks ('Fugues Familles') with preferential rates on interconnecting rooms and a free session in the children's club. Note that there's a free hotel seaboat from Dinard to St-Malo between May and September.

*46 avenue George V, Dinard, ☎ 02 99 88 26 26, **www.lucienbarriere.com**. 90 rooms. Double rooms € 140–220 (£ 92–145); interconnecting double at € 185 per night for parents' room and € 92.5 per night for room for children under 12; suites € 230 to € 440; extra bed – € 40 per day; cot free of charge. Amenities: restaurant, bar, indoor pool, gym, indoor tennis courts, golf circuit, 24hr room service, babysitting, drycleaning/laundry service. In room: cable/Sat TV, minibar, safe.*

**under-12s menu:*

STARTERS

Vegetable soup

Tomato and mozzarella salad

Cold-meat platter

MAIN COURSES

Fish fillet and green vegetables

Hamburger with chips

Fish or chicken nuggets and rice

Tagliatelle Carbonara or Bolognese

DESSERTS

Cream cheese

Fruit salad

Chocolate cake

Ice creams or sorbets

Waffle and chantilly cream

Ile Flottante (fluffy egg whites floating on a sea of custard)

INEXPENSIVE

La Pensée ★ FIND This exceptional little place in the charming resort of St-Lunaire (p. 66) offers double B&B rooms with kitchenettes, plus self-catering apartments and houses for 2–5 people, most of it year-round. Styles vary, but all accommodation has lovely wooden furniture and decor, mosaic-tiled bathrooms and kitchens, and pretty colour combinations – Ariane, for instance, is a house for 4–5 with a colour scheme of pale and hot pinks, plus some sweet wrought-metal furniture (maybe not one for the guys, then). Some rooms have views of the former Grand Hôtel, and most have their own little garden or verandah. You're also just moments from the lovely Grande Plage. Your hosts will advise on which is best-suited to your needs (one or two have spiral staircases unsuitable for toddlers). A delicious breakfast featuring home-made jams and scones can be provided even in the self-catering apartments.

*5 rue de la Grève, St-Lunaire, ☎ 02 99 46 03 82, **www.la-pensee.fr/**. Apartment for four € 275–710 (£ 186–479) per week (midweek and weekend rates available). In room: kitchen including dishwasher, washing machine (in some), TV. B&B closed July and Aug.*

Village Mahana ★★★ FIND A well-thought-out gîte complex a couple of kilometres inland from Dinard and St-Lunaire, on the site of the proprietress's childhood home, Mahana is focused around a great mid-sized outdoor pool fenced off from straying toddlers, with pool games and balls, plus loungers for parents. Children also have use of a little play area, table tennis and some baby toys. The five attractive stone gîtes, reassuringly situated in a dead-end street away from main roads, sleep 2-7 (note that a few have spiral staircases that might be a problem for those with tots). All have satellite TV; some have washing machines and others share the use of a communal laundry and freezer room where you'll also find some board games and beach items. A cot, highchair, changing mat and baby bath can be provided, and the owner is pleased to babysit if you want to follow up any of her restaurant tips.

Look out for great last-minute midweek offers on the website.

*La Vallée Piet, near Pleurtuit, 5km (3 miles) south of Dinard on D266, ☎ 02 99 88 73 21, **www.gites-mahana.com**. Gîtes € 270–630 (£ 182–425) per week (weekend rates available). Amenities: outdoor pool (Apr–mid-Oct) laundry room, Internet access, games and toys, babysitting. In room: kitchen, washing machine (some), TV, Playstation (extra fee), baby equipment by request.*

FAMILY-FRIENDLY DINING

Baie du Mont-St-Michel

Normandy with Your Family, a companion volume to this guide, lists other dining options around the bay.

EXPENSIVE

Olivier Roellinger of the **Maisons de Bricourt** (p. 90) runs the area's gourmet hotspots, although you'd be better off leaving the children with a babysitter if you want to experience their delights.

MODERATE

Auberge de la Cour Verte ★

FIND If you don't mind straying inland a little, a rural treat awaits you here in an old stone farmhouse now housing a restaurant offering a versatile choice of local country fare, grills and crêpes. You can enjoy a house cocktail (or your entire meal) outdoors on the flower-filled terrace while the children work up an appetite on the play equipment provided in the courtyard. Inside, it's all very cosy and intimate, with beams, old photos, a log fire over which local meats are expertly grilled, and views of the chef at work in the kitchen. There's a small and fairly standard children's menu (€ 8.50 (£ 5.70)), but the menu is so wide-ranging – it takes in soups, salads, omelettes, mussels, galettes and crêpes, and ice cream – that it's unlikely that even the fussiest eater will go hungry. You can also order smaller portions according to how hungry you are. Make sure to leave room for the home-made rice pudding or *crême brûlée*. The young English-speaking staff are delightful with children and adults alike – if you don't finish your wine they'll pack it up for you to take away.

Route de Rennes, Dol-de-Bretagne, ☎ 02 99 48 41 41. Menus € 8–29 (£ 5.40–19.50). Open Wed–Mon noon–2.30pm and 7–10pm. Highchair.

INEXPENSIVE

Café du Port In a picturesque port with its fair share of tourist traps, this laidback little bar, pub and café is the real thing – full of locals shooting the breeze over an aperitif. It's a little cramped inside, and can get smoky, but it's the decked terrace that will lure you anyway, for warm tarts (such as Auvergne ham with goats' cheese and salad, or three cheeses with basil and tomatoes), paninis, great salads (including mozzarella and tomato with basil), steaks, burgers, ham and chips and more. It's an especially handy place to know about if you've tired of Continental breakfasts – here you can get egg and bacon with toast, plus freshly squeezed grapefruit and other juices, at fair prices given the seafront location. On a sweltering day, try the iced chocolate drinks. Or parents might prefer wine by the glass, Irish coffee or grog.

2 place du Calvaire, Cancale, 15km (9 miles) east of St-Malo on D355, ☎ 02 99 89 62 85. Main courses € 6–12 (£ 4–8). Open 9am–late (times vary).

Around Bécherel & the Fôret de Brocéliande

MODERATE

Hôtel du Lac Beautifully situated on a lake in the shadow of a castle that was once home to writer Chateaubriand, and handy for the Bourbansais zoo (p. 73), this two-star hotel has three pleasant dining rooms (one air-conditioned), plus a pretty lakeside terrace and garden where you can relax over an aperitif as the children have fun in the play area provided. The two *menus* feature mainly local ingredients, with the accent on seafood – king prawns with mango and light spices, lemon sole with orange butter, and turbot with chitterling sausage. For children there's a good € 8 (£ 5.30) menu starting with a mini-pizza or melon, followed by creamy chicken casserole with

A Lot of Hot Air

Le Tertre Gris, a hill east of the Brocéliande forest and south of Rennes, was once thought to be a very old volcano, after thick black smoke was seen coming out of it. The smoke was later found to be due to the spontaneous combustion of organic materials that were mined there. A pleasant place for a stroll, it is also home to the very family-friendly **Halte du Volcan** restaurant (Le Châtellier, ☎ *02 99 43 75 65*, ***www.halteduvolcan.com***), which has a play area and a riverside animal park with llamas, Vietnamese potbellied pigs, kangaroos and more. You can also play quoits or *boules*, and fish nearby. The homely, moderately priced cuisine can be enjoyed on a shady terrace in fine weather, or in a cool bright dining room with forest murals.

Vietnamese Potbellied Pig

bacon and mushrooms or fillet of fish, then ice cream.

*2 place Chateaubriand, Combourg, 18km (11 miles) south of Dol-de-Bretagne on D795, 02 99 73 05 65, **www.hotel-restaurant-du-lac.com**. Menus € 13.50–33 (£ 9–22). Open July and Aug Sat–Thur noon–2.15pm and 7.30–9.15pm, Fri 7.30–9.15pm; rest of year Mon–Thur noon–2.15pm and 7.30–9.15pm, Sat 7.30–9.15pm, Sun noon–2.15pm. Highchair.*

INEXPENSIVE

The **Domaine des Trémélins** (p. 85) at Iffendic has a child-friendly restaurant.

Le Pressoir This is a handy crêperie if you're heading north out of the Fôret de Brocéliande towards Bécherel or the coast, set in a tiny town just north of Montfort-sur-Meu. Bright and welcoming, it offers almost 50 kinds of *blé noir* galettes, many quite unusual – parents might like to try La Lucette with homemade steak tartare (raw mince), egg and Emmenthal cheese; children might like the house speciality, the prawn-cocktail-like Le Pressoir with avocado, crab and prawns. They'd be wise to leave room for the dessert crêpes, though – try La Rousse, a gorgeous combination of vanilla ice cream and homemade caramel with salted butter. For non-pancake fans, there are also main-course salads and grilled meats, including a good-value daily special. There's a new farm-produced cider each month, or choose from a good range of inexpensive wines.

16 place de l'Eglise, Romillé, 18km (11 miles) northwest of Rennes on D21, 02 99 23 28 59. Main courses € 5–11 (£ 3.30–7). Open Tue–Sun noon–2.30pm and 7–10pm. Highchair.

St-Malo

EXPENSIVE

Le Bénétin Well away from the tourist hordes of St-Malo *intra-muros*, at the tip of the bay by the Rochers Sculptés de

Rothéneuf (p. 69), this stylish restaurant boasts a splendid big decked terrace with unobstructed views out into the wide blue bay with its rocky clusters of islands. Don't worry if the weather's not up to it, though – the dining room has huge bay windows from which to enjoy the same vista. Though the standard of cuisine is high and the decor fashionable, the atmosphere is relaxed, and there's a little lounge corner where you can sit if the children get twitchy at the table. The sophisticated menu changes with the seasons and what's available at the market each day but might include Cancale oysters, scallops with leeks and truffle oil, pollack with sweet potato and celeriac mash, monkfish carpaccio with vanilla, lamb with thyme and potato galette, dark-chocolate mousse with pistachio sorbet, and caramel-apple crumble with gingerbread ice cream. Children pay a good-value € 10 (£ 6.60) for smaller versions of any of the meat or fish dishes plus a dessert. There's an enormous wine and champagne list, reinforcing this as a great place for a treat. Note that at weekends – or daily in high season (June–Aug) – it also opens in the afternoon as a *salon de thé*.

Rochers Sculptés, Rothéneuf, St-Malo, ☎ 02 99 56 97 64. Main courses € 12–21 (£ 8–14). Open July and Aug Thur–Tue noon–2.30pm and 7.30–10pm; rest of year Thur-Mon 12–2.30pm and 7.30–10pm. Highchair.

MODERATE

Chez Jean-Pierre VALUE You won't come away from this restaurant-pizzeria-grill thinking you've had the best Italian food of your life, but you'll be heartened by the warm welcome, sea views and well-priced food. On the Sillon coast road leading away from St-Malo *intra-muros*, it's a bright place decorated with old posters. Children are made very welcome: there are chair-stilts for young children as well as normal highchairs, and an under-12s menu (€ 7.80 (£ 5.20)) with a wide choice – steak, turkey escalope or ham with spaghetti or chips, spaghetti bolognaise, spaghetti carbonara or pasta with butter, or five varieties of pizza (including a spicy Vesuvio with chorizo), finished off with plain or fruit yogurt, ice cream or seasonal fruit, plus juice or a soft drink. The main menu runs from open sandwiches via good pizzas and pasta dishes to steak and other meats served with pasta, chips or green beans. If you're tired of *kir bretons*, try an Italian version with amarena syrup and cherries, or save your sweet tooth for home-made chocolate mousse or *crème brûlée*, or the speciality apple pizza with rum and raisin ice cream. My only gripe is that as a result of being next to an Ibis hotel, JP's can get inundated with tourists (look for the hilarious English mis-translations on the menu), with the inevitable impact on service. Note, however, that there's a takeaway/delivery service for pizzas, sandwiches, Tex Mex fare and more.

60 Chaussée du Sillon, St-Malo, ☎ 02 99 40 40 48. Main courses € 9–13 (£ 6–8.60). Open daily noon–2pm and 7pm-midnight. Highchairs and chair-stilts.

INEXPENSIVE

Le Café Bleu ★★★ FIND In the shadow of the ramparts, a minute's walk from the Plage de Bon Secours (p. 63), this relative newcomer to St-Malo's crêperie scene stands out for its personal welcome and its delicious food made freshly from organic, Fair Trade ingredients. Choose from tasty galettes such as Baltique (smoked salmon, *crème fraîche* and chives) or Grècque (Feta and sundried tomatoes), savoury crêpes with cheese, egg or ham, veggie salads, hearty sandwiches, and dessert crêpes including an amazing caramelised apple. You may get a free *dégustation* of veggie pâté and bread before your main course. In addition to juices, teas and coffees, there's beer, wine and cider by the glass or *bolée*. The cosy space has a sofa area with Internet access and is dotted with eclectic ornaments – an old rocking horse, a Buddha-like figure – and jugs of flowers. Shelves hold Ecover cleaning products and organic mueslis, tuna terrines, Fair Trade coffee and so on – you might like to stock up if you're self-catering. With its mellow, jazzy soundtrack, it will tempt you to linger in the heat of the day, and the cheerful owners won't make you feel you have to hurry away. But if you can't tear yourself away from the beach, all dishes can be provided as takeaways.

2 rue du Boyer, St-Malo intra-muros, ☎ 02 99 40 98 38. Main course € 4.50–8.50 (£ 3–5.70). Open Sun and Mon 11am–2.30pm, Tue, Wed, Fri and Sat 11am–2.30pm and 6.30–10pm, but times may vary slightly.

St-Lunaire & Around

EXPENSIVE

The *bateau-promenades* on the Rance run by **Croisières Chateaubriand** (p. 81) include lunch and dinner trips with children's menus.

MODERATE

L'Arganier ★ FIND This attractive Moroccan tucked away up a street behind Dinard's seafront is worth making a detour for, especially if you're overdone it on the seafood platters and crêpes. Named after an oil-producing tree, it serves well-prepared tagines and coucous, from vegetable to Royal (with a bit of everything – lamb, spicy merguez sausage, chicken and vegetables) or fish, if you think it's not right being so close to the sea and not eating seafood. Although it's inherently child-friendly fare, there is a children's menu (€ 7 (£ 4.70)) with smaller portions of what's on the main *carte*, followed by ice cream and accompanied by a drink, though normal portions are on the large side so if you have tots you may be able to get away with sharing your dish.

The English-speaking staff couldn't be friendlier or more obliging, often offering a free glass of mint tea at the end of your meal. It's worth asking them for recommendations from among the Moroccan reds and rosés on the wine list. Try to come when there's a special event in town, as the restaurant puts on North African dance displays.

3 rue Winston Churchill, Dinard, ☎ 02 99 16 90 39. Main course € 9–15 (£ 6–10). Open daily noon–2pm and 7.30–9.30pm. Closed mid-Oct–mid-Mar.

INEXPENSIVE

Le Surf ★★★ FIND VALUE A blink-and-you'll miss it *snack de plage* overlooking St-Lunaire's best beach (p. 66), this beach hut is the kind of place you want to keep to yourself but know may not survive unless you spread the word. Little more than a covered terrace and a line of blue plastic tables and chairs along the sea wall, it has one tiny kitchen that somehow produces an amazingly wide choice of wonderful food. Come just for paninis (from smoked salmon to nutella with banana), *croques* or crêpes, or treat yourself to steak, *moules de bouchot*, whole lobsters (order a day in advance) or salads simple or elaborate – my Indonesian salad of grilled king prawns with seaweed butter, basmati rice, rocket and shallots cooked in lemon juice was one of the highlights of our most recent trip, and a steal at € 12 (£ 8) (you'd pay three times that in a fancy London restaurant). The children's menu (ham or frankfurters with chips, € 3.50 (£ 2.40)) is rather unimaginative, but there's so much on the menu, plus an ice-cream cabinet, that everyone will come away happy, if you can bring yourself to leave – it's all too easy to linger over a kir, cider, herbal tea or hot chocolate as the children explore the rockpools below.

Plage de Longchamp, St-Lunaire, ☎ 06 80 26 08 58. Main courses € 3–12 (£ 2–8). No credit cards. Open daily to 10pm; hours vary widely by season and weather.

4 Côtes d'Armor

Continuing the sparkling Côte d'Emeraude that began in the Ille-et-Vilaine and then swooping round the awesome Baie de St-Brieuc, the Côtes d'Armor becomes the jagged, rocky coast for which Brittany is renowned on the Goëlo coast up to Paimpol. But it's at the Côte du Granit Rose west of here that the real fun starts, with its famous boulders twisted by the elements into all manner of odd shapes – and stained pink, according to legend, by the blood of persecuted saints. Here, too, signs begin appearing in French and Breton, giving you a sense of having entered a different world.

Most tourists, French and English, head for this 'pink granite coast', and the Côtes d'Armor is indeed prime Breton beach holiday territory, with some fabulous boat trips out to nearby islands. You might even like to try scouting out likely locations for Astérix's village, which some claim to be the Cap d'Erquy towards the eastern end of the Côtes d'Armor. Yet there are many charming inland spots that might lure you away from the sea, especially the pretty Lac de Guerlédan with its lake resorts, the horse stud at Lamballe and the shops of St-Brieuc. In summer, the town of Guingamp is a great place for family-oriented entertainment.

St-Brieuc, the Côtes d'Armor's main city, is a good base if you want to visit the Côte du Granit Rose, Côte d'Emeraude and some of the inland attractions. Otherwise, there are some splendid accommodation options both inland and on the coast.

ESSENTIALS

Getting There

By Air The nearest airport receiving flights from the UK is Dinard in the Ille-et-Vilaine, about 55km (35 miles) northeast of Lamballe.

By the Côte du Granit Rose, **Lannion** has daily flights to and from **Paris** on Air France (p. 31), plus links with various other French cities.

By Boat There are no cross-Channel ferries to the Côtes d'Armor: the nearest terminals are **St-Malo** in the Ille-et-Vilaine (p. 57) and **Roscoff** in Finistère (p. 146).

By Train TGVs on the Paris–Brest line pass through **Lamballe**, **St-Brieuc** (about 3 hours from Paris), **Guingamp** and **Plouaret**, but not all trains stop at every station. There is also a branch line to **Lannion**. For the SNCF, see p. 41.

VISITOR INFORMATION

The CDT website, ***www.cotes-darmor.com***, an excellent source of info on the Côtes d'Armor, has a links page with all the contact details of the *département* tourist offices – click on 'Offices de tourisme et Pays touristiques'.

CÔTES D'ARMOR

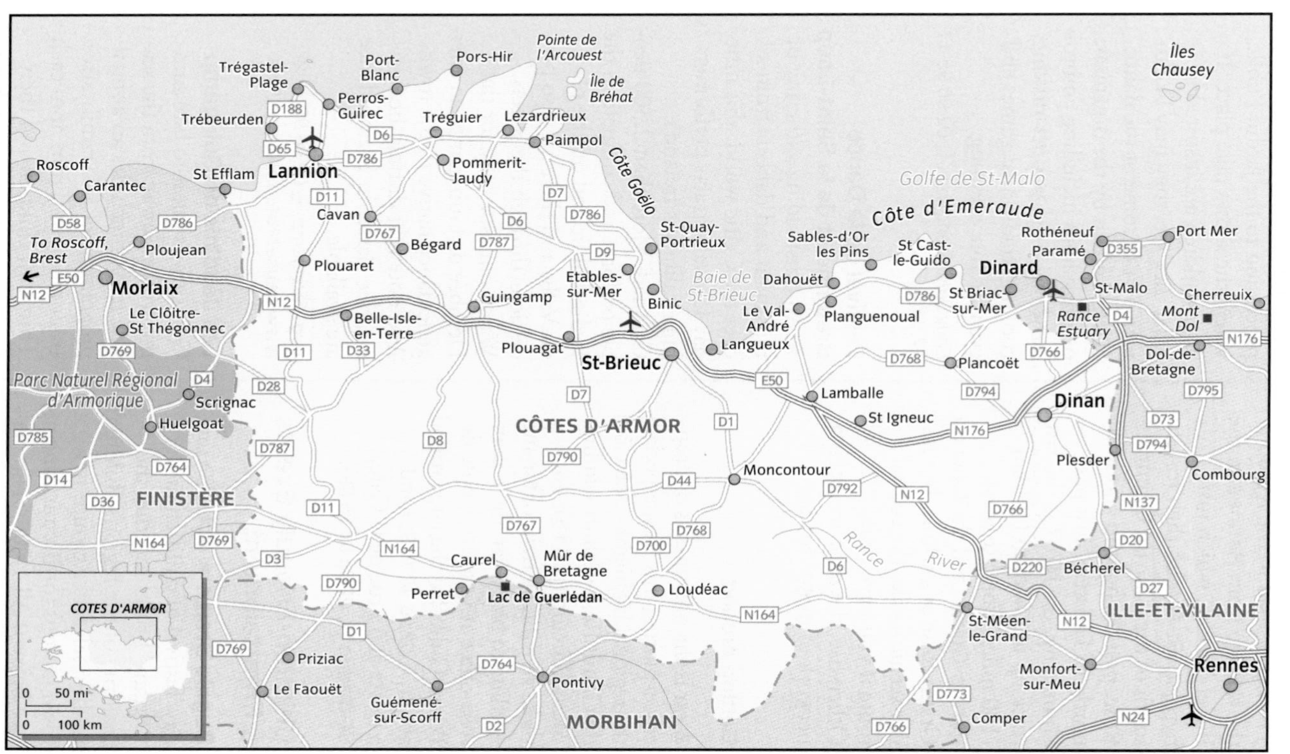

Orientation

The major road in the region is the **N12 up from Rennes** in the Ille-et-Vilaine, which just bypasses **St-Brieuc** then travels south of the Côte du Granit Rose, past **Guingamp** and into northern Finistère. Just past Guingamp, the **N767** is the fast track up to **Lannion** (160km (100 miles) from Rennes), **Perros-Guirec** and the Côte du Granit Rose as a whole, but it's not scenic – take the coastal route if you have time. Otherwise, the *département* is a network of minor roads.

Getting Around

A car is the only means of properly exploring this area, especially the regional highlight – the Côte du Granit Rose with its winding coastal 'circuit' (p. 115). For those arriving by train or air and needing to **hire** a car, there is an **Avis** office at **Lannion** (route de Perros-Guirec, at the large roundabout, *02 96 48 10 98*) and a **Hertz** at 53 rue de la Gare, **St-Brieuc** (*02 96 94 25 89*).

Children-Friendly Events & Entertainment

Bugale Breizh ★★★ The one-day 'festival of children in Brittany' brings together the majority of the region's children's traditional dance groups in a town famous for Breton dancing (see below). All 1,000-or-so performers, some as young as five, dress in historical costume – elaborate white headgear for the girls, cute waistcoats for the boys. The day begins with a 2pm procession to the Jardin Public, where the shows take place. If your children are inspired by what they see, they may like to take part in some of the dance classes laid on by the organisers, or workshops including embroidery, make-up, puppet-making, cooking, traditional games and even Breton wrestling.

Early July. Guingamp, 02 96 95 11 27. Free.

Festival de la Danse Bretonne et de la Saint-Loup

★ An outstanding gathering of musicians and dancers from all over the Celtic world, this nine-day festival attracts performers as high-calibre as Ireland's Clannad. More than 2,500 people perform and compete in the Jardin Public and on the place du Vally, and there are also processions through the streets. Watch out especially for the Dérobée de Guingamp, an energetic dance native to the town. And note that during the festival, free classes in Breton dance are available.

Aug. Guingamp, 02 96 95 11 27, ***www.dansebretonne.com****. Free.*

Les Jeud'his de Guingamp

Guingamp's quest to lure summer visitors away from the seaside resorts includes an annual programme of free family street entertainment. From 3pm each Thursday, children and their parents can come to watch puppetry, singing, dancing, comedy, circus acts and more; at 6pm there is also a show – street theatre, music, dance – by the local theatre.

Mid-July–early Aug. Place du Centre and Jardin Public, Guingamp, 02 96 43 73 89 (tourist office). Free.

Les Marionnet'ic Binic's week-long marionette festival offers both indoor and outdoor shows and related exhibitions by puppetry artists from all over Europe, giving you the chance to see how puppets have evolved across the Continent – witness the similarities between the Italian Pulcinella, English Punch, French Polichinelle, Spanish Don Cristobal and Russian Petrouchk, for example. The decade-old festival has now overspilled the resort of Binic itself, with some events held in nearby towns. Ask about related workshops.

May. Binic (and around), 10km (6 miles) north of St-Brieuc on D786, 02 96 73 60 12. Prices vary; some shows free.

Les Mediévales de Moncontour de Bretagne ★★ Held every other year (the next one is due in August 2007), this festival celebrates the fortified town of Moncontour's medieval heritage with a mass in the church of St-Mathurin followed by all kinds of costumed fun and frolics – fire-eaters, jugglers, stilt walkers, dancing, archery, horse-back jousting, plays, falconry displays, a procession and much more, culminating in an open-air ball in the evening. You can even eat medieval food if you like, although you'll need to book a place ahead of time. Note that you get into the festival free of charge if you come dressed up in medieval costume, though you won't actually save any money if you have to pay for costume hire (the organisers' website gives an address).

*Aug every other year. Moncontour, 27km (17 miles) southeast of St-Brieuc on D1, 02 96 73 49 57 (tourist office), **www.moncontour-medievale.com**. Tickets: € 10 (£ 6.70), under-12s free.*

Breton Puppets

Tournoi de Lutte Bretonne ★ Breton wrestling (*gouren*) is celebrated at this day-long tournament, in which participants shake an oath of loyalty before starting combat, the objective of which is to pin both your opponent's shoulders to the floor. Very like Cornish wrestling, this ancient sport was practised by Breton warriors. Spectators can also watch caber-tossing, discus-throwing, tug-of-war competitions and other displays of brute strength. If your interest is piqued, the town museum has displays on the traditions, rules and past masters of the sport, as well as other traditional Breton games.

July. Belle-Isle-sur-Terre, 15km (9 miles) west of Guingamp off N12, 02 96 43 01 71 (tourist office). Free.

WHAT TO SEE & DO

Children's Top 10 Attractions

❶ **Spotting** witches, crêpes, tortoises and other shapes in the contorted rocks of the **Côte du Granit Rose**. See p. 115.

❷ **Sailing to** the **Sept Iles** bird reserve with its puffins and gannets, looking out for seals on the way. See p. 122.

❸ **Playing** Celtic-themed games in a setting out of an Astérix book at the **Village Gaulois**. See p. 128.

❹ **Watching** 1,000 local children dance in traditional costume at the **Bugale Breizh**. See p. 110.

❺ **Meeting** mighty Breton stallions at the **Haras National** stud. See p. 119.

❻ **Going medieval** with children's trails, games and workshops at the 13th century **Château de la Hunaudaye**. See p. 123.

❼ **Steaming through** woods and valleys on the **Vapeur du Trieux**. See p. 126.

❽ **Messing about** on the water at the lovely **Lac de Guerlédan**. See p. 114.

❾ **Lunching on** pork hotpot and rhubarb crêpes, playing on the wooden fort and riding ponies at the eccentric 'green B&B' **Au Char à Bancs**. See p. 134.

❿ **Exploring** the string of family-friendly resorts on the **Côte d'Emeraude**. See p. 112.

Beaches & Resorts

Binic ★ Part of the rocky Goëlo coast sweeping up from St-Brieuc to Paimpol, this pretty resort with its charming harbour has three sheltered sandy beaches, including Plage de la Banche near the centre, with seawater and paddling pools. It's a great place to come in summer, with a raft of family activities, including monthly 'seaside safaris' – guided tours of the shore at low tide – trips around the port in fishing and pleasure boats, children's treasure hunts (*jeux de piste*) with the town's mascot Moni'c the cod (for 7–12-year-olds, accompanied by an adult), beach clubs, gymnastics clubs and trampolining, and free weekly children's shows ('Place aux Mômes') by the Théâtre de Verdure, including songs, storytelling and puppets. Puppets also make an appearance at a special May festival (p. 111); that month also sees the **Fête de la Morue**, a 'cod festival' with sailors' songs, trips on old fishing boats and fireworks.

10km (6 miles) north of St-Brieuc on D786, Tourist office: avenue Général de Gaulle, 02 96 73 60 12, www.ville-binic.fr.

Côte d'Emeraude ★ The easternmost coast of the Côtes d'Armor, continuing the lovely

Binic

'Emerald Coast' that began in the Ille-et-Vilaine (p. 55), is studded with family-friendly resorts and fine wide strands. They include **Lancieux**, famous for its red-streaked rocks claimed to be stained by the blood of St Siog; **St Cast-le-Guildo**, where you can choose from seven beaches and make boat trips around the Cap Fréhel (p. 124) or to St-Malo (p. 63); **Sables-d'Or-les-Pins**, with its wonderful beach; **Erquy**, which may have inspired the creators of Astérix (p. 114); and **Le Val-André**, with its expansive flat central beach that is great for children, plus some wilder stretches popular with surfers, sandyachters and paragliders This last resort also has great views over towards St-Brieuc, stylish little shops selling everything from trendy home decor to buckets and spades, and a very good fish restaurant, **Au Biniou** (p. 138). It's also famous for its lollies, the **Sucettes du Val-André**, which you can buy in the shop in town or at the factory on the way out of it (where short guided visits are given; ✆ *02 96 32 93 93*).

St Cast-le-Guildo and Erquy have free '**Place aux Mômes**' open-air children's shows in July and August, featuring acrobatics, dancing, electro-pop, theatre, circus, juggling, puppets and more. The tourist offices in each town have details.

*Tourist offices: Lancieux ✆ 02 96 86 25 37, **www.lancieux-tourisme.fr**; St Cast-le-Guildo ✆ 02 96 41 81 52, **www.ot-st-cast-le-guildo.fr**; Sables-d'Or-les-Pins ✆ 02 96 41 53 81, **www.pays-de-frehel.com**; Erquy ✆ 02 96 72 30 12, **www.erquy-tourisme.com**; Le Val-André ✆ 02 96 72 20 55, **www.val-andre.org**.*

St Cast-le-Guildo

The Elusive Gaul: in Search of Astérix

Astérix the Gaul and his companion Obélix first appeared in the comic *Pilote* in 1959, and went on to star in more than 50 adventures of their own, which sold more than 280 million copies round the world. There's long been debate among fans about the location of the nameless village in which the Gaulois heroes form a stronghold against the Roman invaders, with many people pointing to the similarities between the Cap d'Erquy on the Côte d'Emeraude and the terrain of the fictional village, especially the three rocks out to sea at the Anse de Port-Blanc.

In an interview, one of the creators of the *bande dessinée*, Albert Uderzo, said that although he didn't consciously choose to base Astérix's village on Erquy, he realised that he had been greatly inspired by the coast of the Côtes d'Armor, and especially the Cap d'Erquy, to which he had been sent with his brother as a child during World War II, and where he had subsequently spent family holidays. It's more likely than not, however, that the cape *did* succumb to the Roman invaders: in 1979 the domestic baths of a Gallo-Roman villa were found here.

Lac de Guerlédan ★ It's not the seaside, but this beautiful lake on the southern boundary of the *département* that is a brilliant place to spend a day or two *en famille*, with its safe artificial beaches. The lake is long – 12km – and narrow, with resorts dotted around its shore, notably **Beau Rivage** near Caurel, popular for watersports and boat trips, and **L'Anse de Sordan** near St Aignan (actually in the Morbihan), with boat hire and a stylish restaurant, the **Merlin** (✆ *02 97 27 52 36*), offering tapas, snacks and full meals, including pasta dishes and pizzas, and a basic children's menu. You can mess about in the water on anything from pedaloes and canoes to windsurfers and waterskis, and also fish and play *boules*. Bring a picnic to walk off in the lovely pine forest to the south. If you want to stay, there's a campsite with games and play areas, **Camping Anse de Sordan** (✆ *02 97 27 52 36*), and an inexpensive six-room hotel on the shore, the **Beau Rivage** (✆ *02 96 28 52 15*), with a restaurant with a € 10 (£ 6.70) children's menu.

If you're here in August, the evening *son-et-lumière* shows (✆ *02 96 24 85 28*) at the **Abbaye de Bon Repos** at the western tip of the lake, recounting the history of the region, are quite spectacular. Nearby Perret is also home to an old iron-working village, the **Forges-des-Salles**, that older children might enjoy.

40km (25 miles) south of Guingamp off N164. Tourist office: Mûr-de-Bretagne, ✆ 02 96 28 51 41, www.guerledan.fr.

Perros-Guirec ★ This is not the most attractive resort in

Brittany – it's too sprawling and impersonal in feel for that – but its position on the Côte du Granit Rose and outstanding range of activities make it a good bet for those with children (the tourist office has won awards for its services for children). The main beaches, the **Plage de Trestignel** and larger and more commercialised **Plage de Trestraou**, on the northern shore, are very toddler friendly. In high summer, the latter has a sailing club that runs the **Jardin des Mers**, an introduction to sailing for 3–8-year-olds (☎ *02 96 49 81 21*), and a surf club (☎ *02 96 23 18 38*). Both beaches host **Clubs de Plage** for children aged 2–11 in July and August, offered by the half-day, day or week. On the square near Trestraou beach there's also an old-fashioned **carousel** (Easter–Sept). For beach gear and other toys, try **L'Ile aux Jouets** (☎ *02 96 23 16 02*) at 41 place de l'Hôtel de Ville near the tourist office.

On Thursdays in July and August (and on occasional dates the rest of the year), the **Place aux Mômes** at the Palais des Congrès just behind Trestraou beach is a free family programme of burlesque circus, theatre, *guignol*, acrobatic dance, poetry, singing, electro-pop concerts and more. **Les Estivales**, in the same months, is another programme of free activities, including beach volley, mountain biking, archery and health workshops. If all that's not enough, a fair trek from the beaches, at the marina on the east side of town, you'll find a fun **Miniature Port** (Bassin du Linkin, ☎ *02 96 91 06 11*) where children aged three and up (plus adults) can sail model ferries and other boats (Apr–June public holidays and long weekends, July and Aug daily). Or you can make an unforgettable boat trip out to the **Sept Iles** archipelago (see p. 122) with its puffin colony, perhaps glimpsing seals en route. Walkers like the old **coast-guard's path**, an 8.5km round-trip on the GR34 route, taking in not only the pink rocks but also animals and wildflowers.

If it's raining, the **Musée du Cire** (boulevard du Linkin, ☎ *02 96 91 23 45*) has waxwork tableaux of great moments in French history that might divert you for an hour, plus an exhibition on Breton *coiffes* (p. 145). In April, the town hosts a *bande dessinée* exhibition.

INSIDER TIP

If you read French, ask the tourist office for *Kid*, a free magazine with info on Perros-Guirec's beach clubs and the like, plus comic strips and quizzes.

*Tourist office: 21 place de l'Hôtel de Ville, ☎ 02 96 23 21 15, **www.perros-guirec.com***

Other Natural Wonders & Spectacular Views

Côte du Granit Rose ★★

Although only about 15km in length as the crow flies, this is one of France's best-known strips of coastline, because of its pinky-brown rocks that erosion has contorted, in many cases, into odd shapes. It begins, in the west, around **Trégastel-Plage**, where it's fun to spot rock formations named after objects they resemble, including the *Sorcière* (Witch), *Tas de Crêpes* (Pile of Crêpes), *Tortues* (Tortoises) and *Tête de Mort* (Skull). Around the coast at **Ploumanach**, on the old coastguards' path, **La Maison du Littoral** (*02 96 9 62 77*) explains how the granite here was formed over millions of years. The spectacular golden-sanded **Plage de St-Guirec** precedes **Perros-Guirec**, the Côte's main resort (p. 114).

Past Perros-Guirec, the pink rockscapes continue up as far as **Pors-Hir**. You can follow a signposted driving circuit, the '**Côte des Ajoncs**' ('Gorse Coast'), around a series of boat-filled bays with breathtaking turquoise waters; highlights are **Trévou-Tréguignec**, **Port-Blanc** and **Buguélès**. At the Gouermel-Plage there's the sweetest little brasserie-crêperie, **Le Gouermel** (*02 96 92 55 26*), with a seaview terrace. At Buguélès you will begin to see houses built in-between the boulders, often so closely that they are seemingly wedged in. Walking around on the beaches themselves, children might enjoy trying to see shapes in the boulders, such as hands and faces.

Stunning overviews of the coast can be had during half-hour **flights** run by the Aéroport de Lannion (*02 96 48 06 49*, ***http://perso.orange.fr/acl.ulm***, € 70 (£ 47) per person).

For Perros-Guirec tourist office, see p. 115.

Ile de Bréhat Bréhat, a pretty car-free archipelago with a dramatic jagged coastline, curiously shaped pinkish rocks and a mild climate, makes for a lovely day out. There's little to do on the Ile de Bréhat, the 3.5 by 1.5km main island, other than walk or cycle among the imported exotic vegetation (eucalyptus, palm

Houses in the Rocks

Trégastel

trees, mimosa and aloes), look at the restored tidal mill and the Phare de Paon, a lighthouse next to a wave-smashed chasm, sunbathe and picnic on the beaches. Bikes can be hired by the jetty, though they are not allowed on the coastal paths.

Ferries leave the Pointe de l'Arcouest north of Paimpol, Erquy or Dahouët, St Quay-Portrieux or Binic, and Perros-Guirec. Direct trips take as little as 10 minutes, but there are a number of route options, including a 45-minute cruise around the island followed by free time. In summer you need to book well in advance, but because Bréhat has a very delicate ecosystem and is vulnerable to high-season hordes, it's better for both you and the island if you try to come at a quieter time. If you want to stay over, there's a reasonable hotel, the **Bellevue** (*02 96 20 00 05, **www.hotel-bellevue-brehat.fr***) with duplex rooms for families and a restaurant amenable to children's requests.

*Tourist office (syndicat d'initiative): Le Bourg, 02 96 20 04 15, **www.ile-de-brehat-org**. Cruisers: 02 96 55 86 99, **www.vedettesdebrehat.com**, direct crossing adults € 8 (£ 5.30), children 4–11 € 6.50 (£ 4.30).*

Sillon de Talbert ★ This thin spit on the peninsula north of Lézardrieux is a real oddity – it curves out almost 3km into the sea, seemingly resistant to the tides that ought to wash it away. In fact, it was created by two converging currents and powerful northwesterly swells, and is stretching northeast, which means it will eventually break away from the coast. Storms can be so forceful here that pebbles are tossed into the air. This being Brittany, there are numerous legends associated with the spit: according to one, Merlin placed millions of pebbles here to get closer to the fairy Viviane. Up close, it's difficult to get the measure of it, though driving down towards it you get glimpses of its spectacular extent. To appreciate its wonder properly, you need to walk out along it, taking care not to tread on the terns' and plovers' eggs at the end (they blend in spookily

Rocky Horror

Travelling away from the Côte du Granit Rose, on your way into Finistère, try to stop in the unspoilt Baie de Lannion, particularly at St Efflam, from which you can look across to the Lieue de Grève with its **Roche Rouge** – a rock that looks like a bit like a dragon, complete with knobbly spine and tail. Indeed, according to legend this was the place where a monstrous red dragon with a human head, snake's body and fish's tail came to die after being slain by King Arthur and St Efflam. The dragon had lived inside the nearby **Grand Rocher**, or Roch hr glas, causing such terror among local people that they tried to appease it with human sacrifices, including unbaptised children.

with the pebbles, so some areas have been marked off for their protection) or the sea kale that grows here. From the tip you a good view of the 45m Phare des Héaux-de-Bréhat about 10km (6 miles) northwest of Bréhat; four times further out, towards Guernsey, is the Phare des Roches-Douves (p. 164)

35km (22 miles) northeast of Lannion on D20. Access all year excluding during seabird nesting.

Aquaria & Animal Parks

At the time of writing the old **Zoo de Trégomeur** just northwest of St-Brieuc had been demolished and a brand-new Asian-themed zoo, run by the owners of the Zoo de la Bourbansais in Ille-et-Vilaine (see p. 73), was due to open on the site in April 2007. For the latest, see ***www.zoo-tregomeur.com***.

Aquarium Marin Set amidst a mass of huge pink-granite boulders, in caves that once served as a chapel and as a World War II weapons store, Trégastel's small aquarium has been modernised in recent years. Visits actually begin outside, in the Zone des Embruns ('Seaspray Zone'), where a combination of rain, wind and salt make the terrain inhospitable for all but lichens, life forms halfway between seaweed and mushrooms, sea snails and sea roaches, which you can see amongst the rocks or in the touching pool. Inside, the Zone des Marées (notice its 5,500-tonne ceiling consisting of a single slab of rock) is full of hardy types who can survive the constant movement of the tides, including lobsters, scallops, seahorses, sea bream and abalone. Interactive displays allow you to understand the tides, especially their links with the stars and planets. Last comes the Deep Zone, with its anemones, sponges and sea-fans, plus fish such as rays, conger eels and rock salmon, which have evolved to deal with the lack of light.

You'll need about 90 minutes for your visit. If that's whetted your appetite, ask about the *Sorties sur l'Estran* – French-language 2-hour tours of the coast between the highest and lowest tides, which include fun seaweed and animal hunts and identification sessions (€ 3 (£ 2), under-5s free, booking required).

*Boulevard du Coz-Pors, Trégastel-Plage, 5km (3 miles) west of Perros-Guirec on D788, 02 96 23 48 58, **www.aquarium-tregastel.com**. Open generally 10am–6pm Tue–Sun, daily May–Sept, but call ahead for seasonal variations and closures. Adm: adults € 7 (£ 4.70), children 4–16 € 5 (£ 3.30), family ticket (2+2) € 20 (£ 13.50), then extra child € 3 (£ 2).*

La Ferme d'Antan As the name ('Farm of Yesteryear') suggests, this an old farm reincarnated as a museum of rural life. Guides in period costume escort you around a restored farmhouse, cowshed, stables, pigsty and hen-house, complete with resident animals the children can get to know – including Olive, a piebald Breton cow, and Jolie, a Jersey cow. It's chastening to see how three generations would have lived together in the one main room of the farmhouse. You can explore the storeroom where cider was made, with its 1750 apple press, and the barn with its collection of early agricultural machinery. The garden is planted with old crops, including flax, Jerusalem artichokes and *blé noir* or buckwheat, the chief ingredient of Breton galettes. At the end of the tour, there's a short film on daily life on the farm in 1925.

Look out for occasional events, such as the festival of breadmaking and old crafts, the chestnut festival, and workshops on basket-making and wool-spinning.

*St-Esprit-des-Bois, Plédéliac, 10km (6 miles) southeast of Lamballe on D55, 02 96 34 80 77, **www.ferme-dantan22.com**. Open afternoons in school hols (call for times), June–Aug daily 10am–6.30pm. Guided tour adults € 3.50 (£ 2.35), children € 2.50 (£ 1.65).*

Haras National ★ Lamballe's stud farm – once France's biggest, and still one of Brittany's most important – runs guided tours (occasionally in English) of its 12 impressive stables, built in 1825 under Charles X and home to about 50 Breton stallions. These powerful, hardy but good-natured horses divide into *chevaux de trait*, which were employed for farm tasks, and *postiers*, a cross between *traits* and Norfolk horses, which are lighter and were used for pulling carriages, including postal carts and cannons in World War I. There are also French trotters, English thoroughbreds, Arabians, French saddle horses and ponies, Connemaras and a lone black donkey, though be aware that in the breeding season (mid-Mar–mid-July) all but about 20 of the residents are 'out visiting'. As well as admiring the handsome beasts, you can see demonstrations by saddlers and blacksmiths, displays of riding and driving, and an array of carriages. There's a new space for local art and heritage exhibitions too.

Haras National, Lamballe

*Place du Champ de Foire, Lamballe, ☎ 02 96 50 06 98, **www.haraspatrimoine.com**. Open for guided tours mid-June–mid-Sept daily 10am–5.30pm (last tour at 5.30pm), with tours at least every hour; school hols tours daily 3pm and 4.30pm, rest of year Wed, Sat and Sun 3pm and 4.30pm. Tickets: adults € 5 (£ 3.30), children € 2.50 (£ 1.65).*

Maison de la Baie ★ High on a windswept bluff with superb views over the Baie de St-Brieuc, this little local-environment museum is focused around a small but interactive Galerie des Oiseaux that gets even little children interested in the 50,000 or so birds that winter in this immense bay, where the tide can retreat by more than 7km. The centrepiece is a re-created stretch of seashore with life-size bird models and real fish; little screens show related videos and let you hear the cries each bird makes. There are also terminals with in-depth bird files and related games for both children and adults (in French only), microscopes, and a big screen showing short films that explain, for instance, why some local birds have such long beaks (for digging oysters out of the sand). Perhaps the best feature is the wall of illuminated boxes that gets you guessing which animal might have inspired a certain tool – crabs and pincers, or long-billed birds and tweezers, for example. Occasional temporary exhibitions on themes such as 'Maths and Nature' are held, and there are nature rambles for all ages. The little shop stocks bug viewers, marine stickers and so on.

There's an outside children's play area on site and an 'interpretation path' (part of the GR34 route) round this part of the coast (a *réserve naturelle* out of bounds to horseriders and mountain bikers). The wild **Dunes de Bonabri** with their amphibians, orchids and other species are worth visiting, as is the **Plage de la Granville**, though signs alert you to the dangers of sudden flooding due to the presence of a dam. **Hillion** itself is on the site of an ancient Celtic settlement and has the remains of a Roman path.

Note that you can get joint tickets with **La Briqueterie** (☎ *02 96 63 36 66*), an old brick and slate factory at nearby Langueux, with displays on the bay's history and industry, including a model railway, and creative workshops for children.

If you want to spend more time here, ask about the very keenly priced **studios** with kitchenettes offered by the Maison.

Camargue Horses

Site de l'Etoile, Hillion, 10km (6 miles) east of St-Brieuc on D80, ☎ 02 96 32 27 98. Open June and Sept Wed–Fri and Sun 2–6, July and Aug Mon–Fri 10.30am–6.30pm, Sat and Sun 1.30–6.30pm, Oct–May Wed, Fri and Sun 2–6pm. Tickets: adults € 3 (£ 2), children 6–12 € 2 (£ 1.35).

Terrarium de Kerdanet This jungle-like reptile and amphibian discovery centre, run by a man who has been a passionate collector since boyhood, is home to all manner of creatures, from affable plodding tortoises to some of the world's deadliest snakes. You can only visit by guided tour, in French; this leads you through the outside space with its mainly native species, then inside to the vivarium, where more exotic specimens are found. At the end comes a touching session for the brave, with pythons, boa constrictors and adders.

Plouagat, 10km (6 miles) east of Guingamp off N12, ☎ 02 96 32 64 49, ***http://terrariumdekerdanet.over-blog.com****. Open May–Sept Wed, Sat and Sun; call ahead for times. Adm: € 5.50 (£ 3.70), under-12s € 4.50 (£ 3).*

Nature Reserves, Parks & Gardens

Marais du Quellen Just west of Perros-Guirec and north of Trébeurden lies a protected area of freshwater marshland separated from Goas Treiz beach by a string of dunes. It's a lovely place for a nature walk, especially given the presence of some beautiful white Camargue horses. Normally seen in southeastern France, this ancient breed is thought to be descended from a Paleolithic horse crossbred with other races, including Arabian horses. A number of the little horses were brought to this area in 1989 – there are only about 30 herds in the world – and have had a profound effect on the vegetation. The marsh has a network of paths for walkers, with sections on stilts where the ground is boggy. Observatories allow you to watch the rich birdlife of the marshes.

*Trébeurden tourist office: place de Crec'h Hery, ☎ 02 96 23 51 64, **www.trebeurden.fr**.*

Station LPO de l'Ile Grande/ Réserve Naturelle des Sept Iles ★★★ The only one of its kind in France, this clinic was set up by the Ligue pour la Protection des Oiseaux in 1984 to treat and rehabilitate seabirds who have fallen victim to oil slicks in Brittany – several hundred a year, about half of whom eventually return to the sea. As well as visiting the lab where the unfortunate creatures are cleaned up (July and Aug only), visitors can see a permanent exhibition on seabirds, including their biology and migration habits, ecological issues and the care of petrol-damaged birds; watch live footage of gannets relayed from a remote-controlled camera on nearby Ile Rouzic; and follow guided tours of the coast to discover its bird- and plantlife.

Ile Rouzic, the only place that gannets come to mate in France (the presence of up to 20,000 pairs here can make it look like it's covered in snow), is part of the **Sept Iles,** France's most important bird reserve. Vedettes de Perros-Guirec (☎ *02 96 91 10 00*, ***www.armor-decouverte.fr***) run boat trips around this stunning archipelago, where you can also see puffins, cormorants and razorbills (p. 122) – plus seals in the surrounding waters.

*Pleumeur-Bodou, 7km (4.5 miles) northwest of Lannion on D21, ☎ 02 96 91 91 40, **http://bretagne.lpo.fr/dept/22**. Open school hols and June daily 2–6pm, rest of year Sat and Sun 2–6pm. Adm: € 2.50 (£ 1.65), under-12s € 1.50 (£ 1), family ticket € 6.50 (£ 4.40). Boat trips from € 16 (£ 10.65), under-12s € 10 (£ 6.65).*

Historic Buildings & Monuments

Abbaye de Beauport ★ This ruined Gothic abbey set atmospherically on the coast near Paimpol, with lovely bay views, can be explored freely or by hourly guided tour (in French), which takes you through the parlour, cellars, kitchen, cloister with Mediterranean plants, abbey church, refectory and more. There are also French-language 'discovery walks' on themes such as nature around Beauport (this includes tastings of freshly picked

In the Swim

Known as 'petit pingouins' in French because of their resemblance to penguins, razorbills are so adept in the water that they can actually swim before they can fly, and in late summer they moult so much that they can't take to the air at all for a while. You may see some of these elegant birds on the cliffs of Brittany, or on the waters, where they often bob up and down together in 'rafts'. They spend so much time at sea, far from land, that sadly they are some of the most common victims of oil slicks.

Abbaye de Beauport

samphire) and medieval food, and imaginative two-hour children's workshops: youngsters might go in search of wildflowers with which to create a box of scents, or learn about strange sea creatures and make their own sea monster out of clay. Some of the workshops are linked to the excellent temporary exhibitions here. Another great family option, for those with older children, may be the night walks in July and August (10pm–1am), with stunning depictions of the monks' daily life through dreamlike projected images of talking apples, a library illuminated by fireflies and other oddities.

*Kérity, 2km (1.25 miles) from Paimpol on D786, 📞 02 96 55 18 58, **www.abbaye-beauport.com**. Open daily mid-June–mid-Sept 10am–7pm, rest of year 10am–noon and 2–5pm. Adm: (abbey and temporary exhibitions) € 5 (£ 3.30), children 11–18 € 3 (£ 2), children 5–10 € 2.50 (£ 1.65), family (2+2) € 12 (£ 8) then extra child € 1 (£ 0.70) (reduced adm Oct–Mar); (abbey, temporary exhibitions and walk) € 8.50 (£ 5.65), children 11–18 € 4.50 (£ 3), children 5–10 € 3 (£ 2), family (2+2) € 20 (£ 13.50), then extra child € 2.50 (£ 1.65).*

Château de la Hunaudaye ★

As part of a three-year restoration and general overhaul that began in summer 2005, this partially ruined 13th century castle, rebuilt in the 15th, is sharpening its focus for visiting families – the French-language guides take time to explain things to children during tours; a € 2 (£ 1.35) booklet 'Y'a pas d'âge pour le Moyen Age' (roughly: 'You're Never too Young for the Middle Ages') for 7–12-year-olds explains the castle's history from a fun and accessible angle, and suggests two trails to follow; and if one of the annual exhibitions is too complicated for little ones, related children's workshops are held so that parents get time to discover the castle alone. In high summer, there are free daily workshops for 7–12-year-olds, on archaeology and weaving, and in September a Children's Day features games and workshops, including chainmail, stained glass and paper making. Watch out, too, for evening *son-et-lumière* shows in summer.

*13km (8 miles) east of Lamballe off D16, 📞 02 96 34 82 10, **www.la-hunaudaye.com**, Open Apr–mid-June and mid-Sept–Oct public hols and Sun 2.30–6pm, mid-June–mid-Sept daily 10.30am–6pm. Adm: adults € 3 (£ 2), children 6–16 € 2 (£ 1.35).*

Fort la Latte ★ One of the most dramatic sights on the Breton coast, this fortified medieval castle looks almost as if it has been sculpted out of the

Fort la Latte

jagged 70m cliffs on which it is perched, against a backdrop of blue sea. Set a fair trek from the main roads, it nonetheless attracts tourists by the coachload in summer due to its fame as a location for the rip roaring final scenes in the 1958 film *The Vikings*, starring Kirk Douglas and Tony Curtis. Some of the structure dates back to the 14th century – curtain walls, rampart towers, two drawbridges and the dungeon – but most of what you can see now dates back to 1690–1715, and that has been subject to more or less continuous restoration over the past century. Once you've followed the winding forest footpath down to the fort (there's a wider track for those less sure on their feet or with buggies) and crossed its first drawbridge, there's not a huge amount to see inside – and certainly not the swooping bats that my son was hoping for – but the views *are* incredible, especially from the roof of the keep, and the 18th century oven used to 'cook' cannonballs (to set enemy ships on fire) is a thought-provoking remnant.

The fort is on a headland of the Cap Fréhel peninsula; over to your left as you look out to sea you can spot the **Cap Fréhel** itself, an ornithological reserve (cormorants, razorbills – see box p. 122 – gannets and other seabirds nest here) with a nature centre and the 33m high **Phare du Fréhel**, a 1950s lighthouse – climb its 145 steps for views of the western Manche coast in Normandy, the Iles Chausey off it, and the Ile de Bréhat (p. 116) on very clear days.

*Cap Fréhel, 40km (25 miles) north-east of St-Brieuc on D34, ☎ 02 96 41 40 31, **www.castlelalatte.com**. Open Apr–early June and late Aug–Sept 10am–12.30pm and 2–6pm, early July to late Aug daily 10am–7pm, rest of year school and bank hols, Sat and Sun 2–6pm. Adm: € 4.30 (£ 2.85), children 5–11 € 2.40 (£ 1.60).*

The Top Museums

Cité des Télécoms ★ A bit of an anomaly just inland of the seaside resorts of the Côte du Granit Rose, this telecommunications museum – set up by France Télécom and occupying, in part, a huge dome used for the first satellite broadcast of images between France and the States, in 1962 – has plenty to occupy tech-heads from ages five or so and up. The Râdome itself hosts a show that allows spectators to relive that first broadcast of TV images – you can still see the 340-tonne cone-shaped antenna that was used – plus a further video, laser and sound show. A separate building is home to an exhibition on the history of telecommunications from the first undersea cables to the Internet; plenty of interactive exhibits allow you to, for instance, snowboard against a projected background, save the Earth from a hail of meteorites or steer a satellite. Don't miss the satellite images of Brittany taken from Space – try to spot the places you've been to. There are also periodic temporary exhibitions and a shop with wacky gifts and knick-knacks ideal for keeping children occupied during car journeys. You can get joint tickets to the Cité and the Planétarium de Bretagne (p. 126).

Cosmopolis, Pleumeur-Bodou, 7km (4.5 miles) northwest of Lannion on D21, 02 96 46 63 80, ***www.leradome.com****. Open early Feb–early Mar Sun–Fri 2–6pm, early Mar, Apr and Sept Mon–Fri 11am–6pm, Sat and Sun 2–6pm, May and June daily 11am–6pm, July and Aug daily 11am–7pm, Oct–Dec very limited opening, call for details. Adm: (museum and one show in Râdome) adults € 7 (£ 4.70), children 5–17 € 5.60 (£ 3.75), family (2+2) € 19.60 (£ 13.25), then additional child € 3.50 (£ 2.35); (with second show) extra € 3 (£ 2) per person, € 9 (£ 6) family.*

Maison de la Harpe It won't be everyone's cup of tea, but this unique museum of the Celtic harp, located in the heart of the medieval city of Dinan, will delight young musicians – not least because of its fun Celtic harp discovery workshops for 6–12-year-olds, held every school holiday and June–Sept. Lasting about an hour and costing € 5 (£ 3.30) per child, they can only be booked a day in advance or in the morning of the workshop itself. The museum also hosts changing exhibitions on this medieval harp, which enjoyed its golden age in Ireland but was popular across Europe in the epoch of Arthur, Merlin and Tristan, and accompanied troubadours' songs.

The Maison extends its opening times for part of July, when it's the focal point of the **International Celtic Harp Festival**, and hosts extra displays (concerts take place all over the city).

6 rue de l'Horloge, Dinan, 02 96 87 36 69, ***www.harpe-celtique.com****. Open early Feb–early Mar Tue–Fri 2–5.30pm, early Apr–early May and June–Sept Tue, Wed, Fri and Sat 3–7pm, Thur 11am–5pm. Adm: € 2 (£ 1.35), under-10s free.*

Musée du Rail Situated in part of the eastern wing of Dinan's train station, this railway buff's dream has both glass cases full of scale models of trains and a vast track on which you can watch them operate – about 170m of it, with scale models of local buildings, the result of 16 years' work by a couple of enthusiasts. There are also old station clocks, signs, platform lanterns, scales and other objects. Don't worry if trains aren't your bag, though – leave the boys to their toys and take a look at the wonderful collection of old French railway posters from various eras and in a wide range of styles, most of them showing landmarks of the region, including Carnac, the Mont-St-Michel and the Côte d'Emeraude. The collection has also been extended into old movie posters with a railway connection. Allow an hour or slightly more for a proper look around.

*Train station, Dinan, ☎ 02 96 39 53 48, **www.museedurail-dinan.com**. Open late May–mid-Sept daily 2–6pm. Adm: adults € 4 (£ 2.65), children under-12 € 3.25 (£ 2.15).*

Planétarium de Bretagne On the same site as the Cité des Télécoms (p. 124; combined tickets available), Brittany's planetarium will be another hit with scientifically minded children. Its hemispheric projection room, where you can see images of the heavens in 3D, hosts shows in French, English, German, Dutch, Italian and, for groups by reservation, Spanish. That said, the best shows for children – *Si La Lune m'etait Contée*, with a magician (for ages three and up), and *L'Aveugle aux Yeux d'Etoiles*, which takes the form of a fairy story to explain the rotation of the Earth and so on (for ages five and up) – are in French only. You'll also need good French to enjoy the expert-led workshops and Q&A sessions. The shop has gifts, books, DVDS and more.

*Cosmopolis, Pleumeur-Bodou, 7km (4.5 miles) northwest of Lannion on D21, ☎ 02 96 15 80 30, **www.planetarium-bretagne.fr**. Open Feb–Apr, July–Dec daily, May and June Sun–Fri; call for show times. Adm: adults € 7.20 (£ 4.80), children 5–17 € 5.80 (£ 3.90), family (2+2) € 23.20 (£ 15.65), then extra children € 4.65 (£ 3.15).*

Children-Friendly Tours

Vapeur du Trieux ★ Accessing parts of the Trieux valley otherwise unseen by visitors, this steam train chugs its way between Paimpol and Pontrieux at a leisurely 30km/h (19mph), leaving you free to enjoy sights such as the 15th century Château de la Roche-Jagu, the Leff–Pontrieux viaduct, a tidal mill and the town of Pontrieux, famous for its old public washhouses now embellished with flowers. As the costumed guides explain (in French or English), the 104-tonne engine that pulls the carriages with their wooden seats has covered more than a million kilometres since it was made in 1922. It all makes for a lively family day out, even more so given that the train stops in the heart of the forest, at the Maison de l'Estuaire de Traou Nez, to let you enjoy Breton music, look at an exhibition on the surroundings, and taste local produce. Booking is required.

*Train station, avenue du Général de Gaulle, Paimpol, ☎ 08 92 39 14 27, **www.connextradition.com**. Open Tue/Wed–Sun; call for times. Return*

Steam Train, Paimpol

trip € 21 (£ 14), children 4–11 € 10.50 (£ 7), family (2+2) € 59 (£ 39.85).

For Active Families

See also '**Beaches & Resorts**, p. 112.

Armoripark A 6 hectare (15 acre) activity park between Lannion and Guingamp, this is a tacky but fun standby for moments when children have had their fill of beaches and aquariums (yes, it happens!) – the park has a waterpark, trampolines, pedal karts, human table football, a luge track, bouncy castles, and less rowdy pleasures such as a mini-farm, deforming mirrors and displays of old farm machines and tools beside a stone dovecote. You can picnic here, or there's a snack bar with outside seating. In late April the three-day Clown Festival is a hit with tots.

*Bégard, 12km (7.5 miles) northwest of Guingamp off D767, ☎ 02 96 45 36 36, **www.armoripark.com**. Open mid-June–late Aug daily 11am–7pm, rest of year call for days and times. Adm: (inc waterpark) € 9.50 (£ 6.40), under-12s € 8.50 (£ 5.75), family (2+2) € 31 (£ 21); reduced rates outside high season.*

Centre de Découverte du Son ★ The oddball Sound Discovery Centre consists of a 'magic pathway' through a natural setting. On your way along it, you listen to, produce and play with sounds of various kinds – from waterfalls to fairy music. Children love the open-air, hands-on installations, which include huge xylophones and musical pulleys. There's a picnic space and snack bar at the end of the circuit.

*Kérouspic, Cavan, 18km (11 miles) southeast of Lannion on D767, ☎ 02 96 54 61 99, **http://decouverte.son.free.fr**. Open Apr–Nov Sun and public hols 1–6pm, daily in school hols. Adm: adults € 6 (£ 4), children 3–14 € 4 (£ 2.70), family ticket (2+2) € 18.50 (£ 12.50).*

Labyrinthe Végétal de Paimpol This huge summer corn maze 2km (1.25 miles)

*Belle-Isle-en-Terre, 15km (9 miles) west of Guingamp on N12, ☎ 02 96 43 30 03, **www.biscuiterie-des-iles.com**. Open daily 9am–7pm.*

Le Blé en Herbe ★ St-Brieuc is blessed with good independent toyshops; this one, with its motto 'Adventure makes us big', is perhaps its best. It's not huge, but within its four colourful walls it crams a vast array of toys, games and books for everyone from babies to teens. All the stock has been selected lovingly, whether high-quality wooden toys for tots (including the French Vilac range of pull-alongs), fantasy models and figurines for older children, or Czech handpuppets. The ranges of model animals and of books are especially impressive. This is also a good place to pick up cards and postcards, and CDs with classic stories such as *Le Petit Prince* – handy for road trips.

There's another very good toyshop, **Pastel**, at no.20 (☎ *02 96 61 71 44*); it's smaller but also has a lots of top-quality wooden toys.

13 rue Saint-Gouéno, St-Brieuc, ☎ 02 96 61 95 55. Open Mon 2–7pm, Tue–Sat 10am–12.30pm and 2.30–7pm.

Comptoirs de l'Ouest A barn-like building on the port of Dahouët, leading out of Le Val-André (p. 113), this antiques/*brocante* (junk) store has the feel of an old-fashioned curiosity shop – it's the type of place you imagine you might unearth a real treasure, buried amidst the old furniture, secondhand books (adults' and children's), trinkets and ancient toys, which include metal cars big enough for tots to ride in, metal tanks and cars, and teddies, all reasonably priced.

Dahouët, 35km (22 miles) northeast of St-Brieuc on D786, ☎ 02 96 63 18 84. Open Thur and Fri 2–5pm, Sat and Sun 10.30am–2.30pm and 3–6.30pm.

INSIDER TIP

Comploirs de la Mer have free 'Horaire des Marées' booklets, which as well as the tide tables contain handy advice on how to fish for and cook various shellfish.

Counters to Count On

A veritable marine empire, the Coopérative Maritime – a fishermen's society set up in the late 1900s – now owns almost 60 **Comptoir de la Mer** shops in ports around France, many of them in Brittany, including Paimpol (quai Armand Dayot, ☎ *02 96 20 80 22, **www.comptoirdelamer.net***). Catering to adults and children, to expert sailors and to people who just love the sea, they stock everything from fishing and sailing gear to nautically inspired clothing and decorative items, including ships' models. Among the lines of clothes are Royal Mer, with bright, soft knits for men, women and children, and Guy Cotten, with its plain practical children's activitywear. Staff are unfailingly cheery and helpful.

Patt'ine ★ Just around the corner from Le Blé en Herbe (p. 130), this fantastic children's shoe shop has a well-selected range of funky footwear from Kickers Junior, Mod8, elefanten and more, with most pairs costing € 50–100 (£ 33–66). In hot weather, come for Geox trainers and sandals, designed not to absorb sweat and thus remain odour-free. The colourful store has a large play area at the rear, with a playtable, blocks, comics and puzzles, and offers a first-class measuring service.

The children might also want to drag you into **Planète Cartoon** a couple of doors away, where the Petit Prince and fox figurines make unusual souvenir purchases.

10 rue Charbonnerie, St-Brieuc, ☎ 02 96 77 03 31. Open Mon 2–7pm, Tue–Fri 9.30am–12.15pm and 2–7pm, Sat 9.30am–12.30pm and 2–7pm.

FAMILY-FRIENDLY ACCOMMODATION

Côte d'Emeraude

MODERATE

Hôtel-Restaurant de l'Abbaye ★ VALUE A short distance inland, in a pleasant riverside village, this quite chic option stands out for its lovely large garden with swings beneath the trees, fine outdoor pool, tennis court and ping-pong table. The rooms are quite plain given the elegance of the building (an old convent) – hence the very fair prices. However, in keeping with the overall atmosphere of the hotel, they are muted and easy on the eye, and bathrooms are very up-to-date, with trendy sinks and mosaic tiling. For families, there are two 'apartments' (interconnecting rooms) or a number of triples or quadruples that will also fit a cot. Staff at the bar will provide you with a flask of hot water if you want to make a cuppa or heat a baby's bottle.

This is the kind of restful place where – unless you've got very young children, that is – you awake to birdsong, and where breakfast (€ 9 (£ 6), free for children) can be brought to your room if you don't feel up to descending to the pleasant *salon*. The restaurant, **Le 18.43**, is quite formal, with linen tablecloths and polished wineglasses – try to get a table on the terrace if you can. Menus, which start at € 27.50 (£ 18.50), have an emphasis on seafood and regional produce – think local lobster with ginger and asparagus *velouté*. The quite expensive but quality children's menu (€ 13 (£ 8.65)) offers a platter of cold meats and *crudités*, then chicken with potatoes or vegetables, and a choice from the dessert menu.

*12 rue Marie Paule Salonne, Plancöet, 24km (15 miles) east of Lamballe on D768, ☎ 02 96 84 05 01, **www.abbaye-hotel.com**. Double € 65–75 (£ 44–50), triple/quad € 85 (£ 57), 'apartment' € 115 (£ 77). Cot free. Amenities: restaurant, bar, tennis court, outdoor pool, sauna, free parking, Wi-Fi Internet access. In room: TV.*

Château de Galinée

INEXPENSIVE

Camping Caravaning Château de Galinée ★ Camping always seems like a more elegant proposition when you're doing it in the grounds of a French château – as at this four-star site in a four hectare (10 acre) wooded park five minutes' from the sea. Accommodation is in mobile homes or 'bungalow tents' with or without private facilities, or you can set up your own tent. Surrounded by pretty stone buildings and exotic foliage, the waterpark here is superior to most, with three slides, two toddlers' pools, a variety of games, whirlpools and a Jacuzzi. Additionally, families have access to a farmyard with goats and other friendly beasties, a tennis court and table tennis, volleyball and basketball pitches, crazy golf, *pétanque*, a large pond you can fish on, and bouncy castles and other games. A children's club operates during the busier months. Amenities include a games room, bar, takeaway food counter, laundrette and baby-changing facility.

St Cast-le-Guildo, 25km (16 miles) northwest of Dinan on D19, ☎ *02 96 41 10 56,* ***www.chateaudegalinee.com****. Mobile homes € 245–800 (£ 165–540) per week, bungalow tents € 220–580 (£ 148–390) per week, campsite pitch € 12.25–19.80 (£ 8.10–13.20) per day for one person, then € 3.85–5.80 (£ 2.55–3.85) per person, under-7s € 2.30–4 (£ 1.55–2.65). Amenities: swimming pools, tennis court, fishing games, children's club, farmyard, bar, food counter, laundrette, babychanging.*

Ecurie du Gallais ★ FIND A great spot for horse-lovers, this stable less than a kilometre from the shore offers farm accommodation you can combine with accompanied horse rides lasting from one hour to four days – destinations include the Cap Fréhel and Fort la Latte (p. 123) and the Ile des Ebihens, which is reached across the sands at low tide. Even tots are catered for, with rides around the farm on resident ponies Bouboule,

Capora and Couette-Couette. The rooms, located in a sweet stone building with a terrace, are basic, as the prices reflect, but great care has been taken to make them bright and welcoming, with equine motifs and homely touches such as teddy bears. The family room for four, with a sparkling clean bathroom, is a steal considering breakfast is included. Children also have the run of the pretty garden with its play equipment.

Le Logis du Gallais, rue du Bois-es-Lucas, St Cast-le-Guildo, 25km (16 miles) northwest of Dinan on D19, ☎ 02 96 41 04 90, ***www.ecurie-du-gallais.com****. Three rooms. Double € 42 (£ 28), family room for four € 75 (£ 50). Amenities: horse rides, play equipment. Closed Oct–Easter (horse rides all year).*

La Julerie ★ FIND These English-run **gîtes**, renovated to retain their traditional Breton style, are a great find given that they share the use of a heated indoor pool – a blessing on wet days when the beaches 20km away lose their appeal. Next to the pool is a games room with table tennis; outside are sun loungers, grassy play areas, a swing, a slide and a sandpit. The setting is peaceful – at night you will hear little except owls – and the main roads are far away. The four gîtes, which sleep 4, 5 and 7–8 people, are all part of the same long building but have their own patio/lawn areas. The best, and most expensive, is Le Grenier, complete with terracotta and wooden floors, wood-burning stove and a French-style bath. Children get a lovely attic floor to themselves, with twin beds and a private bathroom. Note that, for once, guests here don't have to pay extra for things such as linen and towels – everything is included.

Corseul, 10km (6 miles) northwest of Dinan on D794, ☎ 02 96 27 24 23, ***www.lajulerie-gites.com****. Four rooms. Rates: € 275–1125 (£ 185–760) per week (weekend rates available). Amenities: indoor pool, table tennis, barbecue equipment, children's games. In room: TV, full kitchen inc dishwasher (except in one gîte), washing machine, heating, cot (by request).*

Baie de St-Brieuc

EXPENSIVE

Domaine et Château du Val

★ A fantasy French château with garden statuary and extraordinary wine cellars, this is a surprisingly good place for children by virtue of its heated indoor pool, its proximity to the beach (less than 1km away via a trail through the woods) and its flexible accommodation – in spacious family suites in the château itself, in self-catering 4–6-person duplex apartments or 2–3-bedroom houses in outbuildings dotted throughout the 11 hectare (27 acre) grounds, or in bedrooms or self-catering studios also in the grounds. Fans of classic French chintz appreciate the decor – *bateaux-lits* or canopied four-posters, leather sofas and deep armchairs – but it's gourmets who are best satisfied, feasting in the expensive restaurant on the likes of house foie gras, smoked salmon, local oysters and grilled lobster, plus produce from the hotel garden. Children get a very good € 15 (£ 10) menu of *crudités* or terrine, roast chicken or fish with pasta or fresh vegetables, and a dessert from the changing selection. It's the kind of place with lots of chi chi little dining spaces, accommodating from two to 40 people depending on how sociable you're feeling, although in summer and at breakfast you can also sit by the pool. Work it all off afterwards in the gym or on the grass or indoor tennis courts, or relax in the sauna and Jacuzzi (rather cheekily, there are extra charges for some of these). The attentive staff – who are welcoming to children – will tell you about nearby activities, including horseriding and quadbiking.

The low point is the breakfasts: limited choice makes them poor value at € 12 (£ 8) (less for children according to age).

*Le Val, Planguenoual, 15km (9 miles) east of St-Brieuc on D786, ☏ 02 96 32 75 40, **www.chateau-du-val.com**. 25 units. Double € 96–230 (£ 64–155), suite for three € 180 (£ 120), 2-bedroom apartment € 180–210 (£ 120–135), 2-bedroom house € 300–700 (£ 200–470) per week. Cot free. Amenities: restaurant, indoor pool (mid-Apr–mid-Sept), tennis court, gym, sauna, Jacuzzi, Internet access, babysitting, laundry service. In room: TV, hairdryer, telephone, kitchen (some).*

MODERATE

Au Char à Bancs ★★★ This extraordinary, eccentric place about 10 minutes inland of Binic (and close to the shortly-to-reopen zoo at Trégomeur; p. 118) is run by the aptly named Lamour family, who over the last 35 years have embraced 'green tourism' as a way of bringing new life to the working farm that passed down to them. It's most famous for its utterly charming inn, which combines rustic period details (old milling wheels turned into tables and curlicued radiators) with funky modern touches such as fairy lights. As it's only open Saturday evenings and Sunday lunchtimes except in July and August (when it's open daily except Tuesday), it gets besieged by local families, who come for the famous *pot au porc* and divinely caramelised rhubarb crêpes. As a result, service can be slow, but you can take children to play on the large wooden fort outside, by a little hill crisscrossed with tunnels to climb through, a slide and swings, a wooden horse, a field full of real ponies they can pet (and ride in summer), and a river with pedalo hire in summer. Some locals bring their children here just to play, thinking it's a public space, but the Lamours don't mind – the more the merrier. They've even set up a junk shop under the restaurant (where you can also buy farm cider and rhubarb jam), and the grounds are dotted with animals and old farm equipment.

The Wooden Play Fort, Au Char à Bancs

INSIDER TIP

A single portion of *pot au porc*, a delicious ham and sausage hot-pot, is more than enough for two

Accommodation is up a winding road, next to the ancestors' farm – until recently an unofficial museum but shortly to be transformed into a house for one of the sisters, Céline, and her young family. Céline runs the B&B – five shabby-chic rooms for up to four people, filled with quirky objects (old birdcages, radios and crockery) and bearing names such as The Hat Room and The Clock Room. You reach the rooms via a wonderful decked terrace with a swinging hammock, loungers and pots of herbs and flowers, where you can browse the old French books and 1960s *National Geographics* left in your room or let the peace and quiet wash over you. A decent Continental breakfast is served in the delightful breakfast 'café' full of tourist guidebooks and 1960s Italian design magazines, though at 9–10am it might be rather late for some. If I had to pick other holes, it would be that the double beds are a bit short and the lack of blinds on the skylights can make for very early mornings for toddlers. Bathtubs would be nice, too, but the power showers are superb. And at these prices and with this degree of charm, it's a shame to carp.

At the time of writing, Céline was thinking of creating a couple of gîtes here. In the meantime, her Irish sister-in-law Lizzy has a gorgeously appointed cottage, **La Maison à Rose** (*☎ 02 96 79 52 39*, ***www.roselouisemarie.com***), 3km north of here, with space for 2–3 people plus a baby.

Moulin de la Ville Geffroy, Plélo, 20km (12 miles) northwest of St-Brieuc on D4, ☎ 02 96 74 13 63, ***www.auchar abanc.com/****. Double € 64 (£ 43), family room for four € 103–109 (£ 68–72). Cot free. Amenities: animals, games, highchair (restaurant), baby-changing (restaurant), TV (breakfast room).*

INEXPENSIVE

Ferme de Malido ★ Four kilometres from the sea, this working

Shetland Pony at Char à Bancs

farm offering six homely B&B rooms is a great summer base – from mid-July to August (and some weekends in September) it has its own mystery maze dotted with playful artworks, two themed mini-mazes, and an area of wooden balancing and skill games, with the chance to win a basket of farm produce. Watch out, too, for special events as Celtic music evenings, visiting circus acts and spit-roast pig dinners. There are also night tours of the maze: bring a torch and, if you like, meat to cook on the campfire. Crêpes, galettes and drinks are also available, and you can find an open-air leisure park right nearby. If you come out of season, there's still a play area on the farm for children.

The basic but pleasantly decorated rooms, in a self-contained annexe with private entrances, include two triples and two two-roomed family units sleeping four and five respectively, one with a balcony. All have showers rather than baths, but they share the use of a cosy breakfast salon and a kitchenette for limited self-catering. For proper self-catering, there are two five-bedroom gîtes.

St Alban, 10km (6 miles) north of Lamballe on D17A, ☎ 02 96 32 94 74, ***www.labymalido.chez-alice.fr****. Eight units, including two gîtes. Double € 38–42 (£ 25.60–28.30), family room for four € 66 (£ 44). Amenities: shared kitchenette, play area, summer mazes, games and events.*

Côte du Granit Rose

MODERATE

Aigue Marine ★ This option on the marina of a pretty cathedral town is a good family bet for a variety of reasons: its pretty outdoor pool; its fabulous gourmet restaurant, **Les 3 rivières**, with a special family area overlooking the garden and pool and a € 10 (£ 6.70) children's menu (tomato salad, melon or cold meats, followed by fish, chicken breast or *steak haché* with vegetables, rice, pasta or chips, then fresh fruit salad or ice cream); and its good-value (if blandly furnished) family rooms for four, consisting of a small room with bunk beds, a large double bedroom, a seating area with table and chairs, a handy fridge, a terrace or balcony, and a bathroom with tub. There are also a number of L-shaped triples without a fridge or seating area; if there are three of you, you may prefer to get a large double with these extras, and ask for another bed. Note that children also get reductions if you stay half board (50% for 3–6-year-olds, 30% for 7–10-year-olds.) Gripes are that you have to pre-book one-hour slots at the small gym and sauna, and that the cancellation conditions are extraordinarily punitive.

Tréguier, although not a destination in its own right, is a good stopping-off point, with a central square full of useful all-day brasseries and crêperies, including **Le Martray** (*02 96 92 20 71*) and **Resto Bar les Vieilles Poutres** (*02 96 92 45 73*). On the quays, the **Crêperie la Dinette** (*02 96 92 93 22*) is a decent spot with a courtyard children's play area.

*Port de Plaisance, Tréguier, 15km (9 miles) east of Lannion on D786, 02 96 92 97 00, **www.aiguemarine.fr**. 48 rooms. Doubles € 72–126 (£ 48–85), family room for four € 101–126 (£ 66–85). Cot € 8 (£ 5.30), extra bed € 19 (£ 13). Amenities: restaurant, bar, lounge, outdoor pool, gym, sauna, Jacuzzi, safe, concierge. In room: Sat TV, telephone, fridge (some).*

Château de Kermezen ★ A gorgeous little château at the end of a sweeping driveway lined by oaks, surrounded by splendid grounds, Kermezen is owned by a real-life count and countess yet is remarkably laidback and unstuffy – the genial hosts embrace families with open arms, dispensing coffee or homemade cider to parents and providing them with all sorts of practical facilities – highchairs, changing mats, bottle warmers and even a babysitting service. Of the five spacious and very flowery B&B rooms – think Louis Seize meets Laura Ashley, with the requisite period furniture – one is a twin with a cosy sleeping alcove that might appeal to older children, two are triples with single beds on a separate mezzanine. Downstairs is a homely, beamed dining room with a large table around which guests congregate for copious Continental breakfasts and a comfy *salon* in which to relax and admire the family portraits. You're just a five-minute drive from the coast, and there's plenty else to do nearby, including cycling and riding. There's also table tennis on site for guests' use.

*Pommerit-Jaudy, 20km (12 miles) north of Guingamp on D8, 02 96 91 35 75, **www.chateaux-france.com**. 5 rooms. Double € 85–99 (£ 57–66), family room for three € 105 (£ 70). Cot free. Amenities: lounge, table tennis, babysitting service, babychanging, highchairs, bottlewarmers. In room: hairdryer (in one).*

INEXPENSIVE

Camping Claire Fontaine

VALUE 'Camping' is somewhat of a misnomer for this pretty site based around a cute old Breton farmhouse a five-minute walk from Perros-Guirec's toddler-friendly beaches (p. 114) – as well as sites for tents and caravans, it has some quite pretty (given the rock bottom prices) double and triple rooms with access to self-catering kitchens, a gîte for four, comfy bungalows for up to six, and caravans, all well spaced out over its leafy three hectare (seven acre) site. It lacks the bells-and-whistles facilities of some of the big-hitting four-star campsites in the area, but given Perros-Guirec's bursting-full programme of family activities, you probably won't miss them – and will probably appreciate the relative calm (and much lower prices) here. In any case, the place does have basics such as a children's play area, table tennis, sheltered picnic spots, a common room with TV, a small grocery, a laundrette and a baby-changing room. It's the kind of place where you'll meet more French than foreign guests, which is no bad thing at all.

*Toul ar Lan, Perros-Guirec, 📞 02 96 23 03 55, **http://perso.orange.fr/claire-fontaine**. Double room € 38 (£ 25), triple € 42 (£ 28) a night; caravan for four € 230–320 (£ 155–216) per week, gîte for four € 350–450 (£ 236–304) per week, bungalow for six € 400–600 (£ 266–405) per week, tent pitch € 15–17 (£ 10–10.70) a night including 1st adult, subsequent adults € 6–8 (£ 4–6), under-7s € 3.50–4 (£ 2.35–2.65). Amenities: play area, games, TV lounge, shop, laundrette, baby-changing.*

Auberge de Jeunesse Les Korrigans ★ This remarkable youth hostel in a handsome blue-shuttered stone building in the centre of Lannion, 10 minutes inland and next to the train station, is named after the mischievous fairies said to populate the area (p. 3). Its 12 rooms, all with two brightly painted bunkbeds and a table and chairs, bear magical names such as Mare aux Fées ('Fairies' Pond') and Vent des Songes ('Wind of Dreams') and have doors adorned with little fairy paintings. But they are practical too – all have private showers and toilets. Linen and Continental breakfast are included in the rates, and low-priced meals and picnics are available, though there's also a shared kitchen for making your own meals. Other communal facilities include an attractive, buzzy 'tavern' with Internet access, a pool table and occasional events, such as concerts and exhibitions. Guests can hire mountain bikes, and coastal hiking packages are offered.

*6 rue du 73eme territorial, Lannion, 📞 02 96 37 91 28, **www.fuaj.org**. 12 rooms. From € 15.70 (£ 10.50) per person. Amenities: garden, self-catering kitchen, bar, games, Internet access, laundrette, linen hire, cycle hire, cycle store, luggage store.*

FAMILY-FRIENDLY DINING

Côte d'Emeraude

EXPENSIVE

Au Biniou ★★ With its minimalist grey-painted facade and its clean, pared-down dining room, this stylish fish restaurant is a minute's walk from the seafront of the family resort of Le Val-André (p. 113) and doesn't look an obvious choice for those with children. But it was a surprise hit of our most recent trip, eliciting the cry 'That was a lovely dinner' from my three-year-old – high praise indeed! The under-10s menu (€ 12 (£ 8)) that tickled his tastebuds wasn't cheap or wide-ranging, but both dishes on offer – roast pollack with creamy rice, and roast chicken breast with tagliatelle – are perfectly cooked and appealingly presented. Desserts of chocolate mousse and ice cream are topnotch, too. Staff are unusually attentive to safety issues, moving knives and glasses away from grabbing little fingers, for instance; service itself is a little cool, but then you can't ask for everything.

As for the adult food, starters include *moules marinières* from the bay of Hillion just down the road, while main courses differ according to the daily catch but might include utterly delicious John Dory with coriander and chive noodles and *nuoc-mam* (Vietnamese fish sauce) butter; seabass with steamed garden vegetables, tomato conserve and a beetroot *jus*; or a sumptuous shellfish platter. If you don't fancy fish, there's a good choice of meats, including roast pigeon with orange and ginger. Desserts are too tempting to pass up on – think old-fashioned (very thick) *crème brûlée* with Bourban vanilla, or pear crumble with caramel sauce and *crème fraîche*. Unsurprisingly, this is a favourite with locals, so book ahead, especially at weekends. On the other hand, it's not at all touristy, so don't expect English-language menus or English-speaking staff.

121 rue Clemenceau, Le Val-André, 12km (7.5 miles) north of Lamballe on D786, ☏ 02 96 72 24 35. Main courses € 19.50–29.50 (£ 13–19). Highchair and booster.

MODERATE

La Stalla Come early evening to this welcoming seafront Italian and you may walk in on the chef still eating with his own children, which inspires confidence from the start. It would be a mistake to come expecting the best Italian food of your life, but you will get no-nonsense, good-value renditions of the basics in an unpretentious decor of wood and red-checked tablecloths, plus smiling service. There is a *menu bambino* for under-12s (€ 6.80 (£ 4.60)), with ham and cheese pizza, spaghetti bolognaise, ham and pasta, or nuggets and chips, followed by ice cream or chocolate mousse and accompanied by a soft drink, but, as in most Italians, there's plenty on the main menu to appeal to junior palates, including a huge selection of pizzas (available to take-away), a small selection of pasta dishes and substantial omelettes. Parents might be tempted by the *moules-frites*, the steak or veal with chips, pasta, green salad or green beans, or the hearty salads.

48 rue du Port, Erquy, 20km (12 miles) northeast of Lamballe on D786, ☏ 02 96 72 01 03. Main courses € 6.10–13.60 (£ 4.10–9.15). Highchair.

INEXPENSIVE

Crêperie Chez Marie ★★ Decorated with an eye for the quirky, with goblins, witches, frogs and pigs among its inhabitants, and walls covered with outsized flower frescoes, this is a child-pleasing seaside crêperie and snack bar that will also appeal to parents because of its handy

Erquy Harbour

all-day service, making it a good option for an early dinner – especially given its wide-ranging menu. As well as galettes (from ham, egg and cheese combos to more adult fare such as chitterling sausage from Guémené-sur-Scorff in the Morbihan) and crêpes (including a wonderful blueberry and a parent-pleasing cider jelly), there's steak and chips, fish or cheese tartlets, feta and olive salads, omelettes, and the town's mussels (June onwards). Under-12s get a menu (€ 6 (£ 4)) of butter, cheese or ham galette or a slice of ham with potatoes, a sugar or honey crêpe or sorbet, and a *sirop à l'eau* (p. 254). Even adults should check out the ice cream menu, which includes oddities such as violet or buckwheat. Note that since everything is freshly prepared to order, there might be a bit of a wait, especially at busy times, although the friendly staff do try to prioritise those with little ones. On warmer days, take advantage of the front terrace safely set on a pedestrianised street.

Les Mielles, St Cast-le-Guildo, 25km (16 miles) northwest of Dinan on D19, ☎ 02 96 41 98 66. Open Feb–Oct Sat to Wed 11am–9.30pm (daily in school hols). Main courses € 5–9 (£ 3.30–6).

Baie de St-Brieuc

MODERATE–EXPENSIVE

Via Costa ★★ FIND The beach itself might be nothing out of the ordinary, but this camp Brazilian-themed 'fashion lounge' down by the sands provides a blast of originality in a sea of crêperies and seafood joints. Inside, it's all fairy lights, funky lightshades and exotic flowers; outside there's a central circular bar surrounded by slinky plastic chairs in hot pink and cool blue – an excellent place for moonlit frozen margaritas to a cheesy, jazzy soundtrack if you've got a sitter. Food-wise, the place runs the gamut from pizzas – including a very good *bambino* pizza with tomato, oregano, mozzarella and ham, supposed to be for an under-8 but big enough for two of them, and the speciality 'Brazilian' with mozzarella, chocolate and banana (yes, you did read that right) – to tandoori chicken brochettes with mango chutney; pollack in a sesame crust with lemon butter and cherry tomatoes; and Thai salad with pork and prawns, let down by overcooked meat but with a wonderful flavour combination of ginger, fresh mint and Asian spices. The children's menu itself (€ 7 (£ 4.70)) is surprisingly basic, so stick to pizza and save room for an outlandish dessert – try crêpe 'tagliatelle' with red fruits, *sirop de menthe* and basil; or dark chocolate *mi-cuit* (a cake left gooeily undercooked inside) with custard and vanilla ice cream.

Even out of season, on a weekday lunch, this crazy place gets very busy – a great recommendation for somewhere off-the-beaten track. Service is surprisingly toddler-friendly given the pouting pretty boys who do it, some of whom speak English, but can be very slow. If you're in a hurry, tapas are served in the bar.

Plage du Moulin, Etables-sur-Mer, 15km (9 miles) north of St-Brieuc on

D786, ☎ 02 96 70 79 57. Main courses € 9–19 (£ 6–13). Open noon–2.30pm and 7–11pm (bar 11am–2am) Mar–Sept and school hols daily, Oct–Feb Fri–Mon. Highchairs and boosters.

MODERATE

La Moana Staff could be warmer at this cosy restaurant one street back from Binic's marina, on a pedestrianised lane, but there's no arguing with the genuine Italian fare, which includes homemade pasta, pizzas (including takeaways) and grown-up dishes such as *osso bucco à la milanaise.* There's no children's menu, and portions can be terrifyingly huge, so consult your server, then pick maybe two or three dishes to share between four – perhaps a Ronde des Dieux ravioli sampler plate, a Dolce Vita pasta sampler plate, and a pizza. This being the seaside, there's a good choice of fish-based pasta dishes, plus *moules-frites* and some interesting seafood-based salads. Beware that some pasta dishes – including the good *cochiglie del mare* – have curry spices in them: again, check with your waiter (the pesto is a good standby if you have fussy children). Everyone will be happy with the dessert menu, which includes strawberries and cream, *fromage blanc* (p. 255), frozen nougat, fruit pizza and – naturally – plenty of ice-cream concoctions. The front room can get smoky; the back one feels a bit cutoff but you get an in-your-face view of the chefs in the semi-open kitchen.

32 rue Maréchal Joffre, Binic, 10km (6 miles) north of St-Brieuc on D786, ☎ 02 96 73 65 89. Main courses € 8.20–15.70 (£ 5.50–10.50). Open Wed–Mon 11.45am–2pm and 6.45pm–midnight (noon–midnight in July and Aug). Highchairs.

INEXPENSIVE

Crêperie des Grèves ★★★ Immensely welcoming, this crêperie occupies the former home and bistro of the owner's great-grandparents. You fight your way in past a bustling front counter, providing locals with takeaway galettes, to reach an appealing dining room with touches of nautical décor – sails, nets, framed old photos and lighthouse paintings. Celtic music plays unobtrusively as you browse the menu of galettes made using mainly local farm produce and organic crêpes, and while your children look at the children's books piled by the hearth, or even wander out to the adjacent seaside play area that you can keep an eye on from the window. Good-value menus include the Tradition, including an organic salad and a *bolée* of cider, and a children's menu (€ 9.50 (£ 6.30)) offering an egg, ham or cheese galette, a sugar/butter or chocolate crêpe, an ice cream or a choc-ice, and a soft drink or *sirop* (p. 254). Children might also like the speciality Terra Neuvas, a galette filled with plump cod. Grown-up highlights include smoked Plémet chitterling sausage, scallops with *julienne* of vegetables, and L'Ouessant, with goats' cheese, blue cheese, Gruyère and salad. Among the dessert crêpes, which come decorated with fresh mint leaves, are honey from the restaurant's own hive and homemade caramel; there are also good handmade ice creams.

23 rue des Grèves, Langueux, 2km (1.25 miles) east of St-Brieuc on D786, ✆ 02 96 72 56 96. Main courses € 1.40–12 (£ 1–8). Open July and Aug Tue–Sat noon–2.30pm, Sun and Mon 7–11pm; rest of year Wed, Thur and Fri noon–2.30pm and Sat and Sun 7–11pm. Highchairs.

Côte du Granit Rose

Tréguier, at the gateway to the Côte du Granit Rose, is a good place for all-day eating options; see p. 137.

MODERATE

Le Ker Bleu This handy option beautifully sited on the least touristy of Perros-Guirec's child-friendly beaches (p. 114) serves galettes, crêpes and drinks all day, plus, at standard restaurant opening times (or all day in July and August), 25 kinds of handmade pizza, pasta dishes, Italian classics such as beef carpaccio and *osso bucco*, fish of the day, seafood platters, and main-course salads containing the likes of scallops and langoustines. The dining room is bright and breezy (and air-conditioned in sweltering weather), but the decked terrace with its view of the Sept Iles bird reserve (p. 122) is the place to be, especially if you want to enjoy one of the excellent ice-cream *coupes*.

17 boulevard Joseph Le Bihan, Perros-Guirec, ✆ 02 96 91 14 69. Main courses € 7–15 (£ 4.60–10). Open July and Aug daily noon–11pm, Sept–Nov and Feb–June Thur–Mon noon–2pm and 7–10pm, Tue noon–2pm.

INEXPENSIVE

Digor Kalon ★ Describing itself as a 'Café Restaurant Tapas', Digor Kalon is in fact impossible to define – as one glance at the multi-coloured façade and equally vivid interior cluttered with bizarre knick-knacks and old furniture confirms. A lively venue for offbeat musical performances, it offers a suitably eclectic range of food, including three tapas plates containing the likes of *pissaladière* (a kind of French pizza with anchovies and onions), dips, *empanadas* (Latin American filled pastries) and naan breads – perfect snack fare if you had a full lunch and just want a bite to eat with a drink in an informal setting. The main menu continues the tapas theme, with plates of *patatas bravas* (fried potato chunks), prawns, squid, or Serrano ham and chorizo sausage. Mussels, served with rice or *patatas*, come in a variety of interesting ways, including cooked with Dremmwel Rousse (an amber Breton beer), and there are also paella or couscous evenings. The children's menu (€ 7 (£ 4.70)) offers ham and chips or mussels and chips, together with a dessert from the main menu – perhaps a dish of *tergoule*. You can sit in the back yard in warm weather, or in any number of little nooks and crannies inside.

89 rue du Maréchal Joffre, Perros-Guirec, ✆ 02 96 49 03 63. Main courses € 7.20–14.70 (£ 4.80–9.80). Open daily 6.30–late.

5 Finistère

FINISTÈRE

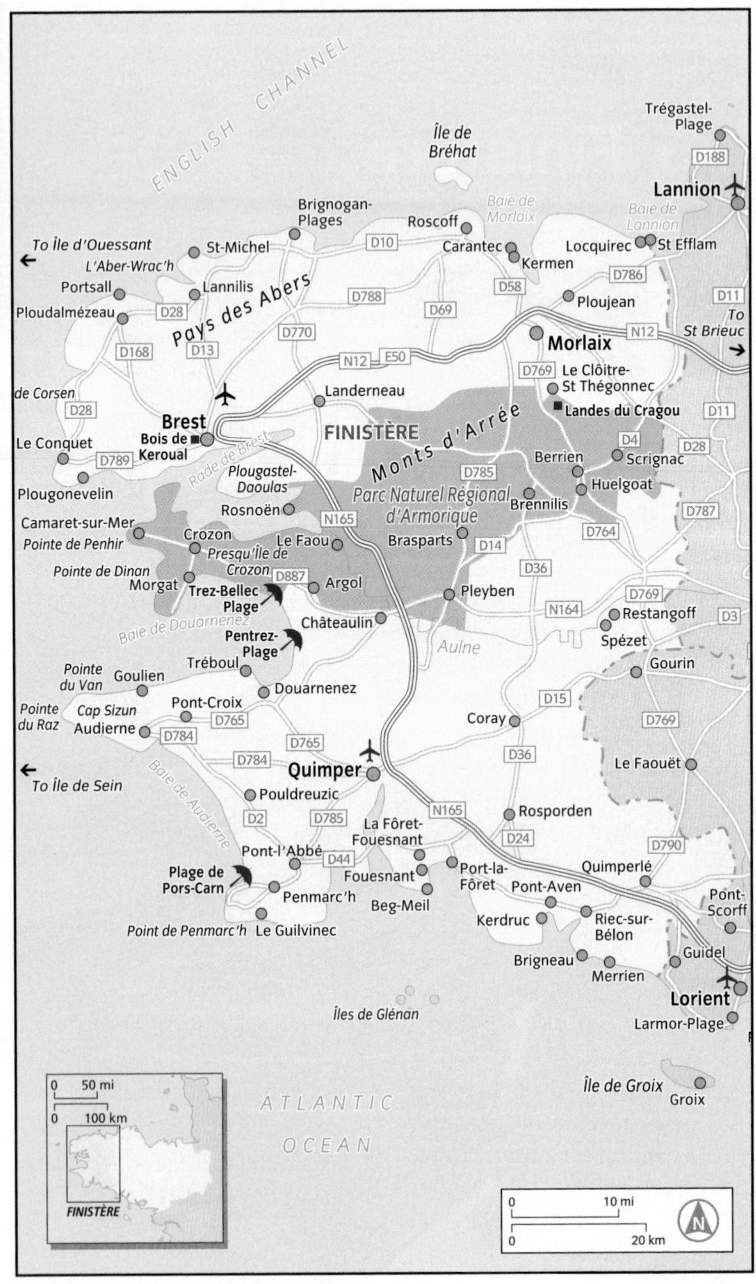
ENGLISH CHANNEL
Île de Bréhat
Trégastel-Plage
D188
Lannion
Baie de Lannion
Baie de Morlaix
Brignogan-Plages
Roscoff
To Île d'Ouessant
St-Michel
D10
Carantec
Locquirec
St Efflam
L'Aber-Wrac'h
Kermen
D786
Portsall
Lannilis
Pays des Abers
D58
D11
D788
Ploujean
To St Brieuc
Ploudalmézeau
D28
D69
D770
N12
Morlaix
D168
D13
N12
E50
D769
Le Cloître-St Thégonnec
de Corsen
Landerneau
Landes du Cragou
D28
Brest
D11
Bois de Keroual
FINISTÈRE
Monts d'Arrée
D4
Le Conquet
D789
Rade de Brest
Berrien
Scrignac
D28
Plougastel-Daoulas
D785
Huelgoat
Plougonevelin
Parc Naturel Régional d'Armorique
Brennilis
Rosnoën
D787
Camaret-sur-Mer
N165
Crozon
Le Faou
Brasparts
D764
Pointe de Penhir
Presqu'Île de Crozon
D14
Pointe de Dinan
D887
D36
Morgat
Trez-Bellec Plage
Argol
Pleyben
D769
N164
Restangoff
D3
Baie de Douarnenez
Châteaulin
Spézet
Pentrez-Plage
Aulne
Gourin
Pointe du Van
Goulien
Tréboul
Douarnenez
D15
Pointe du Raz
Cap Sizun
Pont-Croix
Coray
Audierne
D765
D784
D769
D765
To Île de Sein
D784
Quimper
D36
Le Faouët
Baie de Audierne
Pouldreuzic
Rosporden
D2
D785
N165
La Fôret-Fouesnant
D24
D790
Pont-l'Abbé
D44
Quimperlé
Plage de Pors-Carn
Fouesnant
Port-la-Fôret
Pont-Aven
Pont-Scorff
Penmarc'h
Beg-Meil
Kerdruc
Riec-sur-Bélon
Point de Penmarc'h
Le Guilvinec
Brigneau
Merrien
Guidel
Lorient
Îles de Glénan
Larmor-Plage
Île de Groix
Groix
ATLANTIC OCEAN
0 50 mi
0 100 km
FINISTÈRE
0 10 mi
0 20 km
N

Coast, coast and more coast – for many people, Finistère is synonymous with Breton beach holidays and stunning shorelines (the very name means 'where the earth [*terre*] finishes'). Yet the interior of this *département*, much of which is subsumed by the vast Parc Naturel Régional d'Armorique, merits exploration, especially the Monts d'Arrée, which has much to offer active families as well as those who want to experience some authentic Breton culture. This is a fiercely Breton region where pride in local traditions can be seen in the many *fest noz* (p. 26) and other celebrations, some attracting Celts from around the world.

This is also a region of tall things – soaring lighthouses that count among the world's highest and most powerful, and towering *coiffes*: lacy headgear that you now only see at traditional festivals and other cultural gatherings, or in museums. Lace is not just one of the country's finest products; it inspired some of its famous biscuits, *crêpes dentelles* ('lace crêpes'). Those who don't have a sweet tooth will find plenty to tempt them in the local seafood and seaweed specialities, sold spanking-fresh in markets in towns all over the region, or even direct from the boats, as at Beg-Meil near Bénodet. Something else to look out for at markets are the famous cherries (*cérises griottes*) from the Fouesnant area and strawberries from the peninsula of Plougastel-Daoulas, which even get their own little museum (☎ *02 98 40 21 18*).

But back to that famous coastline: this dips out in a series of sweeping bays and dramatic headlands that are home to some splendid beaches and beautiful unspoilt resorts well geared towards families in terms of hotels, restaurants and facilities, including beach and watersports clubs. The Crozon peninsula, in particular, is absolutely breathtaking.

As for larger towns and cities, Concarneau is a fascinating tuna fishing port with lots of attractions for tourists, and the naval port of Brest has some real gems amidst its sprawling, modern bulk.

ESSENTIALS

Getting There

By Air **Ryanair** (p. 31) runs budget flights between **London-Luton** and **Brest** airport, 10km (6 miles) east of the city, taking 1 hour 10 minutes. **Flybe** (p. 31) flies there from **Exeter** (50 minutes), **Southampton** (65 minutes) and **Birmingham** (1 hour 20 minutes). For up-to-the-minute schedules, see the Brest airport website, *www.airport.cci-brest.fr/en/*.

For those coming from **Paris**, **Air France** (p. 31) flies between Brest from both Charles de Gaulle and Orly airports, taking about 1 hour 15 minutes. Flights from other French cities are also available. Air France also flies to **Quimper** airport (☎ *02 98 94 30 30*, *www.quimper.cci.fr*) from Paris Orly in roughly the same time.

By Ferry If you're bringing your car to France and staying exclusively on the west coast, it's worth coming into **Roscoff** because it's the only port west of St-Malo back over in the Ille-et-Vilaine (p. 57). **Brittany Ferries** (p. 32) sail there from **Plymouth** up to three times a day, with daytime trips lasting from 5 hours 30 minutes to 6 hours and night sailings of 8 hours. You may want to check for crossings on the *Pont-Aven*, the company's luxurious flagship ferry, which as well as standard facilities such as children's play areas and entertainment, has a small swimming pool and a cinema.

The *Pont-Aven* also makes one night-sailing a week between Roscoff and **Cork** in **Ireland**, taking 13 hours. Or you can sail from **Rosslare** with **Irish Ferries** (p. 33) in 17 hours; the ship, the *Normandy*, has play areas for different age groups and children's entertainment in high season, plus a cinema.

By Train **TGVs** from **Paris** (via Rennes in the Ille-et-Vilaine; to **Brest** and to **Quimper** each take about 4 hours 20 minutes; see p. 41 for SNCF details. Some trains to Brest also stop at **Morlaix** and **Landerneau**; some to Quimper also stop at **Quimperlé** and **Rosporden**.

VISITOR INFORMATION

The very good CDT website, ***www.finisteretourism.com***, has a links page (under 'Useful Tips') to all the tourist information offices within the region.

Orientation

The **N165**, which begins down in Nantes in the Loire Atlantique, slices up through the region via Vannes and Lorient in the Morbihan. From just south of **Quimperlé** past **Quimper** and up to **Brest**, it's a fast non-toll motorway.

From Brest running east, the **N12** is also a non-toll motorway taking you round **Morlaix** and into the Côtes d'Armor, to St-Brieuc. Then it goes on to Rennes in the Ille-et-Vilaine and ultimately right on to Paris via the Mayenne and Normandy, though it's a *route nationale* for some of the way.

Off these roads, including north of Brest towards Roscoff, you're confined to *routes départementales* and rural roads and should allow more time for journeys.

Getting Around

Finistère, more than any other area of Brittany, is very difficult to explore by **public transport**, and any holiday will be severely limited if you attempt to use the scant local buses and even scanter train services, though local tourist offices always do their best to provide details.

If you don't bring your own vehicle, there are five **car-hire** firms at **Brest airport** (see ***www.airport.cci-brest.fr/en/***, under

'Services') and four at **Quimper airport** (*www.quimper.cci.fr*). For those coming by train, there's a **Europcar** (*www.europcar.fr*) office outside **Brest train station** and one right by **Quimper train station**. Or for those arriving by ferry at **Roscoff**, the firm also has an office at the Gare Maritime.

Children-Friendly Events & Entertainment

Festival de Cornouaille ★★ This major Breton festival, lasting a week, has been running since the 1920s, and as well as performers as high profile as The Chieftains features a 'village' on the banks of the Odet, with stalls selling Breton crafts, specialities and more, demonstrations of old trades, pony rides and parades, and traditional sailor's songs and *bagadou* (bagpipe bands). It all comes to a head on the Sunday, when there's a 'traditional day' with a procession of more than 3500 people in Breton costume. Those who want to get fully involved can sign up for free workshops, which include ones for children aged 6–12 on themes such as art, storytelling, traditional games, *gouren* (Breton wrestling), singing, the Breton language, crêpe-making and embroidery.

Mid–late July. Quimper, ☎ 02 98 55 53 53, www.festival-cornouaille.com. Adm free; tickets for some concerts, prices vary.

Festival de Cornouaille

Fête des Brodeuses The family highlight of this four-day 'embroiderers' festival' – for which read 'Breton culture' – is the street parade of 200 children in traditional regional costume, looking almost unbearably cute, followed by a dance show involving them all and then group performances. There is also lots of music, including bagpipe bands, Breton dance lessons and competitions, *son-et-lumière* galas and a firework spectacular over Pont-l'Abbé's little lake. Note that the town also has an interesting **Fête de la Langoustine** ('prawn festival') in August, with trips in old fishing boats, a 'Bumpy Boats' children's ride, seafood stalls, sailors' songs, lifesaving demos and fireworks.

Mid-July. Pont-l'Abbé, 15km (9 miles) southwest of Quimper on D785, ☎ 02 98 82 37 99 (tourist office), www.fetedesbrodeuses.com. Free.

Fort de Bertheaume ★★ Just along the coast from Brest, overlooking its glorious Rade (p. 149), this ruined island-fort designed by the famous military architect Vauban and accessible by a footbridge has an open-air theatre hosting dramatic evening *son-et-lumière* sessions (Weds, July and Aug) recounting some of its legends and history, as well as plays, dance, concerts by artists as hip and internationally renowned as Sonic Youth and firework displays against a background of old boats on the water. Children can also see special shows in their own little theatre, while parents enjoy a cider in the nearby traditional crêperie, Le Blé Noir (*02 98 07 57 40*), and there's a *via ferrata* (a sort of rock-climbing course involving both hiking and climbing) and hair-raising ropeswings over the water (see ***www.arbreizh.com***; the firm has another adventure course through the treetops of the Bois de Keroual just outside Brest).

Plougonvelin, 15km (9 miles) west of Brest on D789, 02 98 48 30 18 (tourist office). Open June and Sept Sat, Sun and hols 2–6pm, July and Aug daily 11am–7pm. Adm: island € 2.50 (£ 1.65), tickets for performances vary.

WHAT TO SEE & DO

Children's Top 10 Attractions

1 **Observing** the penguin colony or experiencing a multi-screen helicopter ride over Antarctica at Brest's **Océanopolis**. See p. 160.

2 **Braving** the wind-lashed island of **Ouessant**, with the world's most powerful lighthouse and a unique lighthouse museum. See p. 153.

3 **Exploring** the **Glénan isles** by family canoe or glass-bottomed catamaran. See p. 170.

4 **Following** a nocturnal storytelling and music walk run by the **Musée du Loup**, a wolf museum. See p. 166.

5 **Climbing** the **Phare d'Eckmühl**, France's second-tallest lighthouse. See p. 164.

6 **Discovering** the animals, marshes and forests of the Monts d'Arrée at the **Domaine de Ménez-Meur** animal park. See p. 159.

7 **Seeing** the crazy boulders and legend-shrouded ponds and grottoes of **Huelgoat** and its valley. See p. 156.

8 **Wondering at** the cliffs, headlands and sea caves of the **Crozon peninsula**, with its family resorts. See p. 157.

9 **Staying on** a working honey farm, the **Ferme Apicole de Térenez**, complete with a playground and friendly farm animals. See p. 183.

10 **Taking in** a rock concert or traditional show at the **Fort de Bertheaume**, a ruined island-fort. See p. 147.

Towns & Cities

Brest ★ This naval port isn't an obvious destination – it's huge, sprawling and in parts extraordinarily ugly (it was largely rebuilt after World War II, when the Allied forces bombed the German navy here). Nor is it blessed with any outstanding family eating or sleeping options. But for all that, if you fly into Brest (p. 148), pass by on your way to the ferry terminal at Roscoff (p. 32) or head here for the wonderful **Océanopolis** (p. 160), there are plenty of reasons to spare it a day or two – not least the **Rade de Brest**, its breathtaking natural bay, which you can experience in its full glory on a boat trip from the marina (✆ *02 98 41 46 23*, ***www.azenor.com***; lunch and dinner cruises available). The most dramatic bit is the narrow Goulet ('throat'), through which massive cargo and military ships squeeze into the bay; you get right up close to them.

Otherwise, there's a botanical park, the **Conservatoire National**, in the Stang Ar valley north of Océanopolis, just east of the city, and beside it a good public park with playgrounds and a branch of **Le Blé Noir** crêperie (✆ *02 98 41 84 66*) also found at the nearby Fort de Bertheaume (p. 147). For culture lovers, there's a fine-arts museum, maritime museum and free music concerts beside the Port de Commerce in summer. Brest's commercial docks lie between this port and Océanopolis, impressive but surrounded by an urban wasteland of derelict buildings. On no account cross this by foot, but on your way to or from Océanopolis you won't fail to notice the truly incredible **graffiti** – gangsters, superheroes and more – bearing witness to a vast store of artistic talent among the city's youth.

If you do want to stay in Brest, the **Auberge de Jeunesse** (✆ *02 98 41 90 41*, ***www.aj-iledebatz.org***), a good modern youth hostel in leafy grounds, with rooms for four with sinks, is near Océanopolis and the beaches east of town.

Tourist office: Place de la Liberté, ✆ *02 98 44 24 96,* ***www.brest-metropole-tourisme.fr.***

Brest Graffiti

Concarneau ★★ One of France's biggest working fishing ports, Concarneau has a tourist heart in the form of its **Ville Close** – a little walled island in its river estuary, accessed via a bridge and enclosed by ramparts that you can stroll around. Some might find it all a little too twee, with its gift shops and seafood restaurants (most of which, I hasten to add, have highchairs and children's menus, and many of which serve all through the day), but explore beyond its main street and you'll find some gems, including 'the world's shortest sea cruise' – a two-minute **ferry service** that's run since the 17th century. If you take this rickety little *bac* across to the other shore, you can link up with the GR4 long-distance footpath to get wonderful views back over Concarneau and its bay. This is also the way to the **Le Porzou** city sports complex (*02 98 50 14 50*), with tennis courts, an indoor pool and a six hectare (15 acre) seaside park with children's play areas and picnic areas. Five kilometres from the beach there's also the **Parc Kersimonou** (*02 98 97 81 44*; open July and Aug), with a pirate ship, comedy bikes, bouncy castles and a mini-golf course set amidst lots of sculptures and trees.

Back near the ferry point in the Ville Close is the **Carré des Larrons**, a little open-air amphitheatre hosting free shows all summer. The Ville Close is also the location of the interesting **Musée de la Pêche** (p. 167).

Entrance to Ville Close, Concarneau

*Tourist office: quai d'Aiguillon, 02 98 97 01 44, **www.tourisme concarneau.fr**.*

Beaches & Resorts

Anse de Bénodet ★ A gentle bay that comes as no small relief after the harsh Baie d'Audierne (p. 151), this has two gorgeous resorts, Ste-Marine and Bénodet, that face each other across the **Odet estuary**; you can explore the latter's charming creeks aboard little cruisers (*0825 80 08 01*, ***www.vedettes-odet.com***; see also p. 170). Bounded to the west by a superb beach leading from Ile-Tudy, **Ste-Marine** consists of a handful of restaurants and cafés nestled around a little port. Nearby, at Combrit, is a botanic garden with a museum of minerals. Across the Pont de Cornouaille with its stunning views, **Bénodet** is much larger, with a bustling marina. As well as its 'seaside museum' with model boats (Musee du Bord de Mer, *02 98 57 00 14*; mid-July–mid-Sept), it has a *petit train touristique* (*02 98 73 37 92*), two lighthouses (one pyramid-shaped) and four beaches – the central **Plage du Trez** has pedaloes, sea canoes and other sporting equipment for hire and two children's clubs in high summer; the little **Plage St-Gilles** is popular with youngsters for its rockpools full of crabs and shrimps. The **Ferme du Letty** (*02 98 57 01 27*), once a Michelin-starred restaurant, is a great place to stock up on Breton caramels (these have won prizes), jams, chutneys and spices.

Rounding the Pointe de Mousterlin, you'll come to **Cap-Coz**, a serene spot with an island atmosphere (it's actually a sandy spit) and pine-fringed beaches.

Bénodet tourist office: 29 avenue de la Mer, 02 98 57 00 14, ***www.benodet.fr****.*

Baie d'Audierne This immense, wild bay south of the Cap Sizun is most famous for the grim autobiography *Le Cheval d'orgueil*, by Pierre Jakez Hélias, about peasant life around **Pouldreuzic** in the early 20th century, when children slept on seaweed-stuffed bedding. Today the town is worth visiting for its shell and seabird museum (p. 159). Further south, the wind- and wave-pounded **Pointe de la Torche** has achieved fame as a location for the World Windsurfing Championships, and is a good spot for funboarding, sand-yachting, surfing and fly-surfing. The lovely crescent-shaped **Plage de Pors-Carn** leading south of the headland can also be good for surfing. Close to here, **Penmarc'h** is the starting point for transatlantic telephone cables linking it with Rhode Island and New York in the USA and Land's End in the UK (a distance of 6321km), and with Sesimbra in Portugal (1600km). It has France's second-tallest lighthouse, which you can climb if you've got the stamina (see p. 164), and a seaside museum.

Penmarc'h tourist office: place du Maréchal Davout, 02 98 58 81 44, ***www.penmarch.fr****.*

Audierne Bay

Baie de Douarnenez Cutting back into the land south of the Crozon peninsula (p. 157), the bay of Douarnenez is made up of lovely untouristy beaches and countryside rich in legends. The waters themselves are supposed to be the home of the mythical drowned citadel of Ys. On the northern side of the bay, eastwards from Morgat, are huge unspoilt beaches with dunes and areas of pebbles that local families use to build walls to demarcate their 'patch', including the open, tranquil **Plage de l'Aber**, **Trez-Bellec Plage** and **Pentrez-Plage**. The southern side, dominated by the fishing town of **Douarnenez**, is speckled with less accessible sandy beaches. It's best appreciated by walking along the coastal path from **Tréboul**; the **Pointe du Millier** is a viewing post with a squat lighthouse jutting strangely from the façade of its keeper's house. Alternatively, explore the bay on a reconstructed *chaloupe sardinière* (sardine fishing boat), on trips run by the **Centre Nautique** (*02 98 74 13 79*, ***www.centre-nautique-douarnenez.fr***) in Douarnenez or the town's **Port-Musée** (*02 98 92 65 20*, ***www.port-musee.org***). This museum of traditional boats reopened in 2006 with new image and sound installations, displays on fish canning, workshops on navigation and nautical radio operating, and, for children aged 6–12, guided tours followed by workshops, including boat decoration and marine communication.

Fish-lovers shouldn't miss **Penn Sardin** (7 rue Le Breton, *02 98 92 70 83*), a shop stocking more than 100 types of canned sardines, beautifully packaged.

Douarnenez tourist office: 2 rue du Dr Mével, 02 98 92 13 35, ***www.douarnenez-tourisme.com****.*

Carantec ★ On its own peninsula reaching up the western side of the Rade de Morlaix near the ferry port of Roscoff, this relaxed family resort is reminiscent of Perros-Guirec on the Côte du Granit Rose (p. 115) but smaller and more chic. Like Perros-Guirec, it erupts with children's activities in summer, including beach clubs (one dedicated to sailing tuition) and the **Place aux Mômes** free festival of electropop concerts, dance, a circus and more. From 2006 visitors have also been able to take **guided tours of the Baie de Morlaix by sea canoe** (ages 14 and up), in addition to cruiser trips around the bay with its bird reserve (home to puffins, terns and others) and the Ile-de-Batz with its untouristy beaches, lighthouses and residential sailing centre. Also, since 2006 are two-hour trips out to the bay's sea fort and former prison, the **Château du Taureau** (Apr–Oct).

Among the six beaches are the **Plage de Kélenn** with its sailing centre, play area, volleyball pitch, picnic site and café terraces – plus pretty blue-and-white and red-and-white striped bathing huts in high season. You can also walk out, at low tide, to the fine sand beaches and protected creeks of the **Ile Callot**, and take drawing and painting lessons there in the Easter and summer holidays, as well as elsewhere in town (for ages 12 and up, but there are also courses for 6–11-year-olds). If that's not enough, there's a small **maritime museum** (*02 98 67 01 46*) and a nature trail for over-6s through the **Parc Claude-Goude** – it's free from the tourist office, which can provide information on everything mentioned above.

*10km (6 miles) northwest of Morlaix on D73. Tourist office: 4 rue Pasteur, 02 98 67 00 43, **www.ville-carantec.com**.*

Ile d'Ouessant ★ The wind-lashed, treeless island of Ouessant in the Atlantic Ocean, 20km (12 miles) from the French coast and shaped a bit like a crab's claw, doesn't sound like the most enticing place. Yet with its wild landscapes, its amazing light and its romantic 'end-of-the-world' atmosphere – countless ships have been wrecked on the rocks surrounding it, despite its five soaring lighthouses (including the Phare du Créac'h, the world's most powerful; p. 164) – it's well worth the 75 minute boat trip from Le Conquet (you can also make a longer trip from Brest, or fly from there in 15 minutes). The focus of interest is its lighthouse museum (p. 168), but there's also an *écomusée*, the **Maisons du Niou-Huella** (*02 98 48 86 37*), in two traditional houses. Here you can learn about the life of Ouessant's womenfolk (the men were more or less constantly at sea, from which they often failed to return) through displays of

The Black Sheep of the Family

Ouessant 's famous black dwarf sheep are Europe's smallest breed and perhaps the world's smallest natural breed, reaching just 45–50cm (18–20 inches) at the shoulder. Until the early 20th century they were only seen on Ouessant itself, providing islanders with wool, but now you can see them in farm parks around France – you may even spot rare white or caramel-coloured ('red') ones.

Ouessants are descended from two breeds: the Morbihan, from southern Brittany, and the Vendéen from further south. The first was small and black, brown or white; the latter larger, purely black and endowed with quite spectacular horns – Ouessant rams still have impressive curly horns. The two lines merged, but the new breed nearly died out in the mid-1900s due to the barrenness of the island (which contributed to their small size). They were saved from extinction by rich locals, who let them graze on their land. Today, ironically, they are nicknamed *tondeuses ecologiques* ('eco-lawnmowers') because they can subsist on small plots and are resistant to many modern sheep diseases.

costumes, tools and furniture made from wood from shipwrecks. There's also the **Centre d'Etude du Milieu de l'Ile d'Ouessant** (*02 98 48 82 65*), an ornithological centre running nature outings – the islands are a bird reserve. Ouessant is also well known for its dwarf black sheep (p. 153), but there are not many left (don't worry – you can see them in animal parks across Brittany). You might also be lucky and spot seals off the northern coast. You can explore the island on foot, by bike, on horseback and by pony and trap. The only settlement of any size is **Lampaul**, which is your best bet for hiring bikes, sleeping (p. 180) and eating, although there are few very interesting lunch or dinner options on the island – try the windswept-looking **Crêperie Ty à Dreuz** (*02 98 48 83 01*) with its marine-inspired decor and lovingly prepared galettes and crêpes, filled with the likes of Camaret sea trout or local scallops.

Fun at Concarneau

Ouessant is surrounded by some even smaller islands; the largest is **Molène**, to which you can also sail from the mainland. Its main sight is the **Musée du Drummond Castle** (*02 98 07 38 41*), which tells of the shipwreck of an English cruise liner en route from South Africa in 1886. The British flag you can see was presented to the island by the Queen in 1996 in thanks for the islanders' work in recovering and burying the bodies. **La Maison de l'Environnement Insulaire** (*02 98 07 38 92*) is a little natural heritage museum that organises guided visits and sea trips with fishermen, during which you might see seals and dolphins.

*Tourist office: place de l'Eglise, Lampaul, 02 98 48 85 83, **www.ot-ouessant.fr**. Boats: 02 98 80 80 80, **www.pennarbed.fr**. Flights: 02 98 84 64 87, **www.finistair.fr**.*

Pays des Abers The stretch of coast northwest of Brest is named after the river estuaries that cut into the jagged shore, forming deep, narrow inlets. In many ways it's a rather inhospitable place, home to mighty lighthouses that warn ships away from the rocks, or try to – they weren't successful in preventing the sinking of the *Amoco Cadiz* oil tanker off Portsall in 1978, causing an ecological disaster of epic proportions. Yet for all that, it has some splendid wide beaches popular with sand-yachters, especially around surprisingly untouristy little **Brignogan-Plages** with its lovely hotel (p. 179) and restaurant (p. 190) and north of **Plouguerneau**. This latter has a unique **Musée des Goémoniers** (📞 *02 98 37 132 35*) or 'seaweed-gatherers' museum devoted to the algae trade prevalent along this coast, with old tools, films and seaweed-cookery demonstrations. On the coast near St Michel is the medieval necropolis of **Iliz-Koz** (p. 163), while over the **L'Aber-Wrac'h** ('Fairy's Estuary') between Plouguerneau and Lannilis is a partially destroyed bridge, the Pont Krac'h (covered at high tide), said to have been built by the Devil in the course of one night but more likely constructed by mere mortals in the Iron Age and reworked in the Middle Ages. **Les Amis de Jeudi-Dimanche** (📞 *02 98 04 90 92*, ***www.bel-espoir.com***) runs boat trips in L'Aber-Wrac'h, plus prawn fishing and other excursions.

Further south, past Aber Ildut, at Plouarzel, there are guided tours of the 37m (120 ft) **Phare de Trézien** (📞 *02 98 99 69 46*), an automated lighthouse with amazing views of the Ile d'Ouessant (p. 153) from the top of its 182 steps. Next you'll come to the **Pointe de Corsen**, a headland with a signpost to New York 5080km away – this is apparently the nearest point on the French mainland to North America. There's also a sign to London 430km away. South of it lies the vast, quite wild, curving beach of the **Anse des Blancs Sablons**, a protected site where you might see dolphins leaping (be advised that it has a naturist section).

Tourist office: 1 place de l'Eglise, Lannilis, 📞 *02 98 04 05 43,* ***www.abers-tourisme.com.***

Other Natural Wonders & Spectacular Views

Cap Sizun ★ Squeezed out between the bays of Douarnenez (p. 152) and Audierne (p. 151) like a tongue, this is the French equivalent of Britain's Land's End. The shorter and less touristy of its stunning promontories is the **Pointe du Van**, a good place from which to view the more famous **Pointe du Raz** to the south, from which Celtic Druids may have believed they could depart for the afterlife. To get from one to the other, you cross the **Baie des Trépassés** or 'Bay of the Dead', shrouded in many a legend – among them the story of the drowned city of Ys. This has

Pointe du Raz

some charming caves to explore at low tide. The Pointe du Raz itself can get inundated by visitors – there are nearby paying carparks with a shuttle bus to the headland itself, from which you gain amazing views of the wild waves, the coastline and a pair of iconic lighthouses, plus, in the distance on a clear day, the Ile-de-Sein. A new heritage centre has displays on the natural environment, shops and restaurants.

As well as coastal paths along the northern and southern shores, there are some fine beaches on the mainly rocky Cap, especially in the **Anse de Cabestan** and at **Ste Evette** near **Audierne**. The latter is a fishing port with some huge seafood tanks, **Les Viviers** (1 rue du Môle, ☎ *02 98 70 10 04*), which you can tour even if you don't want to buy anything, and an aquarium (p. 158). At nearby Goulien there's a **bird sanctuary** (☎ *02 98 70 13 53*) where you can see guillemots, fulmars, storm petrels and more, daily from April to August.

*Audierne tourist office: 8 rue Victor Hugo, ☎ 02 98 70 12 20, **www.audierne-tourisme.com/www.pointe-du-raz.com**.*

Huelgoat ★★ Part of the Monts d'Arrée, a sweep of hills that forms one of inland

The Huelgoat Valley

Camaret-sur-Mer

Finistère's main attractions, the valley of Huelgoat is strewn with as many legends (some of them Arthurian) as it is strangely shaped rocks – it seems no one was content with the natural explanation for them (river erosion). The most famous is the **Roche Tremblante** or 'trembling rock', which is huge (about 100 tonnes) but balanced so precariously that even a child can make it move if they touch it in the right spot. Twice as big but unbudgeable is the mushroom-like 'Champignon', and some people claim to make out wild boars' heads in the rocks of the Mare aux Sangliers, where film director Roger Vadim came to shoot in the 1960s, while his then-wife Jane Fonda learnt to make crêpes in the absurdly pretty **Crêperie des Myrtilles** in the centre of Huelgoat. By moonlight visit the Mare aux Fées to see if you can glimpse fairies bathing here, preening themselves with golden combs. And the fit can descend (with the help of a narrow ladder) into the Grotte du Diable or 'Devil's Grotto', supposed to be a gateway to Hell...

All these sights are accessed via the signposted *sentier pittoresque*. More prosaically, you can visit the vestiges of a Gallo-Roman camp later occupied by Julius Caesar's armies, or feed the ducks and swans on Huelgoat's town lake.

Huelgoat tourist office (syndicat d'initiative): place Alphonse-Penven, ☎ 02 98 99 72 32.

Presqu'île de Crozon ★★

This spectacular portion of coast with its awesome headlands and cliffs is one of Brittany's highlights, and with some great family accommodation (p. 182) it makes an excellent base for a seaside holiday. Its main resort is **Morgat**, in a sheltered bay on the south side of the peninsula, with fine sand beaches (hosting children's clubs in summer) and some famous **sea caves** (*grottes marines*) you can visit by guided boat trip (Vedettes Rosmeur, *02 98 27 10 71*), including the 80m (250 ft) long 'cave of the altar' and the funnel-shaped 'devil's chimney'. The Peugeot car family founded this resort in 1884, building the strange white metal villa, Ker Ar Bruck, that you can still see by the sea (it was falsely attributed to Gustav Eiffel), and the clan still holidays here today.

Another scenic spot is **Camaret-sur-Mer** with its natural jetty of pebbles ballooning out into the bay, dotted with old fishing boats and a decapitated chapel. You can take boat trips from here, including dawn and evening sea-fishing excursions (Compagnie Pesquetour, *02 98 27 98 44*). From Camaret it's a short trip to the dramatic **Pointe du Toulinguet** to the north and the **Pointe de Penhir** to the south, with the huge rocks of the Tas de Pois ('pile of peas') speckling the Atlantic. Still further south, the Anse de Dinan is a vast bay from which you can see the **Pointe de Dinan**, dubbed the 'Château' because it resembles a castle with a drawbridge. Nearby is a mineral museum (p. 166).

*Camaret-sur-Mer tourist office: 15 quai Kléber, 02 98 27 93 60, **www.camaret-sur-mer.org**. Crozon tourist office: boulevard de Pralognan, 02 98 27 07 92, **www.crozon.com**.*

Aquaria & Animal Parks

The **Aquarium-Musée** at Roscoff is closed for renovation until 2009/10.

L'Aquashow Set in Audierne, famous for its giant seafood tanks, this smallish aquarium focuses on sealife from around the Breton coast. Its more than 180 species include sharks, giant lobsters, octopuses, hermit crabs and sea urchins, and there's a touchpool where you can stroke starfish as well as the more usual rays, plus a 3D cinema. Rather oddly, however, the place is better known for its seabird and falconry displays hosted in an outdoor arena from April to October, though these do feature cormorants hunting underwater.

Children under 14 get free entry until noon, and if you order a seafood platter in the adjoining crêperie built on stilts over the water, you get free entry to the aquarium (it also serves good Breton omelettes and ice cream). There's a little gift shop too.

Rue du Goyen, Audierne, 30km (19 miles) west of Quimper on D784,

L'Aquashow

☎ 02 98 70 03 03, ***www.aquarium.fr****. Open Apr–Sept daily 10am–7pm, Oct Sun–Thur 2–7pm, Nov–Mar school hols daily 2–7pm. Adm: Apr–Oct adults € 11.50 (£ 7.75), children 4–14 € 8.50 (£ 5.75), family (2+3) € 41.50 (£ 28); Nov–Mar adults € 7 (£ 4.70), children 4–14 € 5 (£ 3.35).*

Domaine de Ménez-Meur
★★★ The 520 hectare (1300 acre) 'Big Mountain' park, set up by a gold prospector who made a fortune in America to preserve the local countryside and animal species, forms the heart of the Monts d'Arrée and the **Parc Régional Naturel d'Armorique** (p. 162) as a whole. Visitors have a choice of circuits, the most obvious one for children being the 3.3km 'animal circuit' around a renovated farm, with spacious enclosures housing wild animals such as wolves, boar and deer, and mainly Breton endangered farm breeds such as Armorican and piebald Breton cows and Ouessant dwarf black sheep (p. 153). There are also some aurochs – an ox-like species that became extinct in the Bronze Age but has been reproduced (albeit incompletely) by breeding domestic cattle strains. In July and August you can join 2-hour guided tours of this circuit on Mondays, Thursdays, Fridays and Sundays (or 3–4 hour guided tours of the Monts d'Arrée).

Then there's a 2.5km path through the forest, where there are several observation hides with information boards on the animal and plantlife here. If you're feeling very energetic, the 8.5km 'countryside circuit' takes you through the farm and the forest then out over heaths, marshes and peat bogs dotted with viewing points over the Monts d'Arrée and the Rade de Brest (p. 149). If you're not feeling energetic, on Tuesday and Wednesday afternoons in high summer you can see some of the Domaine by pony-and-trap.

Children are well catered for, with regular nature-related activities (including a 'wolf week' with the Musée du Loup; p. 166) and good play equipment, and there are also interactive temporary exhibitions and a permanent one on the Parc Régional Naturel d'Armorique and France's regional natural parks in general. Note that this is a lovely place for a picnic; a number of shady areas are set aside.

Near Hanvec, 25km (16 miles) south-east of Brest off D18, ☎ 02 98 68 81 71, ***www.pnr-armorique.fr****. Open Mar, Apr, Oct and Nov Wed, Sun, public and school hols 1–5.30pm, May, June and Sept daily 10am–6pm, July and Aug daily 10am–7pm, Dec, Jan and Feb school hols except public hols (call to check) 1–5pm. Adm free.*

Maison de l'Amiral This seaside museum of shells and seabirds is old-fashioned and all the more charming for that. Its 2500 shells of all shapes and sizes from around the world include a giant clam nearly 1m long. There are exotic items here, but also lots of shells collected on the beaches of Brittany. The stuffed bird collection is smaller, but among the 200 specimens are rarities such as a great bittern and grey heron. French-language display boards and a booklet give you the lowdown. Dotted throughout the room are also minerals, fossils and corals, plus some impressive sharks' heads, and you can watch a loop of short videos on themes such as fishing, seaweed gathering, the treatment of birds damaged by oil slicks, and Tahitian black pearls. Right on the shore of the Baie d'Audierne – which can be bleak but is alive with birdlife – the museum has a playground, picnic tables and views of the famous Pointe du Raz (p. 155).

*Penhors, 20km (12 miles) west of Quimper on D40, ☎ 02 98 51 52 52, **www.maison-de-l-amiral.com**. Open Tue–Sat 10.30am–6pm. Adm: adult € 4.85 (£ 3.25), children 5–15 € 2.50 (£ 1.65).*

Le Marinarium This working research lab in the world's oldest marine biology station, dating back to 1859 (when it was a breeding centre) and now part of France's natural history museum, allows fans of the deep a close-up view of science in action. Many important discoveries have taken place in this slightly dilapidated building, as the displays point out. Permanent exhibitions focus on the biodiversity of the oceans; the role of plankton; tides and the coast; ecology; the Glénan islands (p. 172); and the laboratory's history and current scientific work. Temporary exhibitions look at the latest in marine biotechnology, and there's also an aquarium including a large tank with local fish such as pollack and sea bream and a demonstration pool used during guided tours. Children love the microscopes they can peer down, the touching pools to forage in and the fishing excursions on the beach at low tide – the latter being great value at € 3 (£ 2) (€ 1.50 (£ 1) for children).

*Place de la Croix, Concarneau, ☎ 02 98 50 81 64, **www.mnhn.fr**. Open daily Apr–June and Sept 10am–noon and 2–6pm, July and Aug daily 10am–7pm, Oct–Dec, Feb and Mar 2–6pm. Adm: adults € 5 (£ 3.35), children 6–12 € 3 (£ 2) .*

Océanopolis ★★★ Amid Brittany's host of great aquaria, Brest's sealife centre is in a league of its own. Away from the centre past the sprawling docks, it looks a bit like a space station, and its size may daunt you. Allow a full day to visit it at leisure; there are lots of facilities, from restaurants to sandwich counters. Exhibitions are spaced over three 'pavilions'; the most awesome is the Polaire, where you can observe a colony of penguins swimming through vast tanks and watch the multiscreen film *Antarctica*, which takes you on a tummy tickling helicopter flight over the icy continent – worth the entry fee alone.

As well as being large, each animal's habitat is beautifully designed and lit, making the whole place a true pleasure to visit. As you continue up past the sea lions in the Polaire pavilion, for instance, you'll find little 'caves' where you can sit and

Sharks at Océanopolis

watch films (in French only, as with most of the display boards), plus little crevasses in the fake ice-walls where you can watch snatches of footage of underwater life. Each area also has its own flashy multimedia space where you can deepen your knowledge of what you have just ogled should you so desire. The temporary exhibitions, on themes such as mermaids or sea monsters, are always colourful and conceived very much with young visitors in mind.

It's hard to pick highlights, but the two daily seal shows, designed not to entertain but to train the animals to accept examinations by vets, should be on your list, as well as a ride in the glass lift down the side of the shark tank, giving you 'submarine vision'. Above all, don't rush your visit, or you'll miss the host of interactive gizmos dotted throughout, such as the periscope viewers and the quotes from *20,000 Leagues under the Sea* painted on the walls. The Temperate Zone is the place to head if your children love hands-on displays that can teach them about the tides, currents and so on, or getting up-close and personal with marine life in the touching pools. Little ones will also love the indoor model boats they can steer, and the great nautically themed outside play area, and everyone will find something pleasing in the huge gift shop or separate bookshop.

INSIDER TIP

At busy periods, save time by pre-buying Océanopolis tickets at the Fnac bookshop or local Géant, Carrefour, Auchan or Leclerc supermarkets, so you can pass through the barriers without having to queue.

Port de Plaisance du Moulin Blanc, Brest, ☎ 02 98 34 40 40, www.oceanopolis.com. Open early Apr–early Sept daily 9am–6pm, rest of year Tue–Sun 10am–5pm (plus Mon 10am–6pm public and school hols); last adm 1 hour before closing. Adm: adults € 15.40 (£ 10.40), children 4–17 € 10.80 (£ 7.30), family (2+3) € 58 (£ 39).

Nature Reserves, Parks & Gardens

Jardins de Suscinio ★ If you're passing through Morlaix with its dramatic 19th century viaduct and its drawbridge through which Mary Queen of Scots passed as a girl, make time for a detour to this three hectare (7.5 acre) botanical garden set around a 16th century turreted manor. Its 1100-plus species are divided into imaginative areas such as the lush 'Valley of Lost Worlds'; the 'Corsaire's Garden', where famous pirate Charles Croisic used to walk (he owned the manor); the 'Garden of the Round Table' with its ring of lime trees; and a terraced kitchen garden. It's a great place to just amble, discovering secret corners, but children will want to make for their very own area, the 'Village des Enfants', where they'll find rush cabins, a ropebridge and a delightful treehouse (the gardens have received awards for their remarkable trees). There's also an aviary and a small animal enclosure. As for the manor – it hosts varied temporary exhibitions, and has a good little shop selling plants, books, postcards and more.

Château de Suscinio, Ploujean, 2km (1.25 miles) north of Morlaix on D46, ☎ 02 98 72 05 86. Open daily Apr and May 2–6pm, June–Sept 10am–6pm, Oct–Mar 2–7pm. Adm: adults € 4.50 (£ 3), children € 2.50 (£ 1.65).

Passport to Breton Nature & Culture

One of 43 Regional Natural Parks in France, designated such to protect their fragile ecosystems and rich cultural heritage, the **Parc Régional Naturel d'Armorique ★★★** (***www.pnr-armorique.fr***) covers a hefty 172,000 hectares (around 660 square miles), of which 60,000 (around 230 square miles) are part of the ocean. The area is split across the islands of Ouessant and Molène (p. 154) and Sein (off the Pointe du Raz), the Crozon peninsula (p. 157), the Aulne estuary, and the Monts d'Arrée (p. 180), and comprises a huge range of attractions that could fill a book of their own. When you visit one attraction within this park, you'll be given a **Passeport Finistére** that qualifies you for reduced ticket prices at all the others.

Venues include the **Domaine de Ménez-Meur** (p. 159), **Musée du Loup** (p. 166), **Musée des Phares et Balises** (p. 168), **Maisons du Niou-Huella** (p. 153), **Centre d'Etudes du Milieu de l'Ile d'Ouessant** (p. 154) and **Musée des Vieux Métiers Vivants** (p. 169). A slightly smaller-scale museum is the **Maison de la Faune Sauvage et de la Chasse** (☎ *02 98 78 25 00*) in the old station at Scrignac, with more than 70 stuffed local mammals and birds, including boars, badgers, hares and woodcocks, plus videos and discovery walks. Those interested in traditional Breton games and sports, meanwhile, especially *gouren* (a form of wrestling once practised by local warriors and nobles, then by peasants), should go on a course at **Ti-ar-Gouren** (☎ *02 98 99 03 80*), the 'Maison de la Lutte et des Sports Bretons', at nearby Berrien.

Historic Buildings & Monuments

Iliz-Koz A veritable medieval necropolis, 'The Old Church' consists of the substantial vestiges of the parish church of Tremenac'h, which – together with its village on Finistère's north coast – became buried by rising sands in the early 18th century and lay forgotten until the 1960s, when it was uncovered by building work. A signposted circuit takes you to the churchyard, where you can see more than 100 extraordinary, elaborately carved tombs of local nobles, cavaliers, merchants, priests and sailors – it's fun to spot the likes of swords and scissors on the stonework. You can also see the remains of the nobles' chapel, the ossuary, a medieval alleyway and, in a tiny museum, 13th–15th century murals from the church's north wall. It's all the more spooky when you know that the rest of the village is still under the surrounding dunes.

St Michel, 30km (19 miles) north of Brest off D10, ☎ 02 98 37 13 35. Open mid June–mid Sept Tue–Sun 2–6pm, rest of year Sun and public hols. Adm: € 2 (£ 1.35).

The Top Museums

Haliotika ★ 'Grandad, tell me about fishing' ran the tagline for one exhibition at this 'seafishing discovery centre' in France's third-largest fishing port, and indeed, there's a real feeling of history being handed down through the generations here – you can even meet and chat to fishermen about their work. Some of the retired ones began work at the tender age of 14, or went as far as the Irish Sea, hunting Norway lobsters, and their stories are fascinating.

Centre de Decouverte Maritime and Phare d'Eckmühl

Phare Out: Brittany's Lighthouses

With its vicious coastline, Brittany is dotted with some of the world's most majestic lighthouses, among them the **Phare de l'Ile Vierge** in the Pays des Abers (p. 154). Constructed between 1897 and 1902 and attaining a height of 82.5m (270 ft), this is Europe's tallest lighthouse, and the world's tallest stone lighthouse. Still standing next to it, the island's previous lighthouse looks comically small. You can't visit it, but from parts of the coast north of Plouguerneau you can watch its light ease the passage from the Atlantic Ocean into the Channel every five seconds, carrying a distance of 52km. The horn of the smaller lighthouse, which now houses the lighthouse-keepers (it's one of only five lighthouses in France to still have keepers), emits a 1200-watt, three-second sound every minute.

Built in 1859–63, the striped **Phare du Créac'h** at the northwest tip of the shipwreck-plagued island of Ouessant 20km from the French coast (p. 153) may not reach the heights of the Ile Vierge, at 55m (180 ft), but its scope of 63km makes it the world's most powerful. To ensure safe passage into the Channel, though, it has also had a variety of sirens, including an underwater one. A system of lights at its summit stops migrating birds crashing into it. You can't go inside, but you can visit the **Musée des Phares et Balises** (p. 168) in its old electrical station.

As for the second-tallest lighthouse, that's the **Phare d'Eckmühl** built at Penmarc'h at the southern end of the Baie d'Audierne in 1897. You can climb this *phare*, rising to 65m (213 ft, with 307 steps) and with a range of 30km (☎ *02 98 58 60 19*; Apr–Sept daily if weather allows). Beside it, the old lighthouse now contains the **Centre de Découverte Maritime** (☎ *02 98 58 72 87*), with changing displays in the old lighthouse-keeper's quarters on maritime themes such as the invention of seabathing, plus a little museum on prehistoric Finistère and a gallery of contemporary local art. At the port nearby is *Papa Poydenot*, a restored 1901 lifeboat with oars.

Outside Finistère, Brittany's third-highest lighthouse, the 58m (190 ft) **Phare des Roches-Douves** off the Sillon de Talbert (p. 117) on the Côtes d'Armor, is the furthest lighthouse in Europe from a coast (it's more than 40km into the sea, towards Guernsey). Built in 1867–69 but reconstructed after being destroyed in World War II, it was manned until as recently as 2000, with one keeper spending 20 years there.

Visitors also learn about fishing techniques, identifying different species, life at the port, recognising the various types of boat, and the challenges for fishing in the modern world. Children 7–12 can take part in 90 minute workshops (€ 5 (£ 3.35)) during which they get to know local species and fishing techniques, with the opportunity to touch, cook and taste the fish. You can also go on fishing walks along the shore (adults € 5 (£ 3.35), children € 3 (£ 2)), learning to catch fish by hand; and on two-hour or day-long trips on a fishing boat (ages 13 and up; € 30 (£ 20) a day; 48 hour advance booking).

After your visit, relax on the terrace with its prime views of the colourful fishing fleet returning with the day's catch from about 4pm. In the week the centre also runs 30 minute guided tours (French or English) of the raucous town fish auctions (*criée*), and there are € 1 (£ 0.70) English audiotours of it. Note, too, that the town has various sea festivals and free open-air festivals in summer.

Le Guilvinec, 25km (16 miles) southwest of Quimper on D57, ☎ 02 98 58 28 38, www.leguilvinec.com. Open early Apr–June, Sept–early Oct and school hols Mon–Fri 2.30–7pm and Sun 3–6.30pm, July and Aug Mon–Fri 10.30am–12.30pm and 2.30–7pm, Sat and Sun 3–6.30pm. Adm: adults € 4.90 (£ 3.30), children 4–16 € 3.70 (£ 2.50), family ticket € 13.50 (£ 9.10); museum and guided tour of criée: adults € 6.30 (£ 4.25), children 4–16 € 2.80 (£ 1.90), family € 17.30 (£ 11.65).

Maison des Johnnies et de l'Oignon Rosé This eccentric museum about an eccentric trade tells about the Roscoff onion-sellers who, in the 19th century, began to cross the Channel every August to ply their wares in Britain – hence the British stereotype of a Frenchman with a string of onions around his neck or the handlebars of his bike. You'll be astonished to discover that about 15 'Johnnies' (as they're called) carry on the profession today – the pink Roscoff onion is in demand for both its flavour and its nutritional benefits – and that boys as young as 14 used to set out for Britain.

A Johnny's bike in Roscoff

Housed in a restored farm, once home to a family of Johnnies, the museum is accessible only by one-hour guided tours (French or English), which take you through the history of the onions and of the Johnnies and their way of life both in France and the UK, backed up by photos and a video. On Tuesdays you get to meet a Johnny, farmer or local restaurateur after the tour, and in August the town has a Pink Onion Festival with music, dance, activities and exhibitions, and stalls selling onions or recipes featuring them. Displays of how to 'weave' a string of onions can be arranged at the museum.

Roscoff also has a *petit train touristique* in summer.

48 rue Brizeux, Roscoff, ☎ 02 98 61 25 48. Guided tours mid-June–mid-Sept Mon–Fri 11am, 2pm, 3.30pm and 5pm, Sun 2pm, 3.30pm and 5pm, school hols Mon, Tue, Thur, Fri and Sun 2.30pm, rest of year (except Jan)

Tue 10.30am and Thu 2.30pm. Adm: adults € 4 (£ 2.70), children 10–18 € 2.50 (£ 1.65), family (2+2) € 12 (£ 8) then extra child € 2 (£ 1.35).

Maison des Minéraux The highlight of this geology museum in an old rural school is the darkened room with Europe's largest collection of fluorescent rocks, including quartz and manganese – red, yellow, orange, mauve and green rocks twinkle at you from every corner like fireflies. The items on display, backed up by photos and texts in French, come from the Crozon peninsula itself (p. 157), which is rich in marine fossils; from farther afield in Finistère; or from the Armorican Massif – a vast plain covering much of Brittany, parts of Normandy and a few *départements* outside them. As well as seeing display cases full of rocks, visitors can go on geology and nature walks (Apr–Sept) and sign up for interactive conferences and science workshops in the laboratory of Professor Kaolin, an expert on the peninsula. The shop has some interesting souvenir items, including geological maps of French regions.

*Route du Cap de la Chèvre, St Hernot, 5km (3 miles) south of Morgat on D887, ☎ 02 98 27 19 73, **www.maison-des-mineraux.org**. Open July–mid-Sept daily 10am–7pm, mid-Sept–Dec and Feb–June Mon–Fri 10am–noon and 2–5pm, Sun 2–5pm, Jan Mon–Fri 10am–noon and 2–5pm. Adm: adults € 4 (£ 2.70), children 8–14 € 2.50 (£ 1.65).*

Musee de l'Ecole Rurale ★ Opened around 1910 for more than 100 local children and closed in the 1970s when the total had shrunk to just five due to rural depopulation, this school has recently been restored as a museum with a reconstructed 1920s classroom hosting rather dry permanent and temporary exhibitions on the history of rural schooling in France. Come in summer, though, and your children (and sometimes you too) can join in with a host of imaginative activities, all free with museum entrance – they include dictation using quills and violet ink; gym lessons in the pretty schoolyard with its lime trees; paper pine-cone making; sessions with homemade countryside toys, including marbles, skipping ropes and whirligigs; traditional games such as hopscotch; science experiments; and drawing and poetry competitions for children and adults, including a prizegiving ceremony. It's a lovely way to experience some true Breton culture.

*Trégarvan, 18km (11 miles) east of Crozon off D60, ☎ 02 98 26 04 72, **www.pnr-armorique.fr**. Open Dec–mid-Feb Mon–Fri 2–5pm, mid Feb–Apr, Oct and Nov Sun–Fri 2–6pm, May, June and Sept daily 2–6pm, July and Aug daily 10.30am–7pm, Oct and Nov Sun–Fri. Adm: adults € 4 (£ 2.70), children over-8 € 2.30 (£ 1.55).*

Musée du Loup ★ Another fascinating nature site within the Parc Régional Naturel d'Armorique (p. 162), this unique 'wolf museum' tells the story of the wolves who roamed this area little over a century ago, striking

The Height of Fashion

Though you're very unlikely to see any worn in the street, you will probably see women or girls sporting the tall *coiffe* lace headdresses that are such an iconic image of Brittany at one of the region's festivals or celebrations. The town of **Pont-l'Abbé**, famous as the home of a particularly skyscraping and richly embroidered form of the *coiffe* that attained a height of 32cm (13 inches), has a large number of them on display in its **Musée Bigouden** (*02 98 66 09 03*), housed in the medieval dungeons of the Château des Barons. You can also see peasant furniture, seaside crafts and other local costumes here.

A Girl Wearing a *Coiffe*

fear into the hearts of locals, who received rewards for killing them. Ironically, today they are a protected species, and at this museum you learn about modern-day preservation measures, as well as about wolves from a biological viewpoint and in legends, stories, superstition and art, including 'Le Petit Chaperon Rouge' ('Little Red Riding Hood') and cave paintings in the Dordogne. There are stuffed wolves aplenty, plus a video, a library, multimedia terminals, an art gallery and a slide show with commentary by a storyteller. It's good to time your visit with an event, such as a Nuit du Loup nocturnal visit to the museum followed by a walk in the nearby former wolf-habitat of the Landes du Cragou with a storyteller and musician. There's also an annual 'wolf week' in association with the Domaine de Ménez-Meur (p. 159), with exhibitions, storytelling, walks and feeding sessions.

The **Restaurant–Crêperie Le Capsell** in Le Cloître-St Thégonnec (*02 98 79 70 60*) runs a special menu on the 'wolf nights'. Don't miss the striking fountain covered with carved wolves in the town's place de la Mairie.

1 rue du Calvaire, Le Cloître-St Thégonnec, 12km (7.5 miles) south of Morlaix on D111, 02 98 79 73 45, www.pnr-armorique.fr. Open July and Aug daily 2–6pm, mid-Feb–June and Sept—mid-Dec Sun 2–6pm. Adm: € 5 (£ 3.35), children 5–12 € 3 (£ 2).

Musee de la Pêche A highlight of the fishing (and fish canning) port of Concarneau (p. 150), set at the entrance to the touristy

Ville Close, this museum looks at maritime traditions and techniques locally and around the world. As well as diverse items such as the frighteningly huge wall-mounted Japanese spider crab (with a leg span of almost 2m or 6 ft!), lobster cages, a reconstructed ship's cabin with radar equipment, tanks with local fish, scale models of the town showing the Ville Close protruding into the bay like an island, and an amazing array of sardine tins, children love the *Hémérica* – a 34m (112 ft) fishing boat permanently moored outside the museum, where the sea sloshes against the rampart. Clamber aboard to see its engine room, bunkrooms, kitchen and more, which really gives you a feel of the ardours of life at sea (you need to be fairly agile to navigate its warren of decks linked by steep steps and ladders). The small shop has a few children's items, including shrimping nets, colouring books, models and other crafts, and candle-powered 'Pop Pop' boats. Allow about two hours for a visit.

For details of tours of the port and/or the early-morning *criée* (fish auctions), contact Vidéo-Mer (☎ *06 80 26 34 25*, ***www.videomer.fr***).

3 rue Vauban, Ville Close, Concarneau, ☎ 02 98 97 10 20. Open daily Apr–June 10am–6pm, July and Aug 9.30am–8pm, Sept–Mar 10am–noon and 2–6pm. Adm: adults € 6 (£ 4), children 5 and up € 3 (£ 2).

Musée des Phares et Balises ★★ In a machine room of the Phare du Creac'h's old electrical station (p. 164), this museum – the only one of its kind in the world – traces the history of lighthouses and maritime signals on the island that saw the world's first automatic lighthouse and the testing of many optical and auditory signals. The navigation lights, beacons and buoys date from the early 1800s to the present day; there are also models that throwing into sharp relief the complicated and often dangerous process of building lighthouses, plus maps, objects from shipwrecks (including the British *Drummond Castle*; p. 154) and displays about lighthouse-keepers' harsh lives. In summer there are two hour tours of the island's signalling system, which includes five lighthouses (not all of them accessible), foghorns, turrets and sea marks.

*Phare du Créac'h, Ouessant, ☎ 02 98 48 80 70, **www.pnr-armorique.fr**. Open daily early Apr–late Sept 10.30am–6.30pm, school hols 10.30am–6pm, rest of year 1.30–5pm. Adm: adults € 4.10 (£ 2.75), children 8–14 € 2.60 (£ 1.75).*

Arts & Crafts Sites

Hangar't ★★ Every June the hamlet of Nizon near Pont-Aven hosts its wonderfully quirky Fête des Cabanes, whereby local children make little huts out of leaves, branches and other natural materials, which are then filled with installation pieces by modern artists. The public can visit on one day only – bring a picnic and wellies to best enjoy the wooded setting with its little islands.

Iles de Kerévennou, Nizon, near Pont-Aven, ☎ 02 98 06 13 03. Open call for date and times. Adm free.

Maison des Vieux Métiers Vivants ★★ This 'living museum' at the entrance to the Crozon peninsula (p. 157) consists of about 15 workshops in which volunteers demonstrate various trades of yesteryear: you simply wander from one to another and watch (and talk to, if you so desire) the artisans, who include a cobbler, a basket-maker, a wool spinner, a rope maker and a turner. Summer is a great time to come by virtue of the many special events, which include a horse festival with wheel waxing, a bread festival with butter-making, Breton dance lessons, and days featuring pony-and-cart rides, sheep-shearing, honey-gathering or crêpe-making over an open fire. The grounds feature a selection of old Breton games to try, including *boultenn*, *kilhoù kozh* and *birinig*, and space for picnics. It's all great fun for both children and parents, as well as an opportunity to immerse yourself in authentic Breton culture.

Argol, 10km (6 miles) east of Crozon on D60, ☎ 02 98 27 79 30, www.argol.fr.st. Open May and school hols daily 2–5.30pm, June and Sept Tue, Thur and Sun 2–5.30pm, July and Aug Tue-Fri 10am–noon and 2.30–6pm, Sat 2.30–6pm. Adm: adults € 4 (£ 2.70), children € 2 (£ 1.35).

Musée des Beaux Arts

Quimper's fine-arts museum has a colourful collection that includes works by Breton artists or inspired by Brittany, including the eerie landscapes of Yves Tanguy, some of which were influenced by his familiarity with the shores of the Cap Sizun (p. 155) and Crozon peninsula (p. 157) at low tide, and with the legend of the drowned City of Ys. Tanguy gets an exhibition all to himself in summer 2007. There's also a permanent homage to Quimper-born painter and poet Max Jacob, with many of his drawings, oil paintings, letters and manuscripts, plus works by friends of Jacob such as Pablo Picasso and Jean Cocteau.

The museum's longstanding creative **workshops** (in French; € 3.20 (£ 2.15)), designed to make the collections accessible to children aged 6–13 through learning painting, drawing, engraving, modelling and collage techniques, begin with a themed tour of the museum, during which they are encouraged to share ideas that come to them. Held in school holidays except at Christmas, the workshops last two and a half hours and have space for just 12, so book well ahead (☎ *02 98 95 52 48*). Artistic children might also like taking a tour (in French or English) of the 17th century **Faïencerie HB-Henriot** (☎ *08 00 62 65 10*), one of the last firms still producing traditional hand-made and hand-decorated Quimper porcelain.

Sun 9am–7pm; rest of year Mon and Thur 1–8pm, Tue and Fri noon–10pm, Wed 10am–8pm, Sat noon–8pm, Sun 9am–7pm. Adm: pools adults € 5.90 (£ 3.95), children 4 and over € 5.10 (£ 2.45); call for prices of other facilities/activities.

Centre International de Plongée/Centre Nautique des Glénans ★ Famous for their shipwrecks (more than 50 boats have come to grief here since the 18th century), the Iles de Glénan, an archipelago of 13 islands and lots of islets and rocks 20km (13 miles) offshore of Concarneau, are some of Europe's best places to learn to sail and dive, although there are no hotels or campsites and only two restaurants – the latter on **St Nicolas**, the only one of the islands to be officially inhabited (by one person!). This is the landing point for cruisers from Concarneau, Port-la-Forêt and Bénodet and the site of the **Centre International de Plongée**, running residential courses for divers aged 14 and up, plus initiation for ages 10 and up, mid-April to mid-October. St Nicolas also has good beaches, a sandy spit linking it with the Ile de Bananec at low tide, and a protected area where the Glénan narcissus, unique to these islands, grows. Meanwhile, **Penfret**, the second-largest island (after the Ile du Loch) has, in addition to a lighthouse, several bases belonging to the residential **Centre Nautique des Glénans**, a top sailing school that also rents some of the other Glénan islands for its activities and runs courses in Paris and in the Mediterranean. Courses cater for ages 13 and up here, and unusually there are some courses run in English, though these are for adults. For boat-trips to the Glénans, see p. 170.

*Centre International de Plongée: ☎ 02 98 50 57 02, **www.cip-glenans.org**; Centre Nautique des Glénans, ☎ 01 53 92 86 00, **www.glenans.asso.fr/**.*

Initiation aux Danses Bretonnes ★★ Here's something that's bound to end up among everyone's dearest (or perhaps that should read 'most embarrassing') holiday memories – lessons in the traditional dances performed at Breton *fest noz* (p. 26), including the *an dro*, *anter dro*, *laridé* and *gavotte*. They're only offered in French, but even if yours is more than a little shaky you should be still be able to keep up and enjoy yourself. Note, however, that though all ages are welcome, the lessons start at 7.30pm and last for an hour and a half, so little children might not last the course. In July and August they are followed by free *fest noz*.

Canoeing on the Atlantic Coast

Also offered by the Penmarc'h tourist board are Breton-language lessons; similarly, all ages are welcome to these, but in order to learn the basic vocabulary, place names, names of boats and so on, and to appreciate the humour of many Breton expressions, you need a good command of French.

Penmarc'h, 25km (16 miles) southwest of Quimper on D785, ☎ 02 98 58 81 44 (tourist office). Adm: € 3.50 (£ 2.35), under-8s free. Classes July and Aug Wed 7.30pm.

Parc d'Attractions Odet Loisirs One of France's trademark rickety but enjoyable leisure parks, this comprises around three leafy hectares (seven acres) of largely tacky fun for family members old and young, including a maze, rope-bridges and pulleys over a lake, 'vélos drôles' (strange bike/cart contraptions), trampolines, a maze, a rodeo ride, pedaloes (extra fee)... the list goes on. If it all gets too frenetic, you're free to stroll in the park with its 600-plus species of trees and shrubs. You can picnic, or there's a bar for snacks/ice cream.

*Route de Quimper, Coray, 15km (9 miles) northeast of Quimper on D15, ☎ 02 98 59 18 25, **www.odet-loisirs.com**. Open July, Aug and early Sept daily 11am–7pm, Apr–June and Oct Wed, Sat, Sun and school and public hols 2–7pm or longer hours in fine weather. Adm: € 6.50 (£ 4.35), under-3s free.*

Les Villages Mer ★ These 'sea villages' in Le Conquet and on the Ile-de-Batz just off Roscoff (p. 152) promise 'freedom for children, relaxation for adults' – the perfect family holiday recipe. On the mainland, where you stay in a holiday village near the beach, with 40 wooden lodges and numerous play areas, you can follow more than 30 walking or cycling routes (with a guide if you wish) or take boat trips out to see dolphins. For the more adventurous there's the Jardin Colonial on Batz, a family holiday centre (and school study centre) near dunes, beaches and an exotic garden, a 20 minute walk from shops and services. Children aged 4–12 are kept busy at the Club Moussaillons (a *moussaillon* is a ship's boy), which offers tuition in kayaking, sailing and fishing, plus crafts such as stone painting. Older children and adults also get to enjoy a range of nautical activities. It's all very flexible: you do as much or as little as you like if you book the *à la carte* option – you pay only for accommodation, then join in individual sessions for an extra € 10 (£ 6.65) a time. At the end of

Lobster Cages in Le Conquet

the day there are convivial seafood suppers (you can also cook for yourself, or get meals to take to your rooms) and music sessions. Accommodation is in basic but comfortable five-person lodges or six-person apartments, and for an extra fee you can leave your car in a secure garage at Roscoff. A fair degree of English is spoken by the friendly staff.

*Le Conquet, 30km (19 miles) west of Brest on D780, and Ile-de-Batz, just off Roscoff, 📞 02 98 89 09 21, **www.lesvillagesmer.com**. Open school hols (spring and summer; accommodation all year). Rates: family accommodation € 325–825 (£ 220–555) per week.*

Shopping

There's a **Fnac** media store in **Brest** (65 rue Jean-Jaurès, 📞 *02 98 33 88 00*).

Biscuitier Chocolatier Glacier Lanicol ★★★ This amazing shop will lure you in with its huge decorative chocolate dolphin and other animals and its luscious displays of specialities such as *kouignettes* (moist little cakes in around 20 flavours, including praline, chocolate and almond, lime and salted-butter caramel made with *fleur de sel*, a special seasalt) and *torchettes* (big round biscuits made without fat of any kind, containing almonds, hazelnuts, raisons and Breton seaweed). Most tempting of all are the giant meringues with or without chocolate, and the riotously colourful *moumettes* – mini meringues with alluring flavours such as raspberry, blackcurrant, orange, lemon, apricot and coffee. Chocaholics won't be able to resist the self-service slabs of chocolate, and the back counter holds an array of sweets and ice creams. A sweet fix to end them all.

9 rue Vauban, Ville Close, Concarneau, 📞 02 98 60 46 87. Open June–Sept daily 10am–8pm, rest of year Mon 2–6pm, Tue–Sat 10am–7pm.

Chocolatier Chatillon This prizewinning producer of fine chocolates, Florentines (almond and chocolate cookies with mint or orange) and Breton biscuits offers short guided tours of its workshops, where you can see specialities such as pink or grey Granit de Bretagne – a white-chocolate confection that doesn't melt up to a temperature of 45 degrees C, handy for picnics – being handmade, plus watch a video and look at various displays. For those who might have difficulty following, translation sheets (in English, German, Dutch, Italian and Spanish) are handed out. After free tastings, it all culminates – as these things do – in a shop, where you can choose from,

Breton Biscuits

Window Shopping, Concarneau

among other things, 17 types of chocolate sweets, made according to Swiss recipes.

46 place Charles De Gaulle, Pleyben, 35km (22 miles) northeast of Quimper on N164, 02 98 26 63 77, ***www.chatillon-chocolat.com****. Open times vary; call ahead. Adm free.*

Miellerie de Fouesnant Tours of this little producer of honey and related products – obvious things such as pollen and royal jelly but also jams, honey vinegar and *chouchenn* (p. 244) – start, logically enough, with the hives, where you can watch bees going about their business behind the safety of glass. From there you wander into the pollen-drying room, then see honey being extracted. The friendly owner is always on hand to answer questions you might have, and you get to taste a selection of different honeys, which may include chestnut, heather, buckwheat and buckthorn. Among the other items on sale are two kinds of gingerbread – 'classic', and a milder variation with choc chips, dried apricots or raisons, hazelnuts and orange peel – plus sweets and soaps.

Crunch Time

Brittany takes its biscuits very seriously indeed, as the number of *biscuiteries* (factories) and boutiques demonstrates. Specialities range from the light *crêpes-dentelles* ('lacy crêpes', a sort of wafer) to butter biscuits called, confusingly, *galettes*. The following are among the best places to buy Breton biscuits and cakes, and sometimes to see them being made and taste some for free:

Biscuiterie de Concarneau, 3 place Saint-Guénolé, Ville Close, Concarneau, *02 98 97 07 67*

Biscuiterie François Garrec, route du Fouesnant, Bénodet, *02 98 57 17 17,* ***www.garrec.com***

Biscuiterie de Quimper-Styvell, 8 rue du Chanoine Moreau, Quimper, *02 98 53 10 13*

Boutique Traou-Mad, 10 place Gauguin and 28 rue du Port, Pont-Aven, *02 98 06 01 94/02 98 06 18 18,* ***www.traoumad.com***

Galettes de Pleyben, rue T. Botrel, Pleyben, *02 98 26 60 21*

Breton Witch Dolls, Concarneau

Pont-Henvez, route de Bénodet, Fouesnant, 12km (7.5 miles) south of Quimper on D45, 02 98 56 59 66. Open July and Aug Tue and Thur 10.30. Adm free.

La Perle Rare Children are drawn as if hypnotised to this shop's colourful window display, which features lots of *jouets d'hier* ('toys of yesteryear'), such as clockwork mice, clowns, elephants and penguins, tin 'Pop Pop boats' (powered by candles), wooden sailboats and fishing games, spinning tops and compasses. It looks tiny from outside, but inside it opens out into an Aladdin's cave with room for masks, jewellery, trinkets, postcards and old posters of Concarneau.

This street, though touristy (it's the Ville Close's main thoroughfare), has some cute shops, including **L'Ilot**, selling interior decor and gifts, among them some funky children's picture frames, mirrors, clothes hangers and so on in pastel shades, and **Le Bois d'Angèle**, a wooden games and toys specialist that also stocks well-made soft toys. On the street's extension, rue Vauban, **Mille et Une Bagues** is a slightly schlocky shop with interesting figurines of *korrigans* (p. 3) and Breton witch dolls, plus carved wooden animals, porcelain snails and lots of grungy jewellery.

6 rue Saint Guénolé, Concarneau, 02 98 97 53 08. Open daily 10.30am–noon and 2–6pm.

Printemps Though Brest's branch of Printemps doesn't live up to the department store brief of stocking 'everything under one roof', and can't hold a candle to its Paris sister in size or prestige, it does have a good childrenswear section stocking designer labels for babies up to teens. The ground-floor accessories department, meanwhile, is a must for teen girls who love glitter and glitz.

There's another branch in Rennes (p. 58).

59 rue Jean Jaurès, Brest, 02 98 44 65 65. Open Mon–Sat 9.30am–7pm.

FAMILY-FRIENDLY ACCOMMODATION

Roscoff & Around

VERY EXPENSIVE

Grand Hôtel des Bains ★★ Wonderfully located at the tip of a peninsula in an out-of-the-way little harbour town near the border with the Côtes d'Armor, the Grand Hôtel des Bains is a rare beast – an elegant late 18th century seafront hotel that eschews the usual chintz in favour of something muted and more modern, with a New England feel that doesn't seem out of place – polished floorboards, grey and eggshell-blue walls and fabrics, and painted wooden furniture. Very comfortable, the majority of rooms have splendid bay views and are flooded with light in the morning (don't worry: heavy curtains keep it out until you're ready); a handful have a view of a 17th century church. Family rooms for three are all on the bay side; they have a double and a single bed but can also fit an extra bed or a cot for an extra fee. Alternatively, you can get interconnecting rooms with a view of the sea from the double room and a church view from the twin room, although this will send your budget through the stratosphere. If terraces are not a safety issue for you, ask for a room on the first floor – you'll be paying a supplement of € 26 (£ 17.50) per day for the privilege, but these are beautiful big decked affairs.

In terms of amenities, as well as direct access to one of Locquirec's nine sandy beaches, the Grand has a large indoor saltwater pool with massage jets and a Jacuzzi with a view out across its grounds with their ancient lime trees, and of the bay. Children are allowed to swim here between noon and 4pm; parents might like to take it in turns to watch over them while the other person benefits from the seawater therapy and beauty treatments in the spa rooms. If you're feeling more active, the helpful but discreet staff will point you in the direction of a sailing and diving school offering tuition for children and adults a short walk away. In keeping with the emphasis on positive living, the restaurant (also with stunning bay views, and a special family room) offers good low-fat cuisine based on seafood and organic produce, along the lines of local lobster with ginger and garden vegetables. Children get a quite sophisticated daily-changing menu at € 13 (£ 8.75). When they're down for the night, there's a luxurious lounge where you can relax over a drink, with a real fire in the cooler months, although unfortunately the hotel doesn't offer babysitting. Note that the rates include breakfast.

Older teens might be interested to learn that *L'Hôtel de la Plage*, a farce about a bunch of French families holidaying in Brittany, was shot here in 1978.

*15 bis rue Eglise, Locquirec, 15km (9 miles) northeast of Morlaix on D64, 📞 02 98 67 41 02, **www.grand-hotel-des-bains.com**. 36 rooms. Double € 145–213 (£ 98–144), 3-person room € 258–284 (£ 175–192), extra bed/child 2–11 € 59 (£ 40), extra child under 2 € 20 (£ 13.50); interconnecting rooms for four € 496 (£ 335). Cot € 15 (£ 10). Amenities: indoor swimming pool, health spa, restaurant, lounge bar. In room: telephone, TV, hairdryer, tea- and coffee-making facilities.*

MODERATE

Hôtel du Centre ★ More than a place to rest your head before catching an early ferry, this long-standing hotel was overhauled in 2003 to give it a resolutely modern look that's still quite rare among French hotels outside the capital. Its 16 rooms, four of which can interconnect to form 'family apartments' and some of which have sea views, are decorated in traffic-light red and grey and have quotes about the sea by Breton poets painted on the walls – bound to impress older children. Downstairs, a former sardine bar where the local onion-selling 'Johnnies' (p. 165) used to come to sign their contracts has been transformed into a tapas bar and restaurant that opens out onto a wide sun-trap of a terrace from where you can watch *boules* matches on the terrain opposite. It's one of those places that's hip but popular with locals, so it's got great atmosphere. In addition to decent breakfasts (€ 8 (£ 5.35)) and the obligatory local seafood in various forms, it serves family-friendly snack options such as sandwiches and salads.

The place shares owners with the nearby **Hôtel Brittany** (☎ *02 98 69 70 78*, ***www.hotelbrittany.com***), another stylish option with expensive junior suites and apartments, children's reductions, and a children's menu in its Restaurant Yachtman.

Le Port, Roscoff, ☎ *02 98 61 24 25,* ***www.chezjanie.com****. 16 rooms. Double € 59–84 (£ 40–56), extra bed € 15–19 (£ 10–12.85). Cot free. Amenities: restaurant, bar, baby-sitting. In room: TV, tel, modem access.*

Manoir de Kervézec On the outskirts of the resort of Carantec (p. 152), this is a classic little turreted château set on an organic farm, and in warm weather you can enjoy your health-conscious Continental breakfast (€ 6 (£ 4)) on a sunny terrace while watching the friendly animals – a llama, horses, donkeys and cows – stroll about. There's a breakfast room for less clement days. In keeping with the building, the five rooms with bath or shower, one for a family of four (with a double and a twin room), are filled with old Breton furniture and have rather chintzy decor, but they're pleasant enough if your tastes are traditional. Some rooms afford you a view as far as the bay a 15 minute walk away. Probably of more interest to most families are the four-person gîtes (occupying one house divided in two) along a little lane, with full kitchens with washing machines and dishwashers, satellite TV and private gardens, as well as the run of the leafy park.

Carantec, 18km (11 miles) southeast of Roscoff via D173, ☎ *02 98 67 00 26. Double € 46–78 (£ 31–52), extra bed € 15 (£ 10); family room for four € 76 (£ 50); gîte € 250–540 (£ 165–360) per week. Amenities: enclosed grounds, lounge. In room (gîtes) satellite TV, kitchen with dish-washer, washing machine, garden, BBQ equipment. Closed Oct–Apr.*

INEXPENSIVE

Camping Les Hortensias/ Gîtes de Kermen ★ FIND It must be something in the air at Carantec, for this friendly campsite is also part of an organic vegetable smallholding (it's beside the farm itself), and you can buy produce during your stay (or in passing). Since 'green' is the watchword here, the site is low-key and lacks the facilities of larger, more touristy (and noisier) sites, but this is reflected in the rock-bottom prices. You do get clean facilities, though, plus bouncy castles where youngsters can burn off some energy. Although it's a kilometre from the sea (2.5km (1½ miles) from the beaches, accessed via direct footpaths), it's high up so you get amazing views over the bay.

If nights under canvas aren't your thing, there are some beautifully decorated gîtes on site, including 'Mer', with charming blue-and-white nautical décor, four bedrooms accommodating a total of five or six, and handicapped access; and 'Campagne', with understated rustic styling and four bedrooms for up to five people (and a view of the lighthouse on the Ile-de-Batz). Smaller cottages are also available on the farm itself, with private gardens and a shared children's play area.

*Kermen, Carantec, 18km (11 miles) southeast of Roscoff via D173, ☎ 02 98 67 08 63, **www.leshortensias.fr**. Tent pitch € 2.50 (£ 1.65), then € 2.80 (£ 1.86) per person, under-7s € 1.50 (£ 1), car € 1.50 (£ 1), motorhome € 1.25 (85p); gîtes € 275–680 (£ 186–460) per week. Amenities: laundrette, phone. Gîtes: TV, kitchen, garden, barbecue, cot, toys and games (some).*

Pays des Abers & Ile d'Ouessant

MODERATE

Castel Régis ★★ VALUE A hotel with a little beach of its own in this price category seems like a dream come true, and in fine weather you won't be able to drag yourself away from the Castel Régis with its crescent of fine sand and lush gardens, set away from town on a little outcrop of rock. The rooms – which include triples, family rooms for four (a double bed and two singles in one large room), interconnecting family rooms (a double and a twin) sharing a bathroom, and a four-person 'gîte' that can be joined with two interconnecting rooms within the same building to accommodate eight – can seem a little plain after the rest of the hotel, but they're extremely spacious, and the bathrooms with their big tubs have an old-fashioned charm. They're set in low-level buildings that border the gardens; a couple of the most expensive ones have sea views. It doesn't seem necessary to fork out for these when you have the use of the panoramic 'salon pieds à l'eau' ('waterside lounge') with books and children's games – a great place to watch the sunset over a glass of wine, perhaps while the children play on the swings a few feet away (you'll have to supervise younger ones as it's next to the car park). There's also a tennis court, canoes for hire, a sauna and an outdoor pool in high summer. The good breakfasts (€ 9 (£ 6), children € 6 (£ 4)) are served in a delightful dining room with views over the bay, or in your room for a small supplement. In all, this is a remarkable place for the price, my only gripe being the 4pm check-in.

*Brignogan–Plages, 35km (22 miles) northeast of Brest on D770, ☎ 02 98 83 40 22, **www.castelregis.com**. 22 rooms. Double € 73–110 (£ 49–74), family room for four € 103–125 (£ 69–84), family 'suite' for four € 125–145 (£ 84–97), four-person gîte € 480–800 (£ 325–540) per week. Extra bed € 15 (£ 10), cot free (linen not provided). Amenities: private beach, outdoor pool (July and Aug), sauna, play area, lounge with books and games. In rooms: TV, telephone.*

INEXPENSIVE

Le Keo ★ FIND Good cheer invades you when you walk into this unpretentious B&B in a characterful old inn 50m from the port in Ouessant's main village, which doubles as a shop selling Breton crafts, puppets, old postcards and beer. There are just three rooms, of which two interconnect to form a family suite with two double beds. Simply furnished, they have a delightful marine theme – blue and white decor, fishing nets, little fish painted on the walls – that is continued in the breakfast room in a former bar. The building also has an old room with its original 1900 carved wood interior, and space for exhibitions on the likes of lighthouse conservation. The kindly owners also run guided taxi tours of the island, and in summer let a nearby gîte for six people.

*Lampaul, Ouessant, ☎ 06 17 88 59 57, **www.lekeo.com**. 3 rooms. Double € 45 (£ 30), family suite for four € 85 (£ 57).*

Monts d'Arrée & Around

INEXPENSIVE–MODERATE

Au Bon Accueil ★ A useful family option on the threshold of the Monts d'Arrée in the Parc Régionel Naturel d'Armorique (p. 162), and also within a 20 minute drive of the beaches of the Baie de Douarnenez (p. 152), this riverside hotel has great amenities for its price range: a heated pool, a sauna and a garden with mini-golf, table tennis and a fishing pontoon. There's also bike hire 2km (1¼ miles) away at Châteaulin, and – if you can summon up a group of six – the possibility of hiring a 15m (45 ft) sailing boat for half-day, day or weekend trips (€ 60 (£ 40) per person a day) into the Baie.

The 42 guestrooms are spread across two buildings; the best have views over the Brest–Nantes canal to the front. Families can choose from four-person rooms (shower only) or suites of two interconnecting rooms sharing a bathroom. Alternatively, there's a new *résidence*, Au Fil de l'Eau, with 12 apartments for two or 3/4 people; they're set back from the road, opposite the pool.

Here you can enjoy hotel services such as breakfast (€ 6.50 (£ 4.40)) and daily cleaning (€ 8 (£ 5.35)) while benefiting from self-catering facilities and the use of a communal laundry. Like the actual hotel rooms, style-wise they're as plain as plain can be but clean and good for the price. Linen in these is extra (€ 17 (£ 11.45)) per week per double bed), as is a TV (€ 48 (£ 32) per week). Guests in both types of accommodation can enjoy decent seasonal local produce in the restaurant, including children's portions.

*Port-Launay, 25km (16 miles) north of Quimper on N165, ☎ 02 98 86 15 77, **www.bon-accueil.com**. Double € 45–67 (£ 30–45), extra bed € 8–17.50 (£ 5.35–11.85), four-person family room € 72–105 (£ 48–70), four -person suite € 105 (£ 70), 3/4-person apartment € 220–500 (£ 148–337) per week. Amenities: outdoor pool (May–mid-Sept), sauna (May–mid-Sept), mini golf, table tennis, fishing, boat hire. In room TV (extra fee in* résidence*).*

INEXPENSIVE

Auberge du Youdig ★ The Unique Selling Point of this gloriously rustic establishment in the heart of the Monts d'Arrée not far from Huelgoat (p. 156) is a museum containing a scale model of the nearby 17th century village of Brasparts, created in 1985 after the collapse of the family farm. Requiring 10000 hours of work and made from discarded roof tiles, it includes a mill, washhouse, well, little lake, chapel and cemetery. One of the friendly family members will show you around, and regale you with legends and choice titbits from local history. A neighbouring building contains four simple B&B rooms with showers, three for three people each (with one double bed and one single; the double room can also fit an extra bed if need be). They're old-fashioned but pretty, with wrought-iron furniture, flowers and personal decorative touches such as murals. The inn on site serves authentic Breton meals (including roast pork in *chouchenn* – weak mead – and *kig ha farz*, buckwheat dumplings with meat and vegetables), which you can burn off by joining in a somewhat frenetic mountain dance. Every Thursday evening in the high season, and sometimes out of season too, there are storytelling sessions on *korrigans* (p. 3) and other local 'characters'.

Those looking for a base while walking, cycling or riding in the Monts might want to enquire about the five gîtes for varying numbers of people in renovated stone buildings on the property, or the new, beautifully simple walkers' *gîte d'étape*, with three rooms sleeping a total of 12 in double and single beds, each with their own bathroom, plus a very well-kitted out and convivial communal kitchen.

*Kerveguenet, Brennilis, 25km (16 miles) south of Morlaix on D36, ☎ 02 98 99 62 36, **www.youdig.fr**. Double € 35 (£ 24) (extra bed € 15 (£ 10)), triple € 50 (£ 33). Gîte for four € 220–570 (£ 149–385) per week. Amenities: restaurant, museum.*

La Crème Maison VALUE South of the Monts d'Arrée, towards the so-called Montagnes Noires (which are hills rather than mountains), this renovated stone house with its original oak beams makes for an unpretentious family base if you don't mind being a little way inland (the coast is a 45 minute drive). Handy for the mad boulders of Huelgoat (p. 156), it's also very close to Gourin in the Morbihan, home to a crêpe festival in July (p. 201). Quietly set in a small hamlet and surrounded by fields, it's a couple of minutes from the typically Breton town of Spézet, which is large enough to have a tourist office and small supermarkets. The accommodation is best suited to four, in a cosy but bright double bedroom and twin, but there's also a large sofa bed in the ground-floor lounge if you want to squeeze in six, and a travel cot. You have to bring your own bed linen. The welcoming lounge has a second sofa and a pine dining table seating six, plus a highchair. Unusually for a French gîte, the adjoining kitchen is very modern and up-to-date. Note, though, that's there's no bath – just a downstairs shower room.

For entertainment, there's a smallish, fully enclosed garden with *boules*, badminton, table tennis and a large paddling pool, plus barbecue equipment, patio furniture and a gazebo for eating outdoors. Indoors is a TV and DVD player with a good choice of English-language films, a CD player, books and games. Note that because the cottage has central heating, it makes a good base for those visiting out-of-season – perhaps to hunt for their own dream holiday home.

Restangoff, near Spézet, 35km (22 miles) northeast of Quimper on D117, ☎ 0151 287 7756 (UK no.), www.crememaison.co.uk. Rates: € 225-450 (£ 150–300) per week. Amenities: garden, games, books, BBQ equipment, TV, DVD player and DVDs, CD player, kitchen, washing machine.

Presqu'île de Crozon

MODERATE

Thalassa ★ Unexciting from the outside, in a bland modern block, the Thalassa is nevertheless a good family choice for its prices, its position 50m (150 ft) from the beach and a five-minute walk from the centre of the pretty resort of Camaret-sur-Mer (p. 158), its outdoor heated seawater pool and its flexible accommodation for those with children – spacious 'Club' doubles with an extra bed, interconnecting rooms for two adults and two children, and apartments with kitchenettes for up to four. There's also a nearby *résidence*, the St Rémy, with apartments for up to seven in a building with a garden. All are relatively basic but have bathtubs; some rooms have enclosed balconies with sea or pool views. If you stay half board, children up to three get free food and board (one child per room); those aged 4–11 get 50% off in the sea-view restaurant, where there's also a € 10 (£ 6.65) children's menu (a fish or meat dish with seasonal vegetables, ice cream, juice or lemonade) and a good main menu of local specialities, especially fish. Breakfast is a reasonable all-you-can-eat buffet affair for € 9 (£ 6) (€ 4.50 (£ 3) for children), and there's a highchair. Parents appreciate the sauna, solarium and gym, and the bar with its terrace. Or for all the family, there's a billiards room and the run of the garden.

*Quai Styvel, Camaret-sur-Mer, 8km (5 miles) northwest of Crozon on D8, ☎ 02 98 27 86 44, **www.hotel-thalassa.com**. Double € 54–130 (£ 36–87), extra bed € 10 (£ 6.65); interconnecting rooms for four € 109–130 (£ 73–87); apartment for four € 398–720 (£ 269–485) (St Rémy € 298–498 (£ 199–336)). Cot free. Amenities: restaurant, bar, billiards room, garden, outdoor pool (summer; months vary), gym, sauna (extra fee), solarium. In room: telephone, TV, kitchen (apartments).*

INEXPENSIVE

Ferme Apicole de Térenez

★★ It's not every day you get to stay on a working honey farm with its own free museum, especially not one that also offers a children's playground, mountain bike hire and animals such as black Ouessant sheep (p. 153), hens and geese to pet, in a wooded garden leading down to the river with views of an ancient abbey (from the top you can see the river winding away to the Rade de Brest; p. 144). Beaches with rock pools and the famous fossils of the Crozon peninsula (p. 157) are a 10 minute drive away. You spend the night in double or four-person rooms with showers, let on a B&B basis. They're fairly spartan, as you'd expect from the prices, but perfectly acceptable. If you have children under six, stress that you need a room with a double bed and two singles rather than bunks. Baby equipment – a cot, changing mat, highchair (for the breakfast room) and baby bath – are all at your disposal.

As for the museum (open daily 9am–7pm), it has displays on bees and their habitat, machinery, a video and free tastings. The farm shop itself sells gingerbread made with 50% honey, cakes, sweets, nougat, biscuits, pollen, royal jelly and more.

*Rosnoën, just south of Le Faou, 35km (22 miles) north of Quimper on N165, ☎ 02 98 81 06 90, **www.ferme-apicole-de-terenez.com**. Double € 37–43 (£ 25–29), room for four € 50 (£ 34). Cot free. Amenities: games, bike hire, museum. In room: telephone, TV.*

Le Grand Large The best thing about this campsite right out on the tip of the Crozon peninsula is its heartstopping views over Camaret-sur-Mer's port, the Goulet de Brest and the open sea. It's a family-oriented site 2km from the port and less than 0.5km from a fine sandy beach, yet there's plenty of facilities to keep you occupied on site: an outdoor pool with a slide, a toddlers' pool, a play area, mini golf, a rather peculiar mini tennis court, table tennis, volleyball, a *boules* terrain, a games room and a TV room. Ask the friendly staff, too, about the reductions they offer at local diving and riding centres.

As well as their own tents (on good pitches separated by tallish hedges), guests can sleep in chalets and mobile homes of varying sizes and degrees of comfort, which out of high season are available by the weekend as well as the week. Bookings are no longer taken for tent pitches; the owners promise that a space can always be made available. As far as practical considerations are concerned, there's a little grocery, a snack bar selling takeaways, and a bar overlooking the pool and the sea beyond it. At night, concerts and discos mean there's little chance you'll fall asleep to the sound of the waves.

Lambézen, 8km (5 miles) northwest of Crozon on D8, ☎ 02 98 27 91 41, ***www.campinglegrandlarge.com****. Tent pitch € 6.20–13 (£ 4.18–8.78), then € 3–4.50 (£ 2–3) per person, under-7s € 1.50–3 (£ 1–2); chalet € 255–555 (£ 172–375) per week; mobile home for four € 250–600 (£ 166–400) per week. Amenities: outdoor pools, play area and games, TV room, snack bar, bar, shop.*

Cap Sizun

MODERATE

Hôtel-Restaurant Le Goyen

★★ A blue-shuttered harbourfront hotel at the northern end of the Baie d'Audierne (p. 151), Le Goyen brings a genteel note to this rather wild yet tourist-swamped headland, with its 26 classically elegant rooms, most with a balcony facing the sea. Families are generally directed to the rear, where there are Junior Suites in which the living room converts into a children's room. The view from these rooms is of the courtyard; if your heart's set on an ocean view, ask for an Océanes room over two levels, with extra beds in the panoramic living room. Better-than-average Continental breakfasts (€ 11.50 (£ 7.75) adults, € 6 (£ 4) 3–12s) can be taken in your room or the panoramic conservatory restaurant, where later in the day you can enjoy such gastronomic delights as cod with chorizo and fresh peas with Breton butter, and carpaccio of scallop with pink bay leaves and a lemon–lobster oil infusion. Children eat a simpler but still sophisticated menu (€ 10–12 (£ 6.65–8)) consisting of an *amuse-bouche*; melon and proscuitto or a market platter of the day with balsamic vinaigrette; fish of the day on crunchy vegetable noodles with seafood sauce or chicken breast on crushed potatoes with Breton butter; and sorbet and fresh fruit with berry *coulis*. There's a highchair.

Look out for special packages including bike hire (the Pointe du Raz (p. 155) is within easy reach) or boat trips to the Ile-de-Sein off the Pointe.

Place Jean-Simon, Audierne, 30km (19 miles) west of Quimper on D784, ☎ 02 98 70 08 88, ***www.legoyen.com****. 26 rooms. Double € 56–114 (£ 37–77), Junior Suite € 56–84 (£ 37–56), Océanes duplex suite € 104–148 (£ 70–99); extra bed € 20 (£ 13.50), children 3–12 € 10 (£ 6.65).*

Cot free. Amenities: restaurant, lounge/bar, dry cleaning, babysitting. In room: Sat TV, mini-bar (most rooms), hairdryer, room service, Internet access. Closed early Nov–mid-Mar.

INEXPENSIVE

Camping-gîte de Loquéran ★ FIND If you're counting the pennies and of a sociable bent, there are few better options than this combined communal gîte and campsite near Audierne. The gîte, an attractive wooden chalet in lovely flower-filled grounds, houses dorms and single and family rooms with their own bathrooms, and a shared kitchen and dining room. If it sounds a bit like a youth hostel, that because it is, but it's a very warm and welcoming one at that. The basic 25-pitch campsite is similarly fresh in feel, with a new toilet and shower block. There are no other facilities, but shops and services are a short walk away – including, at the end of the path, a communal *lavoir* or basin where some locals still come to wash their clothes (they don't mind if you join in!). It's a place to enjoy the peace, pet the horses in the surrounding fields and wander around the atmospheric nearby boat cemetery. The GR4 footpath runs right nearby, and there are lots of mountain bike and riding trails, as well as some fine beaches.

Rue des Lavandières, Plouhinec, 25km (16 miles) west of Quimper on D784, ☎ 02 98 74 95 06, **http://campgite.loqueran.free.fr**. *Family room for four € 42–49 (£ 28–33); tent pitch € 3 (£ 2), then adults € 3 (£ 2), children under-13 € 1.50 (£ 1). Amenities: shared kitchen and dining room (gîte).*

Bénodet & Around

MODERATE

Domaine Ker-Moor ★★ This smart *résidence* a few minutes' walk from the sea offers the freedom of self-catering accommodation with the facilities of a hotel – in this case, Le Ker-Moor just steps away, which has a pool, one squash and five tennis courts, table tennis, two bars and a restaurant. The latter, with its huge bright paintings and airy sea views, serves very good local seafood, and especially good desserts – local Plougastel strawberries, cinnamon *crème brûlée* and *millefeuilles au chocolat*. Children choose a meat or fish dish and a dessert or ice cream for € 8 (£ 5.30). Sometimes there are themed buffets around the pool.

Small enough not to feel impersonal (as many such places do), the Domaine has clean, fresh and modern 2–4-person studios with especially good kitchens with dishwashers and a roomy dining area. Beyond that, there's one double bedroom, a living room with a sofabed, and a separate bathroom and toilet. There's a TV in both the bedroom and the living room. Each unit gets its own parking space within the shady grounds, which you can appreciate from your private terrace or balcony. A swing helps keep children entertained. If you like to keep a handle on the chaos, there's maid service at € 18 (£ 12) a day.

Corniche de la Plage, Bénodet, 15km (9 miles) south of Quimper on D34, ☎ 02 98 57 04 48, ***www.hotel-ker-moor.fr****. 12 units. Studio € 480–700 (£ 320–466) per week. Cot free. Amenities: use of outdoor pool (Easter–late Oct), tennis courts, squash court, table tennis, two bars and restaurant; laundry service, car and bike hire, Wi-Fi and multimedia room. In room: kitchen with dishwasher, TVs, telephone, safe.*

INEXPENSIVE

Aire Naturelle de Keraluic ★★ Although its name lets you know this is a 'green' campsite, this renovated Breton farm also offers B&B accommodation and studios, making it a good flexible option for holidaying families. In the heart of the countryside and surrounded by forests yet only 6km from the coast (you're handy for both Penmarc'h and Bénodet, and the surfer-friendly Pointe de la Torche, p. 151), it comprises a flat campsite dotted with just 25 spaces for tents and caravans, plus very good sanitary blocks. The emphasis being on nature, facilities are kept to a minimum, but there is an unobtrusive play area, table tennis and a *boules* terrain. The rainy-day games room eschews video nasties in favour of wholesome chess, cards and so on, and there's a cosy stone-walled library with books for everyone. Oven-fresh bread is sold in summer.

The three B&B rooms and three studios are in a restored cottage on the edge of the campsite. The rooms are generally for two, though a cot (and highchair) can be provided, and an extra bed can be fitted in the largest. Good, hearty breakfasts are served in a snug dining room with an open hearth. The studios all have bathtubs, and two can accommodate an extra bed. Again, a cot and highchair are available. Out of season they can be rented for three nights rather than a week.

Plomeur, 20km (12 miles) southwest of Quimper on D785, ☎ 02 98 82 10 22, ***www.keraluic.fr****. Tent pitch € 4.50 (£ 3), then € 3.90 (£ 2.60) per person, under-7s € 1.90 (£ 1.25), car € 1.90 (£ 1.25), motorhome € 1.50 (£ 1). Double room € 48–62 (£ 32–42), extra person € 15 (£ 10), under-7s € 11 (£ 7.35). Studio € 215–415 (£ 145–280), extra bed € 32.50 (£ 22), cot € 15 (£ 10), highchair € 7.50 (£ 5). Amenities: play area, games, library. In room: tea- and coffee-making facilities (B&B); kitchen, TV (studio).*

Concarneau & Around

INEXPENSIVE–MODERATE

Hôtel de l'Océan ★ In 2006, the addition of an indoor pool made this three-star with its outdoor pool and seafront location an even more alluring option. Although the rooms, which include triples and 4–5-person duplexes, with pool or sea view, could do with updating and jazzing up, prices are good for what you get – especially the large outdoor pool surrounded by loungers and a children's play area. Room service is also offered, as well as a rather expensive Continental breakfast in bed (€ 18 (£ 12)); for € 12 (£ 8) (children € 5.80 (£ 3.85)) you can take it in the airy bay-view dining room, where you can also enjoy local fare such as pollack in white butter and Concarneau chicken in cider in the evenings. Children 4–10 get reductions if you stay on a half-board basis.

*Plage des Sables Blancs, Concarneau, ☎ 02 98 50 53 50, **www.hotel-ocean.com**. 71 units. Double € 69–125 (£ 46–84), duplex for four € 95–165 (£ 63–112). Cot € 12 (£ 8). Amenities: restaurant, bar, indoor and outdoor pools, room service. In room: Sat TV, telephone.*

INEXPENSIVE

There's a big Siblu (p. 36) campsite, **Domaine de Kerlann**, near Pont-Aven.

Camping Le Ty Nadan ★★★

Although it's a fair way (a 25 minute drive) inland, this four-star campsite on a 24 hectare (60-acre) riverbank estate near the Morbihan border stands out for its excellent range of activities, which include canoeing on the river or the sea (plus lessons for children over six), horseriding (including Shetland pony rides for children aged four and up), mountain biking, Quad biking, walking, trout and salmon fishing, archery, watercycling, rock climbing and even Paintball. There's also an adventure park with treetop acrobatic courses with 'monkeywalks', 'crazy bridges' and the like, for 7–13-year-olds and over-14s, tennis courts, pedaloes and a sauna. This is all in addition to campsite standards such as an indoor pool with waterslides and a paddling pool, outdoor pools, table tennis, volleyball, pool tables, a restaurant/pizzeria/crêperie also offering takeaways, a shop and a bar. Even babysitting is offered here, and there are baby-changing facilities and baby baths in all the attractive stone sanitary blocks.

Most of the non-standard activities cost extra, but prices are reasonable. The highlight is the coastal kayaking for 12-year-olds and up – a 5 hour excursion spent exploring caves and creeks. But don't fret if your children are too young for all this: there are superior children's clubs for ages 4–8, 9–12 and teens, with trips to Pont Scorff zoo in the Morbihan (p. 209), insect hunts, puppet shows, crêpe-making, films (some in English) and much more. Adult-oriented entertainment includes the usual karaoke sessions but also Breton evenings and films in English.

After all this, accommodation almost seems an afterthought. In keeping with the overall rugged countryside feel, the campsite is very green, with lots of trees contributing to a feeling of privacy. Guests with tents can hire fridges, cots and highchairs. There are also decent mobile homes and a couple of apartments, one above the shop and one above the crêperie. Best of all, though, for the feeling of being in nature, are the six-person wooden chalets near the river.

A wooden chalet at Le Ty Nadan

INSIDER TIP

You get 10% discounts on Condor ferry crossings (p. 33) at Le Ty Nadan if you stay here.

*Route d'Arzano, Locunolé, 15km (9 miles) northeast of Quimperlé off D790, ☎ 02 98 71 75 47, **www.camping-ty-nadan.fr.** Tent pitch including car € 8.70–21 (£ 5.80–14), then € 4.30–8.40 (£ 2.90–5.60) per adult, € 1.70–5.20 (£ 1.14–3.51) per child aged 2–6, mobile home for four € 40–110 (£ 27–74) per night, 6-person chalet € 60–152 (£ 40–101) per night. Amenities: indoor and outdoor pools, sauna, adventure park, games, activities programme, children's clubs, restaurant, bar, laundrette, baby-changing, babysitting.*

La Villeneuve ★★★ Another British-owned venture, this complex of eight gîtes in old farm buildings within three and a half hectares (nine acres) is a little paradise for children, with an outdoor pool (fully fenced off), a good play area and woods that are brilliant for making dens. Unusually for gîtes, it's also right by the coast, on the delightful Bélon *aven* or estuary with its boat trips. Gîtes take up to eight, including a baby, in two or three bedrooms; cots are available (without linen), as are high-chairs, and child-safety gates are ready fitted on all staircases. Behind every gîte is a private patio and then your own patch of lawn where youngsters can run around safely, and there's also a *boules* pitch and table tennis. The standard of interior decoration is quite high, and there is central heating, so out-of-season lets are not a problem. There's also a communal laundry room, and babysitting is provided.

*Riec-sur-Bélon, 5km (3 miles) south-east of Pont-Aven on D24, ☎ 02 98 06 99 38, **www.la-villeneuve.co.uk.** Rates: € 370–1170 (£ 250–790) per week. Cot free. Amenities: outdoor pool (May–Sept), play area, games, BBQ equipment, laundry. In room: kitchen.*

FAMILY-FRIENDLY DINING

Roscoff & Around

EXPENSIVE

Restaurant Patrick Jeffroy ★★ Views don't come much better than from the panoramic dining room of the Hôtel de Carantec, the resort's poshest restaurant, with the Baie de Morlaix and its yachts at your feet. Chef Patrick Jeffroy specialises in wonderfully phrased *mariages malicieux* (roughly translating as 'wicked marriages') such as Thai curry of hermit crab with warm artichoke, wakamé, shallot vinaigrette and coconut cream, or a dessert of apple tart with lavender, all gorgeously presented. The dining room suits the food – it's expensive-looking but not overdone (there's no point trying to rival these views, after all) – and the staff are friendly to children, since, as the chef himself points out, they are future customers. For children there is a suitably sophisticated € 18 (£ 12) menu that changes with the seasons and the market's offerings but might feature hermit crab and avocado salad, local pollack with new potatoes, and chocolate cake with strawberry sorbet. Not for the unadventurous, then, or for those with rampaging toddlers, but a great special-occasion venue for those with older children.

*20 rue de Kélenn, Carantec, 18km (11 miles) southeast of Roscoff via D173, ☎ 02 98 67 00 47, **www.hoteldecarantec.com**. Main courses € 38–50 (£ 25–33). Open mid-June–mid-Dec Wed and Fri–Sun noon–2.30pm and 7.30–10pm, Mon, Tue and Thur 7.30–10pm; rest of year Wed–Sun noon–2.30pm and 7.30–10pm. Closed 2 weeks Nov and 2 weeks Jan. Highchair.*

MODERATE

L'Ecume des Jours Occupying a lovely 16th century house in Roscoff's old port, this is a well-respected, longstanding restaurant serving quite refined fare using local produce – including pink onions, artichokes from the 'artichoke coast' west of Roscoff, where the vegetables grow almost right up to the sea, and seafood fresh from the boats – cooked with originality. You might, for instance, enjoy a dish of grilled monkfish medallions with Breton chitterling sausage and Roscoff pink onions, and a dessert of chocolate fondant with a crunchy cocoa dome, filled with cherries. If your children find that all too rich, the obliging staff will point you in the direction of the € 8 (£ 5.35) children's menu of daily-changing basics such as roast chicken or fish, followed by ice cream or a homemade dessert. Choose between a room with exposed stonework and huge fireplaces, best for chillier days, and a small blue-painted room with sea views, opening out onto two terraces for balmier days.

Quai d'Auxerre, Roscoff, ☎ 02 98 61 22 83. Menus: € 21–31 (£ 14–21). Open noon–2.30pm and 7.30–10pm June–Sept daily, Oct, Nov and Mar–May Thur–Mon. Closed Dec and Jan.

INEXPENSIVE–MODERATE

Le Petit Relais ★★★ Located on Carantec's busy Plage de Kélenn and boasting a fine terrace, this brasserie/pub/bar/*glacier* tries to be everything to everyone, at just about all hours of the day – which makes it a very handy family option. If you want to eat between regular mealtimes, you can be assured of a selection of baguette sandwiches (about € 3.80 (£ 2.55)), ice creams and pastries, and children are warmly welcomed with games, books and colouring sheets. You, in the meantime, could be checking your emails for free at the computer terminal. And those with babies will be grateful for the bottle heating and changing facilities.

This is an especially good place to come for a relaxed late family breakfast, particularly if you're fed up with the ubiquitous Continental variety – choices include fried eggs and ham, *madeleines* and brunchy fare such as smoked salmon with scrambled eggs on toast. 'Proper meals' run to all kinds of dishes, French or otherwise: *chili con salsa*, Italian cheese and meat platters, Russian caviar with vodka and *moules breton* all feature. The € 7.50 (£ 5) children's menu is rather uninspiring (ham or sausage with chips); you might want to steer younger diners towards the more interesting tarts, *croques*, pasta dishes and salads.

Plage de Kélenn, Carantec, 18km (11 miles) southeast of Roscoff via D173, ☎ 02 98 78 30 03. Main courses € 4.50–16 (£ 3–11). Open May–Sept daily 10.30am–1am, plus some other times (call for details). Highchairs.

Local Artichokes

Pays des Abers & Ile d'Ouessant

Ouessant can be a less-than-exciting place to eat; see p. 192 for my best option.

EXPENSIVE

La Corniche ★★ This is a funny place – part smoky bar filled with locals and sailors drinking to a cheesy '70s soundtrack, part top-notch seafood restaurant. One of only a couple of eateries in an untouristy little seaside town (p. 155), it can get fiendishly busy on a weekend night, and on holiday weekends staff turn people away in droves – although if you come very early and don't look as if you're going to spend all night here, they might squeeze you in. Not that staff are overly friendly towards those with children, but their coolness (perhaps just a result of being so busy) is more than made up for by the superlative food and the panoramic views of the bay, and they do provide highchairs, which are by no means a standard in French restaurants. The best time to eat here is in high summer, when there's a more child-friendly all-day brasserie service.

The changing menus are written up on large chalkboards that are hefted to your table; you'll need to ask about the good € 8 (£ 5.35) children's menu comprising *steak haché* or creamy white monkfish with chips (the very best *frites* we had during our last trip to France!), tagliatelle or rice, followed by ice cream. The boards feature a large choice of mussel specialities, fish dishes and some meats. You'll need a good knowledge of French, as they're not translated and the staff don't speak English. Recommendations include an exquisite skate wing with capers, sautée potatoes, courgettes, cherry tomatoes and carrots, and 'fisherman's stew' (*cotriade du pêcheur*), with tuna, scallops, monkfish, prawns and more in a dark, buttery sauce. It's hard to resist the desserts, but your curiosity about ice creams such as *chouchenn* (p. 244) or seaweed may be outweighed by the desire for a homemade *fondant au chocolat* (half-mousse, half-cake) with strawberries.

Rue de la Corniche, Brignogan-Plage, 35km (22 miles) northeast of Brest on D770, ☎ 02 98 85 81 07. Main courses € 9–32 (£ 6–21). Open Apr–June Tue–Sun noon–2pm and 7–11pm, July–Sept noon–11pm daily. Highchair.

MODERATE

Restaurant de la Mairie ★★
A little way inland and handy for those who fly into Brest airport but don't want to go into the city itself, this extremely welcoming place is just a couple of minutes' walk from the amazing Pont de Rohan, one of the few remaining European bridges containing inhabited houses. The restaurant is one of those rare places where real thought has gone into making children – and hence parents – feel relaxed and happy: as well as a baby-changing room, there are a selection of toys and a pretty little patio where a real live tortoise lurks amidst the greenery. Inside, paintings by local artists adorn the smart cream walls. The traditional cuisine includes heaps of seafood – the speciality is *timbale Neptune*, a wonderful stew of prawns, scallops and mushrooms in Cognac and cream – but there's also very good duck and, if you like that sort of thing, veal kidneys. If you can drag them away from the toys (or the tortoise), there's a € 7 (£ 4.70) children's menu featuring chicken, ham, *steak haché* or omelette with their choice of accompaniment and dessert.

9 rue de la Tour d'Auvergne, Landerneau, ☎ 02 98 85 01 83. Main courses € 8–17 (£ 5.35–11.45). Open Sun–Mon noon–2.30pm and 7–10.30pm, Tue noon–2.30pm. Highchairs.

INEXPENSIVE

Château d'Eau It doesn't really matter about the food in a place like this – you come to eat in this old 50m (165 ft) high watertower for the 360 degree ocean and countryside views from its dining room – a great thrill for children. It also helps that it's open all day. That's not to say that the food is bad – there's a good choice of galettes in adult and child-friendly guises, from three-cheeses to smoked sausage from the nearby island of Molène (p. 154), then dessert crêpes that can be a meal in themselves: try the house speciality with apple, orange-caramel and vanilla ice cream, the After Eight with custard, or one of the crêpes named in honour of the keepers of local lighthouses such as the Phare de l'Ile Vierge (p. 164).

St Roch, Ploudalmézeau, 18km (11 miles) northwest of Brest on D26, ☎ 02 98 48 15 88. Main courses € 5–12 (£ 3.35–8). Open noon–9.30pm Feb–mid-Nov daily, rest of year Sat, Sun and school hols. Highchair.

Crêperie Le Salamandre ★★ A pretty village crêperie with blue shutters and a sunny terrace, the Salamander was set up by the present owner's granny and has a real family atmosphere, as well as practicalities such as a baby-changing mat. You'll find some really quite adventurous crêpes on the menu, including plum and bacon, and Catalan with tomatoes and anchovies, but also the basics with cheese, eggs and ham for children who like to stick with what they know. Desserts can also be exotic – there are a couple of Canadian-inspired crêpes with maple syrup – and there's a big choice of ice cream *coupes* available in handy half-price mini-portions.

INSIDER TIP

Le Salamandre's very flexible weekday (and Saturday) € 10 (£ 6.65) menu is a great bargain for a family lunch. Note that you can also get takeaway crêpes here.

Place du Général de Gaulle, Ploudalmézeau, 18km (11 miles) northwest of Brest on D26, ☎ 02 98 48 14 00. Main courses € 4.50–9 (£ 3–6). Open Apr–June and Sept Thur–Mon noon–2pm and 7–10pm, Tue noon–2pm; July and Aug daily noon–2pm and 7–10pm; Oct–mid-Nov and mid-Dec–Mar Sat, Sun and school hols noon–2pm and 7–10pm, Tue noon–2pm. Highchair.

Presqu'île de Crozon

MODERATE

The Crozon peninsula is rather disappointing in terms of good child-friendly restaurants; the **Thalassa** hotel (p. 182) in Camaret-sur-Mer is a reliable bet.

INEXPENSIVE

Crêperie du Ménez-Gorre ★ Just inland of Morgat, this crêperie is worth knowing about for its little garden (complete with fountain and plenty of space for toddlers to play beside the wooden benches and tables), its quirky decor, which includes Breton dolls, local paintings and other knick-knacks, and its convenience – it's open every day. Set in a handsome stone building, it offers more than 100 galettes and crêpes, which means every member of the family will find something pleasing, whether it's a filling of seaweed, fresh fish or tasty seasonal veg. The friendly staff pride themselves on cooking everything fresh and never reheating – a fact you can verify by watching your meal being prepared in the semi-open kitchen.

86 rue de Poupatré, Crozon, ☎ 02 98 27 19 66. Main courses € 4.50–11 (£ 3–7.35). Open daily noon–2.30pm and 7–10pm. Highchair.

Cap Sizun

EXPENSIVE

L'Irois ★★ One can eat very well in Audierne. This newish establishment, presided over by a young chef who honed his skills in some of France's top restaurants, has opened to challenge the gastronomic crown of Le Goyen (p. 184), and is situated close to the more established restaurant. A chic stone-walled dining room with large colour-drenched paintings, soft lighting and beautifully dressed tables is the setting for such sophisticated fare as snail and oyster profiteroles, steamed fillet of marinated pollack on a tomato carpaccio, John Dory with rosemary peas and an orange and balsamic vinaigrette, and orange *clafoutis* (in batter) with sangria syrup. It's the kind of place where the children's menu is called a 'taste apprenticeship': for € 15 (£ 10) budding foodies get a plate of Serrano ham, fish of the day or chicken escalope with ultra-creamy mashed potato, and a choice of wonderful sorbets and ice creams. If it's quiet and there's no one enjoying a cigar there, snag the cosy lounge area with its deep sofas for a relaxing apéritif as you browse the menus.

8 quai Camille-Pelletan, Audierne, 30km (19 miles) west of Quimper on D784, ☎ 02 98 70 15 80. Main courses € 24.50–27 (£ 16.55–18.25). Open daily noon–3pm and 7–9pm (or sometimes much later). Highchairs.

INEXPENSIVE

Crêperie L'Epoké A quaint, welcoming pancake house in an extremely picturesque town with steep cobbled streets, set opposite the impressive cathedral, L'Epoké serves up such wonderful fishy crêpes as sardine butter with lemon, salmon with creamy spinach, and scallops, or you can choose from hearty main-course salads bursting with top-quality local ingredients, from seafood to smoked pork and chitterling sausage. For fussy children there are simple crêpes with cheese, ham and so on. Desserts run from elaborate crêpe confections (the caramelised apple with cinnamon ice cream is recommended) and ice-cream coupes to *kouign bigouden* (a buttery Breton yeast cake). The dining room with its log fire in the colder months can get a bit crammed; a better bet is the pretty terrace.

Pont-Croix

If L'Epoké is full, **Le Pub** on rue de la République has great children's *steak haché*.

1 rue des Partisans, Pont-Croix, 30km (19 miles) northwest of Quimper on D765, 02 98 70 58 39. Main courses € 6–15 (£ 4–10). Open noon–2pm and 7–9pm Wed–Sun most of year (call for exceptions), July and Aug daily. Highchair.

Bénodet & Around

Note that the company **Vedettes de l'Odet** (p. 170), which sails from Bénodet, runs gastronomic cruises that include children's menus.

MODERATE

La Brocéliande ★ This traditional restaurant by Bénodet's port is a handy standby when the children want the relative simplicity of a galette or crêpe but you fancy a more substantial seafood meal – perhaps even a gargantuan, super-fresh seafood platter for two. The pancakes, excellent by anyone's standards, include the basics (plain with butter, ham and egg and so on) as well as fancier specialities such as hot Camembert, Breton sausage with mustard, and smoked salmon with *crème fraîche*, all containing the freshest ingredients, whether from nearby or more distant climes (the salmon is Scottish). Fishy treats include mackerel rillettes (p. 246) with mustard, stuffed Glénan clams, and home-smoked haddock with *ratte* potatoes, spinach and poached egg. On hot days there is also a salad menu. On a sour note, staff can be distracted and the decor is fusty, but the homemade ice cream or *entremets* (a plate of chocolate desserts), or the roasted figs with *kouign* (butter cake), put you in a frame of mind to forgive anything.

2 rue de l'Eglise, Bénodet, 15km (9 miles) south of Quimper on D34, 02 98 57 25 71. Main courses € 4.50–18 (£ 3–12). Open Tue–Sun noon–7pm ('til 10pm in July and Aug, and daily school hols). Highchair.

La Couscousserie ★ FIND Couscous is a good bet with most children, and when you've overdone it on the seafood, this Moroccan on the river at Quimper, with its warm and refined Middle Eastern decor, its two red parrots and its lush Arab soundtrack, makes for an excellent change of scene. The staff couldn't be friendlier or more attentive, and that welcome extends to younger diners – who don't get their own menu but can order smaller portions of anything on the proper menu of couscous, tagines (the chicken, prunes and almonds is recommended) and *méchoui* (roast leg of lamb). Alternatively, if you have little ones, think about getting two or three dishes and sharing them between you – portions are large, and you can get free refills of vegetables and couscous. Cocktails from the bar are a good way to start your meal, fresh mint tea an excellent *digestif* at the end.

1 boulevard de Kerguélen, Quimper, ☎ 02 98 95 46 50. Main courses € 12–20 (£ 8–13.50). Open daily noon–1.30pm and 7pm–midnight. Closed most of Aug. Highchair.

INEXPENSIVE

Crêperie Chez Annick Just northeast of Bénodet, in a leafy spot outside the town of Fouesnant, this friendly crêperie stands out for its quiet covered terrace and little garden with a swing for the children to play on while you enjoy a *bolée* of cider. Inside, it's all stone walls, checked tablecloths and old Breton furniture. There's no children's menu, but as with all crêperies, plenty to suit all members of the family among the list of galettes, from melted cheese to chitterling sausage, and the crêpes – children love the fresh raspberry *coulis*, parents the cider jelly.

Route de Gouesnac'h, Clohars-Fouesnant, 12km (7.5 miles) south of Quimper on D34, ☎ 02 98 57 02 98. Main courses € 3–9 (£ 2–6). Open Apr–Sept Wed–Sun noon–2pm and 7–10pm, plus school hols. Highchair.

L'Ilot Jardin Cheap and cheerful, L'Ilot Jardin is a basic restaurant within a leisure park of the same name 3km from Fouesnant, with tennis and squash courts and mini-golf. Handily, the enclosed children's play area is by the restaurant's large terrace, which means the children can blow off some steam on the climbing frame and slide while you enjoy a beer from the bar (you don't have to eat here). It's a useful stopoff on the way home from the beach, whether you want something snacky such as omelette and chips or pizza (also available for takeaway) or proper meals from the *à la carte* menu of steaks and the like. The € 7 (£ 4.70) children's menu runs to the usual *steak haché* and *jambon blanc*.

Route de Mousterlin, just south of Fouesnant, 12km (7.5 miles) south of Quimper off D34, ☎ 02 98 51 69 03. Main courses € 5–15 (£ 3.35–10). Open May–Sept daily noon–2pm and 6–10pm for food (bar open all day). Highchair.

Concarneau & Around

MODERATE

Le Porte au Vin ★ In the heart of Concarneau's picturesque but touristy Ville Close (p. 150), this former fishermen's bistro has little to distinguish it from the host of others that line the street – at least from the outside. Once over the threshold, you may be surprised to find that the cosy rooms are full of locals rather than visitors, tucking into excellent seafood and other dishes from a very wide menu. Highpoints include a house *choucroute* with cod, salmon and smoked mackerel in Breton cider butter with steamed potatoes – a hearty dish that's best washed down with a light Britt Blanche from among the good list of Breton beers – Concarneau fish stew with *rouille* and croutons, and mussels in various guises, including the popular *indienne* (with a creamy curry sauce). Children can choose from the very good and light savoury and sweet crêpes, or there's an excellent, plentiful, very well-priced under-12s menu for € 7.50 (£ 5), which, in addition to nuggets or ham with chips, features *moules marinières* with chips, wonderful fresh breaded fish with rice and new potatoes or chips, or a ham, egg and cheese crêpe, followed by a Nutella, chocolate, strawberry jam or sugar crêpe or ice cream, and accompanied by a fizzy drink, water or juice. The genial English-speaking staff are very solicitous towards both adults and children, bringing highchairs and boosters to the table and pointing you in the direction of the baby-changing facilities. Note also that this has *service crêperie continu*, meaning you can eat crêpes all day, in front of a roaring log fire when it's cool or outside on the people-watching terrace.

9 place St-Guénolé, Ville Close, Concarneau, ☎ 02 98 97 38 11. Main courses € 2.10–19.90 (£ 1.40–13.45). Open daily noon–10.30pm; closed Oct–Feb. Highchairs.

INEXPENSIVE

Le Talisman Though the town of Pont-Aven isn't a favourite of mine, many are seduced by its good looks and artistic heritage, and it is a good central stopoff if you're touring the coast south of Concarneau, especially the *avens* by boat (p. 171). This good-value crêperie with its garden and children's games, books and comic strips is its most child-friendly option. It's set in an old house with the terrace at the back, away from the street; it's a good place to enjoy your complimentary apéritif while the children run around working up an appetite. In addition to plain crêpes or more interesting options such as the house special with *merguez* and smoked sausages, anchovies and garlic, there's a flambéed potato galette that goes down very well with children, plus main-course salads and a good choice of ice creams. You can get takeaway crêpes here, too.

4 rue Paul Sérusier, Pont-Aven, ☎ 02 98 06 02 58. Main courses € 7–15 (£ 4.70–10). Open Tue–Sun noon–2pm and 7–9pm, daily in July and Aug. Highchair.

6 Morbihan

Although the least-known and in many ways least touristy *département* of Brittany, especially among overseas visitors, the **Morbihan** is nevertheless home to the world-famous Carnac – a megalithic site with thousands of stones dating back further than Stonehenge or the Pyramids, to the neolithic period when agriculture developed. Thought by some to have been a lunar observatory, the formations, or at least some of them, have an undeniably mystical atmosphere, since experts are still scratching their heads as to their significance or how the ancients could even have placed some of the stones without powered machinery. Carnac is now largely closed off for much of the year, a victim of the tourist hordes, but happily within a stone's throw there are some good spots where you can still experience the mystery up close.

The Morbihan is not just about old rocks, though: its name means 'little sea'. This refers specifically to the stunning inland Golfe du Morbihan with its magical landscape of tiny islands, but there are some wonderful islands to sail out to, and a selection of fine resorts and beaches. Venturing just inland, meanwhile, will bring you to some wonderful nature parks and an array of quirky little museums that really bring Breton culture alive.

Accommodation-wise, this is a great place for thalassotherapy cures (a bit like spa treatments but with a greater medical basis) in hotels with childcare facilities, or there are some very stylish seaside options. The seafood, unsurprisingly, is first rate.

ESSENTIALS

Getting There

By Air At the time of writing, Ireland's **Aer Arann** (p. 31) has just launched budget flights between **Cork** and **Galway**, and one-way flights from Lorient to **Cardiff**, **Waterford** and **Kerry**. There are also links with **Paris** (Orly) on **Air France** (p. 31). For schedules, see ***www.lorient.aeroport.fr***.

Alternatively, **Ryanair** (p. 31) has low-cost flights from **London Stansted, East Midlands** and **Shannon** (Republic of Ireland) to the city of **Nantes** (115km (72 miles) south of Vannes) in the Loire Atlantique region.

By Boat There are no international ferry points in the Morbihan; your closest is **Roscoff** in Finistère (p. 32), about 140km (88 miles) away.

By Train Some fast **TGVs** between **Paris** and Quimper in Finistère stop at **Vannes**, **Auray** or **Lorient** (about 3 hours 35 minutes from Paris); see p. 41 for SNCF details.

THE **MORBIHAN**

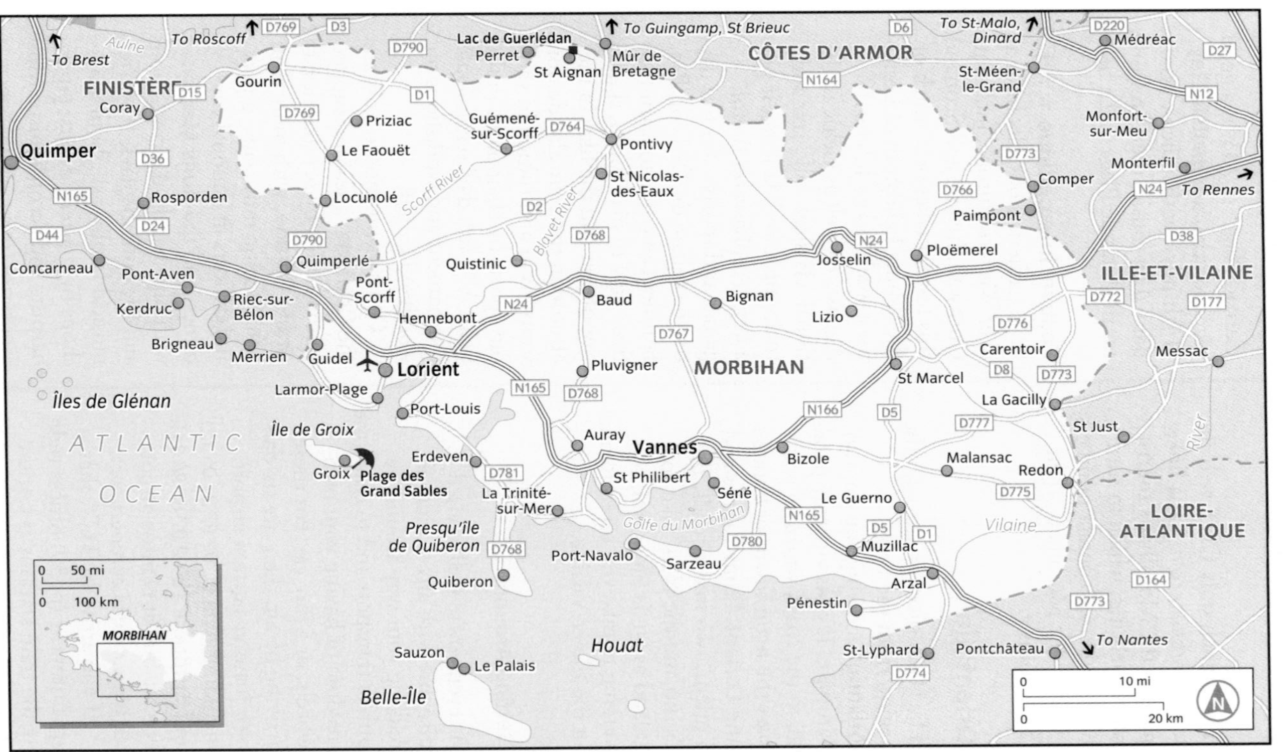

VISITOR INFORMATION

The French-only CDT website, ***www.morbihan.com***, has a links page to the Morbihan's tourist office websites, which in turn have addresses/contact numbers; click on 'Le Morbihan', then 'Sites Amis'.

Orientation

The **N165** slices up through the region from the Loire Atlantique, taking you on into Finistère. It runs virtually parallel to the coast, whizzing you past the main towns of **Vannes** and **Lorient**. From Vannes and Lorient, two major roads, the N166 and the N24, take you inland as far as **Ploërmel**, converging to take you on to Rennes in the Ille-et-Vilaine.

Getting Around

As ever, you're well advised to dispense with any notion of making your way around by public transport and to enjoy the freedom of having your own wheels, or a hire car. For those arriving by air, there are six **car-hire** firms at **Lorient** airport, including **Avis** (☎ *02 97 21 00 12*) and **Europcar** (☎ *02 97 86 28 34*). For car-hire at **Nantes** airport, see ***www.nantes.aeroport.com***.

If you arrive by TGV, there are Europcar (p. 39) offices right by the train stations at **Lorient** (☎ *02 97 21 22 44*), **Auray** (☎ *02 97 24 23 33*) and **Vannes** (☎ *02 97 42 43 43*).

Children-Friendly Events & Entertainment

Carnac-Plage (p. 203) is a good place to celebrate **Bastille Day** (14th July), with a picnic accompanied by music, then fireworks on the Grande Plage and a ball.

Festival Interceltique ★★★ A huge gathering of Celts from all over Western Europe, including Cornwall, Ireland and Scotland, this festival takes over much of the fishing behemoth of Lorient for a week in late July/early August. As well as Celtic traditional, classical, folk, jazz and rock music and dancing, it puts a large emphasis on Breton games and sports – for five days, on the square du Dr Léon Rio, families can come to learn (for free) how to play *boules*, skittles, tug-of-war and the like; in the afternoon there are also demonstrations of and tuition in various sports by champions in their field. A 'youth day' sees a *boules* tournament and workshops on woodland games.

Other events not to miss are the **Cotriade**, a seafood supper accompanied by sea shanties, the **Grand Parade**, with more than 3,000 Celtic musicians, pipers and dancers in national costumes, and the **Nuits Magiques**, with pipe bands, dancers, choirs and firework displays. If you're a musical family, ask about workshops by master fiddlers, pipers, harpists and accordionists. Most events are free; evening concerts require pre-paid tickets. The

Carnac Plage

Marché Interceltique in the city centre is open daily for crafts, books, clothes, music and food.

*Late July/early Aug. Lorient, ☎ 02 97 21 24 29, **www.festival-interceltique.com**. Adm mostly free; ticket prices for concerts vary.*

Fête de la Crêpe ★★ Only in Brittany, surely, would you encounter a crêpe festival, held in a town that holds the crown as the region's biggest industrial crêpe producer. The festival takes place in the grounds of a castle just outside town; over two days you can taste crêpes cooked over an open fire, plus chitterling sausages (for which nearby Guémené-sur-Scorff is famous), watch traditional crêpe-making demonstrations, dancing and Celtic music concerts, see displays and shows about rural traditions, peruse craft stalls, and play traditional Breton wooden games. There's also an attempt to break the local record for the biggest pancake.

Gourin, 55km (35 miles) northwest of Lorient off D769. Tourist office (syndicat d'initative): *24 rue de la Libération, ☎ 02 97 23 66 33. Free.*

WHAT TO SEE & DO

Children's Top 10 Attractions

❶ **Sailing** amidst the beautiful fragmented island landscape of the **Golfe du Morbihan**. See p. 205.

❷ **Going rural** at the **Ferme du Monde** with its farm animals from round the world, children's farm, pony rides, puppet shows and activities. See p. 208.

❸ **Reliving** the life of a submarine crew at the **Tour Davis** in Lorient. See p. 214.

❹ **Discovering** the animated scrap-metal sculptures in the magical universe of the **Poète Ferrailleur** at Lizio. See p. 220.

❺ **Exploring** the château, animal park and botanical garden of the **Parc de Branféré**. See p. 210.

❻ **Puzzling about** how ancient peoples moved the gigantic **Grand Menhir Brisé**. See p. 214.

❼ **Being green-fingered** at Yves Rocher's **Végétarium**, Europe's only dedicated plant museum. See p. 218.

⑧ **Learning about** the amazing 5000km (3125 mile) odyssey of the salmon as it returns from the Atlantic to its birthplace, at the **Odyssaum**. See p. 209.

⑨ **Playing** Breton games and watching fireworks to the strains of Celtic music at the **Festival Interceltique** in Lorient. See p. 200.

⑩ **Having a siesta** under the fruit trees, swimming in the pool and relaxing in the clawfoot bath of your beach-hut-style family suite at the **Lodge Kerisper**. See p. 226.

Beaches, Resorts & Islands

Note that the southern part of the **Lac de Guerlédan** (p. 114) is in the Morbihan.

Belle-Ile ★★ The largest Breton island, 14km (9 miles) off the Quiberon peninsula, Belle-Ile with its mild climate and gorgeous beaches is popular with Parisians as a location for their second homes – and has become accordingly chic and expensive. Like the Parisians, you're most likely to stick to the calm beaches and harbours of the northeast coast; rather confusingly, since it's also the name of part of the mainland coast around Quiberon, Belle-Ile's southwest coast is known as the Côte Sauvage ('Wild Coast') for its vicious cliffs, which inspired some of Monet's Impressionist paintings, especially the Aiguilles ('Needles') de Port Coton. Actress Sarah Bernhardt and writer Alexandre Dumas also loved the island; the latter set part of his adventure yarn *The Man in the Iron Mask* here.

The biggest beach, **Les Grands Sables**, gets crowded in high season; seek out other beaches by hiring bikes or mopeds. Most people leave their cars in car parks on the mainland because it's so expensive to bring them over, and because the spaces for them get booked up well in advance. Most of the good beaches are between

Aiguilles de Port Coton Belle-Ile

Locmaria at the southern tip and the island's capital, **Le Palais**, though local youngsters flock to **Port Donnant** on the west side, which is good for bodyboarding. You can climb the nearby **Phare Grande** lighthouse, if you have enough puff for its 213 steps. Alternatively, take a bus or taxi tour of the island, hire a pony-and-trap at Locmaria (*02 97 31 76 67*) or go horse-riding (*02 97 31 64 32*). If you want to stay, **Hôtel La Désirade** (*02 97 31 70 70*, ***www.hotel-la-desirade.com***) has two family suites (*moderate–expensive*), charming nautical decor and an outdoor pool; **Hôtel Le Clos Fleuri** (*02 97 31 45 45*, ***www.hotel-leclosfleuri.com***) also has family rooms (*inexpensive–moderate*) overlooking its lovely garden, and offers preferential rates with a local babysitting service.

*Tourist office: Quai Bonnelle, 02 97 31 81 93, **www.belle-ile.com**. Ferries from Quiberon to Le Palais (45 minutes, or 20 minutes by fast-craft in summer) and Sauzon (June–Sept, 25 minutes, no cars), or Lorient to Sauzon (50 minutes, mid-July–Aug), 02 97 35 02 00, **www.smn-navigation.fr**; high-season single fares adults around € 14 (£ 9.45), children aged over 3 € 9 (£ 6), smallest model of car € 65 (£ 43.95). (There are also passenger boats from Vannes and Port-Navalo [Apr–Oct] and La Trinité-sur-Mer, 08 25 13 21 00, **www.navix.fr**, and from La Turballe in the Loire Atlantique [May–Sept] 08 25 13 41 00, **www.compagniedesiles.com**.) Flights: daily from Nantes in the Loire Atlantique, 02 40 84 82 41, **www.atlanticairlift.com**; one-way fare adults € 80–120 (£ 54–80), children 2–12 € 50–90 (£ 33–60).*

Phare Grande

Carnac-Plage ★ Virtually synonymous with neolithic megaliths (p. 213), Carnac has its own stylish, sheltered beach resort backed by pine woods, with a **yacht club** (*02 97 52 10 98*, ***www.yccarnac.com***) running introductory courses for 4–7-year-olds, **sand-yachting** (*02 97 52 40 60*, ***www.aeroplage.com***), a **surf and skate school** (*02 97 52 41 18*, ***www.bretagnesurf.net***) and other seaside activities, plus a **thalassotherapy centre**, lots of **children's clubs** on the various beaches, **Place aux Mômes** free children's shows (puppetry, storytelling, clowns) in summer and a carousel. Look out for the **Nocturnes** evening markets in July and August, with local produce and crafts, and if you can drag yourself away from the beach, Carnac's charming upper town, **Carnac-Ville**, is worth a stroll.

*15km (9 miles) southwest of Auray on D186. Tourist office: place de la Chapelle and 74 avenue des Druides, 02 97 52 13 52, **www.carnac.fr**.*

Houat ★ Stranded in the Atlantic between Belle-Ile and the mainland, the islands of Houat and Hoedic derive their names from the Breton for 'duck' and 'duckling'. Houat, the largest (5km or 3 miles long and 1.5km at its widest point), has magnificent unspoilt beaches, **Treac'h er Goured** and **Treac'h er Salus**, where you can hunt for crabs, lobsters, conger eels and colonies of wild mussels and oysters. That may inspire you to visit the **Musée de l'Eclosarium** (May–Sept, *02 97 52 38 38*), which has displays on microscopic life in the sea as well as the island's history.

The population amounts to less than 350, most of whom live in the main village, also named Houat, and home to three hotels, two with restaurants, a crêperie, a brassiere and a bar. Outside this village you will see just one tree on the whole island, which you can explore by mountain bikes hired from Houat Vélo (*02 97 30 68 76*) by the port. There's a new municipal campsite open June–Sept (no bookings), and the *mairie*'s website (below) has a page with rooms and apartments let by islanders.

INSIDER TIP

If you sail to Houat from Vannes, the trip is much longer but lets you take in the Golfe du Morbihan (p. 205) en route, at no extra cost.

14km (9 miles) off Quiberon Peninsula, 02 97 30 68 04 (mairie) *or 02 97 30 66 42 (high season info line),* ***www.ile-de-houat.com****. Ferries to Houat: from La Trinité-sur-Mer (40 minutes; hand luggage only), 02 97 35 02 00,* ***www.smn-navigation.fr****; single fares over-25s about € 13 (£ 8.75), ages 4–25 € 8 (£ 5.40), under 4s € 1 (£ 0.70); also from La Trinité (July and Aug, 45 minutes), 08 25 13 21 00,* ***www.navix.fr****, single fares adults € 27 (£ 18), children 4–14 € 11 (£ 7.45), under 4s € 5 (£ 3.35); from Vannes, Locmariaquer and Port-Navalo (Apr–Sept, 1 hour 45 minutes, 1 hour, and 45 minutes respectively), 08 25 13 41 00,* ***www.compagniedesiles.com****, single fares adults € 11–17 (£ 7.45–11.45), children 4–14 € 7–11 (£ 4.75–7.45), under-4s € 5 (£ 3.35).*

Port-Tudy, Ile de Groix

Ile de Groix The 'Island of the Witch' according to its Breton name (*Enezar Grroac'h*), Groix lies just off Lorient, from which you make the 45 minute boat trip (it should be quicker, but getting out of the congested Rade de Lorient takes forever). Aside from the remains of some megaliths and forts, there is little here but rabbits, honeysuckle plants and some lovely coastline that you can explore on foot or by bike – whether it be the fine sandy beaches of Primiture on the east or the wilder shoreline and cliffs of Piwisy to the west. The former, including the popular **Plage des Grands Sables** (which has the distinction of being one of Europe's few convex beaches, and also of having shifted 160m in just two years), are often streaked with red dust from garnets – an inexpensive gemstone that is abundant in the local rocks – when it has been very windy. **Port-Tudy**, once one of France's biggest tuna fishing ports, has an **Ecomusée** about the island's main industry in a former canning factory, and up the hill at **Groix** (Le Bourg) is a church with a tuna weathervane. But the island's chief claims to fame are **Le Trou de l'Enfer** (Hell's Hole), a huge legend-steeped hole in a cliff, and the **Pointe des Chats** ('Cats' Point'), an area of dazzling multicoloured schist rocks.

Divers can explore various wrecks off the island's coast with Subagrec (*02 97 86 59 79*, ***http://assoc.orange.fr/subagrec***); 80% of the sites it visits, including a German submarine, are accessible to Level 1 divers aged 14 and over.

Mairie: *13 place de l'Eglise, 02 97 86 80 15, **www.groix.fr**. Boats: 02 97 35 02 00, **www.smn-navigation.fr** (prices similar to those to Belle-Ile,* *p. 203**, and places for cars similarly limited).*

Other Natural Wonders & Spectacular Views

Golfe du Morbihan ★★

Covering 100 square kilometres (39 square miles), the Gulf of Morbihan is a gorgeous inland sea busy with fishing vessels, oyster boats, yachts and canoes and sprinkled with lush green islands and islets – one for every day of the year according to legend, and many of them home to neolithic remains. Of the 40 or so islands, most are private; you can only visit the **Ile aux Moines**, full of fishermen's cottages, winding pathways, old fountains, chapels, ruined

Ile aux Moines, Golfe du Morbihan

windmills and megalithic vestiges lurking amidst pine and fig trees, and evocatively named areas ('Love Woods', 'Regret Woods', 'the Sighing Woods'); and the **Ile d'Arz**, with more old windmills, pleasant family beaches and peaceful coves that you can discover by following the coastal path right round the island (guided nature tours are run in high season). You can hire bikes on both islands, and seasonal tourist information points by the boat jetties give out free maps.

Alternatively, fly over the gulf on 30 minute trips run by the **Aéroclub du Pays de Vannes** (*02 97 60 73 08*, ***http://assoc.orange.fr/acpvannes/***, € 120 (£ 80) for three people), or by hot-air balloon (p. 220). The gulf also has its own new museum in Vannes. **Capitaine d'un Jour** ('Captain for a Day'; Parc du Golfe, *02 97 40 40 39*, ***www.capitainedunjour.com***), which has a discovery area with games, films and children's naval modelling workshops.

Ile aux Moines mairie, *02 97 26 32 31*, ***www.ileauxmoines.fr***; *Ile d'Arz* mairie: *02 97 44 31 14*, ***www.iledarz.fr***; *or contact Vannes tourist office (1 rue Thiers, 02 97 47 24 34,* ***www.tourisme-vannes.com****) for both. Boats: Ile aux Moines (5 minutes from Port-Blanc every 30 minutes daily; adult return € 3.80 (£ 2.55), children 4–10 € 2 (£ 1.35)), 02 97 26 31 45,* ***www.izenah-croisieres.com****; Ile d'Arz (20 minutes from Conleau [Vannes] roughly every hour daily; adult return € 7.20 (£ 4.80), children 4–10 € 4 (£ 2.65)) or Séné, 02 97 01 22 80,* ***www.lactm.com****. Other companies sail to both in high season.*

Mine d'Or ★ This 3km (2 mile) beach and listed geological site just south of the Vilaine estuary, unique in Europe, takes its name from a short-lived and unsuccessful gold mine here, but it's entirely apt – at sunset its sandstone and clay cliffs glow the colour of the precious metal. They are part of a 25km (15½ mile) stretch of lovely coastline around Pénestin with pretty, safe, toddler-friendly beaches and wilder creeks, marked walking, mountain-biking and riding tracks, plus the **Maison de la Mytiliculture** little mussel-farming museum in an old lighthouse (this is a good place for shellfishing on foot; the tourist office can provide guidelines and rules). Adventurous types like to see this coastline by *parapente* (paraglider; *06 08 21 95 30*). There's a great hostel and campsite (p. 185) here.

Tourist office: allée du Grand Pré, Pénestin, 45km (28 miles) southeast of Vannes on D34, 02 99 90 37 74, ***www.penestin.com****.*

Aquaria & Animal Parks

L'Abeille Vivante et La Cité des Fourmis Set on a characterful old farm, 'The Living Bee and City of Ants' allows you a close-up view of insect activity, beginning with some working hives of all shapes and sizes. There follow three rooms with displays about bee-keeping through history, including traditional hives from Spain and Morocco. Then comes 'Ant City', where you watch leaf-cutting ants break up leaves, petals and the like to take to the colony, where others grind them into loam in which a special mushroom grows, with strands that constitute their main food source. There's also a larger colony consisting of a metre-high dome made from twigs and pine needles by forest ants; children can get right into the heart of this by means of tunnels leading to glass viewing pods. It's all rounded off by a short video about the importance of ants to the ecology of the forest. There are 90 minute French-language guided tours (€ 5 (£ 3.35)), or free audioguides in French, English, German, Dutch and Spanish.

In the grounds is an attractive communal gîte, with four rooms for three, four and five people with private showers and loos and a shared kitchen. Nearby are a playground, a picnic area, a corn maze and numerous walking paths.

Note: At the time of writing the owner was retiring and new proprietors being sought, so call to check it's open before setting out.

*Kercadoret, Le Faouët, 30km (19 miles) northwest of Lorient on D769, ✆ 02 97 23 08 05, **www.abeilles-et-fourmis.com**. Adults € 6 (£ 4), children 4–15 € 4 (£ 2.70). Open Apr–Sept, call for times.*

Aquarium du Golfe ★ It doesn't scale the heights of Brest's sealife centre (p. 160), but Vannes' aquarium has an original focus – it looks at the Golfe du Morbihan (p. 205), the Red Sea and the Amazon in its three separate sections. Some of the most interesting inhabitants are the Golfe du Morbihan seahorses and the Morgat, a cuttlefish whose eggs can be found on local beaches in summer, resembling bunches of black grapes. From further afield there are the obligatory but no less awesome sharks, piranhas and moray eels, and changing temporary exhibitions investigate such themes as tides and how sea creatures adapt to them (the Golfe du Morbihan has some of Europe's strongest currents). Thought has been put into making visits easier for those with children: there's free use of some rather bizarre wheeled highchairs that mean you can push babies and toddlers round at a height at which they can see into the tanks. There are also changing facilities, and a crêperie and bar May–Sept (plus a lawn for picnics). The shop has the usual trinkets, toys and books.

Your ticket allows half-price entry to **Le Jardin aux Papillons** (✆ *02 97 40 67 40, **www.jardinauxpapillons.com***) 500m away. Formerly Le Papillonneraie, this is a tropical space full of freeflying butterflies that flit about your head or amidst the lush vegetation, which includes orchids from round the world.

*Parc du Golfe du Morbihan, Vannes, ✆ 02 97 40 67 40, **www.aquarium-du-golfe.com**. Open daily Jan–Mar and Oct–Dec 2–6 (plus 10am–noon school hols), Apr, May and Sept 10am–noon and 2–6pm, July and Aug 9am–7pm. Adm: € 8.90 (£ 6), children 4–11 € 5.90 (£ 3.95).*

A Breton Donkey

Barrage d'Arzal ★ This flood dam built at the entrance to the Vilaine estuary in 1970 contains a 70m (230 ft) long *passe à poissons* ('fish pass') that lets migrating fish through on their way back up the river. This pass is fitted with an observation room where you can come to watch, from very close up, the fish on their way through. A guide, meanwhile, tells you (in French) about the various species you might see – mullets, sea trouts, eels, sea lampreys and occasionally salmon – and their habits. There are also display boards and a video. It's a low-key sight, for sure, but a delightful one at that.

Arzal, 35km (22 miles) southeast of Vannes on D139, ☎ 02 99 90 88 44. Adm: € 3 (£ 2), under-18s free. Open 2–6pm May Sat and Sun, June–mid-Sept Mon–Fri, late Sept Wed–Fri.

Ferme du Monde ★★★ One of the most remarkable things about the 'World Farm', home to more than 400 domestic animals in five zones representing the five continents, is that it was conceived and created entirely by handicapped workers, and one of its special events is a festival with open-air performances by handicapped artists. Others from the eclectic list are calf races, balloon sculpting and traditional bread-making. Set in a tranquil wooded park covering 25 hectares (60 acres), it includes yaks, zebus (a humped cow), buffaloes, camels, Texas longhorns and Cameroon sheep, housed in large enclosures. For closer encounters, there's a children's farm where they can pet dwarf goats, Ouessant sheep, ponies, a Vietnamese potbellied pig, donkeys and more. There's also a *petit train* to take you around (lasting about an hour), free pony rides for under-12s, a scale model of a Breton village with automated figures carrying out old professions, and, new in 2006, puppet shows. A play area has mini-tractors, mini-golf, a slide and a basketball hoop. With so much to do, you'll need a good 2–3 hours, or ideally a whole morning or afternoon. Inside the 16th century manor in the grounds you'll find a rather expensive restaurant, a bar and a shop with souvenirs and local produce, including 'milk jam' (nicer than it sounds).

*Entreprise de Travail Adapté, 'Le Bois Brassu', Carentoir, 30km (19 miles) southeast of Ploërmel on D118, ☎ 02 99 93 70 70, **www.lafermedu-monde.com**. Open daily Apr–mid-June and mid-Sept to mid-Nov 10am–6pm, mid-June to mid-Sept 10am–7pm. Adm: adults € 8 (£ 5.40),* *children over 5 € 4.50 (£ 3);* petit train *adults € 2.50 (£ 1.70), children over 5 € 2 (£ 1.35), children 2–5 € 1 (70p). Puppet show: child € 1 (£ 0.70).*

Haras National de Hennebont ★ This stud farm took over a former Cistercian abbey in 1857 and retains some interesting architecture. However, people flock to see the stables, saddlery and smithy, plus its modern 'discovery space' with displays (many of them interactive) on the relationship between Breton horses and humans, and its little screening room. Try to time your visit for one of the frequent events, which include a grand 'Spectacle Equestre', a stallion parade, competitions, demonstrations, riding courses and quizzes.

1 rue Victor Hugo, Hennebont, ☎ 02 97 89 40 30, ***www.haras-nationaux.fr****. Open July and Aug Tue–Fri 9am–7pm, Sat–Mon 9am–12.30pm, Sept–mid-Dec and mid-Jan–June Tue–Fri 9am–12.30pm and 2.30–6pm, Sat–Mon 9am–12.30pm (also Mon mornings in school hols). Adm: € 6.60 (£ 4.40), children € 5.10 (£ 3.45), family (2+2) € 19.90 (£ 13.45), then € 1.50 (£ 1) per additional child.*

Insectarium de Lizio In a town of ceramic and weaving workshops, this old cottage stands out – instead of kilns and looms it houses scorpions, praying mantises, trap-door spiders, millipedes up to 30cm (12 inches) long, stick insects and more. The exhibition spaces focus not only on the insects themselves (housed safely in more than 30 terrariums) but also on their role in maintaining the natural status quo by, as in the example of the ladybird in Brittany, eating aphids before they destroy tomato plants. The diverting display boards (in French) explore others ways that insects help humans, and microscopes and magnifying glasses allow you close-up views. Don't miss the screening room with its fascinating half-hour film on the ethereal life of the *libellule* or dragonfly, or the new ant colony and display of carnivorous plants. Outside is a quiet picnic area.

Rue du Stade, Lizio, 15km (9 miles) southeast of Ploërmel on D174, ☎ 02 97 74 99 12, ***www.insectarium-de-lizio.com****. Open Apr–Sept daily 10am–12.30pm and 1.30–6.30pm, rest of year Sat and Sun 1.30–6.30pm. Adm: adults € 5.50 (£ 3.70), children € 4.50 (£ 3).*

Odyssaum ★★ A perfect counterpoint to the more commercialised zoo nearby (p. 211), this tranquil eco-museum is based around an open-air *station de comptage* where wild salmon are captured and anaesthetised in order to be weighed, measured, aged and sexed during their migration back from the Atlantic to their native river to breed and die – the aim is to keep track of how many make the return journey. Next-door the **Moulin des Princes**, once home to Breton royalty, now houses displays about the salmon's amazing 5000km (3000 mile) odyssey. This centre reopened in mid 2006 after extensive remodelling and is now more hands-on, with lots of images and sounds evoking the salmon's journey.

Afterwards, you go back out into the open, to an island in the middle of the Scorff with display boards on local flora and fauna. Try to coincide your visit with an open-air performance, in summer, about the adventures of Salmo the salmon – great fun for children and parents alike. There is also a salmon festival in July. The chic **Bistrot Saumon** (☎ *02 97 32 42 07*) by the carpark offers gourmet seafood and views over the lovely river and a Roman bridge – though it's about 15km (9 miles) from the sea, seawater can reach as far as this at high tide.

Pont-Scorff, 10km (6 miles) north of Lorient on D6, ☎ 02 97 32 42 00. Open July and Aug daily 9am–7pm, Sept–June Mon 2–6pm, Tue–Sun 9am–12.30pm and 2–6pm (open Mon morning in school hols). Adm: € 5 (£ 3.35), child € 3.50 (£ 2.35).

Parc de Branféré ★★★ Like the Bourbansais in the Ille-et-Vilaine (p. 51), Branféré combines guided visits of its stately château with an animal park containing native and exotic species. It also has a botanical garden full of ancient trees and plants from around the world, and – uniquely – a nature school with a mission to teach children how to live in harmony with the world around them. Called the **Ecole Nicolas Hulot pour la Nature et l'Homme**, this runs weekend and school-holiday residential 'discovery courses' for the general public, with parents and children taking part in the same activities, which can include nature-based sports (canoeing, tree-climbing and hiking), and studies into biodiversity and sustainability (how to make your house more eco-friendly, and so on). There's also a course designed specially for children aged 8–12 and their grandparents, and one in which you hang out with the park's animal-keepers. Accommodation is in 2–5-person rooms with their own loo and shower, and you eat in the park's panoramic restaurant, serving seasonal local produce and crêpes.

Parc de Branféré

A Giraffe at the Zoo de Pont-Scorff

Prices start at a very reasonable € 132.50 (£ 89.50) per child and € 170 (£ 114.80) per adult for two days and two nights, with all meals (not drinks), sheets (not towels), unlimited access to the animal park and botanical garden, and mountain bike loan.

One of the highlights of the animal park itself – a pretty, well-maintained place full of lakes, islands, waterfalls and woods – is the bird show, during which pelicans, storks, ibis, herons, birds of prey and parrots fly right over your head. In the castle – which has attracted visitors as illustrious as Serge Gainsbourg and Jane Birkin – are works by Hélène Jourde, a park founder and talented animal painter. Guided tours of its rooms take place daily in July and August.

Le Guerno, 25km (16 miles) south-east of Vannes on D139, ☎ 02 97 42 94 66, **www.branfere.com**. *Open Feb, Mar, Oct and Nov daily 1.30–5.30pm, early Apr, May, June and Sept Mon–Fri 10am–6.30pm, Sat, Sun and hols 10am–7.30pm, July and Aug daily 10am–7.30pm; last adm 90 minutes before closing. Adm: adults € 11 (£ 7.35), children 4–12 € 8 (£ 5.40) (castle extra € 3 (£ 2), under-12s free).*

Zoo de Pont-Scorff Out-of-the-way but expectedly huge, this zoo has 12 hectares (30 acres) of hilly (if attractive and flower-filled) grounds crossed by steep, winding pathways you need to negotiate to see its 120 species (buggy pushers and toddlers with easily tired legs beware), including elephants, big cats, zebras and rhinos. Enclosures tend to be on the small side, though some imagination has gone into their design – there are Moorish buildings, for instance, for the friendly giraffes who stroll over to eat popcorn from your hands. Other highlights are an area where you have to identify the animal dung used to fertilise certain plants, and a farm enclosure set around an island of monkeys, with tame ducks and sheep. There are good daily shows, including sealions, *mal-aimés* ('unloved' animals, such as snakes and rats) and, most dramatically, seabirds, who swoop and soar above your head, cackling like devils. Allow about four hours for a visit. There are refreshment stops, shops and baby changing facilities.

Pont-Scorff, 10km (6 miles) north of Lorient on D6, 02 97 32 60 86. Open daily Apr, May and Sept 9.30am–6pm, June–Aug 9.30am–7pm, rest of year 9.30am–5pm; last adm 1 hour before closing. Adm: € 13 (£ 8.75), children 3–11 € 8 (£ 5.40).

Nature Reserves, Parks & Gardens

Parc de Préhistoire de Bretagne ★ This 'park to take you back in time' a little way northeast of the Parc de Branféré (p. 210) might be just the ticket for youngsters for whom the ancient alignments at Carnac (p. 213) are too dry. Its circuit takes you past more than 25 life-sized scenes of dinosaurs, animals and early humans, including *Homo erectus* – they're extremely schlocky and not at all convincing, but that's all part of the fun (the Cro-magnon dancing scene will have you in stitches). Unusually, all the information boards are in English, Dutch, German and Spanish as well as French. Things are more low-key elsewhere in the vast and rather wild wooded park, where you can see old wells and slate quarries, and walk around five pretty lakes edged by cliffs. The reception centre has a picnic space, a bar selling snacks and ice creams and a shop with fossils and minerals. In all, you should reckon to spend about two hours here.

*Malansac, 35km (22 miles) east of Vannes on D153, 02 97 43 34 17, **www.prehistoire-bretagne.com**. Open Apr–mid-Nov daily 10.30am–7pm; last adm 2 hours before closure, or 1 hour in July and Aug; mid-Oct–early Oct Sun 1.30–6pm. Adm: € 9 (£ 6), children 5–11 € 5 (£ 3.35).*

Historic Buildings & Monuments

Alignments de Kerzehro ★ If you want to ogle ancient stones without the crowds (or fences) of Carnac (see below), this is your place – you don't even need to get out of your car, as the D781 south from Erdeven takes you through the middle of some of the 1000 stones, which are 10 rows wide at their thickest point. There are also four huge menhirs, the **Giants of Kerzehro**, two standing and two lying on the ground, apparently encircled by stones; one even seems to have a semi-human face, though this is probably due to the elements. As with the Carnac alignments, the signification of the geometric configurations remains a mystery. Ask at the tourist office for their free maps outlining a Circuit des Mégalithes et Châteaux and a Circuit du Grand Arc Mégalithique, and about mountain bike hire.

*South of Erdeven, 15km (9 miles) west of Auray on D781. Erdeven tourist office: 7 rue Abbé Le Barh, 02 97 55 64 60, **www.ot-erdeven.fr/**.*

Carnac ★ Carnac is the most famous (and touristy) of the prehistoric sites that make the area just north of the Golfe du

Ancient Tongues: a Neolithic Vocabulary

Cairn: piles of stones surrounding a tomb or tombs
Cromlech: a circle of standing stones
Dolmen: a megalithic burial monument made of large stone slabs
Enceinte: standing stones forming a circle or quadrilateral
Menhir: a tall, upright stone, isolated or in alignments
Tumulus: a large tomb built of piled-up stones or earth

Morbihan the neolithic capital of the Western world. It bristles with around 3000 megaliths – menhirs, dolmens and tumulus – built between 4500 and 2000 BC. Now generally held to have been a place of worship, or perhaps a lunar observatory that helped the ancients observe the movement of stars, the alignments were believed by some Bretons to have been erected by *korrigans* (p. 3) or giants, and some modern-day theorists even claim they were made by aliens.

Sadly, the number of visitors here in the past caused serious damage to vegetation, which stabilises the stones, and now the area is fenced off and can only be accessed (in part) between November and March – the rest of the year, the Kerzehro alignments (p. 212) are a good alternative. Carnac has three main fields of alignments: **Menec**, the largest, with 1099 menhirs in 11 rows, some up to 4m (13 ft) high; **Kermario**, with 1029 menhirs in 10 rows plus the **Géant du Manio**, the area's tallest menhir at more than 6m (20 ft); and **Kerlescan**, the smallest but best-preserved, with 555 menhirs in 13 rows. Scattered between are some isolated remnants, many concealed in pine-scented woods; the most interesting is the vast **Tumulus St Michel**, covering a dolmen and two burial chambers, and once housing 15 stone chests filled with bone remains, axes, pottery fragments and jewellery that are now in the museum (*below*). The tourist office has free maps.

For background on the megaliths and a useful reminder that they were created by real people like us, visit the **Musee de Prehistorie James Miln – Zacharie le Rouzic ★★** (☎ *02 97 52 22 04*; ***www.museedecarnac.com***), which has an

Kids at Carnac

astonishing 6500-plus objects found during archaeological digs, including ceramics, tools, axes and jewellery, plus maps, models and a film. In school holidays it runs workshops on daily life in neolithic times for 6–12-year-olds, and in summer there are special shows for adults and kids, night visits and demonstrations of prehistoric techniques. French-speaking children should also enjoy the special guided tours for 8–12-year-olds, by a cartoon character called Neo.

For **Carnac-Plage** and **Ville**, see p. 203.

15km (9 miles) southeast of Auray on D781, ☎ 02 97 52 89 99; Centre des Monuments Nationaux, Carnac tourist office: see p. 20.

Grand Menhir Brisé ★ Set on a megalith-rich peninsula south of Carnac, the 'Big Broken Menhir' is one of the largest stones to have been worked on by prehistoric people, at 20m (65 ft) in length (in four sections, after an earthquake in 1722) and weighing about 280 tonnes (more than a jumbo jet). Formerly known as Pierre de la Fée ('Fairytale Peter'), it would have reached a height of almost 18m (60 ft) when standing, and it's mind boggling to think that ancient peoples somehow lifted it into place; no one has explained how, and it is claimed that it is the heaviest object ever moved by humans without the help of powered machinery. Some theorists claim it's the central point of the lunar observatory of Carnac (p. 213).

Locmariaquer peninsula, 12km (7.5 miles) south of Auray on D781, ☎ 02 97 57 33 05 (tourist office). Open daily mid-Jan–Mar and Oct–mid-Dec 2–5pm, Apr and May 10am–1pm and 2–6pm, June–Sept 10am–7pm. Adm: July and Aug € 5 (£ 3.35), Sept–June € 4 (£ 2.70).

Tour Davis ★★ Dubbed the 'museum under the sea', the Davis tower, part of the old Nazi submarine base of Keroman, contains the simulator that was used to train all French submarine crews in evacuation and rescue techniques for more than 50 years after the base was taken over in 1953, including a decompression chamber. Fascinating 50 minute guided tours are run by passionate diving and history specialists (who speak good English). You then visit three exhibition rooms, including an audiovisual space re-creating the experience of life in a submarine in all its claustrophobia and sense of danger, including U-171 as it sank off Groix (p. 204) and other Atlantic wrecks; a soundtrack of a diver's breathing makes it all the more haunting.

Part of the rest of the monstrous concrete base is currently being transformed into the **Cité de la Voile Eric Tabarly**, a space dedicated to the memory of the famous distance racer and to sailing in general, scheduled to open in June 2007. The following year, a submarine, *La Flore*, should be open to the public as well.

*Base des Sous-Marins de Keroman, Lorient, ☎ 06 07 10 69 41, **www.tour-davis.com**. Open July and Aug* *daily 1.30–6.30pm, rest of year Sun 2–6pm. Adm free.*

Village de Poul-Fetan ★ Restoration of this tiny hamlet dating back to the 16th century began in 1979, less than 10 years after the last of its handful of inhabitants left, and was carried out so painstakingly that you might be forgiven for thinking you've walked onto a film set – especially given the presence (every afternoon Apr–Oct) of costumed characters acting out scenes from the daily lives of 19th century peasants, including milking, wool-dying, butter- and crêpe-making and buckwheat cultivation. Children will probably be most taken by the protected domestic animals who populate the 9 hectare (22 acre) farmland, including Breton cows, horses, sheep and pigs, but there are also displays of old farm machinery and peasant costumes, a re-created 1850s interior, a half-hour video on the hamlet's architecture and its restoration, pottery and bakery workshops, a craft shop and a 'tavern' serving local produce.

Quistinic, 30km (19 miles) northeast of Lorient on D156, ☎ 02 97 39 51 74, ***www.poul-fetan.com****. Open early Apr–May and late Sept–late Oct daily 2–4pm, June–late Sept 10.15am–1pm (for guided tours only) and 1–7pm. Adm: adults € 7 (£ 4.70), children 6–12 € 4 (£ 2.70).*

The Top Museums

Musee de la Poupée This famous collection of around 600 antique dolls and items of dolls' house furniture belonged to the improbably named Herminie de La Brousse de Verteillac, who was Princess of Léon and then Duchess of Rohan, as well as a distinguished poet. It's housed in the former stables of the splendid family château, first built (in wood) around 1000AD and currently inhabited by the 14th Duke of Rohan; in recent times

Crepe-Making, Village de Poul-Fetan

Château de Josselin

his guests have included the British Queen Mother. After looking at the dolls, together with a variety of old toys and games, you can take guided tours (Apr–Sept, including two tours a day in English) of some of the ornate rooms full of 17th and 18th century furniture, family portraits and gifts from royals. Don't miss, on your way in or out, the carved dragons and other monsters on the castle's Gothic inner façade.

Château de Josselin, Josselin, 10km (6 miles) northwest of Ploërmel on N24, ☎ 02 97 22 36 45, Open Apr, May and Oct 2–6pm Sat, Sun and school hols, June–mid-July and Sept 2–6pm daily, mid-June–Aug 10am–6pm daily, Nov–Mar 2–6pm school hols. Adm € 6.80 (£ 4.60), children € 4.70 (£ 3.15).

Musée Régional des Petits Commerces et des Métiers

Not one for those who don't like clutter, this repository of more than 30,000 objects dating from the 17th century to the 1950s, amassed by an avid collector, brings to life more around 60 trades of yesteryear through tools, machines, period decor and old posters, crammed into a series of re-created workshops and shops – boot and shoe makers, a carpenter, a barrel maker, a smithy, a barber and so on. The old grocery contains old cake and sweet boxes, while in the chemists there's a mortar, pill maker and so on. There's also a display of traditional lace and Breton *coiffes* and a reconstructed 19th century Breton interior. The highlight for children comes at the end – a 1930s classroom with real desks and old toys. The museum is in a 15th century manor containing an intact 1950s bar where you can still get a drink.

Route du Château de Suscinio, Sarzeau, 25km (16 miles) south of Vannes on D780, ☎ 02 97 41 75 36.

Open July and Aug daily 10am–noon and 2–9pm, rest of year Tue–Sun 2–7pm. Adm: adults € 5 (£ 3.35), children 12 and over € 3 (£ 2).

Musée de la Résistance Bretonne The area around St Marcel was well suited to Allied and French Resistance parachuting expeditions because of its wooded scrubland – easy to both land on and hide in – and a famous battle took on this very spot in June 1944. In July and August there are guided tours (available in English and German as well as French) of the terrain in an old US army vehicle, which children love. The wooded 6 hectare (15 acre) park also has space to run around in, plus a good children's playground, picnic space and crêperie/bar.

Inside, meanwhile, the museum contains plenty of hands-on displays, including a Boeing B17 ('Flying Fortress') simulator that allows you to 'fly' over Lorient at an altitude of 8km (5 miles) and a speed of 300km/h (188mph), plus large-screen presentations. The France Libre parachutists also have their national exhibition here, and there's a re-created shopping street under Occupation.

Les Hardys Béhelec, St Marcel, 35km (22 miles) northeast of Vannes on N166, 📞 02 97 75 16 90, ***www.resistance-bretonne.com****. Open Apr–mid-June daily 10am–noon and 2–6pm, mid-June–mid-Sept daily 10am–7pm, mid-Sept–Mar Wed–Mon 10am–noon and 2–6pm. Adm: museum € 6.60 (£ 4.40), child € 5.10 (£ 3.40); museum and guided tour € 8.85 (£ 5.98), children over 10 € 7.65 (£ 5.15), children 5–9 € 4.30*

Musée de la Résistance Bretonne

(£ 2.90); guided tour without museum € 4.30 (£ 2.90).

La Thalassa Not a seawater spa, as the name might suggest, but an 'oceanology discovery centre', La Thalassa is set partly inside a ship, the *Ifremer*, that covered more than 1509380km (815000 nautical miles) equivalent to nearly 38 trips around the world) in the course of 252 missions to gather scientific data on fishing and the conservation of fish stocks.

Inside are models, including one of the ship itself and almost 30 of Atlantic fish species, sections conserved as they were to give you a flavour of life on board, and displays on fishing techniques and marine biology. There's a fair amount of hands-on action, but it's a good idea to ask at reception for one of the free French-language 'treasure hunt' leaflets for children aged 6–9 and 10–12 if appropriate. After looking round the boat, you hop back on land to see some displays on Lorient's role as France's second-largest fishing port, plus changing temporary exhibitions. In total you'll need about two hours.

Quai de Rohan (Port de Plaisance), Lorient, ☎ 02 97 35 13 00, ***www.sellor.com****. Open July and Aug daily 9am–7pm, rest of year Tue–Fri 9am–12.30pm and 2–6pm, Sat, Sun and Mon 2–6pm (plus Mon morning school hols). Adm: adults € 6.60 (£ 4.40), children € 5.10 (£ 3.45), family ticket (2+2) € 19.90 (£ 13.45).*

Le Végétarium ★★ Unique in Europe, this museum devoted to the plant kingdom is the brainchild of Yves Rocher, the botanical beauty products manufacturer who was born in La Gacilly and was once mayor of the town. Created in collaboration with the national history museum, it begins with a beautiful five-minute video of flowers opening in fast-motion, before proceeding to a room with mock-ups of two ecosystems, the desert and the tropical forest, including a vivarium full of stick insects. Upstairs, 'Refléchir' ('Think') is a great space for children, with quiz questions and hands-on displays, and 'Voyager' ('Travel') has an exhibition on the origins and uses of plants around the world, plus 'magic books' that automatically recount the story as you turn the pages.

Le Végétarium forms part of a 'discovery circuit' that also includes the **Jardin Botanique Yves Rocher**, containing more than 1000 species used in food, medicine, perfume, dyes and fibres (including the Artemisia collection of species dedicated to the goddess Artemis, such as tarragon and absinthe), and the **Espace Yves Rocher**, a reconstruction of the family workshop where Rocher started out. In high season there's a free *petit train* between Le Végétarium and the garden. Each year also sees an open-air summer photographic festival, **Nature and Landscape**, gorgeously set within a scented plant maze.

Route de Sixt-sur-Aff, La Gacilly, 30km (19 miles) southeast of Ploërmel on D8, ☎ 02 99 08 35 84, ***www.yves-rocher.com****. Open late May–mid-June and mid-Sept–mid-Oct Sat, Sun, school and public hols 2–6pm, 2nd half June and 1st half Sept daily 2–6pm, July and Aug daily 10am–7pm (botanical garden open all year). Adm: € 5.50 (£ 3.70), children 10–18 € 4 (£ 2.70);* circuit découverte *€ 6.50 (£ 4.40), children 10 and over € 5.50 (£ 3.70).*

Arts & Crafts Sites

Le Cartopole ★ At any one time, this exhibition space belonging to the Conservatoire Régional de la Carte Postale has around 2000 postcards on display in rooms designed to resemble an early 20th century local village. They provide a wonderful insight into traditional and modern Brittany and the art form as a whole – which, you learn, saw its heyday between 1900 and 1920. An audiovisual display with scenes from farming, sailing and other everyday activities accompanies the displays relating to this era. In the section on the Morbihan you can have fun identifying sights you have been to – perhaps the Grand Menhir Brisé (p. 214) or the resort of Carnac (p. 229). This is followed by a room on unusual postcards, from transparent versions to some with optical illusions (a few are rather risqué) and one on the renaissance of the postcard in the late 20th century. At the end of the visit, a multimedia area lets you zoom in on a huge choice of cards on its database, often revealing unexpected details.

Bibliothèque Municipale (town library), rue d'Auray, Baud, 28km (17.5 miles) northeast of Lorient on D768, 02 97 51 15 14, ***www.cartolis.org/cartopol/****. Open 2nd half of June and 1st half of Sept daily 9.30am–12.30pm and 2–6pm, July and Aug daily 9.30am–12.30pm and 2–7pm, mid-Sept–Dec and Feb–mid-June Wed, Thur and Sat 2–5.30pm, Sun 2–6pm. Adm: € 4 (£ 2.70), children 8–15 € 2 (£ 1.35).*

Domaine de Kerguéhennec ★

An uncompromising contemporary art venue in an 18th century château and its grounds, this contains one of Europe's best sculpture parks. It's great fun to roam the lawns, woods and lakeside in search of the 20 or so works by major artists such as Brit Tony Cragg, whose *Gastéropodes* is a huddle of outsize cast-iron shells in which you might make out tortoises and rifle holsters as well as snails. *Mimi*, by Markus Raetz from Switzerland, is a family of figures of different sizes and materials dotted throughout the grounds, and *Sentier de Charme* by Italian Giuseppe Penone is a bronze figure through the middle of which a tree is growing, gradually incorporating the body. The friendly staff are keen for children to learn about contemporary art, even if that means climbing on some of the pieces. Inside the château you can see temporary exhibitions by modern artists, and enjoy a light meal in the Café du Parc.

Bignan, 25km (16 miles) north of Vannes on D1, 02 97 60 44 44, ***www.art-kerguehennec.com****. Open Tue–Sun mid-June–mid-Sept 10am–7pm, mid-Sept–mid-Dec and mid-Jan–mid-June 10am–6pm. Adm free.*

Moulin à Papier de Pen-Mur

This restored 15th century mill on the edge of an enchanting lake makes paper according to traditional techniques, just as it did in the 1940s, before it fell into abandon. You find out all about these techniques during a half-hour French-language guided tour of the workshops, practical demonstrations, and finally in an exhibition room. There's also the 3m (9 ft) wide wheel to admire – it's a reproduction of the original and took five workers three months to complete – and occasional temporary exhibitions on local traditions, costumes and the like. Allow about an hour for a visit, and don't leave without buying a few reproductions of old postcards (from a choice of nearly 400000) – vastly superior to those you get in souvenir shops. There's also a selection of regional paper-based crafts and specialist writing equipment.

Muzillac, 12km (7.5 miles) southeast of Vannes on D765, 02 97 41 43 79, www.moulin-pen-mur.com. Open Apr–June Mon–Sat 10am–noon and 2–6pm, Sun 2–6pm, July–Sept daily 10am–noon and 2–6pm, Oct–Mar Sat, Sun, public and school hols 10am–noon and 2–5.30pm except Sun morning. Adm: € 5.50 (£ 3.70), under-14s € 3 (£ 2).

Musée des Châteaux en Allumettes ★ FIND The result of one man's obsession over the last quarter-century, this collection of scale models of some of France's most famous castles and other monuments built from matches now counts close to 30 works, each of which takes about a year to complete. Among them you may recognise the nearby Château de Josselin, home to the Musée de la Poupée (p. 215), which consists of 26600 matches, and the Mont-St-Michel (p. 68). There are even buildings from further afield, such as Bavaria's famous Schloss Neuschwanstein. The creator, or sometimes his wife, leads the free guided tours (only available in French).

12 rue du calvaire, Bizole, 8km (5 miles) east of Vannes on D104, ☎ 02 97 43 03 20. Open May–Oct Mon and Tue 2–7pm, Wed–Sun 9am–noon and 2–7pm. Adm free.

L'Univers du Poète Ferrailleur ★★★ Another extraordinary labour of love, this magical little world of animated, musical and aquatic sculptures, automats and kinetic machines was created from scrap metal objects over 15 years by a filmmaker whose imagination is clearly on the wild side. The best thing is that visitors bring the contraptions to life, by pressing buttons, pedalling and turning handles – children are naturally in their element, whereas parents are known to comment that they feel as if they've gone back to their own childhood. If you don't want to break the spell, there are two 20 minute films to watch: *Bricoleur de Lune* ('Moon Maker'), about a child fascinated by a carousel who decides he wants to make one when he grows up, and *Le Secret de Mermoz*, about an outsider whose meeting with a little girl reawakens his childhood dreams of becoming a pilot. On a more sober note, there's a 'maison écologique' here too, demonstrating the use of renewable energy in homes. The town of Lizio, otherwise the site of an Insectarium (p. 209), is a centre for artists and craftspeople, and each August hosts the Festival des Artisans d'Art et Modèle Réduit, with more than 150 artisans and modelmakers displaying/selling their wares to a soundtrack of traditional music. Children are entertained by free face-painting workshops and the like.

La Ville Stéphant, Lizio, 15km (9 miles) southeast of Ploërmel on D174, ☎ 02 97 74 97 94, www.poeteferrailleur.com. Open July–mid-Sept daily 10.30am–12.30pm and 2–7pm. Adm: € 5 (£ 3.35), children 4–14 € 4 (£ 2.70) (3rd child in family free).

Children-Friendly Tours

Montgolfière Morbihan ★★ One of the loveliest ways to see the stunning Golfe du Morbihan (p. 205) and its islands, or inland

A Balloon Ride

Morbihan and its rivers, is by hot-air balloon, and this firm is a trustworthy one with 20 years' experience. There's a maximum passenger quota of 4–5 people in these balloons, depending on weight; under-10s and pregnant women are not allowed. Flights, which depart from near Pluvigner north of Auray or from by the Golfe very early in the morning (when the air is most stable), last around an hour, but with getting there, blowing up the balloon and deflating it, you need to set aside 3–4 hours. Balloons reach an altitude of just 700m (2300 feet) so passengers can get the best views. Wear trousers and sensible shoes, as it's not guaranteed that you'll land near a road and you may have to tramp across a few fields. And don't forget to bring a camera!

Lescouëdec, St Avé, 3km (2 miles) north of Vannes on D126, ☎ *02 97 62 76 00,* ***www.montgolfiere-morbihan.com****. Open daily, depending on weather conditions. Flights: € 230–280 (£ 155–189), children 10+ € 180–210 (£ 120–140).*

For Active Families

See also 'Beaches, Resorts & Islands', p. 202–205. There's also a **Labyrinthe du Corsaire** (p. 86) at Guidel near the Finistère border.

Centre Nautique de Kerguelen ★ Run by a firm with an excellent reputation for watersports and diving tuition at its seven bases, this centre leads canoeing trips on the Laïta, Scorff and Blavet rivers or on the sea, sailing in the Rade de Lorient and diving around the Ile de Groix (p. 204). Set in a protected natural site with good sandy beaches, it offers five-day 'Classes de Mer' for ages eight and up, which include sailing and windsurfing tuition and 'nature discovery' outings – explorations of the seashore and a museum trip, perhaps to La Thalassa (p. 217) or the Ecomusée on Groix (p. 205). Accommodation and food can be provided in a neighbouring *résidence*. In July and August children aged 3–5 can enrol in the Jardin des Mers programme of shellfishing, aquarium-making and other seaside activities, while 5–7s can sign up for the Moussaillons programme of sailing tuition; maximum group size is six, meaning children are kept on a very firm rein, and they need to bring snacks.

Parc Océanique, Larmor-Plage, 3km (2 miles) south of Lorient on

The River Scorff by the Odyssaum (p. 209).

D152, 02 97 33 77 78, ***www.sellor-nautisme.fr****. Open all year. Fees: € 115 (£ 77) for five morning/afternoon Jardin de Mer or Moussaillons sessions.*

Parc Aquanature de Stérou
★★ More than 100 red and fallow deer roam this 70 hectare (174 acre) nature park spread across six valleys and boasting three waterfalls, and you will share their sense of freedom as you choose from the huge range of activities, which include a nature school with school-holiday courses for children 6–14, five walking circuits covering 1–15km (½–9 mile), horse rides, pony and trap rides (in high season), treasure hunts and 35 minute 'Breton safaris' in a 4x4 vehicle. There's also a mill with an aquarium with freshwater fish, two legend-shrouded sites, the Trou du Biniou and Clos des Roches de l'Aër, fishing and displays on local plants and animals. You can picnic here, or there's a restaurant with local products such as deer terrine or stew (maybe a bit close to home for some), plus a 6–8 person gîte.

INSIDER TIP
October can be a surprisingly good time to visit the Park Aquanature, for the stags' autumnal rut, and December for the salmons' return upriver from the ocean.

Priziac, 35km (22 miles) northwest of Lorient on D132, 02 97 34 63 84, ***www.parc-aquanature.com****. Open Easter–early Nov daily 11am–7pm, last 3 weeks Nov and Feb–Easter Sun and school hols 2–6pm. Adm: (including Breton safari) € 9 (£ 6), children € 5.50 (£ 3.70).*

Shopping

Clipper Set in Vannes' pedestrianised quarter, this is an Aladdin's cave of nautical paraphernalia, from furniture painted with marine scenes by local artists, antiques (compasses, buoys and so on, some sourced in a boat graveyard in Bangladesh), children's sailing boats from 1890–1950, sailors' instruments and fishing tools, to stunning craft items, including quirky terracotta figures and sculpted birds and fish, boats in a bottle, and

Breton Colours

Every summertime, from May to September, a host of towns and villages around the Golfe du Morbihan (p. 205) welcome amateur artists of all ages to come and paint them, with the results being entered into contests divided by age group (starting at just 0–3). For details of locations and how to get involved, see ***www.couleursdebretagne.org***.

model 19th century boats from as far afield as Colombia and as near as Séné (famous for its *sinagot*) – choose from clippers, trawlers, tuna and prawn boats and more, made by local sailors or former fishermen. Prices start at about € 8 (£ 5.40) for trinkets and climb into the thousands.

16 rue Saint Salomon, Vannes, ☎ 02 97 54 17 24. Open Tue–Sat 10am–12.30pm and 2–6pm.

Fnac ★★ France's leading bookshop and media specialist is a good bet for English-language books and magazines, and though it does have some specialist children's outlets, its general shops have plenty for children, whether you're looking for books, DVDs, CD-Roms or music, all of them tested by its panel of *Parents Pilotes* and their children.

Shopping, Vannes

All purchases come with a price guarantee: if you find it cheaper elsewhere within 30 days, the difference is refunded. Fnac is also well known for its in-store *billetteries* selling tickets for concerts, theatre and dance, exhibitions, sports events, leisure parks and circuses.

There are other Fnacs in Brittany, in **Brest** (p. 174) and **Rennes** (p. 88).

*Place Aristide Briand, Lorient, ☎ 02 97 84 38 40, **www.fnac.com**. Open Mon 2–7pm, Tue–Sat 10am–7pm.*

Galerie Plisson Philip Plisson is internationally renowned for his seascape photographs, taken around the world but particularly in Brittany – he moved to La Trinité-sur-Mer at the age of four. In his gallery in the town you can buy his works – which include shots of some of Brittany's majestic lighthouses (p. 164) and sea craft – in a range of formats, from calendars to giant 2m posters. If you're looking for a gift, there are limited-edition prints, or you can get particular photos individually framed in the gallery workshop. There's a cosy reading corner where you can look at books of Plisson's works, also sold here.

*Cours des Quais, La Trinité-sur-Mer, 12km (7.5 miles) southwest of Auray on D781, ☎ 02 97 30 15 15, **www.plisson.com**. July, Aug and school hols daily 10am–12.30pm and 2.30–7pm, rest of year Mon–Sat 10.30am–12.30pm and 3–7pm.*

Les Saveurs D'Arvor One of France's most famous biscuit and cake makers, the Biscuiterie La Trinitaine has its massive factory near Vannes, at St Philibert, where more than 200,000 fresh eggs are used every day and 80 tonnes of cake produced. Its shop in Vannes stocks the full range, including its speciality Breton butter biscuits – *galettes*, *palets* and 'cigarettes' – plus traditional Breton madeleines. Some are individually wrapped, making them perfect for picnics or car journeys; others make great gifts in their limited-edition tins. You will also find other Breton specialities: jam, caramels, cider and liqueurs, fish soup, salt, crêpes and earthenware. There are other shops dotted throughout the Morbihan, and a handful in the rest of Brittany and elsewhere.

19 place des Lices, Vannes, ☎ 02 97 42 53 18. Open Mon 2.30–6pm, Tue–Sat 10am–6pm.

FAMILY-FRIENDLY ACCOMMODATION

Around Lorient

EXPENSIVE–VERY EXPENSIVE

Château de Locguénolé ★★ This handsome castle with lawns rolling down to the Rade de Lorient (p. 204) and its own 120 – hectare (297 acre) wooded park offers great themed packages, including trips to the islands of Groix and Houat (p. 204), shark-fishing expeditions and Breton history sorties (trips to various sights, including La Thalassa, p. 217, the Musée de Préhistoire in Carnac, p. 213, and the Haras National de Hennebont; p. 209). You can even book the hotel helicopter, *L'Ecureuil* ('Squirrel'), for flights to Groix, the Golfe du Morbihan (p. 205), Belle-Ile (p. 202) or the Glénans (p. 172); prices start at € 140 (£ 94) per person. If you prefer to stay close to home, as well as its 2km (1½ miles) of private shoreline, the castle boasts a large outdoor pool beside its 'winter garden', which houses two saunas, a Turkish bath and rooms where you can indulge in shiatsu and other massages. There's also a tennis court, bike hire and a private pontoon for those arriving in boats.

Family accommodation in the château is in 'apartments' (interconnecting rooms) with generally quite elegant and restrained decor but the odd splash of chintz; some have beams and huge fireplaces, all have smart marble bathrooms with big tubs that may have a hydrotherapy option. Large duplex rooms with plenty of space for extra single beds and cots can also be booked in the **Chaumières de Kerniaven**, 18th century Breton stone cottages 4km (2½ miles) away towards the beaches but sharing the castle's amenities.

One of the Chaumières de Kerniaven at the Château de Locguénolé

The castle's Michelin-starred **restaurant** is the setting for refined Continental or buffet breakfasts – expensive at € 17 (£ 11.45) or € 23 (£ 15.55) (half for under-12s) but served on gleaming silver – and evening meals featuring local vegetables, line-caught fish, salt-meadow lamb from near the Mont-St-Michel (p. 68) and so on. Don't miss the carpaccio of smoked lobster or the monkfish roasted on a rosemary branch with local artichokes. Options for children are very flexible, including one choice each from the *entrée* and dessert menus for € 15 (£ 10), or a main course and dessert for € 20 (£ 13.50).

Route de Port-Louis, Kervignac, near Hennebont, ☎ 02 97 76 76 7, ***www.chateau-de-locguenole.com****. Double € 112–235 (£ 75–158), suite/ apartment € 325–405 (£ 219–273), extra bed € 31–39 (£ 21–26) (half for children 3–12).* Chaumière *double € 80–112 (£ 54–76), extra bed € 31–39 (£ 21–26) (half for children 3–12), cot free. Amenities: restaurant, lounges, cigar cave, outdoor pool (May–Sept), sauna, Turkish bath, treatment rooms, pontoon, helipad, free Internet access, babysitting. In room: Satellite TV, telephone, hairdryer, minibar, safe, free Wi-Fi Internet access (some rooms). Closed Jan–mid-Feb.*

INEXPENSIVE–MODERATE

La Maison Magique ★ About 15 minutes inland of Lorient in the charming traditional village of St Nicolas-des-Eaux, the 'Magic House' is a self-catering Breton farmhouse set with three gîtes in lovely gardens and woodland on the banks of the Blavet river. Very welcoming to families, the little complex has a large outdoor pool surrounded by loungers and its own bar; crazy golf; a *boules* court; a children's play area; more than 40 bikes for hire (including tandems and children's trailers); a games room with pool and table tennis tables, games, films and books; hammocks; picnic tables; fishing rods for catching carp in the river; and a boat you can rent. Not far away are tow-path walks, riverside bars, crêperies and restaurants, a canoeing club and pedalo hire.

The Maison Magique itself, which has a quirky first-floor balcony, can sleep up to 10. Then there's the old hayloft, Cockatoo Court, with three bedrooms sleeping up to six (including a baby); the old milking parlour, Swift Court, which is fully wheelchair/buggy accessible (with an adapted wet room) and has 2–3 bedrooms sleeping up to six; and the garden-level Heron Court with two bedrooms, sleeping 5–6. All are clean, comfortable and fairly plain in decor; rates include all linen, towels and central heating.

Allée du Vieux Blavet, St Nicolas-des-Eaux, 40km (25 miles) northeast of Lorient on D1, ☎ 02 97 51 86 02 ***www.lamaisonmagique.com****. Four units. Farmhouse € 825–1500 (£ 557–1010) per week, gîte € 375–1500 (£ 253–1010) per week. Amenities: outdoor pool (summer; months vary), play area, games, bike and boat hire, terrace with BBQ. Gîtes: Sat TV, DVD and video player, CD player (some), Internet access, kitchen, BBQ equipment.*

Around the Golfe du Morbihan

MODERATE–EXPENSIVE

Le Lodge Kerisper ★★★ FIND

For parents who don't want to compromise on style, this intimate hotel in a renowned yachting town has a beautiful little outdoor pool (heated year round) edged with decking, loungers and parasols and equipped with games and water-wings; trendy 'beach hut' decor; a space for massages and beauty treatments; and a babysitting service – though you may be happy to stay put once you've clocked the stunning zinc bar (open all day) or the library with its cosy hearth and stone walls. In fact, the charming couple who opened the place in 2005 had children very much in mind during the creation process, having often been disappointed by hotels when travelling with their own. As a result, you'll also find beach games, waterproof coats and boots to borrow, children's books, and children's films to watch in the room.

There are bikes (and child seats) for hire, and staff will organise outings, including sailing trips to nearby islands. Or you can simply doze in the old curate's garden beneath the fruit trees while the children run around. Rooms are tucked away and private, linked by a series of walkways and footbridges. Light and airy, they include three spacious suites with three or four beds, and four connecting rooms, with bathrooms with wooden floorboards, clawfoot baths and two sinks. The very good buffet breakfasts are served on the stilted verandah (€ 12 (£ 8)) or in your room (€ 15 (£ 10), and cost less for children according to age. The home-prepared picnics are great for a day on the beach 100m (300 ft) away. If you're going sailing for the day, a packed lunch can also be provided, and staff

Le Lodge Kerisper

will even rustle up a meal for your children and babysitter, though there are good crêperies within walking distance.

4 rue du Latz, La Trinité-sur-Mer, 12km (7.5 miles) southwest of Auray on D781, ☎ 02 97 52 88 56, ***www.lodge-kerisper.com****. 16 rooms. Double € 80–130 (£ 54–88), suite for four € 160–230 (£ 108–155). Cot free. Amenities: children's meals, outdoor pool with games and children's equipment, beach equipment, garden, library, treatment room, bike hire, free Wi-Fi Internet access, highchair, picnic/lunchbox service. In room TV, DVD player (with DVD loan), telephone. Closed 3 weeks in Jan.*

MODERATE

Hotel Bellevue ★ VALUE Given its three-star rating, outdoor pool and proximity to Quiberon's Grand Plage, one of Brittany's most popular family beaches, the Bellevue is a bargain. Its warmly decorated rooms come in four categories, of which three include family rooms for three or four. The smartest and most modern are Belle-Ile, but all are pleasant, and most have a balcony or patio area. Breakfasts (€ 9.50 (£ 6.40); children € 5 (£ 3.35)) take the form of a plentiful buffet including Continental goodies, cheese, fresh fruit, cereals and hard-boiled eggs, or you can have a Continental breakfast brought to your room. The large, light-flooded restaurant is open for lunch, on tables around the pool in fine weather; the light fare includes a dish of the day, a cheese platter, oysters and a selection of desserts. In high season there is also a poolside menu of club sandwiches, salads and oysters. Evenings you dine on fancier but quite well-priced seafood such as fillet of sole with balsamic vinegar, pistachio oil and creamed cauliflower. For children, there's a selection of *à la carte* dishes, including roast fish or chicken with vegetables (€ 8.50 (£ 5.75)) and fruit compôte (€ 2.50 (£ 1.70)); highchairs are provided. The

Water, Water, Everywhere

If you want to pamper yourself without leaving the children at home, the Morbihan has several **thalassotherapy centres** where the staff will keep children entertained while you kick back and relax. One such is the **Miramar Crouesty** (☎ *02 97 53 49 00*, ***www.miramar-crouesty.com***) at Port du Crouesty on the spit of land curling round between the Golfe du Morbihan and the Atlantic. Resembling an ocean liner in its own artificial seawater lake, its rooms and suites are bland but spacious, with sea or lake views and large balconies. While you're being pummelled in its Institute of Thalassotherapy, your 3–6-year-olds can get creative with playdough, plasticine and the like, explore the shore and enjoy short walks, pony rides, and horse-and-carriage trips; and 6–12-year-olds can discover local menhirs and châteaux, go on picnics or horse rides and play mini-golf or tennis (€ 34 (£ 23) per day per club). There's also a nursery for babies two months and over (€ 11 (£ 7.35) per hour). If you come with a baby, a cot, bottle-warmer, steriliser, highchair and baby bath are provided, and you can partake of a Mother and Baby programme. There's also a pool complex. Pricing is complex due to the range of options and treatments, but expect to pay around € 600 (£ 400) per night for four nights in a lake-view suite with two extra beds, including lunch or dinner for four (the hotel has two restaurants) and four hydrotherapy treatments a day for two.

On Belle-Ile, the **Castel Clara** (☎ *02 97 31 84 21*, ***www.castel-clara.com***) is a similar large modern hotel in a wild setting on the south side of the island. It doesn't have a children's club, but babysitting can be arranged while you enjoy a treatment, and there is an outdoor heated seawater pool, two tennis courts, bike hire and sailing trips.

attractive bar overlooks the pool and flower-filled little garden, so you can relax over a drink while the children carry on playing.

Rue de Tiviec, Quiberon, 25km (16 miles) southwest of Auray on D768, ☎ *02 97 50 16 28,* ***www.bellevue-quiberon.com****. 38 rooms. Double € 58–115 (£ 39–77), family room for four € 93–118 (£ 63–79). Extra bed € 10 (£ 6.65) (free under-12s). Cot free. Amenities: restaurant, bar, outdoor pool (Apr–Sept), garden. In room: TV, telephone, free Wi-Fi access.*

INEXPENSIVE

La Grande Metairie ★ This campsite on the doorstep of some of the famous Carnac alignments (p. 212) has the usual amenities of a four-star facility – including a large pool complex with slides for different ages, one with four lanes – plus its own mini-farm with animals that children can come to help feed and ponies to ride. There are also play areas, a mountain bike track, free children's clubs for

Duplex two-bedroom suites and family apartments, decorated in a modern 'boutique' style, cost € 186–569 (£ 126–385) depending on the view and time of year, without treatments.

But you don't need to break the bank to enjoy this kind of holiday. The **Résidence Carnac** (☏ *02 97 59 53 54*, ***www.thalasso-carnac.com***) 150m from the beach at Carnac-Plage (p. 203) has 34 apartments with kitchenettes, Sat TV and balconies, and access to the **Thalassothérapie de Carnac** centre. In the French school holidays, a club keeps children aged 3–12 occupied. Guests also have access to an indoor heated seawater pool, table tennis and tennis courts, a *pétanque* terrain and bike hire, some at extra cost. Accommodation-only costs € 462–1,029 (£ 312–696) per week for a four-person apartment (double and two single beds). If you don't want to self cater, the complex includes the **Novotel Carnac** hotel, with interconnecting rooms, and the **Ibis Carnac**, with interconnecting rooms and 23 duplex rooms for 2–4, including 10 rooms for new mums, with cots, baby baths, bottle warmers and a laundry service. The six-day 'Young Mother' treatment is available. The three hotel restaurants have children's menus and highchairs.

There's also an Accor Thalassa at nearby **Quiberon** (☏ *02 97 50 20 00*, ***www.accorthalassa.com***); treatments here include 'Connivence', for teenage girls and their mums who want to adopt a healthier lifestyle, boost their self-esteem and have some 'bonding' time. It also offers entertainment for children aged 4–10 in the school holidays. Further afield, there's an Accor Thalassa at **Dinard** in the Ille-et-Vilaine (p. 99).

children aged 4–12, junior discos, a weekly circus, football, basketball, volleyball, table tennis and tennis courts, crazy golf, *boules* and organised trips. Attractive Breton buildings backing the main pool area remind you of where you are (sometimes campsites like this feel a bit cut off from local life), and the site is nicely wooded. In practical terms, there's a grocery and shop, an evening restaurant serving pizzas, pancakes and the like, a takeaway, a bar with concerts and a big-screen Satellite TV, a amphitheatre for barbecues, folk music and shows put on by the children, a cyber-café and a TV room. If this is the kind of holiday you like, La Grande Metairie does it better than most.

INSIDER TIP

La Grande Metairie can be booked via **Siblu** (p. 36) and some of the other camping holiday operators.

La Grande Metairie

*Route des Alignements de Kermario, Carnac, 15km (9 miles) southwest of Auray on D186, ☎ 02 97 52 24 01, **www.lagrandemetairie.com**. Mobile home for four € 245–665 (£ 161–438) per week; pitch € 8–23.90 (£ 5.40–16.15), then € 4–7.20 (£ 2.70–4.80) per person, children 4–6 € 3.50–5.40 (£ 2.35–3.60), under-4s € 2 (£ 1.30 in July and August; rest of time free). Amenities: pool complex, games and sports, children's clubs, mini-farm, shops, restaurant, takeaway counter, bar, cybercafé, TV room. Closed 2nd week Sept–mid-May.*

La Mine d'Or ★ This super-friendly independent youth hostel in which everyone is encouraged to muck in together and socialise is centred around an almost absurdly quaint thatched Breton cottage right by the sea, surrounded by pine trees and cypresses. Its accommodation options are varied – you can stay in a dorm (for 4–9), in one of three bungalows in the grounds sleeping five people, in a four-person tent supplied by the hostel or in your own small tent. As you'd expect, rooms are basic but entirely acceptable. There are also clean, shared facilities, and, if you opt for half- or full-board, traditional meals are enjoyed together in the dining room or outdoors, followed by frequent musical gatherings. There's a great beach (p. 206) two steps away, with a seawater tank where children can bring any crabs, prawns or little fish they have caught for inspection. Hostel staff are more than happy to fill you in on other local activities, which include sailing, cycling, horse-riding, canoeing on the Vilaine, *pétanque* and volleyball, and sometimes volunteers drop by to talk about responsible tourism.

*Pénestin, 45km (28 miles) southeast of Vannes on D34, ☎ 02 99 90 30 22, **http://clajpenestin@free.fr**. 60 places. Rates: € 9 (£ 6) per person per night, including breakfast. Amenities: communal kitchen.*

FAMILY-FRIENDLY DINING

Around Lorient

This is not a great area for eating, though the Michelin-starred restaurant at the **Château de Locguénolé** (p. 224) is a surprisingly flexible sophisticated option.

EXPENSIVE

Le Vivier ★★ Stunningly sited on a rocky outcrop just southwest of Lorient, with views over the sea to the Ile de Groix (p. 204), Le Vivier has long been fêted for its seafood, although other dishes are equally superb. The dining room with its huge windows makes you feel as if the waves are lapping at your feet; it's quite plush and has a trendy modern look, but the staff are welcoming, and that welcome is extended to children, who get a € 13 (£ 8.75) 'gourmet discovery' menu consisting of a starter, a main course (except lobster) and a dessert from the *à la carte* menu, all in smaller portions. It's perfect for those who are trying to re-educate their children's palates away from kiddy fare towards something more adult. Tempting dishes for them might include an *entrée* of crab and artichoke cake, a main of steamed John Dory with mushroom ravioli or baby pigeon with grapes and fondant potatoes, and a dessert of salted-butter caramel mousse with a chocolate doughnut. You, meanwhile, might be tempted to blow the budget on the € 70 (£ 47) lobster menu, which features lobster salad with flavoured oils, a half-lobster in a 'cannelloni' of cabbage leaves, and lobster thermidor (lobster meat with egg yolks and brandy or sherry, stuffed into the shell and served with a cheese crust).

Though the restaurant is not at all touristy, the dishes are described in English on the menu, and good English is spoken. It's part of a hotel with plain but pleasant double rooms (€ 76–95 (£ 51–64)) that can accommodate extra beds (€ 11 (£ 7.45)).

9 route de Beg-Er-Vir, Lomener, 8km (5 miles) southwest of Lorient on D152, ☎ 02 97 82 99 60, ***www.levivier-lomener.com****. Main courses € 16–60 (£ 10.65–40). Open daily noon–2.30pm and 7–10pm. Highchair. Closed late Dec–early Jan.*

La Casa Varadero Tiny from the outside but opening up, like the Tardis, into a fair-sized room, this warm Italian restaurant with its bright red, green and yellow walls decorated with metallic fish gets packed out with locals of all ages, who flock here for the best pizzas in Lorient (including a monthly special), together with authentic main-course dishes such as saltimbocca veal escalope (breaded, with mozzarella and *proscuitto*), carpaccio of beef, pasta dishes and some very good risottos. Staff, though invariably rushed off their feet, are charming, and solicitous to those with children. There's a *menu bambino* for under-10s (€ 8.40 (£ 5.60)), with mini tomato, ham and cheese pizza, *steak haché* or high-quality ham with homemade fries or pasta, and two scoops of ice cream or house chocolate mouse, plus drinks. Prices are very fair given the quality. Come early to secure a place.

19 boulevard Franchet d'Esperey, Lorient, 02 97 64 20 77. Main courses € 6–15 (£ 4–10). Open Mon–Thur noon–2pm and 7–11pm, Fri and Sat noon–2pm and 7–11.30pm, Sun 2–4pm. Booster seat.

INEXPENSIVE

Chez Paule Crêperies don't come much more authentic than this little family-run place in an old fisherman's cottage on the Ile de Groix (p. 204), with net curtains at the windows, a stone floor, a cosy fireplace, and local furniture, including a *lit-clos* (traditional Breton sleeping cabin – left for historical interest only!) and benches in place of chairs. Come early and you may find nobody here (holler and the staff will emerge from the back); come later and you don't have a chance of getting a table without advance reservations. There's no children's menu, but at these almost laughably low prices that's no problem: they can choose from an excellent galette menu of classics such as *jambon-fromage* and *beurre-sucre*, or something more adventurous, perhaps sardines or smoked pollack. Beware of ordering the children's *lait caillé*, a yogurty curd drink with an acquired taste.

6 route de Port-Mélite, Groix (Le Bourg), Ile de Groix, 02 97 86 89 72. Main courses € 2–7.50 (£ 1.35–5). Open Wed–Mon noon–3pm and 7–11pm, plus Tue in school hols. Closed Oct–Mar. Highchair.

Around the Golfe du Morbihan

EXPENSIVE

Le Gavrinis ★★ FIND Behind this ugly modern façade lies a chic hotel and restaurant with muted cream, beige and pale blue decor and quirky but tasteful furniture. Its dining room is great for a special occasion, offering regional specialities with a twist, with the emphasis on seafood, including a duo of veal sweetbreads and warm scallops, and seabass with pea *coulis* and carrot and cumin mousse. Though prices are high,

Le Gavrinis, Baden

there are some good-value *menus* that make this an affordable treat, even in the evening, including a € 20 (£ 13.35) daily Menu du Marché, and the € 28 (£ 18.95) Menu Er-Lannic based on ingredients sourced from local producers and fishermen, including fresh sardine tart with tomatoes and mint, seabream with creamy polenta and *sauce vierge* (an uncooked sauce with olive oil, garlic, tomatoes, coriander seeds and basil), a selection of fine cheeses, and a home-made dessert (for an extra € 2.50 (£ 1.70)). Children can opt for this menu without the cheese plate for € 20 (£ 13.35), or there's a very good € 14.50 (£ 9.75) under-12s menu comprising steamed fish or sirloin of beef with rice or roast potatoes, and ice cream.

The 18 restful double rooms cost € 50–95 (£ 34–64), with a cot provided free.

*1 rue de l'Île Gavrinis, Baden, 15km (9 miles) west of Vannes on D101, ☎ 02 97 57 00 82, **www.gavrinis.com**. Main courses € 17–49 (£ 11.45–33.15). Open mid-June–mid-Sept daily 12.10–1.30pm and 7.10–9.30pm, rest of year Tue–Fri 12.10–1.30pm and 7.10–9.30pm, Sat 7.10–9.30pm and Sun 12.10–1.30pm. Highchair.*

La Côte ★ Close to the Kermario alignments (p. 213), 2km (1½ miles) from the centre of Carnac (and thus mercifully free of the tourist hordes in high season, though you need to book ahead any time of year), this fine restaurant is run by a welcoming (and English-speaking) young husband-and-wife team who took over the family farmhouse with a view to combining local produce and tradition with new flavours and methods. They've largely succeeded, but this is not some sniffy gastronomic temple – among the *menus* is one for children under 13 (€ 9 (£ 6)), comprising oven-roast chicken breast with potato fork-mashed with veal *jus*, then homemade apple tart with a creamy caramel sauce. For adults, there are a variety of *menus* (two devoted to lobster dishes); they change thrice-monthly but may include foie gras terrine with figs; celery soup with mackerel, mustard and onion ravioli; seabream with ginger and a pancake filled with chorizo, tomato and red onion; and crêpes with marmalade butter and bitter orange sorbet. Some of the combinations are a bit overblown, but most dishes hit the spot. The dining rooms couldn't be more inviting: 'Château' has exposed bricks and beams and a wooden floor, 'La Vérandah' has a view over the garden and its ornamental pond, as does the pretty terrace. Specify a non-smoking table when you book, or you risk getting a blast from someone enjoying a cigar from the *cave*.

Kermario, Carnac, ☎ 02 97 52 02 80, 15km (9 miles) southwest of Auray on D186, Menus € 22–52 (£ 14.85–34.85). Open July and Aug Tue 7.15–9.15pm, Wed–Sun 12.15–2.15pm and 7.15–9.15pm; Oct–Dec and Feb–June Tue–Fri 12.15–2.15pm and 7.15–9.15pm, Sat 7.15–9.15pm and Sun 12.15–2.15pm (but closed 2nd week Mar, 1st week Oct and 3rd week Nov). Highchair.

INEXPENSIVE

Crêperie Chez Renée Renée retired years ago, and Président Mitterrand, who used to fly over by helicopter for a simple buckwheat pancake in this pretty traditional house, is no more – yet this local institution keeps on and on, and if you come after 8pm you'll find yourself waiting ages for a table. Once you're ensconced, however, the friendly staff keep things moving, and the galettes and crêpes – fine, crispy yet soft in the middle – are worth the wait. There's no children's menu, but as always in a crêperie, the choice of fillings, from the simple to the elaborate, should embrace something to please everyone. Worth trying are the fresh tomato compôte, thick local bacon, and local cheese and honey – a surprisingly winning combination. The banana and *crème fraîche* crêpe flambéed with rum is popular, whereas for children there are excellent home-made ice creams and sorbets. On a balmy evening, it's worth trying to get a table in the very sweet little garden, although you can't reserve these so it's more a case of luck.

Bangor, Belle-Ile, ☎ 02 97 31 52 87. Main courses € 3.25–9.50 (£ 2.20–6.40). Open Tue–Sun noon–2pm and 7–9.30pm. Highchair.

Crêperie La Taupinière You enter this cute little crêperie by going down into a sort of hole, hence its name, the 'mole hole'. The speciality galette here – foie gras – is best left to parents who like that kind of thing; children will probably prefer basics such as *jambon-fromage*, which are done very well and served in larger-than-average portions. Ingredients are ultra-fresh and everything is made in-house. It's a good-value option for the location, and the genuinely charming staff make for a warm atmosphere, though service can be slow.

9 place des Lices, Vannes, ☎ 02 97 42 57 82. Main courses € 3.50–11 (£ 2.35–7.45). Open July and Aug Mon–Sat noon–3pm and 7–10pm, Sun 7–10pm; rest of year Mon, Tue and Thur–Sat noon–3pm and 7–10pm. Highchair.

Appendix: Useful Terms and Phrases

It's not essential to speak French when visiting France, but outside Paris – and especially in the furthest reaches of rural Brittany – you will certainly struggle if no one in the family has some degree of proficiency in the language. Certainly, any stay in France is immeasurably enhanced if you all speak decent French, and children, who will be able to mix with French children and join in French-language activities at museums, farms and so on, will get much more out of their trip abroad. Remember, too, that being seen to be making an effort will predispose you well to local people.

Children pick up new languages much more easily than adults – at the end of our most recent trip, even my youngest son, not quite two, was happily switching between basic phrases – *bonjour*, *au revoir*, *merci* – in the two languages, depending on who he was talking to. Capitalise on this facility by introducing your children to a fun language-learning programme: one of the most highly regarded is the award winning BBC course *Muzzy*, which includes DVDs with cartoons, available at **www.bbcshop.com** or **www.muzzyonline.co.uk**. There's nothing to say that adults can't learn from it too by watching with their children! Alternatively, use the language options available on many DVDs to allow your children to watch their existing favourite shows and films in French.

Children love stories, and the best way of interesting them in the sights of Brittany is to tell them the legends and histories surrounding them during the visit, many of which I've summarised in this book. Once you're in France, stock up at media stores such as Fnac (p. 223) with French-language story books for your child's age group, and song and story CDs or cassettes in French – a great way of making long car journeys more productive for all the family. *Le Petit Prince* is a classic; for books specific to Brittany, see p. 49. See the box below for more language-learning recommendations.

Resources: Learning French with Children

The following resources are all available at **www.amazon.co.uk**.

First 100 Words in French Sticker Book (Heather Amery)

French is Fun with Serge, the Cheeky Monkey (BBC Active); includes DVD and CD.

Les Portes Tordues/The Twisted Doors: the Scariest Way in the World to Learn French (Kathie Dior); includes audiobook.

Let's Learn French Colouring Book (Anne Françoise Hazan)

Let's Sing and Learn in French (Matt Maxwell)

Muzzy (BBC English); see above.

Snap Cards in French (Jo Litchfield)

Lastly, when your child is older, there's no better way of instilling a love of French language and culture than by sending them to stay with a French family – you can arrange this through ***www.french-exchange.co.uk***, or ask the French department of your child's school or French friends who may know people with children the same age as your own.

For information about the Breton language and a basic vocabulary, see p. 5.

Basic Vocabulary and Greetings

English	French	Pronunciation
Yes/No	**Oui/Non**	wee/nohn
Okay	**D'accord**	*dah*-core
Please	**S'il vous plaît**	seel voo play
Thank you	**Merci**	*mair*-see
You're welcome	**De rien**	duh ree-*ehn*
Hello (daytime)	**Bonjour**	bohn-*jhoor*
Good evening	**Bonsoir**	bohn-*swahr*
Goodbye	**Au revoir**	oruh-*vwahr*
What's your name?	**Comment vous appellez-vous?**	ko-*mahn*-voo-za-pell-ay-*voo*?
My name is	**Je m'appelle**	*jhuh* ma-pell
How are you?	**Comment allez-vous?**	kuh-mahn-tahl-ay-*voo*?
I'm sorry/excuse me	**Pardon**	pahr-*dohn*

Getting Around

English	French	Pronunciation
Do you speak English?	**Parlez-vous anglais?**	par-lay-voo-ahn-*glay*?
I don't speak French	**Je ne parle pas français**	jhuh ne parl pah frahn-*say*
I don't understand	**Je ne comprends pas**	jhuh ne kohm-*prahn* pas
Could you speak more loudly/more slowly?	**Pouvez-vous parler plus fort/plus lentement?**	Poo-*vay* voo par-lay ploo for/ploo lan-te-*ment*?
What is it?	**Qu'est-ce que c'est?**	kess-kuh-*say*?
What time is it?	**Qu'elle heure est-il?**	kel uhr eh-*teel*?
What?	**Quoi?**	kwah?
How? or What did you say?	**Comment?**	ko-*mahn*?
When?	**Quand?**	kahn?
Where is?	**Où est?**	oo *eh*?

English	French	Pronunciation
Who?	**Qui?**	kee?
Why?	**Pourquoi?**	poor-*kwah*?
here/there	**ici/là**	ee-*see*/lah
left/right	**à gauche/à droite**	a goash/a drwaht
straight ahead	**tout droit**	too-*drwah*
Fill the tank (of a car), please	**Le plein, s'il vous plaît**	luh plan, seel-voo-*play*
I want to get off at	**Je voudrais descendre à**	jhe voo-*dray* day-son drah-ah
airport	**l'aéroport**	lair-o-*por*
bank	**la banque**	lah bahnk
beach	**la plage**	lah plarj
bridge	**le pont**	luh pohn
broken down (in car)	**en panne**	ahn *pan*
bus station	**la gare routière**	lah *gar* roo-tee-*air*
bus stop	**l'arrêt de bus**	lah-*ray* duh boohss
by car	**en voiture**	ahn vwa-*toor*
cathedral	**la cathédrale**	luh ka-tay-*dral*
church	**l'église**	lay-*gleez*
driver's licence	**le permis de conduire**	luh per-*mee* duh con-*dweer*
entrance (building or city)	**une porte**	ewn port
exit (building or motorway)	**une sortie**	ewn sor-*tee*
first floor	**le premier étage**	luh prem-ee-*ehr* ay-*taj*
hospital	**l'hôpital**	low-pee-*tahl*
lift/elevator	**l'ascenseur**	lah sahn *seuhr*
luggage storage	**la consigne**	lah kohn-*seen*-yuh
museum	**le musée**	luh mew-*zay*
no smoking	**défense de fumer**	day-*fahns* de fu-may
petrol	**du pétrol/de l'essence**	duh pay-*trol*/de lay-*sahns*
one-day pass	**le ticket journalier**	luh tee-*kay* jhoor-nall-ee-*ay*
one-way ticket	**l'aller simple**	lah-*lay sam*-pluh
police	**la police**	lah po-*lees*
return ticket	**l'aller-retour**	lah-*lay* re-*toor*
slow down	**ralentir**	rah-lahn-*teer*
street	**la rue**	lah roo
underground/Tube/subway	**le Métro**	luh *may*-tro
telephone	**le téléphone**	luh tay-lay-*phone*
ticket	**un billet**	uh *bee*-yay
toilets	**les toilettes/les WC**	lay twa-*lets*/les vay-*say*

Shopping

English	French	Pronunciation
How much does it cost?	**C'est combien?/Ça coûte combien?**	say comb-bee-*ehn*?/sah coot comb-bee-*ehn*?
That's expensive	**C'est cher/chère**	say share
Do you take credit cards?	**Acceptez-vous les cartes de crédit?**	aksep-*tay* lay kart duh creh-*dee*?
I'd like	**Je voudrais**	jhe voo-*dray*
I'd like to buy	**Je voudrais acheter**	jhe voo-*dray* ahsh-*tay*
aspirin	**des aspirines/des aspros**	deyz ahs-peer-*een*/deyz ahs-*proh*
boots	**des bottes**	day bot
colouring book	**un livre de coloriage**	uh lee-vr duh colo-ree-*arj*
gift	**un cadeau**	uh kah-*doe*
hat	**un chapeau**	uh shah-*poh*
map of the city	**un plan de ville**	uh plahn de *veel*
newspaper	**un journal**	uh zhoor-*nahl*
phonecard	**une carte téléphonique/télécarte**	uh cart tay-lay-fone-*eek*/*tay-lay* cart
postcard	**une carte postale**	ewn cart pos-*tahl*
raincoat	**un imperméable**	uh am-per-mey-*arbl*
road map	**une carte routière**	ewn cart roo-tee-*air*
shoes	**des chaussures**	day show-*suhr*
soap	**du savon**	dew sah-*vohn*
stamp	**un timbre poste**	uh *tam*-bruh post
sweets	**de la confiserie/des bonbons**	duh lah kohn-feez-ree/day bon-bon
swimming trunks	**un slip de bain**	uh sleep duh ban
swimsuit/swimming costume	**un maillot de bain**	uh *mi*-o duh ban
suntan cream/sunscreen	**de la crème solaire**	duh lah krem sol-*air*
toothpaste	**du pâte dentifrice**	dew pat den-tee-*frees*
shop	**le magasin**	luh ma-ga-*zehn*
bakery	**la boulangerie**	lah boo-*lahn*-jeh-ree
butcher	**la boucherie**	lah *boosh*-ree
cake shop	**la pâtisserie**	lah pah-tees-ree
drycleaners	**la blanchisserie**	lah blon-*shi*-ser-ree
fishmonger	**la poissonnerie**	lah pwah-*sohn*-ree
grocery	**l'épicerie**	lah *pees*-ree
laundrette	**la laverie automatique**	lah la-vairy auto-mah-*teek*

English	French	Pronunciation
market	**le marché**	luh mar-*shay*
farmers' market	**le marché fermier**	luh mar-*shay* fair-mee-*ay*
off licence	**le magasin de vins**	luh mah-gah-zahn day *vahn*
supermarket	**le supermarché**	luh sue-per-mar-*shay*
very large supermarket	**le hypermarché**	luh ee-per-mar-*shay*
shopping trolley	**le caddy**	luh cah-*dee*
shopping bag	**un sac/une poche**	uh sack/ewn posh
till	**la caisse**	lah kes

Children's Stuff

English	French	Pronunciation
babychanging	**un table à langer**	uhn tahb-le a lahn-*gay*
baby equipment	**matériau de puériculture**	ma-tay-re-o de pu-ray-cult-*your*
bottlewarmer	**une chauffe-biberon**	ewn showf-bee-ber-*on*
buggy/pushchair	**une poussette**	ewn poo-*set*
child seat	**un siège enfant**	ehn see-erj on-*fon*
children's Paracetamol	**Paracétamol à dose pédiatrique**	Pa-ray-see-tem-ol a does pay-day-at-*reek*
dummy	**une sucette**	ewn sue-*set*
formula milk (newborn–4 months; 4 months–1 year)	**lait formule** (premier âge; deuxième âge)	lay four-*mule* (pray-may-ehr *arge;* der-zi-em *arge*)
follow-on milk	**lait de croissance**	lay de cwa-*zance*
highchair	**une chaise haute**	ewn chayz *oht*
nappies	**les couches**	lay coo-sh
playground	**aire de jeux**	air de jurs
seesaw/swing	**une balançoire**	ewn bal-on-*swar*
slide	**un toboggan**	uhn tob-o-*gan*
sterilising tablets	**comprimés de stérilisation à froid**	com-pree-*mays* de stery-lee-za-shon a *fwad*
wet wipes	**les lingettes**	lay lan-*jets*

In Your Hotel

English	French	Pronunciation
we're staying for . . . days	**on reste pour . . . jours**	ohn rest poor . . . jhoor
is breakfast included?	**petit déjeuner inclus?**	peh-*tee* day-jheun-*ay* ehn-*klu*?
are taxes included?	**les taxes sont comprises?**	lay taks son com-*preez*?

English	French	Pronunciation
room	**une chambre**	ewn *shawm*-bruh
double room	**une chambre double**	ewn *shawm*-bruh *doo*-bluh
twin room	**une chambre aux lits simples**	ewn*shawm*-bruh o lee *sam*-pluh
triple room	**un triple**	uh *tree*-pluh
family room	**une chambre familiale**	ewn *shawm*-bruh fam-ee-lee-*o*
family suite	**une suite familiale/un appartement familial**	ewn sweet fam-ee-lee-*al*/uhn apart-a-ment fam-ee-lee-*al*
interconnecting rooms	**des chambres communicantes/ un appartement**	day shawm-bruhs com-you-ni-*cont*/ uhn apart-a-*ment*
extra bed	**un lit supplémentaire**	uh lee sup-lay-mon-*tair*
cot	**un lit bébé**	uh lee bay-*bay*
shower	**une douche**	ewn dooch
sink	**un lavabo**	uh la-va-*bow*
suite	**une suite**	ewn sweet
the key	**la clé (la clef)**	la clay
balcony	**un balcon**	uh *bahl*-cohn
bathtub	**une baignoire**	ewn bayn-*nwar*
bathroom	**une salle de bain**	ewn sal duh *ban*
shower room	**une salle de douche**	ewn sal duh *dush*
hot and cold water	**l'eau chaude et froide**	low showed ay fwad
babysitting	**le babysitting/garde d'enfants**	luh bay-bay sitting/gard den-*fons*
swimming pool (heated; indoor)	**une piscine (chauffée, couverte)**	ewn pee-*seen* (show-*fay*, coo-*vair*)

Numbers and Ordinals

English	French	Pronunciation
nought/zero	**zéro**	*zare*-oh
one	**un**	oon
two	**deux**	duh
three	**trois**	twah
four	**quatre**	*kaht*-ruh
five	**cinq**	sank
six	**six**	seess
seven	**sept**	set
eight	**huit**	wheat
nine	**neuf**	noof

English	French	Pronunciation
ten	**dix**	deess
eleven	**onze**	ohnz
twelve	**douze**	dooz
thirteen	**treize**	trehz
fourteen	**quatorze**	kah-*torz*
fifteen	**quinze**	kanz
sixteen	**seize**	sez
seventeen	**dix-sept**	deez-*set*
eighteen	**dix-huit**	deez-*wheat*
nineteen	**dix-neuf**	deez-*noof*
twenty	**vingt**	vehn
thirty	**trente**	tron-te
forty	**quarante**	ka-*rahnt*
fifty	**cinquante**	sang-*kahnt*
sixty	**soixante**	swa-sont
seventy	**soixante-dix**	swa-sont-deess
eighty	**quatre-vingts**	kaht-ruh *vehn*
ninety	**quatre-vingts-dix**	kaht-ruh vehn *deess*
one hundred	**cent**	sahn
one thousand	**mille**	meel
first	**premier**	*preh*-mee-ay
second	**deuxième**	*duhz*-zee-em
third	**troisième**	*twa*-zee-em
fourth	**quatrième**	*kaht*-ree-em
fifth	**cinquième**	*sank*-ee-em
sixth	**sixième**	*sees*-ee-em
seventh	**septième**	*set*-ee-em
eighth	**huitième**	*wheat*-ee-em
ninth	**neuvième**	*neuv*-ee-em
tenth	**dixième**	*dees*-ee-em

The Calendar

English	French	Pronunciation
Sunday	**dimanche**	dee-*mahnsh*
Monday	**lundi**	luhn-*dee*
Tuesday	**mardi**	mahr-*dee*

English	French	Pronunciation
Wednesday	**mercredi**	mair-kruh-*dee*
Thursday	**jeudi**	jheu-*dee*
Friday	**vendredi**	vawn-druh-*dee*
Saturday	**samedi**	sahm-*dee*
yesterday	**hier**	ee-*air*
today	**aujourd'hui**	o-jhord-*dwee*
this morning/this afternoon	**ce matin/cet après-midi**	suh ma-*tan*/set ah-preh mee-*dee*
tonight	**ce soir**	suh *swahr*
tomorrow	**demain**	de-*man*
January	**janvier**	jon-vee-*ay*
February	**février**	fay-vree-*ay*
March	**mars**	mars
April	**avril**	av-*reel*
May	**mai**	may
June	**juin**	juh-wan
July	**juillet**	je-wee-*yay*
August	**août**	oot
September	**septembre**	zept-om-*bruh*
October	**octobre**	oct-oh-*bruh*
November	**novembre**	no-varm-*bruh*
December	**decembre**	day-som-*bruh*

Food/Menu/Cooking Terms

English	French	Pronunciation
I would like	**Je voudrais**	jhe voo-*dray*
to eat	**manger**	mahn-*jhay*
Please give me	**Donnez-moi, s'il vous plaît**	doe-nay-*mwah,* seel-voo-*play*
a bottle of	**une bouteille de**	ewn boo-*tay* duh
a cup of	**une tasse de**	ewn tass duh
a glass of	**un verre de**	uh vair duh
breakfast	**du petit-déjeuner**	dew puh-*tee* day-zhuh-*nay*
the bill	**l'addition/la note**	la-dee-see-*ohn*/la noat
dinner	**le dîner**	luh dee-*nay*
lunch	**le déjeuner**	luh day-zhuh-*nay*
a knife	**un couteau**	uh koo-*toe*
a napkin	**une serviette**	ewn sair-vee-*et*

English	French	Pronunciation
a spoon	**une cuillère**	ewn kwee-*air*
a fork	**une fourchette**	ewn four-*shet*
Cheers!	**A votre santé!**	ah vo-truh sahn-*tay*!
fixed-price menu	**un menu une formule**	uh may-*new*/oon for-mool
menu	**la carte**	la kart
gastronomic tasting menu	**menu dégustation**	may-*new* day-gus-ta-see-*on*
menu based on daily market produce	**le menu du marché**	luh may-*new* dew mar-*shay*
children's menu	**le menu enfant/menu bambino/menu Moussaillons**	luh may-new *en*-fon, may-*new* bam-bee-no/may-*new* moo-*sigh*-ons
extra plate	**une assiette supplémentaire**	ewn ay-see-et sup-lay-mon-*tayr*
small portion	**une petite portion**	ewn puh-*tee* por-cee-*on*
Waiter!/Waitress!	**Monsieur!/Mademoiselle!**	muh-*syuh*/mad-mwa-*zel*
wine list	**la carte des vins**	la kart day *van*
appetiser	**une entrée**	ewn en-*tray*
main course	**un plat principal**	uh plah pran-see-*pahlh*
homemade	**maison**	may-*zon*
dish of the day	**le plat du jour**	luh plah dew jhoor
tip included	**service compris**	sehr-*vees* cohm-*pree*
Is the tip/service included?	**Le service est compris?**	luh ser-*vees* eh com-*pree*?
pancake house	**une crêperie**	ewn *kray*-pay-ree
small informal restaurant	**un bistrot**	uh *bee*-stro
small restaurant and bar with long hours	**une brasserie**	ewn bra-zer-*ee*

Breton Specialities

English	French	Pronunciation
fish stew	**de la cotriade**	duh lah cot-ree-ard
biscuit/savoury buckwheat pancake	**une galette/une galette de blé noir**	ewn ga-*let*/ ga-*let* duh blay *nwah*
wheatflour pancakes	**les crêpes de froment**	lay krayps duh fro-*mon*
butter cake	**kouign amann**	koo-in ah-*man*
prune cake	**far breton**	far bray-*ton*
weak mead made from fermented honey	**chouchenn**	shu-*shen*
fermented milk, like sour yogurt	**du lait ribot**	dew lay ree-*bow*

The Basics

English	French	Pronunciation
organic	biologique	bee-ooh-loj-*eek*
bread	**du pain**	dew pan
wholemeal bread	**du pain complet**	dew pan com-*play*
slice	**une tranche**	ewn tron-*sh*
toast	**du pain grillé/un toast**	dew pan gree-*yay* unh tost
butter	**du beurre**	dew buhr
breakfast cereals	**des céréales**	day say-ray-*al*
sugar	**du sucre**	dew *sooh*-kruh
honey	**du miel**	dew mee-*el*
jam	**de la confiture**	duh lah con-fee-*tyur*
cheese	**du fromage**	dew fro-*mahje*
eggs boiled	**des oeufs à la coque**	day zuhf a lah cok
eggs hardboiled	**des oeufs durs**	day zuhf de-yur
eggs fried	**des oeufs au plat**	day zuhf o plat
eggs poached	**des oeufs pochés**	day zuhf posh-*ay*
eggs scrambled	**des oeufs brouillés**	day zuhf bwee-*yay*
omelette	**une omelette**	ewn om-uh-*let*
pasta	**les pâtes**	lay pahtz
pizza	**un pizza**	uhn pee-*zah*
pizza Margherita (with tomato and cheese, and sometimes ham)	**un pizza margherita**	uhn pee-*zah*mar-zhe-reeta
rice	**du riz**	dew ree
dumplings (egg, chicken, veal or fish)	**des quenelles**	day ke-*nelle*
sauerkraut	**de la choucroûte**	duh lah chew-*kroo*

Snacks

English	French	Pronunciation
sandwich (open sandwich)	**un sandwich/une tartine**	uhn sahn-*weech*/ewn tart-*een*
ham and cheese toastie (with fried egg)	**croque-monsieur (croque-madame)**	crow-kuh muh-*shur* (crow-kuh mah-*dam)*
with ham, cheese and egg	**complète**	com-*play*
buttery bread made with eggs	**du brioche**	dew bree-*osh*
crisps	**les chips**	lay *sheeps*
nuts/walnuts	**les noix**	lay nwa

English	French	Pronunciation
almonds	**les amandes**	lay a-*mahnd*
cashews	**les noix de cajou**	lay nwah duh ca-*yoo*
chestnuts	**les marrons, les châtaignes**	lay mah-*rohn*, lay shah-*tay*-nee-yuh
hazelnuts	**les noisettes**	lay nwah-*zet*
peanuts	**les arachides, les cacahouètes**	lay ah-rah-sheed, lay kah-kah-*wayt*
coconut	**le noix de coco**	luh nwah duh ko-ko
chocolate	**du chocolat**	dew shok-o-*laht*
ice lolly/ice cream	**une glace**	ewn glass
lollipop	**une sucette**	ewn sue-*set*
salted-butter caramels	**des caramels au buerre salé**	day cara-mel o buhr sa-*yay*

Starters and Side Dishes

English	French	Pronunciation
chips	**des pommes frites**	day puhm *freet*
garnish/side vegetables	**la garniture**	lah gar-nee-*tyur*
snails	**des escargots**	dayz ess-car-*goh*
coarse pork (or mackerel)	**pâte des rillettes**	day ree-yett
potted meat/pâté	**une terrine/du pâté**	ewn *tai*-reen/dew pah-*tay*
clear broth	**du consommé**	dew kon-*somay*
onion soup	**de la soupe à l'oignon**	duh lah soop ah low-*nyon*
vegetable soup	**du potage (de légumes)**	dew poh-taj duh lay-*guhm*
creamy soup	**du velouté**	dew veh-loo-*tay*
creamy soup with seafood	**de la bisque**	duh lah beesk
seafood stew	**de la bouillabaisse**	duh lah boo-yah-*bayz*
leek and potato soup	**du vichyssoise**	dew vee-shee-*swahz*
rich consommé with meat and veg	**une petite marmite**	ewn puh-teet mahr-*meet*

Meat

English	French	Pronunciation
meat	**la viande**	lah vee-*ond*
poultry	**les volailles**	lay vol-*eye*
game	**le gibier**	luh *gee*-bee-ay
ham	**du jambon**	dew jham-*bon*

English	French	Pronunciation
pale sliced ham	**du jambon blanc**	dew jham-*bon* blonk
smoked ham	**de la poitrine fumée**	duh la pwa-treen fuw-*may*
chicken	**du poulet**	dew *poo*-lay
duck	**du canard**	dew can-*ahr*
goose	**de l'oie**	duh l'wah
pheasant	**du faisan**	dew fay-*zan*
pigeon	**du pigeon**	dew pee-*zyon*
turkey	**de la dinde**	duh lah dahnd
quail	**de la caille**	duh lah kay-ee
lamb	**de l'agneau**	duh lahn-*nyo*
rabbit	**du lapin**	dew *lah*-pan
sirloin	**de l'aloyau**	duh lahl-why-*yo*
steak	**du bifteck**	dew beef-*tek*
hamburger patty/child's steak	**du steak haché**	dew tek a-*shay*
veal	**du veau**	dew voh
gizzards (ducks' innards)	**les gésiers**	lay *jey*-zee-ay
chitterling (tripe) sausage	**de l'andouille**	duh lon-*dwee*
black pudding (blood sausage)	**le boudin noir**	luh boo-don nwah
frogs' legs	**des cuisses de grenouilles**	day cweess duh gre-*noo*-yuh
goose liver	**du foie gras**	dew fwah *grah*
chicken stew with mushrooms and wine	**du coq au vin**	dew cock o vhin
beef stew	**du pot au feu**	dew poht o *fhe*
meat stew with red wine, onions and garlic	**daube**	dohb

Fish

English	French	Pronunciation
fish (freshwater)	**du poisson de rivière/d'eau douce**	dew pwah-*sson* duh ree-vee-*aire*/d'o *dooss*
fish (saltwater)	**du poisson de mer**	dew pwah-*sson* duh *mehr*
seafood	**les fruits de mer**	lay fwee duh *mehr*
shellfish	**les coquillages**	lay cok-ee-*arj*
crustaceans (crabs, lobsters, shrimps etc)	**les crustacés**	lay kruhz-ta-*say*
catch of the day	**le poisson du jour**	luh pwah-*sson* duh *jhur*
breaded/cooked in breadcrumbs	**pané**	pah-*nay*

English	French	Pronunciation
anchovies	**les anchois**	lay an-*shwa*
clams	**les palourdes**	lay pah-lord
cockles	**des coques**	day cok
dog cockles	**des amandes**	day zah-*mahnd*
cod	**du cabillaud/de la morue**	dew cab-ee-*yode*/duh lah maw-*ru*
crab	**de la crabe**	duh lah crab
hermit crab	**un tourteau**	uhn tor-*toe*
spider crab	**de l'araignée de mer**	duh la-ray-nay duh mehr
herring	**du hareng**	dew ahr-*rahn*
lobster	**du homard**	dew oh-*mahr*
mackerel	**du maquereau**	dew ma-ker-row
monkfish	**de la lotte**	duh lah lot
mussels (grown on posts)	**des moules (au bouchot)**	day moohl (o boo-show)
mussels in white wine with shallots and herbs	**des moules marinières**	day moohl mar-ee-nee-*air*
oysters	**des huîtres**	day *hwee*-truhs
European oysters	**des huîtres plates**	day *hwee*-truhs plat
Pacific oysters	**des huîtres creuses**	day *hwee*-truhs crerz
pollack	**du lieu (lieu jaune)**	dewh lee-ew (lee-ew jawn)
prawns	**les gambas**	lay gahm-bah
red mullet	**du rouget**	dew roo-jhay
sardines	**des sardines**	day sar-*deen*
scallops	**des coquilles St-Jacques/ des noix de St-Jacque**	day cock-*eel* san-jack/ day nwah duh san-jack
bay/Atlantic sea scallops	**des pétoncles**	day pet-*onk*-l
scampi/large prawns	**des langoustines**	day lohn-gus-*teen*
sea bass	**du loup de mer/du bar**	dew loo duh mehr/dew bar
sea bream	**du dorade**	dew door-ard
shrimp/small prawns	**des crevettes**	day kreh-*vet*
skate wing	**un aile de raie**	uhn ay duh ray
smoked salmon	**du saumon fumé**	dew sow-*mohn* fu-*may*
swordfish	**de l'espadon**	duh *lez*-padon
tuna	**du thon**	dew tohn
turbot	**du turbot**	dew ter-bow
trout	**de la truite**	duh lah tru-*eet*
whelks	**des bulots**	day boo-*low*

English	French	Pronunciation
winkles	**des bigorneaux**	day bee-gohr-*no*
seafood with sauerkraut	**de la choucroûte de mer**	duh lah chew-*kroot* duh mehr

Fruits

English	French	Pronunciation
fruit	**les fruits**	lay frwee
citrus fruit	**les agrumes**	lay zag-*room*
berries	**les fruits rouges**	lay frwee rooj
apples	**les pommes**	lay puhm
apricot	**les abricots**	lay *ah*-bree-koh
bananas	**les bananes**	lay bah-*nahnz*
blackberries	**les mûres**	lay myur
blueberries	**les myrtilles**	lay mehr-tee
cherries	**les cérises/les griottes**	lay cay-*rees*/lay gree-*yot*
dates	**les dattes**	lay daht
figs	**les figues**	lay feeg
gooseberries	**les groseilles**	lay grow-*zi*
grapefruit	**un pamplemousse**	uhn pahm-*pluh*-moose
grapes	**les raisins**	lay ray-*zhan*
lemon/lime	**du citron/du citron vert**	dew cee-*tron*/dew cee-tron *vaire*
melon	**du melon**	luh meh-*lohn*
oranges	**les oranges**	lay zor-*ahn*-je
peach	**une pêche**	ewn paysh
pears	**les poires**	lay pwarz
pineapple	**de l'ananas**	duh lah-na-*nas*
plums	**les prunes**	lay prwehn
pomegranate	**une grenade**	ewn greh-*nad*
prunes	**les pruneaux**	lay prweh-*noh*
raspberries	**des framboises**	day fwahm-*bwahz*
strawberries	**des fraises**	day *frez*
watermelon	**une pastèque**	ewn pas-*tek*

Vegetables

English	French	Pronunciation
vegetables	**les légumes**	lay lay-*guhm*
artichoke	**de l'artichaud**	duh larh-tee-*show*

English	French	Pronunciation
asparagus	**des asperges**	day as-*sperj*
aubergine	**de l'aubergine**	duh loh-ber-*jheen*
avocado pear	**de l'avocat**	duh lah-voh-*kah*
beetroot	**de la betterave**	duh lah beht-*rahv*
broccoli	**du brocoli**	du broh-koh-*lee*
cabbage	**du choux**	dew *shoe*
carrots	**les carottes**	lay *cah*-rot
cauliflower	**du chou-fleur**	du *shoo*-fler
celery	**du céleri**	du say-leh-*ree*
courgettes	**des courgettes**	day coor-*jet*
endive	**de la scarole**	duh lah scah-*roll*
fennel	**du fenouil**	du feh-nou-*eel*
garlic	**de l'ail**	duh lie
garlic cloves	**des gousse d'ail**	day goose dye
green beans	**des haricots verts**	day *ahr*-ee-coh *vaire*
leeks	**des poireaux**	day pwah-*row*
mushrooms	**des champignons**	day sham-pin-*yon*
morel mushrooms	**des morilles**	day moh-*ree*
onion	**les oignons**	lay zon-*nyohn*
peas	**des petits pois**	day puh-tee *pwah*
peppers (green, red, yellow)	**les poivrons (verts, rouges, jaunes)**	lay pwah-*vrohn* (vehr, rooj, jorn)
potatoes	**des pommes de terre**	day puhm duh *tehr*
baked potatoes	**des pommes de terre au four**	day puhm duh *tehr* o fooyr
mashed potatoes	**des pommes de terre en purée**	day puhm duh *tehr* ohn *poo*-ray
potatoes au gratin	**des pommes de terre dauphinois**	day puhm duh *tehr* doh-feen-*wah*
shallot	**des échalotes**	lay ay-shaw-*lot*
sorrel	**de l'oseille**	duh low-say-ya
spinach	**des épinards**	dayz ay-pin-*ards*
sweetcorn	**du maïs**	du may-*eez*
truffles	**des truffes**	day truhf
turnips	**des navets**	day nah-*vay*
assortment of vegetables	**un méli mélo de légumes**	uhn may-lee may-lo duh lay-*guhm*
diced mixed vegetables	**une macédoine de légumes**	ewn mah-say-duwhn deh lay-*guhm*

English	French	Pronunciation
steamed vegetables	**des légumes à vapeur**	day lay-*guhm* a vah-*purr*
boiled vegetables	**es légumes bouillis**	day lay-*guhm* buw-*yee*
raw vegetables	**des légumes crus**	day lay-*guhm* crew
raw vegetable sticks	**crudités**	crew-dee-*tay*

Salads

English	French	Pronunciation
green salad	**une salade verte**	ewn sah-lahd *vairt*
main-course salad	**une salade composée**	ewn sah-lahd com-poy-*say*
lettuce	**de la laitue, de la salade**	duh lah lay-*too,* duh lah sah-*lahd*
lettuce leaves	**des feuilles de salade**	day foo-ya deh sah-*lahd*
watercress	**du cresson**	dew creh-sohn
tomatoes	**es tomates**	day toe-*maht*
cucumber	**du concombre**	du kohn-*kohm*-br
radish	**des radis**	day rah-*dee*
spring onions	**les ciboules**	lah see-*bool*
salad dressing	**la sauce de salade/la vinaigrette**	lah saws duh sa-*lahd*/lah veen-ee-ah-*gret*

Herbs

English	French	Pronunciation
herbs	**les herbs**	lays airb
basil	**le basilic**	luh bah-zee-*leek*
bay leave	**la feuille de laurier**	lah foohy duh loh-*ree*-ay
chive	**la ciboulette**	lah see-boo-*leht*
dill	**l'aneth**	lah-ne
lavender	**la lavande**	lah la-vahn
mint	**la menthe**	lah mahnt
oregano	**l'origan**	loh-ree-gahn
parsley	**le persil**	luh par-*seel*
rosemary	**le romarin**	luh row-ma-*ran*
sage	**la sauge**	lah sowj
tarragon	**l'estragon**	lestra-gohn
thyme	**le thym**	luh teehm

Spices and Condiments

English	French	Pronunciation
salt	**du sel**	dew sel
salted	**salé**	sal-ay
pepper	**du poivre**	dew *pwah*-vruh
rock salt	**le gros sel**	leh grow sel
vinegar	**du vinaigre**	du vin-*ay*-gruh
capers	**les câpres**	day *cay*-prus
mayonnaise	**de la mayonnaise**	duh lah mayo-nez
garlic mayonnaise	**de l'aïoli**	duh lah-ee-oh-lee
spicy garlic mayonnaise served with fish soup	**de la rouille**	duh lah rwee
ketchup	**du ketchup**	dew ket-sup
mustard	**de la moutarde**	duh lah moo-*tard*-uh
curry	**le curry**	luh ke-*ree*
cardamom	**la cardamome**	lah car-da-mum
cinnamon	**la cannelle**	lah ka-*nel*
coriander	**la coriandre**	lah ko-ree-*an*-dr
clove	**le clou de girofle**	luh clue deh jee-*ro*-fler
cumin	**le cumin**	luh koo-min
ginger	**le gingembre**	luh jeen-jarm-br
nutmeg	**la noix de muscade**	ah nwah deh moos-cade
pimento	**le piment**	luh pee-mahn
saffron	**le safran**	luh sah-frahn

Cooking Methods

English	French	Pronunciation
fish, meat, vegetables or fruit simmered in a reduction of their own fat or juices	**un confit**	uh khon-*feeh*
baked	**cuit au four**	kweet o foohr
boiled	**bouilli**	boo-ee-*yee*
cooked over a wood fire	**cuit au feu de bois**	kweet o foo dew *bwoi*
cooked in parchment paper	**en papillotte**	on pah-pee-*yott*
cooked on a skewer	**en brochette**	on bro-*shet*
cooked in alcohol set alight	**flambé**	*flom*-bay
cooked with spinach	**florentine**	floh-ren-*teen*
deep fried	**frit**	free

English	French	Pronunciation
grilled	**grillé**	gree-*yay*
marinaded	**mariné**	*ma*-ree-nay
medium (cooked, ie steak)	**à point**	ah-*pwahn*
panfried	**à la poêle**	a lah *pwal*
poached	**poché**	pow-*shay*
Provencal-style (cooked with tomatoes, onions, olives, herbs, perhaps anchovies)	**Provençale**	proh-vahn-*sahl*
puff pastry shell	**vol-au-vent**	vhol-o-*vhen*
rare (cooked, i.e. steak)	**saignant**	say-*gnohn*
roast	**rôti**	row-*tee*
simmered	**mijoté**	mee-jo-*tay*
steamed	**à la vapeur**	ah la va-*poor*
sautéed	**sauté**	so-*tay*
stuffed	**farci**	far-*see*
very rare (cooking, i.e. steak)	**bleu**	blew
well done (cooking, i.e. steak)	**bien cuit**	byahn *kwee*

Sauces

English	French	Pronunciation
sweet and sour	**sauce aigre-douce**	saws aygr doo
butter and egg with shallots, tarragon and wine	**sauce béarnaise**	saws bare-*neyz*
white with milk, butter and flour	**sauce béchamel**	saws beh-sha-*mel*
creamy white wine and egg	**sauce blanquette**	saws blon-*ket*
white wine with vegetables	**sauce à la bonne femme**	sawz ah lah bon fame
wild mushroom	**sauce forestière**	saws foh-rehs-tee-*air*
egg yolk, butter and lemon/vinegar	**sauce hollandaise**	sawz o-lahn-*dayz*
vegetable	**sauce jardinière**	saws jahr-dee-nee-*air*
butter with parsley and lemon juice	**sauce maître d'hôtel**	saws may-tr do-*tel*
butter, cream and parsley	**meunière**	*muhr*-nee-ayr
white with cheese	**sauce mornay**	saws mohr-*nay*
mayonnaise with mustard	**sauce rémoulade**	saws ray-moo-*lahd*
creamy béchamel and fish/ chicken stock	**sauce velouté**	saws veh-loo-*tay*
wine and grapes	**sauce véronique**	saws vay-ron-*eek*
butter and egg yolk	**sauce hollandaise**	sawz o-lon-*days*

Drink

English	French	Pronunciation
water	**de l'eau**	duh *lo*
drinking water	**de l'eau potable**	duh lo pot-*ah*-bluh
spring water	**de l'eau de source**	duh lo de sors
still mineral water	**de l'eau minérale plat/ sans gaz**	duh lo min-ay-*ral* plat/ sonz gahz
sparkling mineral water	**de l'eau minérale gazeuse/ pétillante**	duh lo min-ay-*ral* gahz-*oze*/ pay-tee-*lahnt*
milk	**du lait**	dew lay
apple juice	**du jus de pomme**	dew joo de puhm
orange juice	**du jus d'orange**	dew joo d'or-*ahn*-jhe
pear juice	**du jus de poire**	dew joo de pwar
lemon juice	**un citron pressé**	dew see-*trohn* preh-*say*
fruit cordial with water	**un sirop (à l'eau)**	uhn see-*ro* (al-o)
fizzy drink	**du soda**	dew so-*dah*
cider	**du cidre**	dew *see*-druh
cider in a traditional porcelain cup	**du cidre en bolée**	dew *see*-druh en bollay
beer	**de la bière**	duh lah bee-*aire*
red wine	**du vin rouge**	dew vhin *rooj*
white wine	**du vin blanc**	dew vhin *blonk*
carafe	**un pichet**	uhn pee-*shay*
white wine with blackcurrant liqueur	**un kir**	uh keer
champagne with blackcurrant liqueur	**un kir royale**	uh keer roy-*al*
coffee (black)	**un café noir**	uh ka-fay *nwahr*
coffee (with cream)	**un café crème**	uh ka-fay *krem*
coffee (with milk)	**un café au lait**	uh ka-fay o *lay*
coffee (decaf)	**un café décaféiné (slang: un déca**)	un ka-fay day-kah-fay-*nay* (uh *day*-kah)
coffee (espresso)	**un café espresso (un express)**	uh ka-fay e-*sprehss-o* (un ek-*sprehss*)
tea	**du thé**	dew tay
herbal tea	**une tisane**	ewn tee-*zahn*
hot chocolate	**un chocolate chaud**	uhn shok-o-laht *showd*

Desserts

English	French	Pronunciation
dessert	**le dessert**	luh deh-*sehr*
fruit salad	**une salade de fruit/une macédoine de fruits**	ewn sah-lahd duh *fwee*/ewn mah-*say*-doine duh fwee
ice cream	**de la glace**	duh lah *glass*
vanilla	**...à la vanille**	a lah vah-*nee*-yuh
strawberry	**...à la fraise**	a lah *frays*
chocolate	**...au chocolat**	o shok-o-*laht*
mint	**...à la menthe**	a lah *month*
pistachio	**...à la pistache**	a lah pis-*tash*
ice-cream cone	**un cornet**	uhn kohr-*nay*
scoop	**une boule**	ewn bool
ice-cream sundae	**une coupe glaceé**	ewn coop glah-*say*
multi-flavoured ice-cream dessert	**une bombe**	ewn bohmb
yoghurt	**du yaourt/yogourt**	dew yow-*urt*
creamy white cheese	**le fromage blanc**	le fro-*mahj* blonk
sour thick cream	**la crème fraîche**	lah krem *fresh*
whipped cream with sugar	**la crème Chantilly**	lah krem shon-*tee*
waffles	**les gaufres**	lay gwohfr
pastries	**des pâtisseries**	day pah-tee-ser-*ree*
cake	**du gâteau**	dew *gha*-tow
sponge cake filled with pudding	**une charlotte**	ewn shahr-*loht*
stewed fruit	**de la compôte**	duh lah com-*poht*
chocolate mousse	**de la mousse au chocolat**	duh lah moos o shok-o-*laht*
half-cooked chocolate cake	**du fondant au chocolate**	duh fon-don o shok-o-*laht*
thick custard dessert with caramelised topping	**de la crème brûlée**	duh lah krem bruh-*lay*
egg custard with caramelised topping	**une crème caramel**	ewn krem kah-rah-*mehl*
caramelised upside-down apple pie	**une tarte Tatin**	ewn tart tah-*tihn*
tart	**une tarte**	ewn tart
doughnuts	**des beignets**	day beh-*nyeh*
cream puffs with chocolate sauce	**des profiteroles**	day proh-fee-ter-ohl

English	French	Pronunciation
meringues in custard sauce	**des oeufs à la neige**	day zuhf ah lah nee-age
battered fruit, especially cherries	**du clafoutis**	dew kla-foo-*tee*
poached pears with vanilla ice cream and chocolate sauce	**des poires hélène**	day pwahr zay-lehn
baked Alaska	**une omelette norvégienne**	ewn om-let nohr-*vay*-jee-on
Bavarian cream (cream dessert with custard)	**une bavaroise**	ewn bah-vahr-*wahz*

Family Travel

Travelling as a family can be fun, exciting and create memories to savour, but a bit of preparation will go a long way in forging a smooth journey and holiday. There are plenty of sites providing parents with essential holiday information and even sites popping up for youngsters, too. From what to pack and coping with flights to childcare and accessories, the sites below will help give you a headstart.

www.babygoes2.com: An innovative guide for parents travelling with babies and children with independent recommendations.

www.all4kidsuk.com: Links to tour companies offering family-friendly holidays, some of them in Croatia.

www.youngtravellersclub.co.uk: Currently in its early days, this is a site for children themselves, which deserves to succeed.

www.deabirkett.com: The website of *Guardian* journalist Dea Birkett, who specialises in travelling with children. It includes a very useful Travelling with Kids Forum.

www.babycentre.co.uk: The travel section throws up some interesting articles on family holidays.

www.mumsnet.com: Set up by a journalist, TV producer and radio producer. Product reviews, interviews and planning help.

www.travellingwithchildren.co.uk: Comprehensive site with lots of handy tips for travelling parents.

www.travelforkids.com: An American site that has some good information on different countries with 'what not to leave at home' type tips.

www.familytravelforum.com: Lots of useful stuff on family travel in general.

www.travelwithyourkids.com: Easy to navigate with advice you feel comes from real experience of things having gone wrong!

www.thefamilytravelfiles.com: Heavily American, but with a section on Europe.

www.family-travel.co.uk: Independent advice on travelling with children: Lots of sound general advice.

Responsible Tourism

Although one could argue any holiday including a flight can't be truly 'green', tourism can contribute positively to the environment and communities UK visitors travel to if investment is used wisely. Firstly, by offsetting carbon emissions from your flight, you can lessen the negative environmental impact of your journey. Secondly, by embracing responsible tourism practises you can choose forward looking companies who care about the resorts and countries we visit, preserving them for the future by working alongside local people. Below are a number of sustainable tourism initiatives and associations to help you plan a family trip and leave as small a 'footprint' as possible on the places you visit.

www.responsibletravel.com: A great source of sustainable travel ideas run by a spokesperson for responsible tourism in the travel industry.

www.tourismconcern.org.uk: Working to reduce social and environmental problems connected to tourism and find ways of improving tourism so that local benefits are increased.

www.climatecare.org.uk: Helping UK holidaymakers offset their carbon emissions through flying by funding sustainable energy projects

www.thetravelfoundation.org.uk: Produces excellent material on how to care for the places we visit on holiday. It also produces a special guide for children aged 7–10 and parents incorporating 'Hatch the Hatchling Hawksbill' with a play and puzzle book. Highly recommended.

www.abta.co.uk: The Association of British Travel Agents (ABTA) acts as a focal point for the UK travel industry and is one of the leading groups spearheading responsible tourism.

www.aito.co.uk: The Association of Independent Tour Operators (AITO) is a group of interesting specialist operators leading the field in making holidays sustainable.

Index

See also Accommodations and Restaurant indexes, below.

General

A

Abbaye de Beauport (Kérity), 122–123
Abbaye de Bon Repos, 114
Accommodations, 42–47. *See also* Accommodations Index
best, 10
budget hotel chains, 45
farm stays, 96
price categories, 43
Accor Thalassa (Quiberon), 229
Activity holidays, 34–37
Aer Arann, 31
Aer Lingus, 31
Air Canada, 31–32
Aire Naturelle de Keraluic (Plomeur), 13, 186
Air France, 31, 40
Air tours, Golfe du Morbihan, 206
Air travel, 31, 39–40
American Airlines, 31
Animal parks and zoos
Côtes d'Armor, 118–121
Finistère, 158–161
Ille-et-Vilaine, 70, 73–74
Morbihan, 206–212
Anse de Bénodet, 150–151
Anse de Dinan, 158
Anse des Blancs Sablons, 155
Anse de Sordan, 114
Anse Du Guesclin, 64
Apartments, 44–45
Aquariums
Aquarium du Golfe (Vannes), 207
Aquarium Marin (Trégastel-Plage), 118–119
Grand Aquarium (St-Malo), 6, 72
L'Aquashow (Audierne), 158–159
Petit Aquarium (St-Malo), 63
Aquarive (Quimper), 171–172
Archéoscope (Mont-St-Michel), 68
Armoripark (Bégard), 127
Astérix the Gaul, 114
Atelier-Musée de l'Horlogerie Ancienne (Fougères), 76
ATMs (automated teller machines), 23–24
Audierne, 156

B

Babychanging, 54
Baby equipment, 49–50
Babysitters, 50
Baie d'Audierne, 151
Baie de Lannion, 118
Baie de St-Brieuc
accommodations, 133–134
restaurants, 140–142
Baie des Trépassés, 155
Baie du Mont-St-Michel, 68, 90, 101
Balade Découverte, 69
Banks, 50
Barrage d'Arzal, 208
Beaches
best resorts, 6
Côtes d'Armor, 112–115
Finistère, 150–155
Morbihan, 202–205
Rothéneuf, 70
safety concerns, 28
St-Lunaire, 66
St-Malo, 64
Beau Rivage, 114
Bébétel Baby Monitor, 25
Bécherel, Cité du Livre, 61–63
Bed and breakfasts (B&Bs), 43
Belle-Ile, 6, 202–203
Bénodet, 150, 185–186
restaurants, 194–195
Bicycling, 42
Houat, 204
St-Lunaire, 66
tours, 35
Vélo Rail (Médréac), 88
Binic, 112
Bird-watching
Goulien, 156
Ile des Landes, 65
Parc Ornithologique de Bretagne (Bruz), 73
Sept Iles, 122
Biscuiterie de Concarneau, 175
Biscuiterie de Quimper-Styvell, 175
Biscuiterie des Iles One (Belle-Isle-en-Terre), 129–130
Biscuiterie François Garrec (Bénodet), 175
Biscuitier Chocolatier Glacier Lanicol (Concarneau), 9, 174
Biscuits, 175
Boardbug Baby and Toddler Monitor, 25
Boat hire. *See also* Canoeing
Côtes d'Armor, 114
Ille-et-Vilaine, 78, 84
Boat trips and tours. *See also* Ferries
best, 7
Finistère, 155, 158, 170, 171
Sept Iles, 122
Books, recommended, 49
Boutique Traou-Mad (Pont-Aven), 175
Breastfeeding, 50
Bréhat, 116–117
Brest, 3, 148–149
Breton Bikes, 35
Breton language, 5
Brignogan-Plages, 155
British Airways, 31
Brittany Ferries, 32, 35–36
Brocéliande Forest (Fôret de Paimpont), 7, 67
Bugale Breizh (Guingamp), 3, 110
Business hours, 50
Bus travel, 34, 42

C

Camaret-sur-Mer, 158
Camargue horses, 121
Camping, 43, 47
Aire Naturelle de Keraluic (Plomeur), 13, 186
best, 13
Camping Anse de Sordan, 114
Camping Caravaning Château de Galinée (St Cast-le-Guildo), 132
Camping Claire Fontaine (Perros-Guirec), 137–138
Camping d'Alet (St-Malo), 98–99

Camping-gîte de Loquéran (Plouhinec), 185
Camping Les Hortensias/ Gîtes de Kermen (Carantec), 179
La Grande Metairie (Carnac), 228–230
Le Ty Nadan (Locunolé), 13, 187–188
Cancale, 64–65
Canoeing
Côtes d'Armor, 114, 128
Finistère, 151, 152, 170, 172, 180, 187
Ille-et-Vilaine, 66, 77, 78, 84, 85, 95
Morbihan, 205, 210, 221, 226, 230
Canvas Holidays, 36
Cap Armor programme, 7, 128
Capitaine d'un Jour (Vannes), 206
Capitaine Némo (Bénodet), 170
Cap Sizun, 155–156
accommodations, 184–185
restaurants, 193–194
Carantec, 6, 152–153
Car hires, 38–39
Carnac, 212–214
Carnac-Plage, 200, 203
Car travel, 37–40
Cashpoint machines, 23–24
Castel Clara (Belle-Ile), 228–229
Castles
best, 9
Château de la Hunaudaye, 9, 123
Fort la Latte, 9, 123–124
Centre Culturel Juliet Drouet (Fougères), 59
Centre d'Activités et de Loisirs de Chênedet (Landéan), 84
Centre de Découverte des Algues (Roscoff), 170–171
Centre de Découverte du Son (Cavan), 127
Centre de l'Imaginaire Arthurien (Château de Comper), 68
Centre d'Etude du Milieu de l'Ile d'Ouessant, 154
Centre International de Plongée/Centre Nautique des Glénans, 172
Centre Nautique de Kerguelen (Larmor-Plage), 221
Centre Nautique de Rance (St Suliac), 84
Château de Comper (near Rennes), 67–68
Château de la Hunaudaye, 9, 123
Chemists, 50–51
Child seats, 40–41
Chocolatier Chatillon (Pleyben), 174–175
Cîté des Télécoms (Pleumeur-Bodou), 124–125
Clipper (Vannes), 222–223
Coach travel, 34, 42
Cobac Parc (Lanhélin), 85
Coiffe, 167
Colette, 64
Comité Régionale de Tourisme (CRT), 20
Comités Départmentales de Tourisme (CDTs), 20
Comptoir de la Mer, 130
Comptoirs de l'Ouest (Dahouët), 130
Concarneau, 150
accommodations, 186–188
restaurants in and around, 195–196
Condor Ferries, 33
Conservatoire National (Brest), 149
Continental Airlines, 31
Côte d'Emeraude, 112–113
accommodations, 131–133
restaurants, 138–140
Côte du Granit Rose, 4, 115–116
accommodations, 136–138
restaurants, 142
Côtes d'Armor, 107–142
accommodations, 131–138
for active families, 127–129
beaches and resorts, 112–115
events and entertainment, 110–112
getting around, 110
orientation, 110
restaurants, 138–142
shopping, 129–131
sights and attractions, 112–129
aquaria and animal parks, 118–121
beaches and resorts, 112–115
historic buildings and monuments, 122–124
museums, 124–126
natural wonders and spectacular views, 115–118
nature reserves, parks, and gardens, 121–122
top 10 attractions, 112
tours, 126–127
traveling to, 108
visitor information, 108
Credit cards, 22
Croisières Chateaubriand (Dinard), 81–82
Crown Blue Line, 36
Cycling, 34, 42

D

Debit cards, 22
Delta Air Lines, 31
Demoiselles de Cojoux (Roches Piquées), 76
Dentists, 51
Diving
Ile de Groix, 205
Larmor-Plage, 221
Doctors, 51
Domaine de Kerguéhennec (Bignan), 219
Domaine de Ménez-Meur (near Hanvec), 6, 159
Domaine de Tremelin (Lac de Tremelin), 85
Driving rules and advice, 38
Dunes de Bonabri, 120
Dwarf black sheep, 153, 159

E

Ecomusée (Ile de Groix), 205
Ecomusée du Pays de Montfort (Montfort-sur-Meu), 77
Ecomusée du Pays de Rennes, 71
EHIC (European Health Insurance Card), 26–27
Electricity, 51
Embassies and high commissions, 51
Emergencies, 51
Enigmaparc (Janzé), 85–86
Entry requirements, 21–22
Erquy, 113, 114
Espace des Sciences (Rennes), 8, 78–79
Espace Ferrié (Cesson-Sévigné), 77
Etincelles Aquatiques (Martigné-Ferchaud), 59–60
The euro, 22
Eurocamp, 36
Eurolines, 34
Europ Assistance, 40
European Health Insurance Card (EHIC), 26–27
Eurostar, 34
Eurotunnel shuttle train, 34

F

Faïencerie HB-Henriot (Quimper), 169
Family Travel, 256
Farm stays, 96
Ferme d'Antan (Plédéliac), 119
Ferme de la Bintinais, 71
Ferme du Monde, 6, 208
Ferme du Tessonnet, 71
Ferme Marine (Cancale), 82
Ferré, Leo, 64
Ferries, 32–33
  St-Malo, 57, 64
Festival de Cornouaille (Quimper), 147
Festival de la Danse Bretonne et de la Saint-Loup (Guingamp), 110
Festival Interceltique (Lorient), 3, 200
Festivals and events, 26
  best, 3
Fest noz, 26
Fête de la Crêpe (Gourin), 201
Fête des Brodeuses (Pont-l'Abbé), 147
Finistère, 143–196
  accommodations, 176–188
  for active families, 171–174
  events and entertainment, 147–148
  getting around, 146–147
  orientation, 146
  restaurants, 189–196
  shopping, 174–176
  sights and attractions, 148–174
    aquaria and animal parks, 158–161
    arts and crafts sites, 168–170
    beaches and resorts, 150–155
    museums, 163–168
    natural wonders and spectacular views, 155–158
    nature reserves, parks, and gardens, 161–162
    top 10 attractions, 148
  tours, 170–171
  traveling to, 145–146
  visitor information, 146
Fishing, 128
  Haliotika (Le Guilvinec), 163–165
  Musée de la Pêche (Concarneau), 167–168
Flybe, 31
Fnac (Lorient), 223
Folle Pensée, 68
Fontaine de Barenton (Château de Comper), 68
Fôret de Brocéliande (Fôret de Paimpont), 7, 67
Fôret de Villecartier, 15
Forges-des-Salles, 114
Fort de Bertheaume (Plougonvelin), 147–148
Fort la Latte, 9, 123–124
Fort National (St-Malo), 63

G

Galerie Plisson (La Trinité-sur-Mer), 223
Galettes de Pleyben, 175
Gingerbread, 29
Gîtes, 44–45
  children's, 46
Glénan islands, 172
Golfe du Morbihan, 4, 6, 205–206
  accommodations, 226–230
  restaurants, 232–234
Goulien, 156
Grand Aquarium (St-Malo), 6, 72
Grand Bé, 63
Grand Menhir Brisé (near Carnac), 214
Grandparents, 29
Groix (Le Bourg), 205
Grotte du Diable, 157
Guingamp, events and entertainment, 110–111

H

Haliotika (Le Guilvinec), 163–165
Hangar't (Nizon), 9, 168–169
Haras National (Lamballe), 119–120
Haras National de Hennebont, 209
Health concerns, 27–28
Health insurance, 26–27
Highchairs, portable, 25
Hillion, 120
Holidays, 25–26
Horseback riding, 85, 87–88, 222. *See also* Pony rides
Hôtel-résidences, 44
Hotels, 42–47. *See also* Accommodations Index
  best, 10
  budget hotel chains, 45
  farm stays, 96
  price categories, 43
Houat, 204
Huelgoat, 4, 156–157

I

Ile Callot, 153
Ile de Bréhat, 116–117
Ile de Groix, 204–205
Ile des Landes, 65
Ile d'Ouessant, 6, 153–154
  accommodations, 179–180
  restaurants, 190–192
Ile Rouzic, 122
Iles de Glénan, 172
Iliz-Koz (St Michel), 163
Ille-et-Vilaine, 55–106
  accommodations, 90–101
  for active families, 83–88
  events and entertainment, 59–61
  getting around, 58–59
  restaurants, 101–106
  shopping, 88–90
  sights and attractions, 61–81
    aquaria and animal parks, 70–74
    art and craft sites, 80–81
    beaches and resorts, 64–67
    historic buildings and monuments, 75–76
    museums, 76–80
    natural wonders and spectacular views, 67–70
    nature reserves, parks, and gardens, 74–75
    top 10 attractions, 61
    towns and cities, 61–64
  tours, 81–83
  traveling to, 57–58
  visitor information, 58
Initiation aux Danses Bretonnes (Penmarc'h), 172–173
Insectarium de Lizio, 209
Insurance, 26–27
Internet access, 30–31
Irish Ferries, 33

J

Jardin du Thabor (Rennes), 74–75
Jardins de Suscinio (Ploujean), 161–162

K

Kayaking, 173, 187
Kerzehro Alignments (near Erdeven), 212
Keycamp, 36

L

L'Abeille Vivante et La Cité des Fourmis (Le Faouët), 206–207
L'Aber-Wrac'h, 155
La Bintinais, 71
Laboratoire de Merlin (Rennes), 79
La Boutique Sentimentale (St-Malo), 88–89
Labyrinthe du Corsaire (St-Malo), 86
Labyrinthe Végétal de Paimpol, 127–128
La Cancalaise (Cancale), 83–84
Lac de Comper, 68
Lac de Guerlédan, 114
Lac de Tremelin, 85
La Chêvrerie du Désert (Plerguer), 70
La Cité des Fourmis (Le Faouët), 206–207
La Droguerie de Marine (St-Malo), 9, 89
La Ferme d'Antan (Plédéliac), 119
La Grande Metairie, 36
La Grande Ourse (St-Malo), 89
La Grande Plage (St-Lunaire), 66
La Maison de l'Environnement Insulaire (Molène), 154
Lampaul, 154
Lancieux, 113
La Perle Rare (Concarneau), 176
L'Aquashow (Audierne), 158–159
La Roche aux Fées (near Essé), 75
L'Atelier Manoli (La Richardais), 80
La Thalassa (Lorient), 217–218
Le Blé en Herbe (St-Brieuc), 130
Le Cartopole (Baud), 218–219
Le Marinarium (Concarneau), 160
Les Amis de Jeudi-Dimanche (L'Aber-Wrac'h), 155
Les Ecuries (St-Lunaire), 66
Les Grands Sables (Belle-Ile), 202
Les Jeud'his de Guingamp, 110–111
Les Marionnet'ic (Binic), 111
Les Mediévales de Moncontour de Bretagne, 111
Les Saveurs D'Arvor (Vannes), 224
Les Secrets du Soie (Campel), 79–80
Les Villages Mer (Le Conquet), 173–174
Les Viviers (Audierne), 156
Le Tertre Gris, 102
Le Trou de l'Enfer (Ile de Groix), 205
Le Ty Nadan (Locunolé), 13, 36, 187–188
Le Val-André, 113
Le Végétarium (La Gacilly), 218
Librairie Guriziem (Bécherel), 62
Librairie Neiges d'Antan (Bécherel), 62–63
Lighthouses, 164
Littlelife Baby Carriers, 25
Locmaria, 203
Lorient
  accommodations around, 224–226
  restaurants, 231–232
Lost property, 51–52
L'Univers du Poète Ferrailleur (Lizio), 220

M

Magazines, 52
Mail, 52
Maison de la Baie (Hillion), 120–121
Maison de la Baie du Vivier sur Mer (near St-Malo), 69
Maison de la Faune Sauvage et de la Chasse (Scrignac), 162
Maison de la Harpe (Dinan), 125
Maison de l'Amiral (Penhors), 159–160
Maison de l'Environnement Insulaire (Molène), 154
Maison des Jeux et Sports Traditionnels de Bretagne Le Jaupitre (Monterfil), 86–87
Maison des Johnnies et de l'Oignon Rosé (Roscoff), 165–166
Maison des Minéraux (St Hernot), 166
Maison des Vieux Métiers Vivants (Argol), 169
Mammoth skeleton, 64
Manoir de l'Automobile et des Vieux Métiers (Lohéac), 77–78
Maps, 52
Marais du Quellen, 121–122
Mare aux Fées, 157
MedicAlert, 28
Medical insurance, 26–27
Merlin's Tomb (near Folle Pensée), 68–69
Mine d'Or (Pénestin), 206
Miramar Crouesty (Port du Crouesty), 228
Mobile phones, 29–30
Molène, 154
Money matters, 22–24
Mont-Dol, 64
Montgolfière Morbihan (St Avé), 220–221
Mont-St-Michel, 67–69
Monts d'Arrée, 145, 156, 159
  accommodations, 180–182
Morbihan, 197–234
  accommodations, 224–230
  for active families, 221–222
  events and entertainment, 200–201
  getting around, 200
  orientation, 200
  restaurants, 231–234
  shopping, 222–224
  sights and attractions, 201–222
    aquaria and animal parks, 206–212
    arts and crafts sites, 218–220
    beaches, resorts, and islands, 202–205
    historic buildings and monuments, 212–215
    museums, 215–218
    natural wonders and spectacular views, 205–206
    top 10 attractions, 201–202
  tours, 220–221
  traveling to, 198
  visitor information, 200
Morgat, 157–158
Motorhomes, 39
Moulin à Papier de Pen-Mur (Muzillac), 219–220
Musée de Bretagne/Espace de Sciences (Rennes), 8, 78–79
Musée de l'Abeille Vivante (Vitré), 72–73

Musée de la Pêche (Concarneau), 167–168
Musée de la Poupée (Josselin), 215–216
Musée de la Résistance (St Marcel), 217
Musée de l'Ecole Rurale (Trégarvan), 166
Musée des Beaux Arts (Quimper), 169–170
Musée des Beaux-Arts (Rennes), 80–81
Musée des Châteaux en Allumettes (Bizole), 220
Musée des Goémoniers (Plouguerneau), 155
Musée des Phares et Balises (Ouessant), 8–9, 168
Musée du Cire (Perros-Guirec), 115
Musée du Drummond Castle (Molène), 154
Musée du Loup (Le Cloître-St Thégonnec), 166–167
Musée du Rail (Dinan), 125–126
Musée Louison Bobet (St-Méen-le-Grand), 79
Musée Maritime (Mont-St-Michel), 68
Musée Régional des Petits Commerces et des Métiers (Sarzeau), 216

N

Nature reserves, parks, and gardens
  Côtes d'Armor, 121–122
  Finistère, 161–162
  Ille-et-Vilaine, 74
Newspapers and magazines, 52
Nocturnes evening markets, 9, 203
Nouvelles Impressions (Dinard), 89

O

Océanopolis (Brest), 6, 149, 160–161
Odyssaum (Pont-Scorff), 209–210
One Parent Families, 29
Ouessant, 6, 153–154
  accommodations, 179–180
  restaurants, 190–192
Oysters, 64, 65

P

Package deals, 34–37
Packing tips, 24
Paimpont, 67, 69
Paramé, 64
Parc Aquanature de Stérou (Priziac), 222
Parc Claude-Goude, 153
Parc d'Attractions Odet Loisirs (Coray), 173
Parc de Branféré (Le Guerno), 210–211
Parc de Port Breton (Dinard), 74
Parc de Préhistoire de Bretagne (Malansac), 212
Parc des Grands Chênes (Villecartier forest), 7, 87
Parc du Golfe (Vannes), 206
Parc Ornithologique de Bretagne (Bruz), 73
Parc Régional Naturel d'Armorique, 162
Passports, 21
Patt'ine, 131
Pays des Abers, 154–155
  accommodations, 179–180
  restaurants, 190–192
Pêche en Mer, 128
Penfret, 172
Perret, 114
Perros-Guirec, 114–115
Petit Aquarium (St-Malo), 63
Pets, 21–22
Phare d'Eckmühl, 163, 164
Phare de l'Ile Vierge, 164
Phare des Roches-Douves (near Finistère), 164
Phare de Trézien, 155
Phare du Créac'h, 164
Phare Grande, 203
Place aux Mômes (Carnac), 203
Place des Frères Lamennais (St-Malo), 63
Plage de Kélenn, 152–153
Plage de la Granville, 120
Plage de la Touesse, 64
Plage de Longchamp, 66
Plage de St-Guirec, 116
Plage des Grands Sables (Ile de Groix), 205
Plage du Bon Secours (St-Malo), 63
Planétarium de Bretagne (Pleumeur-Bodou), 126
Plouarzel, 155
Pointe de Corsen, 155
Pointe de Dinan, 158
Pointe de la Varde, 70
Pointe de Penhir, 158
Pointe des Grands Nez, 64
Pointe du Grouin, 65
Pointe du Raz, 156
Pointe du Toulinguet, 158
Pointe du Van, 155
Point Passion Plage (St-Lunaire), 66
Police, 52
Pont-l'Abbé, 167
Pony rides, 60, 66, 71, 92, 96, 147, 154, 159, 187, 203, 208, 222
Port Donnant, 203
Port-Mer, 65
Port Miniature (Villecartier forest), 7, 87
Port-Tudy, 205
Post offices, 52
Prescription medicines, 27–28
Presqu'île de Crozon, 157–158
  accommodations, 182–184
  restaurants, 192–193
Printemps (Brest), 176
Puppet shows, 6, 80, 110–112, 208

Q

Quai des Bulles (St-Malo), 60
Quartiers d'Eté (Rennes), 60
Quimper porcelain, 169–170

R

Rainfall, average, 24
Ranch de la Foucheraie (Cardroc), 87–88
Rennes, 57, 58
Rennes sur Roulettes, 60–61
Responsible Tourism, 257
Restaurants, 47–48
  best, 13–16
  price categories, 48
Roche Rouge, 118
Rochers Sculptés de Rothéneuf, 69–70
Roches Piquées (Demoiselles de Cojoux), 76
Roche Tremblante, 157
Rollerblading festival (Rennes), 60–61
Roscoff
  accommodations in or near, 176–179
  restaurants in and around, 189–190
Ryanair, 31

S

Sables d'Or-les-Pins, 113
Safety, 28
Safety concerns, 52–53
Sailing
 Centre Nautique de Rance (St Suliac), 84
 La Cancalaise (Cancale), 83–84
 Morbihan, 221
 Penfret, 172
 Port-Mer, 65
 St-Lunaire, 66
St Briac-sur-Mer, 66–67
St-Brieuc, 108
 accommodations in or near, 133–136
 restaurants in or near, 140–142
St Cast-le-Guildo, 113
St Efflam, 118
St Just, 75–76
St-Lunaire, 6, 66–67
 accommodations in or near, 99–101
St-Malo, 3, 57, 63–65
 accommodations, 97–99
St Nicolas, 172
School holidays, 26
Seasons, 24–25
Sept Iles, 122
Siblu, 36
Sillon de Talbert, 117–118
Single parents, 28–29
South African Airways, 32
Special needs, families with, 29
Speed limits, 38
Sportmer (St-Malo), 90
Station LPO de l'Ile Grande/ Réserve Naturelle des Sept Iles, 122
Stud farms, 119–120, 209

T

Tas de Pois, 158
Taxes, 53
Taxis, 53
Télégraphe de Chappe (St Marcan), 76
Telephone, 53
Temperature, average daytime, 24
Tennis, 66
Terrarium de Kerdanet (Plouagat), 121
Thalassothérapie de Carnac, 229
Thalassotherapy centres, 228–229
Thomson Al Fresco, 36
Time zone, 53
Tipping, 53–54
Toilets, 54
Tombées de la Nuit (Rennes), 61
Tour Davis (Lorient), 214
Tournoi de Lutte Bretonne (Belle-Isle-sur-Terre), 111
Toyshops, 90, 130
Traffic rules, 38
Train Marin (Cherrueix), 82–83
Train travel, 34, 41–42
 Musée du Rail (Dinan), 125–126
 Vapeur du Trieux (Paimpol), 126
Transportation, 37–42
Traveling to Brittany, 31–34
Travel insurance, 26–27
Traveller's cheques, 22–23
Treac'h er Goured (Houat), 204
Treac'h er Salus (Houat), 204
Tumulus St Michel, 213

V

Vannes, 206
Vapeur du Trieux (Paimpol), 126
VAT (value-added tax), 53
Vedettes Aven-Bélon (Moëlan-sur-Mer), 171
Vélo Rail (Médréac), 7, 88
VFB Holidays, 36
Village de Poul-Fetan (Quistinic), 215
Village Gaulois, 9, 128–129
Ville Close (Concarneau), 150
Visas, 21
Visitor information, 20–21
VVF Vacances, 37

W

Water, drinking, 54
Weather, 24–25
Websites, child-specific, 21
Wi-Fi access, 30–31
Windsurfing, 85, 97, 151, 221

Y

Youth hostels, 43

Z

Zoo de la Bourbansais (Pleugueneuc), 73–74
Zoo de Pont-Scorff, 211–212

Accommodations

Accor Thalassa (Dinard), 99
Aigue Marine (Tréguier), 136
Auberge de Jeunesse (Brest), 149
Auberge de Jeunesse Les Korrigans (Lannion), 138
Auberge du Youdig (Brennilis), 181
Au Bon Accueil (Port-Launay), 180–181
Au Char à Bancs (near St-Brieuc), 12, 134
Beau Rivage (Anse de Sordan), 114
Camping Caravaning Château de Galinée (St Cast-le-Guildo), 132
Camping Claire Fontaine (Perros-Guirec), 137–138
Camping-gîte de Loquéran (Plouhinec), 185
Camping Les Hortensias/ Gîtes de Kermen (Carantec), 179
Camping Le Ty Nadan (Locunolé), 13, 187–188
Castel Régis (Brignogan), 11, 179–180
Château de Kermezen (Pommerit-Jaudy), 137
Château de Locguénolé (Lorient), 10, 224–11
Château du Pin (Iffendic), 94–95
Domaine des Ormes (Epiniac), 92–93
Domaine du Logis (La Chapelle-aux-Filtzméens), 95
Domaine et Château du Val (Planguenoual), 133–134
Domaine Ker-Moor (Bénodet), 185–186
Ecurie du Gallais (St Cast-le-Guildo), 132–133
Ferme Apicole de Térenez (Rosnoën), 12, 183
Ferme de la Vieuville (Cancale), 93
Ferme de Malido (St Alban), 135–136
Grand Hôtel Barrière (Dinard), 99–100
Grand Hôtel des Bains (Locquirec), 10, 176–177
Hotel Bellevue (Quiberon), 227–228
Hôtel de l'Océan (Concarneau), 186–187
Hôtel du Centre (Roscoff), 11, 178
Hôtel La Désirade (Locmaria), 203
Hôtel Le Clos Fleuri (Belle-Ile), 203

Hôtel-Restaurant de l'Abbaye (Plancöet), 131
Hôtel-Restaurant Le Goyen (Audierne), 11, 184–185
La Clef du Four (Plesder), 95
La Crème Maison (near Spézet), 182
La Grande Metairie (Carnac), 228–230
La Julerie (Corseul), 133
La Maison Magique (St Nicolas-des-Eaux), 225–226
La Mine d'Or (Pénestin), 230
La Motte Beaumanoir (Pleugueneuc-Plesder), 93–94
La Pensée (St-Lunaire), 100
La Villeneuve (Riec-sur-Bélon), 13, 188
Le Gîtes de Kersillac, 95–96
Le Grand Large (Lambézen), 183–184
Le Grénier d'Ernestine (Bréal-sous-Montfort), 96–97
Le Keo (Ouessant), 180
Le Lodge Kerisper (La Trinité-sur-Mer), 11–12, 226–227
Les Maisons de Bricourt (Cancale), 12–13, 90–92
Les Villages Mer (Le Conquet), 173–174
Manoir de Kervézec (Carantec), 178
The Résidence Carnac, 229
Résidence Reine Marine (St-Malo), 10, 97–98
Thalassa (Camaret-sur-Mer), 182–183
Village Mahana (near Dinard), 100–101

Restaurants

Auberge de la Cour Verte (Dol-de-Bretagne), 101–102
Au Biniou (Le Val-André), 14, 138–139
Café du Port (Cancale), 16, 102
Château d'Eau (Ploudalmézeau), 15, 192
Chez Jean-Pierre (St-Malo), 104–105
Chez Paule Crêperies (Ile de Groix), 232
Crêperie Chez Annick (Clohars-Fouesnant), 195
Crêperie Chez Marie (St Cast-le-Guildo), 14–15, 139–140
Crêperie Chez Renée (Belle-Ile), 234
Crêperie des Grèves (Langueux), 14, 141–142
Crêperie du Ménez-Gorre (Crozon), 192–193
Crêperie La Taupinière (Vannes), 234
Crêperie L'Epoké (Pont-Croix), 193–194
Crêperie Le Salamandre (Ploudalmézeau), 192
Crêperie Ty à Dreuz (Ouessant), 154
Digor Kalon (Perros-Guirec), 142
Halte du Volcan (Le Tertre Gris), 102
Hôtel du Lac (Combourg), 102–103
La Brocéliande (Bénodet), 194
La Casa Varadero (Lorient), 231–232
La Corniche (Brignogan-Plages), 14, 190–191
La Côte (Carnac), 233
La Couscousserie (Quimper), 194–195
La Moana (Binic), 141
L'Arganier (Dinard), 105–106
La Stalla (Erquy), 139
Le Bénétin (St-Malo), 104
Le Café Bleu (St-Malo), 15, 105
L'Ecume des Jours (Roscoff), 189
Le Gavrinis (Baden), 232–233
Le Gouermel (Gouermel-Plage), 116
Le Ker Bleu (Perros-Guirec), 142
Le Petit Relais (Carantec), 13, 190
Le Porte au Vin (Concarneau), 195–196
Le Pressoir (Romillé), 103
L'Escale Gourmande (St-Malo), 72
Le Surf (St-Lunaire), 15, 106
Le Talisman (Pont-Aven), 196
Le Vivier (Lomener), 231
L'Ilot Jardin (near Fouesnant), 195
L'Irois (Audierne), 193
Merlin (L'Anse de Sordan), 114
Restaurant-Crêperie Le Capsell (Le Cloître-St Thégonnec), 167
Restaurant de la Mairie (Landerneau), 13–14, 191
Restaurant Patrick Jeffroy (Carantec), 16, 189
Via Costa (Etablessur-Mer), 15, 140

Notes

Notes

Notes

Notes

Notes

Notes